BK 791.43 R264c

D0026596

791.43 R264c
RAY

SEP 8 1986

A CERTAIN TENDENCY OF THE HOLLY-
WOOD CINEMA, 1930-1980

45.00
FPCC

INVENTORY 98

 St. Louis Community
College

Library

5801 Wilson Avenue
St. Louis, Missouri 63110

A Certain Tendency
of the Hollywood Cinema,
1930–1980

A Certain Tendency
of the Hollywood Cinema,
1930–1980

ROBERT B. RAY

PRINCETON UNIVERSITY PRESS

Princeton, New Jersey

Copyright © 1985 by Princeton University Press

Published by Princeton University Press, 41 William Street, Princeton,
New Jersey 08540
In the United Kingdom: Princeton University Press, Guildford, Surrey

All Rights Reserved

Library of Congress Cataloging in Publication Data will be found
on the last printed page of this book

ISBN 0-691-04727-8 (cloth)   0-691-10174-4 (paper)

This book has been composed in Linotron Century Schoolbook

Clothbound editions of Princeton University Press books are printed on
acid-free paper, and binding materials are chosen for strength and durability.
Paperbacks, although satisfactory for personal collections, are not usually
suitable for library rebinding

Printed in the United States of America by Princeton University Press
Princeton, New Jersey

For Helen

Contents

Acknowledgments

ANY WRITER whose first book happens to be about Hollywood composes the acknowledgment section under the specter of that most dire of genres, the Oscar acceptance speech. Heeding that minatory example, I will be brief.

Although the book that follows proposes an anti-auteurist accounting for the American Cinema, I wish to state explicitly my debt to Andrew Sarris who, in many ways, invented film studies in this country. I also wish to acknowledge the (often contradictory) influences of Michael Wood and Noël Burch, whose writings on the movies first set me to thinking about Hollywood's thematic and formal transactions with myths and ideologies.

As teachers, William Hatchett, Sherman Hawkins, Lawrance Thompson, Patrick Lyles, Steven Lavine, and Paul Elledge encouraged me and often changed the way I thought. Three others have had particular influence on this book. Harry Geduld introduced me to film scholarship, and Willis Barnstone to the modernist tradition that shadows Hollywood's own stubborn conservatism. David Pace read the book's first draft and accurately pointed out that it had been written from within the very mythologies it meant to criticize. His remarks suggested the major direction for all subsequent revisions.

The University of Florida has provided me with release time for research and writing, with funding for film rentals and frame enlargements, and with teaching assignments that any full professor would envy.

Marie Nelson typed the book's entire second draft before the University of Florida English Department had acquired its word processor. Bonnie Jo DeCourcey prepared the index and caught mistakes missed by everyone who came before her.

I am especially grateful to Joanna Hitchcock, my editor at Princeton, who has been unvaryingly punctual, generous, and helpful with her advice and strategy; and to Marilyn Campbell, whose film knowledge and grammatical expertise make her the copy editor one could only wish for (she knows the difference between *The Conqueror* and *The Conquerors*).

Finally, I owe the most to my three colleagues at the University of Florida, Robert D'Amico, Alistair Duckworth, and Gregory Ulmer, who have read and commented on the manuscript while simultaneously serving as my postgraduate instructors in contemporary critical theory; and above all, to James Naremore, who in seeing this project through from its inception, has never once mentioned how many of his own ideas appear in it.

A Certain Tendency
of the Hollywood Cinema,
1930–1980

Introduction

[The study of film and television] shouldn't simply be training more appreciative consumers, which is what film appreciation clubs did, or encouraging the "mystique of making" by giving people glimpses of the studio, but, *within a more general body of cultural studies, admitting the social relations which have been excluded from education.*—Raymond Williams[1]

Ideology is, in effect, the imaginary of an epoch, the Cinema of a society.—Roland Barthes[2]

ON NOVEMBER 15, 1981, CBS's "60 Minutes," at the time the most popular television show in the United States, offered its estimated 45 million viewers a twenty-minute segment teasingly entitled "The Best Movie Ever Made?" Harry Reasoner's opening prolonged the suspense by carefully avoiding an immediate answer to this rhetorical question:

The best movie ever made? It was filmed in 1942 on a budget of about a million dollars. It was based on a play that had never been produced. It had writers like some houses have mice, but the script was still done more or less a day at a time. It changed the image of its stars, none of whom were particularly enthusiastic about being in the movie. Is it the best movie ever made? Those who say it is are passionate about it. They've become a cult, and I'm a member.

The unmistakable film clip that followed immediately gave away the game: Humphrey Bogart toasting Ingrid Bergman with the line "Here's looking at you, kid," as an offscreen piano played "As Times Goes By"—*Casablanca*.

Few "serious" critics would designate *Casablanca* as the best movie ever made. At the very least, however, *Casablanca* is one of the handful of films that have lodged in the collective American imagination, movies whose stories, characters, and images everyone knows: *King Kong, The Wizard of Oz, Gone With the Wind, Citizen Kane, Casablanca, Shane, On the Waterfront, Bonnie and Clyde, The Godfather, Taxi Driver, Star Wars.* Of these pictures, *Casablanca* may be the most recognizable. Even those who have never seen the movie itself respond instantly to all the advertisements, TV skits, and Woody Allen parodies that use the image of a brooding man in a white dinner jacket to evoke an entire world.

For over forty years, in other words, *Casablanca* has remained an immensely popular movie. Significantly, "60 Minutes" made no real effort to account for that fact, falling back instead on film criticism's by-now standard portrayal of the movie as an unforeseen, unrepeatable, miraculous accident, the result of its heroic producer's struggle with reluctant actors and a jerry-built script.[3] Indeed, this "explanation" of *Casablanca* is so entrenched that most of its fans are surprised to discover that, far from beginning as a little-known cult film, the movie won the 1943 Best Picture Academy Award. Clearly, the idea of *Casablanca* as an underdog movie issuing from a stubborn, serendipitous individualism has proved more appealing, perhaps because that explanation forestalls analysis. Its insistence on the film's fortunate independence from Hollywood's normal production protocols is in complicity with *Casablanca*'s own ideological message—but I am getting ahead of my argument.

I like *Casablanca* very much myself. But while the majority of the film's critics regard *Casablanca* as a sport in the Hollywood lineage, I have always been struck by how *typical* it seemed. Far from being an isolated case, *Casablanca* appeared both to sum up a whole era of the American cinema (now known as the Studio Era) and to predict the way in which the patterns established by that era would both persist and evolve. In hindsight, *Casablanca* reverberates with echoes of films coming before and after it, not even counting those like *To Have and Have Not* and *Play It Again, Sam* consciously modeled on it. *Casablanca*'s Rick Blaine, for example, clearly descends from *Gone With the Wind*'s Rhett Butler, and both of these characters provide the source for *Star Wars*'s Han Solo. Further, *The Man Who Shot Liberty Valance*'s western exterior conceals an almost exact reworking of *Casa-*

blanca, and *Star Wars* (one of the three most profitable films in history) works variations on the same plot.

With *Casablanca*, then, we have a remarkable case: an American movie at once both immensely popular and immensely typical (arguably *the* most popular and typical) that no one seems to know anything about. If *Casablanca* is in fact so representative of Hollywood, our ignorance about it and its relationship to other movies suggests that we also know less about the shape of the American cinema as a whole than we have thought.

What exactly do we need to know about the American cinema? My own preference would be for a knowledge at once theoretical and historical—theoretical because the sheer number of movies released in this country (35,483 between 1917 and 1979[4]) necessitates an accounting that would work for a large class; historical because the discovery of any common patterns in those movies demands a recognition that such patterns developed over time and in response to material determinations.

In terms of theory, film study has benefited enormously from the contemporary critical project known loosely as structuralism, which has affected film scholarship more rapidly, completely, and profoundly than it has any of the other humanities. Ironically, however, by calling into question investigatory procedures previously taken for granted, this same critical project has brought historical studies of the cinema to a standstill. As Geoffrey Nowell-Smith complains in an article significantly titled, "On the Writing of the History of the Cinema: Some Problems":

> Meanwhile—and it is a substantial meanwhile—the loss of confidence in traditional historiographic procedures and the turn towards non-historical modes of theorisation have produced a severe hiatus in the study of the cinema. No one now accepts accounts of film history (or of film in history) which pass blandly from one "fact" to another, alternately making technology the cause of style, directional intention the cause of a film's reception or public taste the arbiter of economic demand, without ever posing the problem of the articulation of different orders of structures and events. And yet no one knows how to do much better, except at the cost of a sceptical unwillingness to do anything.[5]

Even while despairing of the possibilities for film history, Nowell-Smith acutely locates the principal roadblock as "the problem of articulation," by which he means the obvious, but generally ignored fact that the cinema exists in a dense, shifting network of relationships with other processes or discourses, each with its own history and determinations, each influencing and influenced by the others. Specifically, as a technologically dependent, capital-intensive, commercial, collaborative medium regulated by the government and financially linked to mass audiences, the movies find themselves immersed at the least in the histories of:

1. technology: developments in photography, the motion picture camera (e.g., sound, color, deep focus), projection systems, and rival media (e.g., radio, television, electronic games)
2. economics: changes in the conditions of production, distribution, and consumption
3. competing commercial forms: developments in, for example, vaudeville, theater, dime novels, comic books, television, radio, newspapers, magazines, electronic games
4. filmmakers: e.g., producers, directors, actors, scriptwriters, musicians, set designers
5. other media: particularly those like the novel and television that emphasize the commercial cinema's preferred mode, narrative
6. politics: the censoring power (implicit or explicit) of prevailing ideologies
7. the audience: both the sociological (demographic) and the psychoanalytic dimensions[6]

Moreover, the cinema is not simply the sum of these extracinematic processes; as Nowell-Smith rightly observes, "cinema also has (or historically has acquired) its own specificity, insofar as its rise to be a mass art inaugurates a new apparatus that joins together the existing determinations in a new way."

Confronted by this entanglement, what can a would-be film historian say? I propose the following only as a suggestion and as a guide to the assumptions underlying this book. First, the cinema as a whole, and, even more emphatically, any individual movie, is massively overdetermined. No film results from a single cause, even if its maker thinks it does; as a discourse, the cinema, especially the commercial cinema, is simply too exposed, too public, to permit such circumspection. Second (and this point follows from the first), in terms of originating causes, the cinema as an institution, and any single film, is thoroughly decentered. The prospective historian must approach it in the frame of mind required of a spectator at one of Robert Wilson's plays, which, as Leo Bersani describes, use multiple actions occurring simultaneously:

> at any one moment, several of these elements were competing for our attention [Bersani writes]. As a result, we were continually discovering that we were in the "wrong place"—or, more accurately, that there was no right place, or that there were always other places. Instead of discovering where to look most intently, we were constantly seeing things we hadn't noticed before. And it can't be said that these distracted our attention, for there was nothing genuinely central from which our attention might be distracted. The action was always somewhere else, but not because we haven't yet reached the right place (the sacred depository of a central truth), but because nothing was ever "entirely" in one place.[7]

The film historian, in other words, has an array of factors to consider, each of them "right" as an object of study, each becoming "wrong" only if the historian's attention fixes on one as the sole explanation of cinema.

It follows from these two assumptions that an ideal film history would be supple and diversified, marked by a willingness both to keep moving and to acknowledge that film history is by definition "interminable." While seemingly reasonable enough, these criteria have in practice proved so strenuous that the history of film theory has consisted almost entirely of a continuous search for a single masterplot. McLuhan's and Bazin's technological determinism, the auteurists' concentration on filmmakers (whether producers, directors, actors, or scriptwriters), the neoformalists' insistence on the aesthetic conventions specific to the movies, Kracauer's socio-historical explanation of the German cinema, the sociological studies of the film audience—each has concentrated on one of the cinema's determinants at the expense of the rest.

Despite my own call for diversification, I am not completely immune to the idea of a masterplot. My own preference is for that synthesis of formalism and materialism fathered by Brecht and taken up by Noël Burch, and the groups surrounding *Screen* and *Jump Cut*,[8] who have unfortunately transformed that position's original populism into a thoroughgoing critique of commercial cinema in the name of textual avant-gardism. At its best, however, this approach, unlike most previous theories, does not disregard the array of processes in which film is implicated, but rather seeks to subsume them under the master term "ideology." Thus, for example, we now have ideological explanations for the consolidation of the American film industry and its decision to concentrate almost exclusively on feature-length, big-budget fictional narratives using stars;[9] for the continuity style in general[10] and for its individual components such as shot-reverse shot and deep focus;[11] for genres;[12] and even for the camera itself.[13]

This project has remained voraciously assimilative, ransacking such disparate disciplines as anthropology, linguistics, political science, communications theory, semiotics, sociology, and even literary criticism. Nevertheless, this position's bedrock, unwavering leftism renders it susceptible to a materialism that if not quite vulgar is at times predictable. Current film reviews appearing in *Jump Cut* and *Cinéaste*, for example, invariably denounce Hollywood's product on political grounds. Similarly, the textual materialism of Burch and *Screen* (objected to by *Jump Cut* as a textual idealism in disguise) has often taken the paradoxical shape of a formalist essentialism in which certain stylistic procedures are labeled in advance as inherently "repressive" or "alienating" regardless of the ends they serve or the contexts in which they appear.[14] Armed with this approach, a critic can simply ignore the American Cinema with its "realist," "transparent" style whose political effect can be read off in advance.

The lure of materialism as a master explanation can influence even a rigorously self-conscious critic like Brian Henderson, whose recent article "A Musical Comedy of Empire"[15] argues that the Astaire-Rogers musical *Flying Down to Rio* resulted directly from RCA-RKO's desire to promote Pan American Airway's nearly exclusive air routes to South America. As satisfying as Henderson's thesis is, it fails to see that in terms of the film's effect, any conscious economic intention has long since been blunted by the film's other determinants, chiefly Astaire and Rogers. For regardless of *Flying Down to Rio*'s original publicity function, the movie almost immediately became a genre film, part of a cycle in which Astaire and Rogers appeared throughout the 1930s.

In addition, the proponents of ideology as the masterplot of the American Cinema have often ignored Marx's own warnings about fetishism. Ideology is not a thing that dictates such formations as the cinema, but rather a set of social relationships fought out in different arenas of which film is among the most prominent.[16] Within the cinematic area, the ringmaster is constantly changing; indeed, as each determinant enters the arena, it is mediated by all the others who are in turn affected by the newcomer. In concrete terms, RCA's economic project in *Flying Down to Rio* had to confront (among other things) the physical presences of Astaire and Rogers, the technical limitations of 1933 filmmaking, the musical genre, the preexisting stereotypes associated with Latin America, and the U.S. government's diplomatic relationship with Brazil. One might argue that each of these factors is determined "in the last instance" by material circumstances, by ideology in short, and I would rush to agree. But I cannot help thinking that even issuing from the same public relations motive, *Flying Down to Rio* with (let us speculate wildly here) the Ramones instead of Astaire-Rogers would have had a somewhat different effect.

The movies, in other words, are implicated in too many processes (both cinematic and extracinematic) for one explanation to prevail. Does the complexity of cinema's articulations finally discredit a materialist, historical approach? I think not. Althusser has offered one way out of this impasse with his formulation of the social totality as

constituted by a certain type of complexity, the unity of a structured whole containing what can be called levels or instances which are distinct and "relatively autonomous," and coexist within this complex structural unity, articulated with one another according to specific determinations, fixed in the last instance by the level or instance of the economy.[17]

Applied to the cinema (as it has often been), this description encourages historical work, prompting investigations both of the various "relatively autonomous" determinants of film (e.g., technology, economics, actors and directors, styles of lighting and editing, political circumstances) and of their specific articulations in individual movies or groups of movies.

Having proposed this image of social relationships, however, and with it an implied research program into its different components, Althusser then scrupulously retracts his own masterplot, economic conditions:

> the economic dialectic is never active *in the pure state*; in History, these instances, the superstructures, etc.—are never seen to step respectfully aside when their work is done or, when the Time comes . . . to scatter before His Majesty the Economy as he strides along the royal road of the Dialectic. From the first moment to the last, the lonely hour of the "last instance" never comes.[18]

Traditional Marxists have protested that, with this admission, Althusser has eliminated the sine qua non of materialism.[19] Certainly that self-cancellation has proved costly both to Althusser's own work and to his reputation in Marxist circles. Nevertheless, we should regard his boldest move as a sign of his honesty. The masterplot is a fiction, but that fact alone should not disallow it. What counts is not its status as "truth" but its value as a heuristic opening up lines of inquiry.

Even Jacques Derrida, the principal philosophic critic of the longing for masterplots (or "centers," as he calls them) in Western metaphysics, has asserted their necessity.[20] We have not yet learned to think without them. I raise this point as an apologia for my study, whose argument, despite its diversity, inevitably rests on a tacit masterplot—in this case, the notion of ideology.

I would like to describe briefly the theoretical basis of the book that follows, a feat less imposing than it may seem, since as Derrida has revealed (thus betraying every writer's secret), these "introductions" are always written last.[21] I can "begin," therefore, by saying that recent film scholarship's obsessive concern with theory has often proved disabling, forcing a would-be practical critic to build the ladder as he climbs it, to provide theoretical justifications for any individual readings advanced.[22] Nevertheless, this new attention to theory has had distinct advantages. First, it has repeatedly demonstrated the falseness of the standard distinction between theoretical and nontheoretical books. We have now been made to see that every book is theoretical; some merely conceal their assumptions. Second, by forcing a writer to lay his cards on the table, the recent demand for explicit theorizing forestalls the arguments at cross-purposes that, while apparently about interpretations, the logic of arguments, vocabulary, and even "facts," are often theoretical differences in disguise. We have been made to recognize that any theoretical position constitutes its object of study and encourages its practitioner to attend to some things while slighting others. Refusing to acknowledge that inevitability leads to silly quarrels. A Marxist who objects to a formalist's failure to mention conditions of distribution, for example, is like a geologist who complains that a botany textbook ignores rocks.

The first draft of this book proceeded from a naïve reflection theory that sought to explain the evolution of the popular American Cinema in terms of the movies' response to changing historical conditions. Eventually I realized that the movies not only reflected but also excluded the world,[23] and that I needed an approach that would account for both a reflection more complicated that I had originally granted and an exclusion more systematic than I had reckoned on. In short, I needed theories of overdetermination and transformation. I found them in three schools of thought that have converged in recent film scholarship: Marxism (especially Althusser's discussions of ideology); myth study (especially Lévi-Strauss's notion that myths are transformations of basic dilemmas or contradictions that in reality cannot be solved); and psychoanalysis (especially Freud's dream work and its notions of condensation and displacement).[24]

Each of these schools entails a particular assumption about film. For Marxism, movies are ideological formations, screened and shaped by political censorship. For myth study, movies are myths whose individual shapes arise from the "rules of transformation." For psychoanalysis, movies are dreams, screened and reshaped by a culture's collective psychic censorship.

The merger of these three methodologies (especially in *Screen* and the *Cahiers du cinéma*) derives from their two basic similarities: all three are theories of both overdeterminism and transformation. Althusserian Marxism proposes that any phenomenon at any level of society results from multiple determinations (economic, cultural, political, personal, traditional, aesthetic).[25] Lévi-Strauss suggests that each version of a myth results from those multiple determinations that have shaped the rules of transformation—that flexibility which enables a single cultural anxiety to assume different shapes in response to an audience's changing needs.[26] Freud refers to dream images as condensations and displacements resulting from multiple dream thoughts.[27]

All three methodologies attempt to define the rules of transformation or censorship, the system that enables a message to cross a boundary and enter another domain. Thus, analysis in all three cases becomes an attempt to trace the path of that message back to its previous site. Marxism wants to discover the "cause" of a culture's particular way of representing material conditions (i.e., its ideology)—in the case of Hollywood movies, for example, the material origins of melodrama. Lévi-Strauss asks why a body of myths has appeal for a given culture: what dilemma does it attempt to solve? Freud wants to locate the repressed anxiety or wish behind the overdetermined dream images. Thus, according to these theories, *Casablanca*, for example, becomes, as ideology, a representation of an unsolvable dilemma—the conflicting appeals of intervention and isolationism; as myth, an attempt to resolve that dilemma; as dream, a displaced condensation of the anxiety generated by that contradiction.

Since the beginning, however, film theory's particular preference for the psychoanalytic accounting (the movie-as-dream) has resulted in an impasse. Certainly, Freud's condensation and displacement (and his insistence on the dream's need for concrete representation) offered rules by which latent dream thoughts (wishes, anxieties) get transformed into dream images. But the associative chains by which Freud retraced these images to their unconscious sources were utterly private, available only to the particular dreamer (and, after enormous effort, to Freud himself). Dream images, in other words, are at best *subjective* correlatives whose import typically remains hidden from even the dreamer.

To the extent that movies do work like dreams, Hollywood's challenge lay in developing rules of condensation and displacement that would work for the audience as a whole, or, to put it another way, that would provide immediately (albeit unconsciously) recognizable objective (?) correlatives for the common wishes and fears of the mass audience. Hollywood's enormous commercial success proves that it met this challenge. As I will argue, it did so by becoming intuitively Lévi-Straussian: the American film industry discovered and used the existing body of mythic oppositions provided it by the local culture. In effect, the great Hollywood czars became naïve, prodigious anthropologists.

The determinedly commercial nature of the American movie business, however, and its financial servitude to the politically powerful eastern banks, insured that Hollywood's elaborations of American mythology would not proceed according to the mathematically indifferent rules of transformation posited by Lévi-Strauss, but rather according to the ideologically censoring standards posited by Marx in a famous passage:

The ideas of the ruling class are in every epoch the ruling ideas, *i.e.*, the class which is the ruling *material* force of society, is at the same time its ruling *intellectual* force. The class which has the means of material production at its disposal has control at the same time over the means of mental production, so that thereby, generally speaking, the ideas of those who lack the means of mental production are subject to it.[28]

Thus, each variation of what I will call the thematic paradigm (in westerns, musicals, gangster movies, etc.) could pose issues only in terms allowed by the prevailing ideology—or could refuse to acknowledge that ideological disposition only at its own commercial risk. *Casablanca*, as I will argue, could deal with the intervention-isolationism opposition only by displacing it into the ideologically favored realm of melodrama, where (since such displacements were traditional to American culture) ample mythic types, images, and stories were available.

I will be talking throughout this book about the "ideology," "myths," and "artistic conventions" of the American Cinema. Certainly, I would not argue that these three terms are interchangeable. I would insist, however, that they are not nearly so distinct as traditional literary scholarship has maintained. Indeed, I have worked from the premise that myths and artistic conventions, far from existing in some politically neutral realm of archetypes or aesthetics, are always socially produced and consumed, and thus always implicated in ideology. In fact, Hollywood cinema confirms the theoretical speculation that ideology is most effectively "naturalized" (that is, made to appear the inevitable product of nature's laws rather than of history) through its most efficient vehicles: popular mythology and well-established artistic conventions.

Thus, although this book takes shape around the three theories of overdeterminism and transformation mentioned above, its masterplot (its provisional "center") is the notion of ideology, a vexed term much confused by careless usage.[29] My own argument derives from Althusser's definition of ideology as "a system . . . of representations (images, myths, ideas, or concepts, depending on the case) endowed with a historical existence and role within a given society."[30] Althusser repeatedly warns that no culture can exist without ideology, for ideology provides a culture with its way of perceiving the world. In a crucial passage, often introduced into recent film scholarship, Althusser elaborates:

> It is customary to suggest that ideology belongs to the region of "consciousness." We must not be misled by this appellation. . . . In truth, ideology has very little to do with "consciousness," even supposing this term to have an unambiguous meaning. It is profoundly *unconscious*, even when it presents itself in a reflected form. . . . Ideology is indeed a system of representations, but in the majority of cases these representations have nothing to do with "consciousness": they are usually images and occasionally concepts, but it is above all as *structures* that they impose on the vast majority of men, not via their "consciousness."[31]

If ideology provides a culture with its structures of perception, its window on the world. a critical theory examines those structures not simply for their distortions or exclusions (present by definition in all ideologies), but for those distortions or exclusions that have become crippling.[32]

Those perceptual structures, the means by which a culture organizes its experience of the world, appear most compellingly in popular myths. In the context of this argument, I am using "myths" to mean not transhistorical, transcultural, Jungian archetypes, but rather the "mythologies" of Roland Barthes, those (disingenuous) representations that transform the historical and the man-made into the timeless and the natural. As Barthes writes in his Preface to *Mythologies*:

> The starting point of these reflections was usually a feeling of impatience at the sight of the "naturalness" with which newspapers, art and common sense constantly dress up reality which, even though it is the one we live in, is undoubtedly determined by history. In short ... I resented seeing Nature and History confused at every turn, and I wanted to track down, in the decorative display of *what-goes-without-saying*, the ideological abuse which, in my view, is hidden there.[33]

For example, while the cumulative effects of Hollywood and American literary tradition conspire to make what I will call the myth of the outlaw hero seem to be the "natural" and "right" solution to such historical events as World War II (*Casablanca*) and urban crime (*Death Wish, Dirty Harry*), that myth in fact chronically distorts our perception of such events and potentially cripples our response to them.

Although I will spend some time demonstrating the American Cinema's (probably unconscious) thematic links to traditional nineteenth-century American literature, I would insist that, regardless of their origins or presence in other dissimilar contexts, myths are always deployed and experienced in specific historical circumstances and thus cannot escape ideological "contamination." Throughout this book, I will focus on how myths appear at specific moments in Hollywood's history. This theoretical perspective renders irrelevant a myth's "original" ideological disposition. Thus, the critical, minority, dissident background of so many of the thematic elements borrowed by Hollywood matters less for my purposes than does Hollywood's repeatedly demonstrated ability to appropriate, defuse, and deploy those elements for entirely different ends.

The caveat about recontextualization's effect on ideological function applies with particular force to the American Cinema's continual appropriations of formal departures conceived of as disruptions of Hollywood's standard continuity style. Thus, Orson Welles's proto-*noir* mannerisms and Jean-Luc Godard's New Wave dislocations became the American Cinema's cosmetic refurbishments. I was struck while watching *Reds* (a movie that certainly conforms to the traditional pattern of displacing politics into romantic melodrama) by how Eisenstein's montage, designed as a tool for precisely that kind of dialectical analysis forbidden in the American Cinema, became Hollywood's Vorkapich montage, the favorite device for compressing (and finessing) social issues and historical background into two minutes of flurried shots. Beatty revives the Vorkapich montage in *Reds*, using it most typically in an early sequence in which John Reed airs his political views to Louise Bryant in an all-night session, reduced to a few seconds of screen time and punctuated not by the elided political opinions, but by the erotic/romantic glances passing between the aroused Reed and the teasing Bryant.

My perspective implies a modification of formalism's politically neutral stance. I regard artistic conventions as the formal equivalents of myth—that is, as another embodiment and conveyor of ideology. In doing so, I am drawing on a later, revisionist development in Russian Formalism, which, as Raymond Williams has recently pointed out,[34] reconnects formalism to a materialist tradition. As developed by Vološinov, Bakhtin, and Mukařovský,[35] this neoformalism emphasizes that artistic conventions are always produced, chosen, and consumed at specific historical junctures. Inevitably, therefore, a well-established convention represents a ratification of a particular world view. Significant departures from major artistic conventions generally meet with surprising emotional resistance from those members of the audience who are neither practitioners nor cognoscenti. See, for example, the hostility directed at Elvis Presley's break with Tin Pan Alley's well-made song and at Godard's departures from Hollywood's paradigms.

Two positions have arisen to account for the relationship between aesthetic conventions and ideology. The essentialist position argues that certain cinematic figures (most prominently shot-reverse shot) are inherently bound up with capitalism's determined appellation of individual "subjects," concealment of "work" (the production process), and enticements to avoid critical thinking. The more moderate instrumentalist position, on the other hand, maintains that aesthetic forms can be perpetually remotivated, and thus that these same cinematic figures, while historically contaminated by capitalist filmmaking, can serve other ends. In this book, I tacitly argue for the latter position. But while the typical instrumentalist critic celebrates the capacity of leftist filmmaking to reappropriate continuity forms for subversive purposes, I am interested in describing the converse: the American Cinema's consistent ability to assimilate formal devices initially conceived as critical departures.

I began this Introduction with a call for a diversified approach to film study; I may seem to be ending it by espousing a theoretical method whose narrowness betrays my own manifesto. Nevertheless, in choosing ideology as the masterplot of my argument, I do not think that I have sacrificed the capaciousness a useful history of the American Cinema requires. On the contrary, I would maintain that the continued power of ideological criticism (known generally as "Marxist" or "materialist" criticism) has consisted precisely of its flexibility, its capacity to infuse and direct the various investigatory disciplines of the humanities. Indeed, if the diffuse project of "structuralism" has not yet disintegrated, it is due in no small part to ideological criticism's underlying role in such disparate fields as linguistics, anthropology, semiotics, psychoanalysis, deconstruction, history, and literary criticism. Even within a single field, the notion of ideology proves particularly useful for the critic. For film history, I have found no other approach that provides the means of analyzing so many of the American Cinema's determinants: the film text (both form and content); conditions of production, distribution, and consumption; extracinematic factors (e.g., historical events, technological developments in rival media); and even the psychoanalytic dimensions of the audience.

Despite the expansiveness of this ideological approach, however, it will inevitably cause me to slight some elements of film history previously regarded as central. In particular, I may appear at times to concentrate on Classic Hollywood's basic formulae (which I will designate as the thematic and formal paradigms) at the expense of the rich variations that have made the American Cinema great. In those cases, I will be arguing that the ideological disposition of Hollywood's principal *modus operandi* overdetermines individual variations to the extent that *in terms of their ideological effect*, no variations can be privileged in the abstract. I would argue, for example, that, ideologically, *The Grapes of Wrath* and *Norma Rae* are virtually the same movie, regardless of their superficial differences: male hero versus female hero, right-wing director versus left-wing director, farm work versus city work, and so on. Both films propose that political problems can only be solved by messianic, individualistic leaders; both portray workers as powerless, lazy, and fearful. *Norma Rae seems* different because it employs the standard Hollywood strategy of assimilating (and co-opting) a fashionably dissident *topos* potentially threatening to the prevailing ideology—in this case, feminism, defused by having Norma Rae appear dependent on the male labor organizer.

Have dissident variations (thematic or stylistic) *any* chance of disrupting or subverting a movie's intended ideological effect? This question seems to me the most interesting thing we can ask about the American Cinema. Unfortunately, we still have to ask it on a case-by-case basis. I have not been able to develop a general theory that would account in the abstract for a dissident thematic variation's ability to outfight the context that seeks to subdue it. (With formal variations, I have more of a clue: a stylistic device remains disruptive by avoiding motivation. The alienating effect of an extreme overhead angle, for instance, dissipates immediately when identified as a character's point of view.) I do not want to fall back on a lame imitation of Potter Stewart's famous "I-know-it-when-I-see-it" definition of obscenity, but for the present, I can only suggest the value of a thesis proposed by Charles Eckert in an article that deserves to be far more famous than it is: writing about *Marked Woman*, Eckert argues that truly effective challenges to Hollywood's prevailing ideology surface in those moments within a movie when the emotional quotient is simply excessive in terms of the narrative's needs—emotion, in other words, that remains inadequately motivated. (Clearly Eckert's theory of thematic variations parallels the stylistic argument made above.)

Significantly, some of the most abidingly interesting American movies display precisely these moments of excess. These same films have proved among the most popular ever made in this country, a fact suggesting that the mass audience in this country likes to live dangerously, likes to see the most privileged elements of its ideology sorely challenged, if not defeated. In the chapters on *Casablanca*, *It's a Wonderful Life*, *The Man Who Shot Liberty Valance*, *The Godfather*, and *Taxi Driver*, I will examine five of these special cases, hoping that these close readings will set us on the road to a more precise, more theoretical understanding of this problem.

I referred to these five movies as "special cases." They also seem to me just the opposite: movies that almost perfectly represent Hollywood strategies at particular historical junctures. In the chapters surveying each of the American Cinema's major periods, I will describe those strategies, and it is there that I may appear to be overconcentrating on the general pattern, what I have chosen to call, adapting Truffaut's famous phrase, "a certain tendency" of the American Cinema.[36] In doing so, however, I hope to provide a necessary complement to the two principal traditions of American film history, auteurism and genre study, both of which have made an enormous effort to deny the obvious homogeneity of the American Cinema. With ideological hindsight, one might wish to denigrate both auteurism and genre study as examples of the inadequate, nonconformist liberalism of the 1950s. More reasonably, however, we should see both as enormously useful correctives to the Frankfurt School's sweeping denouncement of popular culture,[37] a position that failed to take account of the unprecedentedly large role assumed by popular culture in England and the United States. Such prominence has insured that Anglo-American popular culture (including the movies) would become a complex hybrid carrying within itself elements of dissident subcultures.

For the most part, however, those dissident elements have been contained. If they had not been, would the movies in which they appeared have been popular?—a devilish question since it points to the great uncharted area of film criticism, the audience. How does one discuss with any confidence "the audience's" reaction to a movie, especially when one is inquiring about precisely those disruptive elements that the surrounding context and the existing ideological predispositions seek to hide? Empirical probes founder on leading questions. (Q: Did you notice Ozu's repeated 180° axis violations? A: Well . . . now that you mention it.)

With its implied equation of dissidence with quality, Godard's famous dictum, "Whenever a great film becomes a commercial success, a mistake has been made," is both more satisfyingly theoretical and more disturbingly dogmatic. Others have argued, for example, that the increasingly homogenized cultural atmosphere of the postindustrial world has insured that dissent survives precisely "in the realm of fantasy and imagination,"[38] in the crevices of conventional modes which never succeed in entirely subduing it.

I am not happy with either of these formulations. The latter too closely resembles auteurism's insistence that quality results from working against the grain of conventional modes and procedures, a too-easy nonconformism for my taste. Godard's proposition, on the other hand, depends on his own estimation of what counts as "great." For now, I can only offer a modification of his slogan, one that seems to me to avoid the necessity of subjective value judgment: I cannot imagine an American movie becoming truly popular if it departs radically from the "certain tendency of the American Cinema" (thematic and formal) which I will describe. Godard, of course, would counter that this "tendency" embodies the dominant American ideology. I would not disagree. I would insist, however, that "popular" is a more verifiable term than "great"—after all, we have box office statistics.

Throughout this book, therefore, I will restrict myself to *popular* American movies. Since as Barthes's *Mythologies* has taught us to see, ideology follows the route of the popular, this focus will, I trust, work as a "control" for the speculations about ideological effect, a notion that implicitly raises the problematic of audience response. The "popular audience," of course, has never been perfectly homogeneous or unchanging, but it has proved more uniform and stable than those perpetual realignments that have constituted the cult and art house audiences. (And, too, we are not without demographic summaries of those shifts that have occurred.) I do not want to fall back on the old formulation that popular movies are all alike, but it is indisputable that *Casablanca* and *The Godfather* have something in common that a film like *Touch of Evil* (much analyzed in contemporary journals) lacks: acceptance by a large audience.

At the outset of this project, I had the grand ambition of accounting "scientifically" for that acceptance—of describing precisely, in other words, those formulae that insure a movie's popularity. Had I succeeded in this effort, of course, I should long ago have sold my prognostic services to Hollywood. I do think, however, that in detailing the "certain tendency" of the American Cinema, the formal and thematic paradigms that commercially successful films in this country have consistently used, I have made theoretical progress toward an understanding of cinematic popularity. This issue is neither trivial nor merely economic. In this century, the movies have provided their audiences with some of the most compelling, most abiding representations of the mental and physical conditions of our lives. As an arena, the movies (and now their offspring, television) have constituted the most visible site of an ideological struggle waged for access to, and control of, these representations. In describing "a certain tendency of the American Cinema," therefore, I am describing a process that has had an enormous influence on what a nineteenth-century novelist once referred to as "the way we live now."[39]

Part One. Classic Hollywood

(1930–1945)

1. A Certain Tendency of the American Cinema: Classic Hollywood's Formal and Thematic Paradigms

To SENSE quickly the importance of the years 1930-1945 for the history of the American Cinema, one only has to realize that:

1. All of the nine major studios (MGM, Twentieth Century-Fox, Warner Brothers, RKO, Paramount, Columbia, Universal, United Artists, and Disney) that have produced and distributed the vast majority of American films came to prominence before 1945. The commonly used term for the 1930-1945 period suggests the extraordinary role of these enterprises during the first two decades of talkies—The Studio Era.

2. Of the great movie stars (Bogart, Cagney, Gable, Wayne, Stewart, Cooper, Rooney, Flynn, Tracy and Hepburn, Astaire and Rogers, Lombard, Loy, Dietrich, Garbo, Davis, Garland, Harlow, and Elizabeth Taylor), only Wayne, Stewart, and Taylor found their greatest success after 1945. Of the postwar stars, none (with the possible exceptions of Brando, Dean, and Monroe) approached the glamor of their predecessors.

3. Of the principal genres that have made up the bulk of American movies (western, gangster, horror, science fiction, screwball comedy, women's melodrama, musical, biography, swashbuckler, costume drama), only the western, science fiction, and horror genres achieved their richest forms after 1945.

Understandably, therefore, film historians have designated the years 1930-1945 as "The Classic Period" of American movies. For despite the American Cinema's enormous silent-era success, the arrival of sound saw Hollywood reach the peak of its narrative and commercial efficiency. Statistics tell part of the story. For those sixteen years, the movies *averaged* 80 million in weekly attendance, a sum representing more than half of the U.S. population of the time. Translated another way, from 1930 to 1945, the movies attracted 83 cents of every U.S. dollar spent on recreation.[1]

Even these remarkable numbers, however, fail to convey the extent of Hollywood's influence. By also dominating the international market,[2] the American Cinema insured that for the vast majority of the audience, both here and abroad, Hollywood's Classic Period films would establish the definition of the medium itself. Henceforth, different ways of making movies would appear as aberrations from some "intrinsic essence of cinema" rather than simply as alternatives to a particular form that had resulted from a unique coincidence of historical accidents—aesthetic, economic, technological, political, cultural, and even geographic. Given the economics of the medium, such a perception had immense consequences: because departures from the American Cinema's dominant paradigms risked not only commercial disaster but critical incomprehension, one form of cinema threatened to drive out all others.

We should realize, therefore, that in examining the movies of Hollywood's Classic Period, we are studying the single most important body of films in the history of cinema, the one that set the terms by which all movies, made before or after, would be seen. The preeminent influence of these films would seem to call for a theoretical description of the basic patterns of Classic Hollywood, locating the sources of those patterns and their connection to the rest of American culture, and accounting for their durability in the face of external and internal pressures for change. Such a theory would not only clarify the shape of American film history; it would also explain why movies operating under different patterns necessarily seem "wrong." It would perhaps provide perspective on the typically normative language of this admonitory passage from a cinematography textbook:

> It is important . . . that ambitious movie makers first *learn the rules* before breaking them. Learn the *right* way to film, learn the *acceptable* methods, learn how audiences become involved in the screen story. . . . Experiment; be bold, shoot in an unorthodox fashion! But, first *learn the correct* way.[3]

The particular path of cinema's evolution has made it especially susceptible to influences from without and within.[4] As an international medium, limited only by a language barrier (appearing long after the movies' establishment and promptly overcome by dubbing and subtitles), film has always been quick to assimilate new cinematic developments as they occur around the world. As an expensive medium, it has generally responded to cultural moods in order to guarantee audience support; at times, it has sought active governmental backing.

The historical nature of American Cinema has made it uniquely vulnerable to influence. Hollywood's early success, the appeal of the United States as a country, and a European political situation that remained unstable from 1914 to 1945 combined to insure that the American film industry would lure many of international cinema's most important figures. Thus actors like Garbo, Jannings, Dietrich, Laughton, Colman, Lamarr, and Negri and directors like Eisenstein, Murnau, Lang, Renoir, Clair, and Pabst all came to Hollywood during the Classic Period, contributing to the melting pot of American Cinema. Innumerable other lesser-known figures—character actors, cameramen, lighting technicians—arrived during the 1930s, bringing with them the modes of German Expressionism and East European, Soviet-influenced montage and making the American style the closest thing to a truly international cinema. *Casablanca*'s extreme cosmopolitanism is merely another sign of its representativeness. Indeed, of that movie's principal contributors, only Bogart, Dooley Wilson, and scriptwriter Howard Koch were Americans. A Hungarian director (Curtiz) orchestrated a cast of one Swede (Bergman), one Austrian (Henreid), two Englishmen (Rains and Greenstreet), one German (Veidt), two Hungarians (Lorre and Sakall), one Norwegian (Qualen), one Russian (Kinskey), and one Frenchman (Dalio) to a musical score composed by an Austrian (Steiner).

If Hollywood's eagerness to exploit any available talent made the American cinematic style a composite of influences, the determinedly commercial nature of the U.S. film industry compelled a kind of filmmaking peculiarly responsive to the dominant ideologies of American life. As Charles Eckert observed,

the industry ... was possibly more exposed to influences emanating from society, and in particular from its economic base, than any other.

To the disruption of production, distribution and consumption shared by all industries [due to the Depression] one must add the intense economically determined ideological pressures that bore upon an industry whose commodities were emotions and ideas.[5]

The self-perpetuating nature of Classic Hollywood's forms, however, made American movies a sociological barometer of the subtlest type. Because commercial exigencies forbade radical departures from established patterns, significant real-world developments often appeared only in the subtexts of superficially traditional movies (as we will see in *Casablanca, It's a Wonderful Life*, and *The Man Who Shot Liberty Valance*). And often, a brief run of movies offering even these slight challenges to Classic Hollywood's paradigms would be followed by a longer string in which the old forms reasserted themselves (as in the post-*Godfather* 1970s with *Star Wars, Heaven Can Wait, Saturday Night Fever, Grease*, and *Urban Cowboy*).

Nevertheless, the sound era American Cinema has been continuously besieged by internal and external factors demanding modifications of the movies' basic strategies. The briefest outline of those factors would include the following:

Internal Influences
1. Technological innovations specific to the cinema (e.g., sound, color, improved lenses and editing facilities, porto-cams)
2. Stylistic innovations (e.g., *Citizen Kane*'s proto-*noir* foregroundings of normally motivated stylistics, Italian Neo-Realism's minimal plots and location shooting, the French New Wave's stylistic self-consciousness)[6]
3. Evolving conditions of production, distribution, and consumption: having deliberately abandoned its original artisanal mode, the American film industry has since evolved from an industrial form (marked by high degrees of standardization, vertical and horizontal integration, and centralized production) to a postindustrial form (distinguished by relative diversification, lack of integration, and centralized distribution)[7]

External Influences
1. Technological developments outside the cinema, particularly television
2. The increasing popularity of other forms of entertainment, particularly popular music and spectator/participant sports

3. Historical events (e.g., the Depression, World War II, the Cold War, Vietnam, Watergate, the energy crisis)

Given this array of stimuli, Hollywood's stability may seem remarkable. In practice, that stability rested on the strategy of avoiding sudden saltations for gradual, often imperceptible modulations. Thus, Hollywood typically adopted only diluted versions of stylistic innovations, which it subsequently devitalized or discarded (the fate of most of the borrowings from the French New Wave). Historical crises, on the other hand (the Depression, World War II, the OPEC embargo), often prompted the most conservative films, as Hollywood sought to fulfill its self-appointed role as public comforter. Inevitably, therefore, most of Hollywood's "new" movies looked like the old ones: *Norma Rae*, for example, as I suggested in the Introduction, provided no surprises for someone who had seen *Grapes of Wrath* forty years earlier.

At times, internal and external influences in concert determined the course of American Cinema. Thus, the beginning of Hollywood's Classic Period saw two key factors converge to encourage a kind of filmmaking that would for the first time draw systematically on a basic American mythology.

The internal factor was sound. Stylistically, sound merely solidified a continuity system that was already highly evolved. In other ways, however, it forced American movies to shed the Victorian trappings which the immense influences of Griffith and Chaplin had encouraged in silent film. First, and most obviously, sound revolutionized cinematic acting. It forced a style that was declamatory, grandiose, and abstract to give way to one that was intimate, vernacular, and specific. "You ain't heard nothin' yet" was the perfect opening for the new age, a slangy wisecrack that banished the universalized mime of the silent era—and with it, many of the European actors who had been playing Americans without being able to speak English. Overnight, merely by the addition of voices, Hollywood films became more American. The movies crackled with the localized inflections that drew an aural map of the United States: Cagney's New Yorkese complementing Cooper's Western laconicism, Hepburn's high-toned Connecticut broad *a*'s matching Jean Arthur's Texas drawl.

Almost immediately, the movie audience rejected the rhetorical manner of the silent era. Henceforth that style would be available to an actor only as a parodic resource, a way of making fun of "acting" that furthered the illusion of the ongoing performance's realism (John Barrymore's 1934 performance in *Twentieth Century* as a hammy impresario being the classic instance). More important, sound and the new indigenous acting style encouraged the flourishing of genres that silence and grandiloquent acting had previously hindered: the musical, the gangster film, the detective story, screwball comedy, and humor that depended on language rather than slapstick (W. C. Fields, the Marx Brothers, Mae West).

Another effect of sound also encouraged the Americanization of Classic Hollywood, albeit indirectly. RCA's and Western Electric's sole control of sound technology and the added expense of producing talkies forced the U.S. film industry, already oligopolistic, into further concentration. Indeed, by 1936, all of Hollywood's major studios had come under the financial control of either the Morgan or Rockefeller interests,[8] a factor that would influence the American Cinema in two ways. First, such concentration clearly led to a homogenized product, fostering Classic Hollywood's tactic of working endless variations around a few basic patterns—a tactic further stimulated by the time pressures involved in producing Classic Hollywood's average of 476 films a year (compared to the 256 per year average of the 1946–1976 period). Second, the financial nature of such control intensified the existing commerciality of the American Cinema, dictating a filmmaking that, for the sake of a regular audience, would consistently deploy the basic ideologies and myths of American culture. The coming of sound, in other words, helped determine two permanent habits of the American Cinema: the tendency to repeat what had worked before, and the inclination, particularly evident during times of financial stress, to return to standard American stories.

Coincidentally, the principal external influences on Classical Hollywood (the Depression and World War II) also encouraged a reformulation of the American Cinema around more traditionally American preoccupations. As perhaps the first significant challenges to American optimism since the Civil War, these two events fostered a moviemaking whose cultural responsiveness revealed itself primarily in displacement and repression.[9] Put simply, the American Cinema was established as escapist. Robert Sklar summarizes the impact of these external factors:

What was different about the movies in the 1930's was not that they were beginning to communicate myths and dreams—they had done that from the beginning—but that the moviemakers were aware in a more sophisticated way of their mythmaking powers, responsibilities and opportunities. Among intellectuals and in centers of political power, the importance of cultural myths to social stability was a seriously debated topic. The Depression had shaken some of the oldest and strongest American cultural myths, particularly the middle-class homilies about the virtues of deferred gratification and assurance that hard work and perseverance would bring success. . . . The widespread doubt about traditional American myths threatened to become a dangerous political weakness. In politics, industry and the media there were men and women . . . who saw the necessity, almost as a patriotic duty, to revitalize and refashion a cultural mythology.[10]

From the outset, that mythology was deliberately traditional, a reassertion of the most fundamental American beliefs in individualism, ad hoc solutions, and the impermanence of all political problems. "We're in the money," Ginger Rogers sang ironically in *The Gold Diggers of 1933*, when one-fourth of the civilian labor force was unemployed, the highest percentage in the history of the United States.

The conservative nature of American Cinema's mythological product should not surprise us. "Statistically," Roland Barthes observed, "myth is on the right," for "*left-wing myth is inessential.*"[11] That nature, however, should alert us to the indirectness of the relationship that American films have consistently maintained with external events. To a great extent, American history's major crises appear in American movies only as "structuring absences"[12]—the unspoken subjects that have determined an aesthetic form designed precisely to conceal these crises' real implications. As we will see in *Casablanca* and *It's a Wonderful Life*, the genuine threats posed by World War II to traditional American ideologies surface only in the cracks of films consciously intended to minimize them. As Sklar observes:

Even satirical movies like the screwball comedies, or socially aware films like the *Grapes of Wrath*, were carefully constructed to stay within the bounds of essential American cultural and political beliefs. . . . Hollywood's contribution to American culture was essentially one of affirmation.[13]

Thus, these historical accidents—the arrival of sound, intensifying economic concentration, and political crisis—resulted in the formation of Classic Hollywood, a cinema whose deliberate evocations of traditional myths effected a new continuity with American culture. Certainly that cinema was never utterly uniform. From the beginning, however, it did display "a certain tendency" that took on both a formal and a thematic pattern. We need now to look more closely at these two patterns, and to observe how both serve the same ideological purpose: the concealment of the necessity for choice.

THE FORMAL PARADIGM—THE INVISIBLE STYLE

Film as a medium, David Thompson has noted, is "intensely decision-based."[14] Each shot results from dozens of choices about such elements as camera placement, lighting, focus, casting, and framing (the components of *mise en scène*); editing adds the further possibilities inherent in every shot-to-shot articulation. Not only do things on the screen appear at the expense of others not shown, the manner in which they appear depends on a selection of one perspective that eliminates (at least temporarily) all others.

The American Cinema's formal paradigm, however, developed precisely as a means for concealing these choices. Its ability to do so turned on this style's most basic procedure: the systematic subordination of every cinematic element to the interests of a movie's narrative. Thus, lighting remained unobtrusive, camera angles predominantly at eye-level, framing centered on the principal business of a scene. Similarly, cuts occurred at logical points in the action and dialogue. Certainly there were shots, scenes, and even movies that did not adhere completely to this tactic. The dominance of this procedure, however, insured the commercial failure of those few Classic Period filmmakers who consistently made style itself the center of attention (Sternberg, Welles).

The American Cinema's habitual subordination of style to story encouraged the audience to assume the existence of an implied contract: at any moment in a movie, the audience was to be given the optimum vantage point on what was occurring on screen. Anything important would not only be shown, but shown from the best angle. This contract could be violated only in the rarest moments, particularly in detective stories, where the audience yielded its normal right to omniscience for the sake of the whodunit game. But because these abridgments, too, were determined by narrative necessity, they went unnoticed. Thus, *The Maltese Falcon*'s deliberately tight framing that conceals Miles Archer's murderer did not shock the audience as a radical departure from the formal paradigm's basic contract.

This tacit guarantee of a constantly optimum vantage point constituted so fundamental a part of Hollywood's stylistic that the best filmmakers, even when working in the detective genre, violated it only surreptitiously. In *Psycho*, Hitchcock twice used an extreme high angle in order to conceal the murderer's identity without appearing to do so. "I deliberately placed the camera very high," Hitchcock told Truffaut, "so that I could shoot down on top of the mother, because if I had shown her back, it might have looked as if I was deliberately concealing her face and the audience would have been leery. I used that angle in order not to give the impression that I was trying to avoid showing her."[15]

The American Cinema's apparently natural subjection of style to narrative in fact depended on a historical accident: the movies' origins lay in a late nineteenth century whose predominant popular arts were the novel and the theater. Had cinema appeared in the Enlightenment or the Romantic period, it might have assumed the shape of the essay or lyric poem. Instead, it adopted the basic tactic and goal of the realistic novel. Conscious "style" would be effaced both to establish the cinema's illusion of reality and to encourage audience identification with the characters on the screen.

This link between Hollywood's continuity style and the narrative tactics of the nineteenth-century novel has been made most compellingly in English by Noël Burch and the *Screen* group of writers, particularly Colin MacCabe and Stephen Heath.[16] The ideological aspect of this argument (that regards a self-effacing, "realistic" style as the embodiment of bourgeois class interests) descends from Roland Barthes's influential critique of nineteenth-century fiction, *Writing Degree Zero*.[17] The counterargument to "the *Screen* position," however, consists in demonstrating the inappropriateness of the novel-film analogy.

This dissent, couched in *Screen*'s own semiotic language, might begin by insisting that realism is merely an effect produced by aesthetic conventions to which an audience has grown accustomed.[18] But since the predominantly working-class audience for the first movies differed significantly in its aesthetic "competencies"[19] from the largely middle-class audience for the nineteenth-century realistic novel, the conventions established by this earlier form would have no effect on the film audience.

In fact, however, this exclusively working-class audience was at most a short-lived phenomenon. Film historians have demonstrated that, from the start, the American movie industry sought to attract the middle-class ticket-buyer.[20] Burch has argued that the industry succeeded in this goal by decisively shifting from the *presentational* modes of such proleterian forms as vaudeville, the circus, and magic shows to the *representational* modes of the bourgeoisie, realistic theater and fiction. Burch insists that Fritz Lang's *Dr. Mabuse, The Gambler* confirms that a cinematic version of this latter mode was perfected as early as 1922.[21] I would disagree and insist on sound as an indispensable unit of the continuity project. In any case, Hollywood's sound era audience (the audience that concerns me in this book) was clearly no longer exclusively (or even primarily) working-class, and was thus unlikely to have received most of its prior aesthetic "training" from presentational modes.

The counterargument poses a second question: how can we be sure that Classic Hollywood's audiences regarded the movies as "real" when so many contemporary filmgoers (those whom I will later describe as the "ironic audience") have learned to see through the cinematic representation to the aesthetic conventions that produce them? The answer is, of course, that we cannot be sure. Indeed, French psychiatrist Octave Mannoni has warned that we have a persisting need to posit "an other scene" of absolute, untroubled faith, whether that "other scene" be primitive cultures, an epoch's own past, an individual's childhood, or even the bumpkin who interrupts a performance of *Julius Caesar* by standing to warn the emperor that his enemies are armed.[22] Certainly, film history has its own version of this last "other scene": the accounts of the frightened first audiences for Lumière's *Arrival of a Train at a Station*.

Mannoni's two articles, "Je sais bien, mais quand même ..." and "L'illusion comique ou le théâtre du point de vue de l'imaginaire," contain superb discussions of how beliefs in illusions (whether theatrical, religious, or traditional) always rest on a delicate balance of faith and disavowal. Moreover, even after such illusions have been exposed, a former believer retains some version of his old faith, a version expressed in what Mannoni observed to be a common formulation: "je sais bien, mais quand même ..." That is, "I know very well that this illusion is only an illusion, but nevertheless, some part of me still believes in it." While Mannoni makes an analogy between this diluted belief and superstition and fetishism, it also seems to approximate precisely the double system of consciousness operating in those moviegoers who "know very well" that onscreen events are not "real" but who "nevertheless" become absorbed in them as if they were.[23]

Just as the transparency (the "realism") of aesthetic conventions depends on their being thoroughly (albeit unconsciously) learned by their audience, the recognition of conventions as conventions also requires learning (or unlearning). Mannoni argues that abandoning a naïve faith in a particular illusion typically involves an *initiation*, a formal process in which the illusion is systematically and thoroughly exposed. An isolated, unintentional revelation will not normally suffice. In support of this assertion, Mannoni cites a story told by a Hopi boy regarding a rite in which masked figures (*Katcina*) appear in the village courting the children with gifts whose sole purpose consists in attracting the children so that the Katcina can eat them. In this grisly version of the Santa Claus story, however, the children win: the parents buy back their children with pieces of meat, and the Katcina seal the bargain by offering magically red ears of corn. During an annual Katcina appearance, the boy happened upon his mother dyeing ears of corn the appropriate red. Despite this revelation of the secret of the Katcina (who were the adult males of the tribe), the boy continued to believe in the illusion until his own proper initiation into the ceremony took place years later.

For film theory, Mannoni's story suggests that any loss of faith in the continuity style as "realistic" would require more than isolated incidental exposures. How are aesthetic conventions systematically exposed as mere convention? I would argue in four ways:

1. When material events consistently contradict the conventions supposedly embodying them. Although I cannot imagine that many ex-prisoners of war would find *Stalag 17* or "Hogan's Heroes" to be accurate portrayals of their own experiences, this mechanism of exposure seems to me to be the *least* important. Hollywood's formulae, after all, proved able to survive such minor distractions as the Depression and World War II.

2. When a commercial art form, trapped by the apparent need to repeat successful formulae, repeats them so often and so obviously that the audience begins to recognize how much of what once seemed "real" is actually convention. This mechanism of exposure, the development of camp responses, arose in the 1960s and 1970s, at the tail end of Hollywood's genre period. It was unlikely to work during the Studio Years when Hollywood was intent on *developing* the genres which still remained relatively fresh.

3. When a consistent pattern of internal self-criticism and self-consciousness foregrounds cinematic mechanisms. This process has never existed systematically in any body of cinema other than the avant-garde. Certainly, Classic Hollywood's films contained few "Godardian" foregroundings of conventions. Comedians occasionally violated certain standard principles of continuity: one thinks of Groucho Marx in *Horsefeathers* turning to address the camera as brother Chico began a piano solo: "I've got to stay here, but there's no reason why you folks shouldn't go out into the lobby until this thing blows over." But such violations were recuperated by being identified precisely as elements of "comedy."

4. When another similar art form intersects obliquely with the

medium in question, thereby providing an unexpected exposure of the latter's established procedures. I will discuss this mechanism at some length in my analysis of television's effect on the film audience.

In sum, none of these mechanisms of exposure operated with any real force during Hollywood's Classic Period. Their weakness was furthered by the industry's self-propagated myth of entertainment which forestalled critical examination of the movies' devices.[24]

Mannoni has also proposed that belief in an illusion rests on identification with some element of the illusion—in the case of theater, for example, with the characters. (Here Mannoni clearly depends on Jacques Lacan's notion of "the mirror stage," a term whose relevance for the American Cinema I wish to raise in a later chapter.[25]) Certainly, as we will see, Hollywood's strategies (formal and thematic) consistently urged the spectator to merge himself with the movies' heroes and heroines. Nevertheless, Hollywood cinema's illusion of reality depended on a far more substantial identification with the film's whole diegesis, that nonexistent, fictional space fabricated out of temporal and spatial fragments, which came to seem more rich, interesting, and fully constituted than the actual, material space of the audience's own lives. It was no accident that such different characters as Buster Keaton's Sherlock Junior and Godard's *carabiniers* would attempt to take up residence there, within the world projected on the screen.

The components of the invisible style gathered around cinema's two fundamental means: *mise en scène* and editing. In *mise en scène*, the invisible style evolved what Burch has called the principal of "centering."[26] Lighting, focus, camera angle, framing, character blocking, set design, costuming, and camera distance all worked to keep what the ongoing narrative defined as the main object of interest in the foreground and center of the frame. The inherent discontinuity of editing, on the other hand, was disguised by rules designed to maintain spatial and temporal continuity from shot to shot. Matching successive shots by graphic similarities, continuing action, connecting glances, or common sounds provided one connecting tactic. Another depended on the 180° system, a procedure of filming all takes in an establishing shot-breakdown shot sequence from the same side of an imaginary 180° axis. The 180° system not only allowed the filmmaker to maintain constant screen direction (particularly important with horizontal movement in the frame); it also enabled him to break down the overall space of a scene into smaller units without confusing the audience about their spatial relationship.[27]

Burch and other French theoreticians have argued that of all the components of the American Cinema's formal paradigm, the most important was the shot-reverse shot figure based on eyeline matches. As Burch puts the case:

> The reverse-field figure with matching eyelines . . . was not merely the last component of the dominant Western editing system; it was, as well, the most crucial. It was this procedure which made it possible to implicate the spectator in the eye contacts of the actor (and ultimately in their "word contacts"), to *include* him or her in the mental and "physical" space of the diegesis. Clearly such a procedure was basic to the illusionist fantasy/identification situation.[28]

Other writers see this trope's importance in its power to attribute a high percentage of a movie's shots to a source within the film, a process that "naturalized" the cinematic narrative by concealing the role of the filmmaker.[29] Thus, while a single shot of a house might have provoked the spectator to wonder "who is showing me this?" a following shot of a man looking offscreen identified the previous image as "his." This "suturing" procedure, whereby one shot "completed" a predecessor, prevented the viewer from becoming conscious of a film's status as an object made by individuals with particular biases. Things on the screen appeared real, unsponsored, and inevitable while the thousands of choices that created the film disappeared.

The shot-reverse shot figure, therefore, played a crucial role in a formal paradigm whose basic tactic was the concealment of the necessity of choice. Whether or not this figure was, as Burch claims, "the keystone" of the whole invisible system, at a minimum it isolated for the viewer a seam of significance within a potentially infinite visual field. For example, when a film narrowed the larger space of a room to the smaller units of a reverse

SPADE: Say, Frank?

FRANK: Oh, hello, Mr. Spade. SPADE: You got plenty of gas? FRANK: Sure thing.

SHOT 2

SPADE: Do you know where Ancho Street or Avenue is in Burlingame? FRANK: Nope. But if she's there we can find her.

SHOT 2

SPADE: Well, twenty-six is the number and the sooner the better. FRANK: Correct!

SHOT 3

SHOT 4

SHOT 4

SHOT 4

SPADE: Keep your motor running.

SHOT 6

SHOT 6

FRANK: Bum steer, Mr. Spade?

SPADE: Yeah. Let's get to a phone booth.

SHOT 7

SHOT 8

SPADE: Hello, Mrs. Perine. Effie there? Yes, please. . . . Hello, precious, what's the good news? No, no, it was a bum steer. Are you sure that was her voice? . . . Well, it was hooey. Everything go all right? . . . Nothing said about the bundle, huh? . . . That's swell. Did they take you down to the hall? . . . Um-huh. All right, precious. You'd better hit the hay and get a good night's rest. You sound all in. . . . Oh, no. Save it for tomorrow. I'm going on home.

SPADE: Thanks. Good night, Frank. FRANK: Good night.

SHOT 8

SHOT 8

SHOT 8

SHOT 8

SHOT 8

SHOT 8

BRIGID: Mr. Spade! I've been hiding in a doorway up the street. I thought you'd never come.

field (say, a man and a woman exchanging glances), the audience assumed that *this* space, at least for the duration of the shot-reverse shots, was the only important one.

Whatever this figure's psychological effect, certainly it constituted a major portion of Classic Hollywood's shot transitions—an average of 30-40 percent according to one researcher. Here again, *Casablanca* provides a perfect example of the period, with fully 50 percent of its transitions employing the reverse-field structure.[30]

Classic Hollywood's invisible style succeeded so well in effacing itself in strong narratives that detecting its workings requires concentration. We can observe its procedures most effectively in short sequences from movies that we know well enough to be able momentarily to suspend our normal interest in the story line. I offer two examples, the first of which involves both spatial and temporal discontinuity, the latter only spatial.

The first sequence is from *The Maltese Falcon*. Having received a phone call from a hysterical and apparently endangered Brigid O'Shaughnessy, Sam Spade (Humphrey Bogart) emerges from a railroad station where he has checked the falcon given him by the dying Captain Jacoby. He takes a cab to an address mentioned by O'Shaughnessy, but the address is a vacant lot. After telephoning further instructions to his secretary, he returns home to find O'Shaughnessy waiting for him.

This sequence compresses an incident requiring at least an hour of real time into eight shots lasting exactly two minutes on the screen. Classic Hollywood's formal conventions also conceal the spatial discontinuity of Spade's roundtrip ride between downtown San Francisco and the Peninsula suburb of Burlingame. No viewer watching this sequence is likely to become aware of the operations of style.

How is this stylistic invisibility accomplished? First, we should note that Classic Hollywood's formal paradigm worked its tricks most effectively around compelling narratives. In bad movies, where the plot's insufficiency allowed the spectator's mind to wander, stylistic mechanics often became glaring. In *The Maltese Falcon*'s scene, on the other hand, one tantalizing narrative movement flows into another, leaving no empty moments where the storyline might stall. The sequence begins immediately after Spade's capture of the falcon, the object previously established as the movie's focus of interest. It shifts to a new development, Brigid's distress call. The vacant lot initiates still another puzzle which Brigid's subsequent appearance at Spade's doorway only partially solves. Thus, even in this two-minute sequence, the narrative's sheer relentlessness forestalls attention to style.

The sequence's eight individual shots and the transitions between them operate further to conceal the traces of the movie's status as manufactured product.

1. Shot 1's framing centers Bogart as he gradually walks into the foreground, the people on the sidewalk seeming to part for his entrance. At this stage in the film, the spectator's concern with Spade has merged with his extra-*Falcon* recognition of Bogart-as-star; the movie trades on the mingling of these two sources of interest to hide the selectivity of a shot that "naturally" finds Bogart-Spade in the center of a street scene.

2. The direct cut to Shot 2 completes the centering begun by Shot 1. The medium shot brings Spade farther into the foreground while keeping him in the middle of the frame. In addition, Shot 2 defines the 180° axis (here, horizontally bisecting the image) for the rest of the sequence and enables the camera following Spade to establish the consistent left-to-right movement of the roundtrip's first half. The dialogue evinces another continuity tactic, as verbal clues smooth the potentially disrupting temporal and spatial ellipses that follow. Spade's question to the cabbie, "You got plenty of gas?" tells the viewer that the forthcoming trip is a relatively long one. For a spectator who knows San Francisco's geography, the name "Burlingame" conveys information still more precise. Although the exact amount of real time elided by the sequence remains indefinite, these verbal clues (and the sequence's consistent night lighting) suggest a duration of only a few hours.

3. The overlapping dissolve connecting Shots 2 and 3 conveys to the spectator that only a brief amount of time has elapsed. (A full fade-out would signal a much larger time gap.) Further, the sustained left-to-right movement of the single tire (a typical Hollywood synecdoche for traveling) implies the continuation of the journey begun in Shot 2.

4. Another dissolve leads to Shot 4, which shows the cab arriving in Burlingame's Ancho Street. Because the camera remains on the same side of the 180° axis as in Shots 1, 2, and 3, the repeated left-to-right motion conveys a trip completed.

5. Shot 5's tracking motion, which keeps Spade center-frame, repeats the pattern of Shot 2. Again, the camera's movement is motivated—i.e., it does not act on its own to scan the neighborhood (an activity whose independence would call attention to the process of filming), but rather moves only to follow a character whose importance to the narrative goes unquestioned. Thus, by either linking most camera movements to a moving character or object, or by attributing them to a source within the story (through reverse-field figures that imply the motions are subjective, point-of-view shots), the invisible style concealed the operations of what otherwise might have been a readily apparent formal mechanism.

As Spade discovers the vacant lot and stops to think, the background music that continues throughout the entire sequence (and thus binds the individual shots together in yet another way) idles momentarily, imitating Spade's hesitation. Because the camera has remained on the same side of the sequence's original 180° axis, Spade's glance and wave to the left invoke the cab sitting in what has become offscreen space.

6. The direct cut to Shot 6 shows the cab pulling up beside Spade, still moving in the left-to-right direction of the trip to Burlingame. Spade's instructions to the cabbie, "Let's get to a phone booth," provide the verbal transition to Shot 7.

7. The dissolve to Shot 7 elides the real time required to reach the phone booth—a period omitted because the narrative defines it as unimportant. The invisible style's continual judgments about the importance of persons, incidents, or activities were powerful precisely because their self-effacing form caused them to go unnoticed. In fact, the sustained use of narratively motivated abridgments encouraged the spectator to regard the vast majority of his own waking hours as insignificant—indeed, all hours that did not fit immediately into some ongoing "plot."

The potential tedium of Shot 7's long take (30 seconds) is overcome by the rapid-fire, bantering dialogue, partially designed to reconfirm the plot turn of the previous shot—that Brigid's address was "a bum steer." Classic Hollywood typically repeated points from shot to shot and scene to scene, removing any potential ambiguity that might cause a viewer confusion. Note, too, that Shot 7 uses an obvious chiaroscuro effect to increase the centering of Spade.

8. Still another dissolve leads to Shot 8, in which the cab's arrival from right-to-left suggests the completion of the round-trip begun in Shot 2. Another motivated camera movement follows the cab leaving, only to pick up Brigid "hiding in a doorway down the street" (thus, a doubled motivation). The camera remains with her as she runs back to Spade, and, perfectly centered, the two enter the building, still accompanied by the background music.

While *The Maltese Falcon* sequence illustrates the ability of Hollywood's formal paradigm to conceal spatial and temporal discontinuities, another example, from *Casablanca*, demonstrates the subtle effects of the shot-reverse shot figure.

This sequence is composed of three linking shot-reverse shot figures: Figure A (Shots 1-3) serves to introduce the movie's protagonist/star (Rick Blaine/Humphrey Bogart); Figure B (Shots 4-8) conveys hints about both Rick's power and his political sympathies; Figure C (Shots 9-11) continues the confrontation between Rick and the German begun in Figure B while introducing, apparently in passing, a character (Ugarte) who possesses the key to the whole film, but whose importance will become apparent only retroactively. Each figure demonstrates a particular facet of Classic Hollywood's formal paradigm.

Figure A: By withholding a view of Rick's face, Shots 1-3 increase the suspense that the film has already established around his character. We have heard Vichy Captain Renault tell the German Major Strasser that "Tonight [the murderer will] be at Rick's. Everybody comes to Rick's." We have also heard Strasser's portentous reply: "I have already heard about this café. And also about Mr. Rick himself." From Carl the waiter, we have gathered another curious bit of information about Rick: "He never drinks with customers. Never! I have never seen him." Shot 1 builds on these mysterious hints, using the waiter's glance to make what is offscreen more intriguing than what is on. The hand extending into the frame further invokes the presence off-

SHOT 1

SHOT 1

SHOT 1

SHOT 2

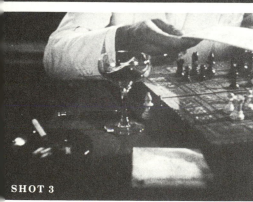

SHOT 3

SHOT 3

SHOT 3

SHOT 3

SHOT 3

SHOT 4

SHOT 5

SHOT 5

SHOT 5

SHOT 5

SHOT 6

SHOT 7

SHOT 8

SHOT 9

ABDUL: I'm sorry, sir. This is a private room.

GERMAN: Of all the nerve! Who do you think—I know there is gambling in there. There is no secret. You dare not keep me out of here.

SHOT 9

RICK: Yes? What's the trouble? ABDUL: Er, this gentleman . . . GERMAN: I have been in every gambling room between Honolulu and Berlin.

SHOT 9

GERMAN: If you think I'm going to be kept out of a saloon like this, you're very much mistaken.

SHOT 9

UGARTE: Um, excuse me, please. Hello, Rick.

SHOT 10

RICK: Your cash is good at the bar. GERMAN: What? Do you know who I am? RICK: I do. You're lucky the bar's open to you.

SHOT 11

GERMAN: This is outrageous! I shall report it to the Angriff!

screen and provides a linking match that connects Shots 1 and 2.

As is often the case of shot-reverse shot figures, the reverse field editing in this first unit pivots around both an object and an action match—here, the check handed to Rick in Shot 1 and signed by him in Shot 2. Both the object and the continued action that flows over the cut enable a viewer to read Shots 1 and 2 as occurring in the same immediate space and time.

The reverse Shot 3's initially odd framing emphasizes objects whose meaning has become coded through repeatedly similar use in Classic Hollywood films: the champagne glass and cigarette suggest both sophistication and jadedness, the solo chess game (an intellectual's solitaire) cleverness and a solitude simultaneously proud and melancholy. In a motivated shot following the hand lifting the cigarette, the camera moves up to reveal Rick's face for the first time. Lighting, framing, and focus keep him perfectly centered.

Figure B: This figure actually begins near the end of Shot 3 with the jaunty piano music (diegetic but offscreen) whose continuation through Shot 11 subtly conveys constant spatial and temporal continuity. Shot 4 begins the sequence proper. As an establishing shot, it sets the 180° axis as a diagonal connecting Rick and the doorman; all subsequent shots in Figure B will be taken from the near side of this line. For the viewer, Shot 4 also determines a temporary seam of significance within the larger space of the café. For the next seven shots, only events occurring within this seam will appear on the screen. Hollywood's implicit contract always to provide the optimum vantage point forestalls the spectator from wondering what might be happening elsewhere.

Shots 5 and 6 are breakdowns, connected by an eyeline match, of Shot 4's two poles. In Shot 5, the doorman, acting on Rick's Shot 4 nod, allows the couple to enter the gambling room; when the German arrives, the doorman looks back at Rick for new instructions. Rick's negative shake in Shot 6 causes the doorman's refusal which begins in Shot 7 and flows over the cut into Shot 8 taken from the other side of the door. During this exchange, adherence to the 180° rule insures that the doorman's and Rick's glances appear to meet.

Figure B's most interesting tactic, however, concerns the way this particular reverse field encourages the viewer to identify with Rick, a process already begun in Shot 2, where one sees the check being signed as if one were in Rick's body. Here, the effect is more subtle, but because of cumulative similar uses throughout the movie, no less powerful: in Shot 5, the doorman's glance directly into the camera suggests that the spectator is seeing him from Rick's point of view. Rick's eyes, on the other hand, do not look into the camera, but rather offscreen-right. This oblique angle replaces the doorman's viewpoint with an apparently neutral perspective. The effectiveness of Classic Hollywood's means of encouraging audience identification always depended on the selectiveness with which they were used. Here, for example, the point-of-view manipulations encourage identification with the protagonist Rick, but not with the inconsequential doorman.

Figure C: Shots 8-11 illustrate how Classic Hollywood's *mise en scène* tactics frequently operate within shot-reverse units. Here, after Shot 8's completion of the action begun in Shot 7, Shot 9 establishes a new 180° axis (extending from just to Rick's left to a point between the doorman and the German). Subsequently, all the visual elements conspire with the dialogue to convey Rick's preeminence over his adversary. First, the normal superiority of the German's centered position is undercut by the blocking that pins him between Rick and Rick's ally the doorman. In contrast to this crowded frame, Shot 10 provides Rick with a much stronger position. Second, the German's centered position, already weakened, is temporarily dislodged by the arrival of a character (Ugarte) who, for the moment, seems unimportant. Finally, Shot 11 sees the exasperated German abandon the privileged center, walking to the rear and out of frame, confirming Rick's victory. In the chapter on *Casablanca*, we will see the ideological effects of mixing *mise en scène* and reverse field strategies.

THESE two examples show Classic Hollywood's formal paradigm at work. In sum, that paradigm disguised an "intensely decision-based" medium as an apparently natural one, concealing the pattern of choices that constitute style in any art form. By eliding all events extraneous to the narrative at hand, by providing the viewer with a constantly shifting, but always ideal, perspective (thereby seeming to anticipate his desires), Classic Hollywood movies already matched Stanislaw Lem's description of an imaginary art form of the future, "the real":

"And what is a real?"
"A real is . . . a real . . ." she repeated helplessly. "They are . . . stories. It's for watching. . . . A real is artificial, but one can't tell the difference. . . ."
My first impression was of sitting near the stage of a theater, or no— on the stage itself, so close were the actors. As though one could reach out and touch them. . . .
The real was more than just a film, because whenever I concentrated on some portion of the scene, it grew larger and expanded; in other words, the viewer himself, by his own choice, determined whether he would see a close-up of the whole picture. Meanwhile the proportions of what remained on the periphery of his field of vision underwent no distortion. It was a diabolically clever optical trick producing an illusion of an extraordinarily vivid, an almost magnified reality.[31]

The ideological power of Classic Hollywood's procedure is obvious: under its sponsorship, even the most manufactured narratives came to seem spontaneous and "real." A spectator prevented from detecting style's role in a mythology's articulation could only accede to that mythology's "truth." When that mythology also denied the necessity for choice, the result was a doubling effect that made the American Cinema one of the most potent ideological tools ever constructed.

THE THEMATIC PARADIGM—THE RESOLUTION OF INCOMPATIBLE VALUES

With Classic Hollywood's formal paradigm, sound technology merely provided the final element in a continuity system that had been evolving since the early days of the silents. With Classic Hollywood's thematic paradigm, on the other hand, sound effected a major shift. Subject to intensifying oligopolistic concentration, increasingly controlled by profit-oriented financiers, more and more standardized, the American film industry perforce took new steps to guarantee a large, regular audience for its product. The key move lay in the thematic paradigm's adoption of the traditional American mythology, a maneuver that involved a decisive break with the silent era. For while the American silent film grew demonstrably out of Victorian melodrama, the talkies clearly derived from an alternate mode, the romance form that Richard Chase has shown to be the basis of nineteenth-century American fiction.[32]

The traditional task of American historians has been the attempt to authenticate this mythology by providing it with indigenously material sources: hence Turner's frontier, David Potter's material abundance, and Erikson's psychological expansiveness. In fact, however, nineteenth-century American fiction's own reliance on preexisting myths suggests that the traditional "American" mythology taken up by the talkies occurs only as part of an infinitely regressing chain of texts, flowing backward from American sound films, to W. S. Hart westerns, to Horatio Alger stories, to Chase's classic nineteenth-century authors (Twain, Cooper, Melville), to frontier tall tales, to Pilgrim captivity narratives, to prospectuses for America, to pre-Columbian myths of the New World, to Eden itself.[33]

American commentators' longstanding pursuit of this mythology's immediate origins, however, indicates the power of that fictional system to assert itself as "true." Ultimately, therefore, the source of this mythology becomes less enlightening than an understanding of the historical circumstances that sustain and modify its particular incarnations.

The American Cinema's version of this traditional mythology rested on two factors. First, Hollywood's power (and need) to produce a steady flow of variations provided the myth with the repetitive elaborations that it required to become convincing. Second, the audience's sense of American exceptionalism (in part authentic, in part itself the product of the myth) encouraged acceptance of a mythology whose fundamental premise was optimistic. For to a large extent, American space, economic abundance, and geographic isolation—and the fictions embroidered around these things—had long been unavailable to the European imagination.

We can begin to describe this mythology by observing that, like the invisible style, it concealed the necessity for choice. As the formal paradigm depended on consciously established rules for shooting and editing, Hollywood's thematic conventions rested on an industrywide consensus defining commercially acceptable filmmaking. This consensus's underlying premise dictated the conversion of all political, sociological, and economic dilemmas into personal melodramas. Thus, *Meet John Doe* transformed unemployment's challenge to American ideology into an individual's credibility crisis. Similarly, *Casablanca* displaced American anxiety about intervention in World War II into Rick's hesitation about helping Victor Laszlo. Even the rare movies purporting to deal directly with general economic and political issues (e.g., *Our Daily Bread, The Grapes of Wrath*) slid inevitably into dramatizations of individual solutions. Warner Brothers, paying lip service to theories of environmental determinism, frequently reduced the Depression to a Vorkapich montage that only briefly interrupted the action (e.g., *The Roaring Twenties*).

Such displacement turned on Classic Hollywood's basic thematic procedure: repeatedly, these movies raised, and then appeared to solve, problems associated with the troubling incompatibility of traditional American myths. *Meet Me in St. Louis*, for example, overcame the opposition inherent in the myth of family (encouraging contentment and permanence) and the myth of success (encouraging ambition and mobility). Similarly, *Gone With the Wind* triumphed over the conflict between Scarlett's incarnation of a classically American self-reliance and her betrayal of the ideal wife and mother image.

This reconciliatory pattern, itself derived largely from earlier American forms, increasingly became the self-perpetuating norm of the American Cinema. Movies that refused to resolve contradictory myths typically found themselves without the large audiences expected by the industry; as a result, directors of such films found themselves without chances to work. Orson Welles's case is the most famous. By basing its story on the life of William Randolph Hearst, Welles was able to make his first film, *Citizen Kane*, a *succès de scandale*. But the movie's dramatization of the irresolvable conflict between American myths of success (celebrating energy and ambition) and of the simple life (warning that power and wealth corrupt) made audiences uneasy and cost

Welles RKO's complete confidence. When his second movie (*The Magnificent Ambersons*) demonstrated the stark incompatibility of nineteenth-century small-town values with those of the modern industrial age, the studio tacked on a wildly inappropriate happy ending and opened the film as the bottom half of double features. Thereafter, Welles rarely worked in America.

In contrast to Welles, the dominant tradition of American Cinema consistently found ways to overcome dichotomies. Often, the movies' reconciliatory pattern concentrated on a single character magically embodying diametrically opposite traits. A sensitive violinist was also a tough boxer (*Golden Boy*); a boxer was a gentle man who cared for pigeons (*On the Waterfront*). A gangster became a coward because he was brave (*Angels with Dirty Faces*); a soldier became brave because he was a coward (*Lives of a Bengal Lancer*). A war hero was a former pacifist (*Sergeant York*); a pacifist was a former war hero (*Billy Jack*). The ideal was a kind of inclusiveness that would permit all decisions to be undertaken with the knowledge that the alternative was equally available. The attractiveness of Destry's refusal to use guns (*Destry Rides Again*) depended on the tacit understanding that he could shoot with the best of them, Katharine Hepburn's and Claudette Colbert's revolts against conventionality (*Holiday, It Happened One Night*) on their status as aristocrats.

Such two-sided characters seemed particularly designed to appeal to a collective American imagination steeped in myths of inclusiveness. Indeed, in creating such characters, Classic Hollywood had connected with what Erik Erikson has described as the fundamental American psychological pattern:

> The functioning American, as the heir of a history of extreme contrasts and abrupt changes, bases his final ego identity on some tentative combination of dynamic polarities such as migratory and sedentary, individualistic and standardized, competitive and co-operative, pious and free-thinking, responsible and cynical, etc. . . .
>
> To leave his choices open, the American, on the whole, lives with two sets of "truths."[34]

The movies traded on one opposition in particular, American culture's traditional dichotomy of individual and community that had generated the most significant pair of competing myths: the outlaw hero and the official hero.[35] Embodied in the adventurer, explorer, gunfighter, wanderer, and loner, the outlaw hero stood for that part of the American imagination valuing self-determination and freedom from entanglements. By contrast, the official hero, normally portrayed as a teacher, lawyer, politician, farmer, or family man, represented the American belief in collective action, and the objective legal process that superseded private notions of right and wrong. While the outlaw hero found incarnations in the mythic figures of Davy Crockett, Jesse James, Huck Finn, and all of Leslie Fiedler's "Good Bad Boys" and Daniel Boorstin's "ring-tailed roarers," the official hero developed around legends associated with Washington, Jefferson, Lincoln, Lee, and other "Good Good Boys."

An extraordinary amount of the traditional American mythology adopted by Classic Hollywood derived from the variations worked by American ideology around this opposition of natural man versus civilized man. To the extent that these variations constituted the main tendency of American literature and legends, Hollywood, in relying on this mythology, committed itself to becoming what Robert Bresson has called "the Cinema."[36] A brief description of the competing values associated with this outlaw hero-official hero opposition will begin to suggest its pervasiveness in traditional American culture.

1. *Aging*: The attractiveness of the outlaw hero's childishness and propensity to whims, tantrums, and emotional decisions derived from America's cult of childhood. Fiedler observed that American literature celebrated "the notion that a mere falling short of adulthood is a guarantee of insight and even innocence." From Huck to Holden Caulfield, children in American literature were privileged, existing beyond society's confining rules. Often, they set the plot in motion (e.g., *Intruder in the Dust, To Kill a Mockingbird*), acting for the adults encumbered by daily affairs. As Fiedler also pointed out, this image of childhood "has impinged upon adult life itself, has become a 'career' like everything else in America,"[37] generating stories like *On the Road* or *Easy Rider* in which adults try desperately to postpone responsibilities by clinging to adolescent lifestyles.

While the outlaw heroes represented a flight from maturity,

the official heroes embodied the best attributes of adulthood: sound reasoning and judgment, wisdom and sympathy based on experience. Franklin's *Autobiography* and *Poor Richard's Almanack* constituted this opposing tradition's basic texts, persuasive enough to appeal even to outsiders (*The Great Gatsby*). Despite the legends surrounding Franklin and the other Founding Fathers, however, the scarcity of mature heroes in American literature and mythology indicated American ideology's fundamental preference for youth, a quality that came to be associated with the country itself. Indeed, American stories often distorted the stock figure of the Wise Old Man, portraying him as mad (Ahab), useless (Rip Van Winkle), or evil (The Godfather).

2. *Society and Women*: The outlaw hero's distrust of civilization, typically represented by women and marriage, constituted a stock motif in American mythology. In his *Studies in Classic American Literature*, D. H. Lawrence detected the recurring pattern of flight, observing that the Founding Fathers had come to America "largely to get *away*. . . . Away from what? In the long run, away from themselves. Away from everything."[38] Sometimes, these heroes undertook this flight alone (Thoreau, *Catcher in the Rye*); more often, they joined ranks with other men: Huck with Jim, Ishmael with Queequeg, Jake Barnes with Bill Gorton. Women were avoided as representing the very entanglements this tradition sought to escape: society, the "settled life," confining responsibilities. The outlaw hero sought only uncompromising relationships, involving either a "bad" woman (whose morals deprived her of all rights to entangling domesticity) or other males (who themselves remained independent). Even the "bad" woman posed a threat, since marriage often uncovered the clinging "good" girl underneath. Typically, therefore, American stories avoided this problem by killing off the "bad" woman before the marriage could transpire (*Destry Rides Again, The Big Heat, The Far Country*). Subsequently, within the all-male group, women became taboo, except as the objects of lust.

The exceptional extent of American outlaw legends suggests an ideological anxiety about civilized life. Often, that anxiety took shape as a romanticizing of the dispossessed, as in the Beat Generation's cult of the bum, or the characters of Huck and

"Thoreau," who worked to remain idle, unemployed, and unattached. A passage from Jerzy Kosinski's *Steps* demonstrated the extreme modern version of this romanticizing:

I envied those [the poor and the criminals] who lived here and seemed so free, having nothing to regret and nothing to look forward to. In the world of birth certificates, medical examinations, punch cards, and computers, in the world of telephone books, passports, bank accounts, insurance plans, wills, credit cards, pensions, mortgages and loans, they lived unattached.[39]

In contrast to the outlaw heroes, the official heroes were preeminently worldly, comfortable in society, and willing to undertake even those public duties demanding personal sacrifice. Political figures, particularly Washington and Lincoln, provided the principal examples of this tradition, but images of family also persisted in popular literature from *Little Women* to *Life with Father* and *Cheaper by the Dozen*. The most crucial figure in this tradition, however, was Horatio Alger, whose heroes' ambition provided the complement to Huck's disinterest. Alger's characters subscribed fully to the codes of civilization, devoting themselves to proper dress, manners, and behavior, and the attainment of the very things despised by the opposing tradition: the settled life and respectability.[40]

3. *Politics and the Law*: Writing about "The Philosophical Approach of the Americans," Tocqueville noted "a general distaste for accepting any man's word as proof of anything." That distaste took shape as a traditional distrust of politics as collective activity, and of ideology as that activity's rationale. Such a disavowal of ideology was, of course, itself ideological, a tactic for discouraging systematic political intervention in a nineteenth-century America whose political and economic power remained in the hands of a privileged few. Tocqueville himself noted the results of this mythology of individualism which "disposes each citizen to isolate himself from the mass of his fellows and withdraw into the circle of family and friends; with this little society formed to his taste, he gladly leaves the greater society to look after itself."[41]

This hostility toward political solutions manifested itself further in an ambivalence about the law. The outlaw mythology portrayed the law, the sum of society's standards, as a collective, impersonal ideology imposed on the individual from without. Thus, the law represented the very thing this mythology sought to avoid. In its place, this tradition offered a natural law discovered intuitively by each man. As Tocqueville observed, Americans wanted

To escape from imposed systems ... to seek by themselves and in themselves for the only reason for things ... in most mental operations each American relies on individual effort and judgment. (p. 429)

This sense of the law's inadequacy to needs detectable only by the heart generated a rich tradition of legends celebrating legal defiance in the name of some "natural" standard: Thoreau went to jail rather than pay taxes, Huck helped Jim (legally a slave) to escape, Billy the Kid murdered the sheriff's posse that had ambushed his boss, Hester Prynne resisted the community's sexual mores. This mythology transformed all outlaws into Robin Hoods, who "correct" socially unjust laws (Jesse James, Bonnie and Clyde, John Wesley Hardin). Furthermore, by customarily portraying the law as the tool of villains (who used it to revoke mining claims, foreclose on mortgages, and disallow election results—all on legal technicalities), this mythology betrayed a profound pessimism about the individual's access to the legal system.

If the outlaw hero's motto was "I don't know what the law says, but I do know what's right and wrong," the official hero's was "We are a nation of laws, not of men," or "No man can place himself above the law." To the outlaw hero's insistence on private standards of right and wrong, the official hero offered the admonition, "You cannot take the law into your own hands." Often, these official heroes were lawyers or politicians, at times (as with Washington and Lincoln), even the executors of the legal system itself. The values accompanying such heroes modified the assurance of Crockett's advice, "Be sure you're right, then go ahead."

In sum, the values associated with these two different sets of heroes contrasted markedly. Clearly, too, each tradition had its good and bad points. If the extreme individualism of the outlaw

hero always verged on selfishness, the respectability of the official hero always threatened to involve either blandness or
repression. If the outlaw tradition promised adventure and freedom, it also offered danger and loneliness. If the official tradition
promised safety and comfort, it also offered entanglements and
boredom.

The evident contradiction between these heroes provoked Daniel Boorstin's observation that "Never did a more incongruous
pair than Davy Crockett and George Washington live together
in a national Valhalla." And yet, as Boorstin admits, "both
Crockett and Washington were popular heroes, and both emerged
into legendary fame during the first half of the 19th century."[42]

The parallel existence of these two contradictory traditions
evinced the general pattern of American mythology: the denial
of the necessity for choice. In fact, this mythology often portrayed situations requiring decision as temporary aberrations from
American life's normal course. By discouraging commitment to
any single set of values, this mythology fostered an ideology of
improvisation, individualism, and ad hoc solutions for problems
depicted as crises. American writers have repeatedly attempted
to justify this mythology in terms of material sources. Hence,
Irving Howe's "explanation":

It is when men no longer feel that they have adequate choices in their
styles of life, when they conclude that there are no longer possibilities
of honorable maneuver and compromise, when they decide that the time
has come for "ultimate" social loyalties and political decisions—it is
then that ideology begins to flourish. Ideology reflects a hardening of
commitment, the freezing of opinion into system. . . . The uniqueness of
our history, the freshness of our land, the plenitude of our resources—
all these have made possible, and rendered plausible, a style of political
improvisation and intellectual free-wheeling.[43]

Despite such an account's pretext of objectivity, its language betrays an acceptance of the mythology it purports to describe:
"honorable maneuver and compromise," "hardening," "freezing,"
"uniqueness," "freshness," and "plenitude" are all assumptive
words from an ideology that denies its own status. Furthermore,
even granting the legitimacy of the historians' authenticating
causes, we are left with a persisting mythology increasingly dis-

credited by historical developments. (In fact, such invalidation began in the early nineteenth century, and perhaps even before.)

The American mythology's refusal to choose between its two heroes went beyond the normal reconciliatory function attributed to myth by Lévi-Strauss. For the American tradition not only overcame binary oppositions; it systematically mythologized the certainty of being able to do so. Part of this process involved blurring the lines between the two sets of heroes. First, legends often brought the solemn official heroes back down to earth, providing the sober Washington with the cherry tree, the prudent Franklin with illegitimate children, and even the upright Jefferson with a slave mistress. On the other side, stories modified the outlaw hero's most potentially damaging quality, his tendency to selfish isolationism, by demonstrating that, however reluctantly, he would act for causes beyond himself. Thus, Huck grudgingly helped Jim escape, and Davy Crockett left the woods for three terms in Congress before dying in the Alamo for Texas independence. In this blurring process, Lincoln, a composite of opposing traits, emerged as the great American figure. His status as president made him an ex officio official hero. But his Western origins, melancholy solitude, and unaided decision-making all qualified him as a member of the other side. Finally, his ambivalent attitude toward the law played the most crucial role in his complex legend. As the Chief Executive, he inevitably stood for the principle that "we are a nation of laws and not men"; as the Great Emancipator, on the other hand, he provided the prime example of taking the law into one's own hands in the name of some higher standard.

Classic Hollywood's gallery of composite heroes (boxing musicians, rebellious aristocrats, pacifist soldiers) clearly derived from this mythology's rejection of final choices, a tendency whose traces Erikson detected in American psychology:

The process of American identity formation seems to support an individual's ego identity as long as he can preserve a certain element of deliberate tentativeness of autonomous choice. The individual must be able to convince himself that the next step is up to him and that no matter where he is staying or going he always has the choice of leaving or turning in the opposite direction if he chooses to do so. In this country the migrant does not want to be told to move on, nor the sedentary man to stay where he is; for the life style (and the family history) of each contains the opposite element as a potential alternative which he wishes to consider his most private and individual decision.[44]

The reconciliatory pattern found its most typical incarnation, however, in one particular narrative: the story of the private man attempting to keep from being drawn into action on any but his own terms. In this story, the reluctant hero's ultimate willingness to help the community satisfied the official values. But by portraying this aid as demanding only a temporary involvement, the story preserved the values of individualism as well.

Like the contrasting heroes' epitomization of basic American dichotomies, the reluctant hero story provided a locus for displacement. Its most famous version, for example, *The Adventures of Huckleberry Finn*, offered a typically individualistic solution to the nation's unresolved racial and sectional anxieties, thereby helping to forestall more systematic governmental measures. In adopting this story, Classic Hollywood retained its censoring power, using it, for example, in *Casablanca* to conceal the realistic threats to American self-determination posed by World War II.

Because the reluctant hero story was clearly the basis of the western, American literature's repeated use of it prompted Leslie Fiedler to call the classic American novels "disguised westerns."[45] In the movies, too, this story appeared in every genre: in westerns, of course (with *Shane* its most schematic articulation), but also in gangster movies (*Angels with Dirty Faces, Key Largo*), musicals (*Swing Time*), detective stories (*The Thin Man*), war films (*Air Force*), screwball comedy (*The Philadelphia Story*), "problem pictures" (*On the Waterfront*), and even science fiction (the Han Solo character in *Star Wars*). *Gone With the Wind*, in fact, had two selfish heroes who came around at the last moment, Scarlett (taking care of Melanie) and Rhett (running the Union blockade), incompatible only because they were so much alike. The natural culmination of this pattern, perfected by Hollywood in the 1930s and early 1940s, was *Casablanca*. Its version of the outlaw hero-official hero struggle (Rick versus Laszlo) proved stunningly effective, its resolution (their collaboration on the war effort) the prototypical Hollywood ending.

The reluctant hero story's tendency to minimize the official hero's role (by making him dependent on the outsider's intervention) suggested an imbalance basic to the American mythology: despite the existence of both heroes, the national ideology clearly preferred the outlaw. This ideology strove to make that figure's origins seem spontaneous, concealing the calculated, commercial efforts behind the mythologizing of typical examples like Billy the Kid and Davy Crockett. Its willingness, on the other hand, to allow the official hero's traces to show enables Daniel Boorstin to observe of one such myth, "There were elements of spontaneity, of course, in the Washington legend, too, but it was, for the most part, a self-conscious product."[46]

The apparent spontaneity of the outlaw heroes assured their popularity. By contrast, the official values had to rely on a rational allegiance that often wavered. These heroes' different statuses accounted for a structure fundamental to American literature, and assumed by Classic Hollywood: a split between the moral center and the interest center of a story. Thus, while the typical western contained warnings against violence as a solution, taking the law into one's own hands, and moral isolationism, it simultaneously glamorized the outlaw hero's intense self-possession and willingness to use force to settle what the law could not. In other circumstances, Ishmael's evenhanded philosophy paled beside Ahab's moral vehemence, consciously recognizable as destructive.

D. H. Lawrence called this split the profound "duplicity" at the heart of nineteenth-century American fiction, charging that the classic novels evinced "a tight mental allegiance to a morality which all [the author's] passion goes to destroy." Certainly, too, this "duplicity" involved the mythology's pattern of obscuring the necessity for choosing between contrasting values. Richard Chase has put the matter less pejoratively in an account that applies equally to the American Cinema:

The American novel tends to rest in contradictions and among extreme ranges of experience. When it attempts to resolve contradictions, it does so in oblique, morally equivocal ways. As a general rule it does so either in melodramatic actions or in pastoral idylls, although intermixed with both one may find the stirring instabilities of "American humor."[47]

Or, in other words, when faced with a difficult choice, American stories resolved it either simplistically (by refusing to acknowledge that a choice is necessary), sentimentally (by blurring the differences between the two sides), or by laughing the whole thing off.

Turner's frontier thesis was the great justification for this pattern, an argument that physical and psychological space had removed American culture from a European imagination whose norms centered on the recognition of limits. Clearly, however, that explanation constituted a key part of the very mythology it pretended to explain. Indeed, in attributing American culture to the values and abilities of a prototypical frontiersman, Turner celebrated a figure whose appeal depended on its remoteness from even his own contemporaries' experience.[48]

The American Cinema's dependence on the mass audience, however, made the truth or falsity of Turner's account irrelevant. For far from relying on historical accuracy for its popularity, Hollywood traded on (and helped to further) an existing ideological projection with a life of its own. Thus, the reluctant hero story's inappropriateness as a solution for contemporary problems mattered far less than the enormous weight of the tradition promoting it. Indeed, the movies' commercial success derived from their ability to insert themselves into the long chain of texts (Turner's being among the most prominent) whose persistent articulation of American exceptionalism had portrayed final choices as unnecessary violations of the national spirit. To a great extent, this tradition of texts operated independently, sustained less by its correspondence to material circumstances than by its own internal determinants. (The reception accorded the frontier thesis, for example, has as much to do with the American Historical Association's imprimatur as with its own historical verifiability.) Further, by the time the movies connected with this tradition, this tradition had long since begun to assert its own authority, often helping to shape historical events. (Turner's frontier thesis, for example, provided the rationale for Woodrow Wilson's interventions into the Mexican War and World War I.)[49]

As a crucial part of this ideological projection, therefore, the American Cinema never simply reflected contemporary events. At the most, the movies responded to what Althusser calls the mass audience's "relationship" to those events[50]—a perception of them determined to a large extent by the movies themselves and the historical weight of the tradition the cinema had adopted. Thus, because external occurrences reached Hollywood only through a filter of its own making, the course of the American Cinema's evolution was always influenced less by external, real-world events than by the self-perpetuating momentum of its own tradition. Not surprisingly, therefore, the majority of American movies of the 1970s looked remarkably similar to those of the 1930s.

The autonomous strength of the American Cinema's mythology not only made it resistant to external pressures for change; it also made the movies an enormously powerful influence on American life. Occasionally, like the frontier thesis, they helped determine major historical events: Nixon's repeated 1970 viewings of *Patton*, for example, directly preceded that year's Cambodian bombings.[51] Less dramatic, but far more pervasive, the American Cinema's significant role in consumer merchandising (through brand-name "tie-ins" of products displayed in films) completed the industrial age's fusion of base and superstructure. For, as Charles Eckert noted, Hollywood's eagerness to use its movies as "living display windows"[52] permanently blurred the lines between material circumstances and the cultural forms previously presumed to be dependent on them. Indeed, by helping to create desires, by reinforcing ideological proclivities, by encouraging certain forms of political action (or inaction), the movies worked to create the very reality they then "reflected."

THE HISTORY of the American Cinema (and to an extent, of world cinema) is the history of the formal and thematic paradigms achieved by Classic Hollywood. Although both paradigms unraveled slightly after World War II, their self-perpetuating authority insured that modifications to them would result only from the convergence of internal and external stimuli for change. (Such changes, in Althusser's terms, would be "overdetermined.") We have observed that the movies' original adoption of the traditional American mythology was prompted both by internal developments (the coming of sound, oligopolistic concentration) and by external factors (the Depression). As we will see, post-World War II changes required a similar confluence of events. In order to understand their impact, however, we need first to look more closely at the variations Classic Hollywood worked around its chosen thematic paradigm—the avoidance of choice.

2. Real and Disguised Westerns: Classic Hollywood's Variations of Its Thematic Paradigm

IN 1953, ROUGHLY the twenty-fifth anniversary of the sound era, a movie appeared that effectively summarized the thematic paradigm adopted and exploited by Classic Hollywood. With (or perhaps despite) its algebraically simple plot, deliberate pacing, and stylized *mise en scène* combining to produce a series of dreamlike, overtly nostalgic tableaux, this film had great commercial success (placing third in the year's box office race, behind only *The Robe* and *From Here to Eternity*), becoming one of the American movies that have contributed some character, image, or dialogue to the collective national imagination. Its careful resumé provides the best introduction to the ways in which Hollywood employed the traditional mythology that concealed the necessity for choice.

The film was *Shane*. In invoking this movie as an ideal recapitulation of Classic Hollywood's thematic paradigm, I am departing from the predominantly chronological path of my overall thesis. Indeed, later (in Chapter 6), I will argue that the western's development into a major fifties' genre depended on material conditions specific to the postwar period. Certainly, *Shane* was a part of that cycle. One might also ask how, as a *western,* *Shane* could possibly be the ideal summary for Classic Hollywood, a period during which the western existed almost entirely as a minor form, relegated to the industry's margins, B-movies and serials.

Here, however, I would insist on the usefulness of theory as a necessary complement to a strictly historical approach. For it seems to me that *Shane* (and perhaps the whole postwar cycle of westerns) functions as, to use Freud's term, a "screen memory" of Classic Hollywood, that is, a particularly vivid recollection of

apparently unimportant structures that embody nearly everything important about the past.[1] As Freud describes them, such
screen memories turn on the dynamics of repression and employ
repression's basic tools, displacement and condensation. Thus,
we remember events from childhood that seem, in comparison
with other largely forgotten moments, utterly trivial, and yet
which, through associative links controlled by displacement and
condensation, actually provide highly compressed clues to decisive moments lost to the conscious memory.

Shane's unqualified adoption of the western formula evoked
memories of a genre that Classic Hollywood seemed to have mar-
ginalized. As a screen memory, however, *Shane* referred back to
Classic Hollywood's double system of repression: first, its deployment of the classic western's structures as a means of displacing
crucial anxieties, and second, the further concealment of that
strategy itself, achieved by displacing those structures into the
disguises they assumed in other genres. In fact, because the
western's formulae had penetrated all of the American Cinema's
gestures, *Shane* made overt narrative structures that were fundamental to Classic Hollywood as a whole.

The movie's story unfolded in a specific place and time—1889
in Wyoming Territory on the eve of statehood—and began with
Shane's arrival into a valley divided between homesteaders and
an open-range cattle baron named Ryker. Offering no accounts
of his past, no explanations for his arrival in the valley, and no
first name, Shane (Alan Ladd) settled in as a hired farmhand
with a struggling but determined family, the Starretts: husband
Joe (Van Heflin), his wife (Jean Arthur), and their son Joey
(Brandon de Wilde). Shane's marksmanship practice behind the
barn and circulating gossip soon intimated that his mysterious
past had included a stretch as a gunfighter, a career that he
claimed to have permanently abandoned. In keeping with this
vow, he remained aloof as Ryker stepped up the pressure on
Starrett and the other small farmers, trying to buy or drive them
out in order to restore the open range for his cattle.

Prompted by his growing friendship with Starrett and by his
own pride, Shane momentarily abandoned his persistent detachment in a barroom confrontation with a gang of Ryker's hired

toughs. Outnumbered, he managed to fight his way out with the help of Starrett, whose normally stolid nature belied his fighting ability. Furious at this humiliation, Ryker sent for a new gunman, Wilson (Jack Palance), a man whose reputation prompted Shane to advise the homesteaders to give up their fight. Angered by his wife's obviously growing attentions to Shane, and frustrated by his hired man's stubborn refusal of involvement, Starrett called a meeting to determine a collective defense strategy against Ryker and Wilson, who had tricked one of the farmers into a fatal gunfight and set fire to another's house. Sensing Starrett's growing authority among the farmers, Ryker laid a trap for him, taunting him to come into town. Finally, Shane took action. Having learned about Ryker's scheme, Shane knocked Starrett unconscious to keep him from his appointment with Wilson, strapped on his own guns, and rode into town for the showdown. In the gunfight, Shane killed both Wilson and Ryker, receiving a slight arm wound himself. In the movie's most remembered moment, Shane said goodbye to a crying Joey who, as Shane rode off toward the mountains, repeatedly called after him, "Come back, Shane, come back."

Clearly, *Shane* was a particularly schematic version of the outlaw hero-official hero confrontation, and Shane's progress from moral detachment to physical involvement a prime example of the reluctant hero story. To Shane's life of solitude, self-determination, and freedom, Starrett opposed the value of family, society, and responsibility. With her affections wavering between the two men, Mrs. Starrett represented the audience's own dilemma about which man and which set of values was to be preferred.

The movie, however, worked to overcome the apparent necessity for choosing between them. First, it carefully portrayed both Shane and Starrett as composites of conflicting impulses, depicting Starrett as a settler capable of fighting if he had to, Shane as a fighter capable of tenderness with Mrs. Starrett and Joey. By thus projecting a coherent personality founded on contradictory urges, each man offered a solution in miniature to the larger oppositions of the film as a whole. Second, the movie consistently demonstrated that the values of Shane and Starrett which appeared to be conflicting were in fact reconcilable, mutually fertile complements. Indeed, the film encouraged its audience to acknowledge the indispensability of both men: while Starrett depended on Shane's intervention for the safety of his farm, Shane depended on Starrett's community for the sense of purpose he had lost. Two particular scenes dramatized the two men's mutual reliance: in the first, Shane and Starrett stood back to back fighting and winning a barroom brawl provoked by Ryker's bullies; in the second, Joey watched as the two men uprooted a decayed tree stump that had resisted Starrett's solitary efforts. Shane's final intervention on Starrett's behalf only completed the merging of their two interests begun early in the movie.

Despite *Shane*'s reconciliatory pattern, the film clearly turned on the gunfighter hero, with the interest center's confirmation of force as the only solution undermining the moral center's condemnation of violence. And, too, despite the overt allegiance paid to the values of the homesteader community, the narrative reinforced the sense of civilization's ultimate dependence on the self-determined, unentangled individual. Nevertheless, the movie's end, with Shane riding away alone, confirmed Robert Warshow's observation that the western form implicitly recognized that individual as an anachronism.

> If justice and order did not continually demand his protection [Warshow wrote of the outlaw hero], he would be without a calling. Indeed, we come upon him often in just that situation, as the reign of law settles over the West and he is forced to see that his day is over; those are the pictures that end with his death or with his departure for some more remote frontier.[2]

In fact, however, movies with the latter conclusion rarely proved sad. By avoiding the outlaw hero's final assimilation into the community (always the greatest threat to his independence), *Shane*'s ending, for example, not only postponed indefinitely that hero's demise, but also preserved the sense of his centrality to American culture.

In dramatizing the cooperation of Shane and Starrett, *Shane* reconciled the two sets of values whose opposition, according to Jim Kitses, had determined the western as a form:[3]

THE WILDERNESS	CIVILIZATION
The Individual	*The Community*
freedom	restriction
honour	institutions
self-knowledge	illusion
integrity	compromise
self-interest	social responsibility
solipsism	democracy
Nature	*Culture*
purity	corruption
experience	knowledge
empiricism	legalism
pragmatism	idealism
brutalization	refinement
savagery	humanity
The West	*The East*
America	Europe
the frontier	America
equality	class
agrarianism	industrialism
tradition	change
the past	the future

The striking point about these oppositions was their general applicability. Certainly, the transposable nature of the western mythology makes it likely that such a chart, meant only to describe the particular structures of the western, would in fact account for the dichotomies basic to all the genres of Classic Hollywood.

As we have seen, the western's importance derived from the national ideology's eagerness to assert an American exceptionalism as the basis for avoiding difficult choices. Typically, that exceptionalism turned on notions about the availability of uncivilized, open land (the frontier) and about the American continent's remoteness from Europe (North America as frontier). In its various guises, the ideology of space supported a large percentage of American policymaking. Transposed into the promise of endless economic growth, the frontier theory provided the rationale for postponing internal reforms (via civil rights or welfare legislation). As the Monroe Doctrine or the Open Door Policy, it prompted repeated American interventions abroad. As the doctrine of common sense, it encouraged active, pragmatic, empirical lifestyles at the expense of contemplative, aesthetic, theoretical ones. Grounded in a frontier mythology concerned almost exclusively with men, this ideology of space minimized, or actively disparaged, women's place in American life.

As a form, the western served as one of the principal displacement mechanisms in a culture obsessed with the inevitable encroachments on its gradually diminishing space. By portraying the advancing society's abiding dependence on the frontier's most representative figure—the individualistic, outlaw hero—the pure western reassured its audience about the permanent availability of both sets of values. In disguised versions, the same story allayed other anxieties left unresolved by the frontier mythology's influence on the various sectors of American experience. Thus, many of Classic Hollywood's genre movies, like many of the most important American novels, were thinly camouflaged westerns. At the least, the period saw the American Cinema increasingly organize its product around the thematic paradigm that dismissed choice as unnecessary.

Angels with Dirty Faces (1938), apparently a straightforward gangster movie, provided a good example of Classic Hollywood's translations of the western story into other genres. In his most characteristic role, James Cagney played Rocky Sullivan, a mobster returning to his old neighborhood after a prison stretch. Back home, Sullivan immediately encountered his boyhood friend, Jerry Connolly (Pat O'Brien), now a priest concerned with an adolescent gang's (the Dead End Kids) reverence for criminals in general, and Sullivan in particular. Recognizing the impossibility of reforming Rocky, Father Connolly concentrated his attentions on Sullivan's influence over the kids, using his friend to encourage the boys to play basketball rather than pool and to avoid crime for school and regular jobs. The priest's escalating public campaigns against hoodlums, however, provoked Sullivan's ex-partners, Frazier (Humphrey Bogart) and Kiefer (George Bancroft), to lay a trap to kill Connolly. Getting wind of the scheme, Sullivan shot and killed Frazier and Kiefer but was arrested and sentenced to death. Minutes before the execution, Connolly pleaded with his friend to use his death to influence the adolescent gang that worshiped him; by dying a coward, Connolly urged, Rocky could destroy his own pernicious glamor. Brave and defiant to the end, however, Rocky refused, walking coolly down the corridor to the death chamber. But there, as the attendants strapped him into the electric chair, and to the astonishment of the journalists present, he began to sob and plead for mercy. Reading about his cowardice in the papers, the boys at last seemed willing to listen to the priest.

In Rocky and Father Connolly, *Angels with Dirty Faces* had its urban versions of the outlaw and official heroes. Indeed, the inherent conflict between mobster and priest seemed to polarize this basic opposition beyond the typical western's gunfighter-homesteader pairing. The movie, however, worked persistently to blur their differences. The story began, in fact, with a scene that identified their common origins—Sullivan and Connolly as boys breaking into a boxcar. Connolly's own ambiguous past, and his ability to throw a punch (he knocked out a poolroom wise guy) complemented his moral earnestness and reinforced his authority to lecture the Dead End Kids against the evils of crime. Ultimately, however, like *Shane*'s Joe Starrett, he had to rely on the outlaw hero's intervention. Typically reluctant, Rocky repeatedly interceded on Connolly's behalf, refereeing the gang's basketball game, giving money to the church, and killing Frazier and Kiefer. Finally, acting for the sake of Connolly's version of the homesteaders (the Dead End Kids), Sullivan renounced even his reputation, deliberately appearing as a coward at the moment of his own death.

Like most Classic Hollywood movies, *Angels with Dirty Faces* had an interest center (Rocky) that overshadowed its moral center (Connolly). For despite the film's overt protestations against crime and violence, the story portrayed Sullivan as the hero without whom all of Connolly's good intentions would have proved worthless. In so doing, the movie provided its audience with a means of displacing the nagging anxieties about ruthless ambition and individualism. By suggesting that the individual, although ultimately sacrificed, had supplied the key contributions to a society's success, *Angels with Dirty Faces* encouraged the audience's acquiescence in a political system committed to laissez faire.

EVEN the musical could take on the western's structure. The opening of the Astaire-Rogers *Swing Time* (1936), for example, offered a prime illustration of the reluctant hero story's protean quality. For a musical, the movie kept its audience waiting a tantalizingly long time for the first dance. In fact, the plot made dancing the equivalent of gunfighting, something that Astaire wanted to renounce. "Hoofing is all right," he announced in the beginning, declaring his intention to retire from the stage, and following with the classic line of all disillusioned fast guns: "But there's no future in it." When he did dance, after nearly thirty-five minutes of a supposed dance movie, the pas de deux with Ginger assumed the overtones of a gunfight. Having met Ginger by chance (and as always, making an unfavorable impression), he traced her to the dance studio where she worked. He hired her for a lesson, pretending to be impossibly awkward (like Johnny Guitar and Destry assuming the characteristics of meekness). Exasperated by his ineptitude, Ginger exploded with the musical's version of the gunfighter's challenge: "You'll *never* learn how to dance." Astaire shrugged, unwilling to be drawn out of retirement that easily. But the studio manager (Eric Blore) supplied the motive for Astaire's intervention, firing Rogers for having failed with her pupil. Astaire's rescuing dance, one of the most exhilarating in any of his films, provided a release comparable to Shane's putting on his guns. The tacit knowledge, however, of Astaire's mastery (and Shane's skill) made "You'll never learn how to dance" an illusory challenge; the tension resided only in the uncertainty about when, or on what terms, the challenge would be met. More subtly, by associating Astaire's dance with the traditional structures of a gunfight, *Swing Time* reinforced a self-contained, aesthetic activity with suggestions of active purposefulness. For only Astaire's dance saved Rogers's job.

OF THE personae of Classic Hollywood's major stars, Clark Gable's most obviously drew on the outlaw hero tradition. His cheerfully self-reliant image occasioned his frequent appearances in disguised westerns that dramatized the conflict between romantic independence and societal responsibility. Typically, these movies were reluctant hero stories that required Gable to play a man who had fled from civilization only to find it at his door, bringing in its train problems that even the audience wanted solved: wrongs to be righted, villains to be fought, women to be protected. Generally, therefore, Gable's films turned on a dilemma: his obligations to some particular community (the moral center) threatened his determination to remain free and unentangled (the interest center). By encouraging the audience to identify with the Gable hero, these movies in turn placed the viewer at a similar impasse, dividing his allegiances between the instinctive appeal of the protagonist's cool aloofness and the obvious moral rightness of the causes that menaced it. Indeed, these films' implication of the audience in the hero's apparent need to choose made their ultimate resolutions all the more satisfying. For in fact, Gable's movies demonstrated once again that an individual's temporary intervention in society's problems compromised none of his freedom. Thus, to the extent that genuine choice involves giving up something, Gable's actions were not choices at all, and individual and collective methods seemed to merge.

Gable's most famous movie, *Gone With the Wind* (1939), perfected the pattern developed throughout the 1930s by many of his other films: *Red Dust* (1932), *No Man of Her Own* (1932), *It Happened One Night* (1934), *Manhattan Melodrama* (1934), *Call of the Wild* (1935), *China Seas* (1935), *San Francisco* (1936), and *Saratoga* (1937). Again and again in these movies, Gable played criminals, gamblers (often named Blackie), unscrupulous reporters, and adventurers trying to get away from manners and customs portrayed as restrictive. Inevitably, however, Gable's characters ended up doing the right thing—taking the rap for a crime committed, renouncing an irresponsible past, or undertaking civic projects for the sake of a larger good.

As particular examples, *Red Dust* and its sequel *China Seas* can stand for the rest. Both recounted the basic American story of the pioneer's flight from civilized society. Indeed, both were disguised westerns that relocated the American frontier in Indochina and transposed continental expansion into colonial imperialism. In each film, Gable played an expatriate soldier-of-fortune, grousing and complaining, but actually thriving on the rough, primitive conditions. Although both stories required Gable to perform some responsible task, the real threat to his detachment was the possibility of marriage—because of its permanence, the most compromising of all involvements. The solution of both movies was to convert marriage into an extension of adventure, and thus to minimize the decision it apparently required.

As the supervisor of a rubber plantation in *Red Dust* and a ship's captain in *China Seas*, Gable reported to no one. In both films, his companion was a woman (Jean Harlow) whose status as a prostitute made her companionship unentangling. In *China Seas*, Gable outlined for her the ground rules of their relationship: "Look, Dolly, we've been friends, and there's no question you're the number one girl in the archipelago, but I don't recall making any vows or asking for any." This speech reconfirmed the American mythology's traditional double standard, which, as Leslie Fiedler observed, permitted the outlaw hero "a certain amount of good clean sex (not as the basis of an adult relationship but as an exhibition of prowess)"[4] that did not cost him his innocence. The woman, however, was allowed no such thing.

In both *Red Dust* and *China Seas*, civilization intruded on Gable's neat little world in its typical guise—the Good Good Girl. *Red Dust* employed the more explicit mythic pattern. Arriving at Gable's jungle rubber plantation carrying tennis rackets and dressed for a grand ball, the nice girl (Mary Astor) and her husband clearly represented society at its most effete. Moreover, the husband's profession (engineer) and his mission (improving the plantation's yield via scientific methods) threatened Gable's frontier sanctuary with the rational, collective values of civilization. By acting for the absentee English owners, the husband demoted the independent Gable to the status of a hired hand.

Immediately, however, the husband signaled his dependence on the outlaw hero by coming down with a fever that only Gable could treat. (Prohibiting reliance on others, the myth of self-sufficiency forbade sending for a specialist: the outsider was always an expert in everything important to a movie's plot.) Reluctant to help a representative of the civilization he had fled, Gable handled the husband roughly. To Astor's protest, "You can't treat him like one of your coolies," Gable responded, "Why not?"—the outlaw hero was always a democrat—"He's just another worker, only less valuable since he's sick."

Harlow, in contrast, could more easily enter Gable's world because, in effect, she was another man, capable of holding her own in the wisecracking that *Red Dust* made the equivalent of tests of physical strength. Asked by Gable to stay up to watch the fever-ridden husband, she shrugged, "I'm not used to sleeping at night anyway." When Gable scolded her for taking a nude bath in front of Astor, Harlow shot back, "Don't you suppose she's ever seen a French postcard?" She even had a crack for the bird whose cage she cleaned: "What've you been eatin', cement?"

Red Dust suggested the outlaw mythology's hostility to women who could not assume characteristics traditionally associated with men. Harlow's occupation, however, made her as much of an outsider as Gable; Astor, on the other hand, embodied diluted versions of the official values. Exasperated by her finicky manners and demands, Gable exploded with the classic rationale of the western hero:

Women don't belong in this country. The white woman can't stand the gaff, and if a native woman comes around, sooner or later she'll be up in the house serving meals, and a man can't take much of that in this country.

Gable's outburst suggested a hint of despair about this self-enforced retreat from civilization and its women, an anxiety about the American myth of self-reliance. Often in Classic Hollywood's westerns or disguised westerns, the outlaw hero's doubt broke through the surface in disturbing confessions that his career as a pioneer, gunfighter, adventurer—even Founding Father?—derived from his failures "back there," his inability to fit into official society, to succeed on its terms. Within the total American ideology, the official heroes' accomplishments served to legitimize an American enterprise eager to deemphasize its origins in bands of European ne'er-do-wells and semi-outlaws. But when

Gable said to Harlow, "We belong here, it's a dirty, rotten country" (*Red Dust*), or "Anywhere else in the world, we'd be pretty
soiled" (*China Seas*), the ideological self-doubts surfaced through
their normal protective veneer.

Classic Hollywood's movies, however, repeatedly demonstrated that yielding to these doubts constituted a betrayal of
the "genuine" American spirit. In falling for the Good Good Girl
(Astor in *Red Dust*, Rosalind Russell in *China Seas*), Gable made
the mistake of trying to escape from his true nature by assuming
the qualities of the opposed tradition. Indeed, from the outset,
the American mythology's project to overcome doubts concerning
its origins involved discrediting all societies and laws that failed
to correspond to "natural" conceptions of justice. The basic western story of the roughneck who falls for the lady, but leaves her
or converts her to a pal, satisfied this project because it represented American primitivism tempted by, but resisting, European sophistication—self-doubts overcome by assertiveness.

Thus, both *Red Dust* and *China Seas* sent the Good Good Girl
packing, back to the rarefied air of England and her manicured
gardens and "fireplace big enough to stand in" (*China Seas*). By
contrast, settling down with Harlow was not settling down at
all; despite her feminine exterior, she was merely another version of the outlaw hero with a good heart. "You sure got the right
feeling though," her maid told her in *China Seas*; "you sure got
the right instincts." Harlow's response confirmed her status: "I
ain't been brought up right, so's all I can say is what's down deep
inside me."

Both *Red Dust* and *China Seas* seemed to confront Gable with
a choice between the two women representing the contradictory
outlaw and official values: the stereotypical madonna and whore.
Both stories demonstrated, however, that in choosing the whore,
Gable did not entirely renounce the other alternative. By decid-
ing to marry Harlow, Gable avoided final choices, simultaneously providing himself with an unentangling companion and
making use of the official code's most basic customs. In *China
Seas*, the abandoned nice girl reassured Gable that nothing important to him had been sacrificed: "You wouldn't have liked
that fireplace in Sussex anyway."

In addition to the sexual resolutions, *Red Dust* and *China Seas* attempted to legitimize adventure by certifying its importance to civilization. The official view of adventure as wasteful and dangerous often appeared in westerns as the gunfighter's desire to hang up his guns (*Shane, High Noon, The Gunfighter*). In the disguised western, *China Seas*, this sense surfaced in Gable's desire to return to England to lead a normal life. Richard Griffith and Arthur Mayer have uncovered this anxiety:

The West was opened by men whose tenacity in the face of hardship was matched by a boyish desire for adventure for its own sake. As the new country developed, this latter quality became an anachronism and soon *only* an outlaw could live what formerly was the normal life of all men on the frontier. . . . The morality of a now-settled country could not permit an outlaw to escape scot-free.[5]

This notion of adventure as an end in itself pervaded *Red Dust* and *China Seas*. In the latter film, Gable's boss, urging him not to return to the quiet life in England, painted a picture of the Orient's drama and the civilizing purpose redeeming the outlaw's code:

My house overlooks the whole of Hong Kong, and I can see ships coming in and out and hear the sound of firing in the night. They were firing when I came thirty years ago, and they'll be firing when I leave. More guns isn't going to stop them. The only things they respect are courage and honor.

By thus providing the outlaw hero's passion for action with official morality's stamp of approval, the American ideology continued to depict the individual as the unknowing vanguard of civilization. Within this mythology, even marriage, when undertaken with a suitable companion, could become an extension of adventure. "Toots," Harlow warned Gable as he proposed in *China Seas*, "a no-good dame like me will always have you in trouble." The movie meant those words not as a threat, but as a promise.

Meet Me in St. Louis (1944) was not a disguised western, but its resolution depended on the traditional ideological translation of the frontier mythology into promises of unlimited opportunities for economic growth. The movie developed around the inherent contradictions between the family and ambition, confronting the father (and the audience) with an apparently difficult choice: whether or not to leave St. Louis for a promotion in New York. Typically, the movie avoided the decision, allowing it to vanish in assertions that opportunities existed everywhere in America, in St. Louis as well as New York.

The film began as a nostalgic idyll in a past when close family life provided the occasion for all pleasure (parties, family dinners, Halloween, long distance calls from beaus, singing around the piano—even making ketchup) and all pains (above all, the pain of moving). Oddly, the threat to this family came disguised as an opportunity, the chance to move to New York. In doing so, the movie anticipated Vance Packard's *A Nation of Strangers*, with its identification of constant executive "re-locations" as a principal cause of modern anxiety. Moving, Packard noted, robbed the family of its roots, of its connection to a past and a future, not to mention its present—all of which the Smith family had in St. Louis, with its three generations (Grandpa to Tootie) living together and coming to each other's rescue: Esther (Judy Garland) beat up the boy next door when she thought he had hit Tootie; Grandpa took Esther to the dance when her beau left his tuxedo in the tailor's shop after closing time.

But what to do about the move? Insisting on moving for the opportunities in New York, the father announced that the family would spend one last Christmas in St. Louis before leaving on the first of the year. The context of loss and regret surrounding it made Garland's "Have Yourself a Merry Little Christmas" one of the most heartbreaking of all Christmas songs, sung under the apparent necessity for choosing an alternative to the domestic values on which the film rested. "Someday soon, we all will be together," she sang, without being at all sure of it.

And then, magically, the need to choose simply disappeared. Father awakened the family just after midnight on Christmas Day to proclaim that "New York doesn't have the monopoly on opportunity. Why, there are plenty of opportunities right here in St. Louis." The film ended with the family sightseeing at the St.

Louis World's Fair, a confirmation of the father's faith, and an assurance to the audience that nothing had been sacrificed by staying home.

OF CLASSIC Hollywood's popular genres, screwball comedy made the most overt use of the oppositions generated by the western. Invariably, these movies divided along lines of class and sex, often scrambling, however, the normal associations of official values with upper-class females and outlaw values with middle-class males. Always these films had as their project what Andrew Bergman called "reconciling the irreconcilable":

> Simply stated, the comic technique of these comedies became a means of unifying what had been splintered and divided. Their "whackiness" cemented social classes and broken marriages; personal relations were smoothed and social discontent quieted. If early thirties comedy was explosive, screwball comedy was implosive: it worked to pull things together.[6]

Significantly, this pulling together involved a synthesis of competing values which sacrificed nothing that these movies allowed to seem important. Indeed, anything forsaken, screwball comedy worked hard to discredit.

Frank Capra's *It Happened One Night* (1934), the first of the screwball cycle (and, with *One Flew Over the Cuckoo's Nest*, one of the only two films to sweep the three major Oscars), borrowed the most directly from the frontier ideology. The movie retained the traditional associations, making Claudette Colbert a slightly stuffy, upper-class heiress and Clark Gable a brash, out-of-work newspaper reporter. Typically, however, the plot blurred the distinctions between the two, portraying Colbert as on the run from her father (an outlaw habit), but for the purpose of marriage (an official custom), and Gable as a no-nonsense pragmatist (an outlaw quality) eager to advance his career (an official goal) by getting a scoop on Colbert's disappearance.

It Happened One Night developed around Colbert's and Gable's mutual education. From Gable, Colbert had to learn the value of money (she gave it away too easily to a hungry family), how to rough it in the outdoors (after having to leave the bus because of being recognized), how to stand in line at a motor camp bathroom (she had obviously never had to wait for anything), how to dunk doughnuts and ride piggyback, and above all how to recognize the importance of other people's feelings (her decision to love Gable, after all, did not decide the matter for him). From Colbert, on the other hand, Gable had to learn to recognize the truth behind appearances (all heiresses were not empty-headed brats to be dealt with only by insults and spankings), and how to admit that his masculinity did not automatically make him the expert on everything (despite his lecture about the subtleties of the use of the thumb in hitchhiking, Colbert's leg got them the ride). The movie's principal image of the barrier between them—the Walls of Jericho, the blanket hung between their beds—came down only with the completion of their joint educations, to consummate a marriage depicted as the merger of apparently irreconcilable traits.

By bringing Colbert down to earth, *It Happened One Night* initiated the screwball tactic of overcoming the class differences denied by American ideology. *The Philadelphia Story* (1941) represented the culmination of a strategy that used the official-outlaw opposition to displace permanent class conflicts into resolvable ethical confrontations. The story opened with heiress Tracy Lord (Katharine Hepburn) on the eve of her marriage to George Kittredge (John Howard), a self-made businessman with political ambitions. Almost immediately, complications arose. Threatening to publish accounts of Tracy's father's affair with a chorus girl, magazine publisher Sidney Kidd (a parody of Henry Luce?) persuaded Tracy's former husband, C. K. Dexter Haven (Cary Grant) to introduce two journalists, Macauley Connor (James Stewart) and Elizabeth Imbrie (Ruth Hussey), into the Lord household. Assigned to produce covertly an exposé on society weddings, Connor and Imbrie encountered an initially hostile reception from Tracy. Gradually, however, she warmed to Connor, piqued by his abandoned career as a serious writer. Connor responded similarly, troubled, nevertheless, by Dexter's blaming the failure of his marriage on Tracy's coolly self-righteous morality. But after the wedding rehearsal party, Tracy (drunk for only the second time in her life) retired with Connor to the family garden. Returning to the house at dawn, Tracy encountered

Kittredge, who immediately suspected the worst. When he patronizingly offered forgiveness, Tracy called off their engagement, and confronted by the crowd gathered for the wedding, went through with the ceremony by remarrying Dexter.

From its beginning, *The Philadelphia Story*'s plot obviously hinged on getting rid of Kittredge, the obstacle impeding Tracy's self-recognition and her remarriage to Dexter. But in a movie that displayed so much anxiety about social divisiveness, Kittredge's lower-class origins made this project difficult. Thus, although Kittredge's deficient graces (he could not ride, for instance) clearly disqualified him as a match for Tracy, the movie could not openly base the broken engagement on such indicators of status without acknowledging the rigid class structures it sought to deny. The movie's solution was to convert these social barriers into moral disagreements, and to attribute incompatibility to the clash between an excessively pure official morality and a more relaxed outlaw standard. Thus, the movie supported both Dexter's and her father's charges that Tracy's puritanism forbade sympathy (although her objections to Dexter's drinking and her father's philandering seemed reasonable positions).

The character of Connor provided the key to this class-into-morals transposition. As a middle-class male, contemptuous of fashionable society, he clearly qualified as a potential outlaw hero. Instead, however, the film made him a lesser version of Tracy, and used his priggishness (underlined by Tracy's calling him "Professor") as the occasion for Tracy's own moral awakening: "You're so much thought and so little feeling," she scolded, before catching herself accidentally repeating Dexter's earlier speech which the movie clearly intended as the ethical equivalent of social egalitarianism. "The fact is, you'll never—you can't be a first-rate writer or a first-rate human being until you learn to have some small regard for . . ." ("for human frailty," Dexter had said). Furthermore, Connor's reverse snobbish disdain for the upper classes allowed Tracy to deny the importance of any social distinctions:

CONNOR: You've got all the arrogance of your class, all right, haven't you?
TRACY: Holy . . . What have classes to do with it? What do they matter—except for the people in them? George comes from the so-called "lower"

class, Dexter comes from the upper. Well? Mac, the night watchman, is a prince among men, Uncle Willie's a pincher.

Here again, Tracy had unconsciously adopted one of Dexter's previous remarks:

DEXTER: Perhaps it offends my vanity to have anyone who was even remotely my wife remarry so obviously beneath her.

TRACY: "Benea . . ." How dare you—any of you—in this day and age use such an . . .

DEXTER: I'm talking about difference in mind and spirit. You could marry Mac, the night watchman, and I'd cheer for you. Kittredge is not for you.

The movie's ultimate discrediting of Kittredge proceeded from his intolerant response to Tracy's apparent improprieties with Connor. (In fact, she had done nothing.) By expressing the same prudery that Tracy needed to shed, Kittredge disqualified himself as a potential husband; he could not provide Dexter's complementary virtues: tolerance, sympathy, understanding. Significantly, too, the greatest damage to Kittredge's image came from the character closest to him in class, with Connor's designation of him as "that fake man-of-the-people." As a result, *The Philadelphia Story* made Kittredge's parting shot seem like Malvolio's sour grapes:

KITTREDGE: [To Dexter] I've got a feeling you had more to do with this than anyone. You and your whole rotten class.

DEXTER: Oh, class my . . .

KITTREDGE: You're all on your way out—the lot of you—and don't think you aren't. Yes, and good riddance.

At this stage of the movie, brightened by the obviously forthcoming rapprochement between a newly sober Dexter and a newly understanding Tracy, the audience could ignore the obvious truth of Kittredge's speech. Instead, the promise of reconciliation between outlaw (Dexter) and official (Tracy) values had become the focus of interest.

In its purest form, screwball comedy ignored class divisions to develop almost allegorical schemas of reconciliation. Howard Hawks's *Bringing Up Baby* (1938) reversed the usual roles, making Katharine Hepburn's rich, scatterbrained Susan the outlaw symbol of adventure that bordered on chaos, and Cary Grant's bespectacled, affianced paleontologist, David Huxley, the official image of domesticity normally represented by women. "But I'm engaged, engaged to be married," Huxley protested to Susan, adopting the female's role. "Then she won't mind waiting," Susan responded, initiating a whirlwind plot of mistaken identities, a lost brontosaural intercostal clavicle, and a tame leopard ("Baby") who caused Huxley no end of troubles.

Bringing Up Baby sought to promote Susan's zany disregard of convention as the necessary complement to Huxley's too-careful life, with its fossils (dead) and near-fossilized fiancée. At one point, the movie even turned on whether or not Huxley would remove his glasses, always Hollywood's symbol for unwarranted repression. In fact, however, by polarizing the values of Huxley and Susan, Hawks (the most reductive and relentlessly optimistic of Classic Hollywood's great directors) made the stock screwball ending (marriage) seem willed and unconvincing. But to object that Huxley made all the compromises missed the point of screwball comedy, which insisted that such apparent polarization merely provided the occasion for the richest mergers.

The skillful displacements of screwball comedies typically made their resolutions seem inevitable. In fact, however, when unprotected by the traditional American ideology, the same données could lead to devastating conclusions: Jean Renoir's *Rules of the Game* (1939) used the same class-divided, "pure" versus "impure" conflicts (André Jurieu and Schumacher versus Robert, Marceau, and Octave) as *The Philadelphia Story*, but ended in tragedy. Similarly, Josef von Sternberg's *The Blue Angel* (1930) turned *Bringing Up Baby*'s domestic professor–hedonist woman pairing into an occasion for sexual degradation and death. By grounding its movies in a thematic paradigm that avoided irreconcilable choices, Classic Hollywood, in contrast, evaded such frankness.

3. The Culmination of Classic Hollywood: *Casablanca*

THIRTY-FIVE minutes into Classic Hollywood's most representative film, an archetypal confrontation occurred between two distinctly different heroes: the European underground fighter, political organizer, and husband, Victor Laszlo (Paul Henreid) and the American expatriate, saloonkeeping loner, Rick Blaine (Humphrey Bogart). Introduced in an establishing shot by Vichy Police Captain Renault (Claude Rains), the two men measured each other across the formal paradigm's essential figure, a shot-reverse shot connected by an eyeline match. With this meeting, *Casablanca* reincarnated in Rick and Laszlo the outlaw hero-official hero opposition, and in doing so, summoned the entire frontier mythology to support its contemporary story of refugees fleeing the Nazis.

The wartime mood prompted the American Cinema's normally camouflaged ideology to become more overt. Thus, with its release timed to coincide with the November 1942 U.S. landings in North Africa, *Casablanca* bristled with references to the anti-intervention sentiments discredited by Pearl Harbor. "My dear Rick," Ferrari (Sydney Greenstreet) counseled, "when will you realize that in this world, today, isolationism is no longer a practical policy." As the culmination of Classic Hollywood's thematic and formal strategies, however, *Casablanca* characteristically transposed its propaganda into melodrama. Thus, by the time Rick asked Sam, "If it's December 1941 in Casablanca, what time is it in New York?" his own answer had come to seem less a retrospective warning about Pearl Harbor than an instance of personal loneliness and despair: "I bet they're asleep in New York. I bet they're asleep all over America."

To effect this displacement from the global to the individual,

RICK: Hello, Ilsa. ILSA: Hello, Rick. RENAULT: Oh, you've already met Rick, Mademoiselle?

RENAULT: Well, then, perhaps you also . . . ILSA: This is Mr. Laszlo. LASZLO: How do you do? RICK: How do you do?

LASZLO: One hears a great deal about Rick in Casablanca.

RICK: And about Victor Laszlo everywhere.

Casablanca, like so many of Classic Hollywood's most popular movies, employed a reluctant hero story, clearly derived from the western, and perfectly tailored for the film's ideological project: the overcoming of its audience's latent anxiety about American intervention in World War II. The narrative traced Rick's progress from self-centered detachment to active involvement in the Allied cause, with the plot turning on whether he would choose to help Laszlo, a major underground leader escaped from a concentration camp. Only Rick could help because only Rick had the crucial letters of transit, obtained from the thief Ugarte (Peter

Lorre) minutes before his capture by the Gestapo. The key to
Rick's decision was Ilsa (Ingrid Bergman), formerly his lover in
prewar Paris, now Laszlo's wife. Initially, her presence merely
abetted Rick's apparently natural selfishness; eventually, however, her explanation of her apparent infidelity (she had been
married to Laszlo when she first met Rick but had thought that
her husband was dead) prompted Rick's ultimate intervention on
Laszlo's behalf. Tricking his friend Renault into thinking that
he would use the letters of transit for Ilsa and himself, Rick gave
them instead to Laszlo and shot the German Major Strasser
(Conrad Veidt) as he tried to prevent their escape. Concealing
Rick's crime by ordering his men to "round up the usual suspects," Renault left with Rick for the Free French garrison in
Brazzaville.

The compelling quality of this narrative effectively concealed
what was at stake in *Casablanca*: the deep-seated, instinctive
anxiety that America's unencumbered autonomy could not survive the global commitments required by another world war. In
fact, this anxiety derived from the national ideology's most fundamental projection: the image of America as separate, unique,
and remote from the Old World's entangling responsibilities. By
portraying all involvements in the larger community as potential threats to American exceptionalism, however, this projection
generated an abiding ideological tension. Indeed, its fundamental disparagement of cooperative behavior necessitated a com-
pensatory mythology whose depiction of commitments as temporary made political activity at least occasionally possible.

This mythology's effectiveness derived from its strategy of reducing national ideological tensions to the manageable size of
outlaw hero-official hero conflicts. Within this pattern (which
typically developed around the western conventions summarized
by *Shane*), the self-determining, morally detached outlaw hero
came to represent America itself. The town's claims on that hero,
by contrast, stood for those historical developments (domestic or
international) that required collective action. The importance of
the reluctant hero story lay in its ability to preserve for the whole
ideology both possibilities: individual autonomy and communitarian participation.

As Classic Hollywood repeatedly demonstrated, the western

conventions proved adaptable to an enormous number of issues confronting the national ideology: the Depression, class divisiveness, conflicts between the family and personal ambition, or between active and contemplative lifestyles. By directly threatening the American ideal of separateness, however, World War II challenged this ideology more thoroughly than any previous issue. For in the need to defeat the Nazis, the war presented the one collective cause critical enough to force the American people to choose—and worse, to choose the kind of cooperative, entangling effort persistently discredited as the very burden the Founding Fathers had sought to escape. *Casablanca*'s ability to acknowledge this challenge, and then triumph over it, established the film's enduring popularity.

The movie's project was to suggest a way that America could fight without losing its autonomy. Inevitably, this enterprise called for the reluctant hero story, whose images of ad hoc interventions and swift victories preserved the traditional ideology's avoidance of final choices. At certain moments, however, *Casablanca* seemed to suggest a new sense of this story's insufficiency. For with Rick's complaint ("Of all the gin joints in all the towns all over the world, she has to walk into mine"), the film allowed to surface the anxieties attending an intuitive recognition of World War II as a watershed that, even in victory, the American dream of unshackled privacy could not survive.

Nevertheless, *Casablanca* was primarily optimistic, offering a solution to an apparently irreconcilable dilemma. Its ability to do so depended first on Classic Hollywood's characteristic movement from a large, abstract issue (American intervention) to a particular melodrama (the Rick-Ilsa-Laszlo triangle). The movie began with one of Warner Brothers' slowly turning globes, with the focus gradually narrowing from a map of the Western Hemisphere, to one of Europe and North Africa, and finally to Casablanca, as a voice-over imitation of Westbrook Pegler accompanied them:

NARRATOR: With the coming of the Second World War, many eyes in imprisoned Europe turned hopefully or desperately toward the freedom of the Americas. Lisbon became the great embarkation point. But not everybody could get to Lisbon directly. And so a tortuous, roundabout refugee trail sprang up. Paris to Marseilles . . . Across the Mediterranean to Oran . . . Then by train or auto or foot across the rim of Africa to Casablanca in French Morocco. Here the fortunate ones, through money or influence or luck, might obtain exit visas and scurry to Lisbon.

By the time the principal characters finally encountered each other thirty minutes further into the film, the sequence's shot-reverse shot figures subtly confirmed the completeness of the transposition from political issue to love story. After Captain Renault's introductions, Rick, Ilsa, and Laszlo joined him at a table.

By this point in *Casablanca*, Victor Laszlo's political importance had been well certified—by Rick, by Renault, by Major Strasser, and by a Norwegian refugee named Berger. Indeed, according to Rick, Laszlo's underground activities had "succeeded in impressing half the world." Deprived of this information, however, someone watching this sequence for the first time would have invariably regarded Laszlo as incidental to *Casablanca*'s main plot. For all the scene's formal elements conspired to bring Rick and Ilsa to the foreground of a viewer's attention. Indeed, by crowding Laszlo to the edge of the frame, by denying him close-ups, by forcing him to share almost all of his shots with one or two other figures, the sequence suggested his peripheral significance to *Casablanca*'s principal business, which the isolating, repeating shot-reverse shots linking Rick and Ilsa intimated was their love affair.

We can observe this stylistic strategy in more detail. By positioning Ilsa between Rick and Laszlo, Shot 1 hinted at her eventual capacity to unite the two men, an intimation repeated by the use of her in Shots 13-15 as the "linking object" around which a reverse field pivoted. Although Shot 2 gave Laszlo his only unaccompanied medium close-up, Shot 3's inclusion of Ilsa in Rick's frame implied her true allegiance. In Shot 4, while Laszlo sat at the extreme right edge of a crowded frame, Renault's and Ilsa's glances offscreen made Rick, even though unseen, the center of attention.

Shots 5-8 used two reverse-field figures to isolate out of the larger space of the table a smaller seam of significance connecting Rick and Ilsa. After the more jumbled grouping of Shot 4,

SHOT 1

LASZLO: Won't you join us for a drink?
RENAULT: Oh, no, Rick never . . . RICK: Thanks,
I will. RENAULT: Well! A precedent is being
broken. Emile . . .

SHOT 1

LASZLO: This is a very interesting café. I
congratulate you. RICK: I congratulate you.
LASZLO: What for? RICK: Your work.

SHOT 2

LASZLO: Thank you. I try.

SHOT 3

RICK: We all try. You succeed.

SHOT 4

RENAULT: I can't get over you two. She was
asking about you earlier, Rick, in a way that
made me extremely jealous.

SHOT 4

ILSA: I wasn't sure you were the same.

SHOT 5

ILSA: Let's see, the last time we met . . . RICK: Was La Belle Aurore.

SHOT 6

ILSA: How nice. You remembered. But, of course, that was the day the Germans marched into Paris.

SHOT 7

RICK: Not an easy day to forget. I remember every detail. The Germans wore gray, you wore blue.

SHOT 8

ILSA: Yes, I put that dress away. When the Germans march out, I'll wear it again.

SHOT 9

RENAULT: Ricky, you're becoming quite human.

SHOT 9

RENAULT: I suppose we have to thank you for that, Mademoiselle.

SHOT 9

LASZLO: Ilsa, I don't wish to be the one to say it, but it's late. RENAULT: So it is. And we have a curfew here in Casablanca. It would never do . . .

SHOT 10

RENAULT: for the Chief of Police to be found drinking after hours and have to fine himself.

SHOT 11

LASZLO: I hope we didn't overstay our welcome. RICK: Not at all.

SHOT 12

WAITER: Your check, sir. RICK: It's my party. RENAULT: Another precedent gone! This has been a very interesting evening.

SHOT 12

RENAULT: I'll call you a cab. Gasoline rationing, time of night. LASZLO: We'll come again. RICK: Any time.

SHOT 12

ILSA: Will you say goodnight to Sam for me? RICK: I will.

SHOT 13

ILSA: There's still nobody in the world who can play "As Time Goes By" like Sam.

SHOT 14

RICK: He hadn't played it in a long time.

SHOT 15

ILSA: Goodnight. LASZLO: Goodnight.

SHOT 16

RICK: Goodnight.

SHOT 16

these uncluttered, highly centered medium close-ups encouraged the sense of the love story's main importance. Significantly, these shots recurred (Shots 10-11) even while Renault and Laszlo talked off screen, a departure from Hollywood's general rule of keeping the camera on the speaker, which further emphasized the Rick-Ilsa story at the expense of Laszlo's

This scene was typical of *Casablanca*. Throughout the movie, stylistic elements worked continually as displacement mechanisms, directing the spectator's attention away from the Laszlo plot about politics to the Rick-Ilsa plot about love. This transposition's supreme effectiveness derived from *Casablanca*'s use of the western conventions and all the associations they provided. Indeed, around the figures of Rick and Laszlo, the movie gathered the most affecting motifs of the traditional American mythology.

Casablanca's plot confronted Rick with a series of choices: Should he help Laszlo to escape and thereby forfeit his own safe neutrality? Should he keep Ilsa with him? Should he avoid the situation altogether and do nothing? In turn, the film appeared to demand that its audience decide between two sets of values, Rick's outlaw hero code and Laszlo's official morality. This dichotomy resulted from the film's sustained contrasting of the two men.

Appearance: As played by Paul Henreid, standing erect in a white dress suit, Victor Laszlo perfectly embodied the official hero.

Indeed, Henreid's clear eyes, chiseled Roman nose, high fore-head, and strong jaw (with the hint of an underbite) made Laszlo resemble George Washington, the arch-official hero of American culture.

If Henreid gave Laszlo a kind of classical good looks, Bogart lent Rick an irregular handsomeness, with weary, cynical eyes, a rather plain nose, and an idiosyncratic mouth. The important thing about this attractiveness was its individuality; its refusal to conform to any preconceived notions of handsomeness dupli-cated the character's stubborn independence.

Attitude toward Women: While Laszlo was married (and even more tellingly, comfortable with being so), Rick was another ex-ample of what Fiedler has called "a long line of heroes in flight from woman and home."[1] An early scene confirmed Rick's atti-tude. Confronted by an ex-girlfriend trying to pin him down to some commitment, he brushed her off with the casual disdain of a man interested in women only for sexual entertainment:

YVONNE: Where were you last night?
RICK: That's so long ago I don't remember.
YVONNE: Will I see you tonight?
RICK: I never make plans that far ahead.

Finally getting the message, Yvonne uttered the classic com-plaint of all women abandoned by an outlaw hero: "What a fool I was to fall for a man like you."

Significantly, too, Rick operated and lived above a saloon, a place which, as Fiedler points out, "was for a long time felt as the anti-type of the home, a refuge for escaping males nearly as archetypal as the wilderness and the sea."[2] Rick's bar was no different, a man's world where women were nightly bought and sold in exchange for exit visas.

Origins: With their different origins, the American Rick and the European Laszlo embodied the contradictory sources of the American ideology. For while the official heroes (e.g., Jefferson, Franklin) provided continuity with the manners, learning, and sophistication of the Old World, the outlaw hero represented the instinctive repudiation of Europe and its culture.

Significantly, Rick's outlaw status depended on more than

simply the imagery of self-containment that surrounded him. Like Shane and the typical gunfighter, he had an ambiguous past: "Richard Blaine, American, Age 37. Cannot return to his country," Strasser read to Rick. "The reason is a little vague." Renault also showed interest:

RENAULT: I've often speculated on why you don't return to America. Did you abscond with the church funds? Did you run off with the Senator's wife? I'd like to think that you killed a man. It's the romantic in me.
RICK: It was a combination of all three.

The truth about Rick's past remained the undisclosed secret of *Casablanca*; the film never revealed why Rick could not go home, as *Shane* refused to specify the exact nature of what its hero refused to discuss.

Casablanca, however, did indicate that while Laszlo was in Morocco for a specific purpose (to escape the Nazis), Rick had come for apparently no reason at all:

RENAULT: And what in heaven's name brought you to Casablanca?
RICK: My health. I came to Casablanca for the waters.
RENAULT: What waters? We're in the desert.
RICK: I was misinformed.

This denial of rational motivation represented a characteristic American ideological tendency to deny past events their capacity to control present circumstances. As an assertion, it derived from the frontier mythology of perpetual renewal which encouraged escapism. Not surprisingly, however, Rick's apparent fresh start concealed a previous disappointment. Like Jay Gatsby (another hero with mysterious origins), he was obsessed with a past that he sought simultaneously to obliterate. In maintaining this ambiguous relationship with his own history, Rick represented not only the typical frontiersman, but also America itself.

Attitudes toward Politics and Ideology: Laszlo was first and foremost a public figure, driven by abstract principles at once rational and supra-individualistic. Trying to explain his character to Rick, Ilsa spoke of "knowledge and thoughts and ideals," the chief symbols of the official values. Significantly, too, Laszlo led a collective movement, the Pan-European underground. Thanking Rick at the end, he spoke of "*our* side."

Rick's pragmatic skepticism contrasted strongly with Laszlo's idealism. "You are a very cynical person," Ugarte told him, and nothing Rick said disproved that characterization. "The problems of the world are not in my department," he insisted, and having heard Ilsa's moralizing about Laszlo's cause, he refused to help: "I'm not fighting for anything anymore except myself. I'm the only cause I'm interested in." With his distrust of abstract principles, Rick confirmed Tocqueville's observation that in America, "each man is narrowly shut up in himself, and from that basis makes the pretension to judge the world."[3]

While Laszlo's absorption in political activities confirmed his official hero status, Rick's evident leisure connected him further to the western hero described by Robert Warshow:

> The Westerner is *par excellence* a man of leisure. Even when he wears the badge of a marshal or, more rarely, owns a ranch, he appears to be unemployed. We see him standing at a bar, or playing poker—a game which expresses perfectly his talent for remaining relaxed in the midst of tension—or perhaps camping out on the plains on some extraordinary errand. If he does own a ranch, it is in the background; we are not actually aware that he owns anything except his horse, his guns, and the one worn suit of clothing which is likely to remain unchanged all through the movie. It comes as a surprise to see him take money from his saddlebags. As a rule we do not even know where he sleeps at night and don't think of asking. Yet it never occurs to us that he is a poor man. . . .[4]

This passage described Rick almost exactly. He owned the casino, but his work seemed limited to signing checks and vouchers, breaking up occasional fights, and refusing to drink with customers. In this context, the information that his cash reserves could withstand the café's closing for "two weeks, maybe three" *was* surprising. He seemed never to think of money.

Attitudes toward the Law: Casablanca repeatedly emphasized Rick's and Laszlo's contrasting views of the law, an issue traditionally dividing the official hero and the renegade. Rick was clearly another version of Robin Hood, operating outside a corrupt legal system in the name of some higher, private notion of justice. Like the original Robin, he made all the decisions for a loyal band of followers (Carl the waiter, Sacha the bartender, the croupier, and most important, Sam the piano player). Like

Robin (or the American gunfighter variants: Jesse James, Bonnie and Clyde, John Wesley Hardin), Rick robbed from the rich to give to the poor, manipulating his own roulette wheel to provide refugees with money for exit visas. When after one instance of remarkable "luck" by one of Rick's favored, another customer asked, "Say, are you sure this place is honest?" Carl's ironic reply reaffirmed the outlaw hero's private standard: "Honest? As honest as the day is long."

While Rick represented an extralegal morality, Laszlo relied on a legal principle for his safety. The movie's basic premise was the neutrality of the "frontier" town Casablanca, an abstract principle that Laszlo repeatedly asserted. "You won't dare to interfere with me here," he warned Strasser. "This is still unoccupied France. Any violation would reflect on Captain Renault."

Having established Laszlo's dependence on the law, however, *Casablanca* used the stock western depiction of the legal system's ultimate inadequacy as a guarantor of the official hero's safety. As in most westerns, the villains in *Casablanca* could control the legal mechanism to their own advantage. "The Germans have *outlawed* miracles," Ferrari warned Laszlo, and Renault used the flimsiest legal pretext to close Rick's café: "I'm shocked! Shocked to find that gambling is going on here!" he proclaimed, pocketing his own roulette winnings. Unlike Laszlo, Rick recognized the Germans' eagerness to manipulate the law. His proposed scheme to deliver Laszlo into the Gestapo's hands offered an apparent certitude of legal proof: Laszlo would be apprehended in the act of purchasing the stolen letters of transit, thereby making himself an accessory to the German couriers' murder.

While Laszlo relied on the law, Rick, like all western heroes, took it into his own hands, replacing an insufficient, corrupt system with his individual standards of right and wrong. His willingness to operate outside the law preserved Laszlo, who, left to his own devices, might never have escaped Casablanca.

ALTHOUGH Rick and Laszlo clearly represented the two strains of American culture, *Casablanca* demonstrated their imbalance.

For Bogart was the film's star, and no matter how badly he be-haved early on, the interest center remained with him. Renault made this focus overt, describing Rick to Ilsa as "the kind of man that, well, if I were a woman, and I weren't around, I should be in love with Rick," an ironic version of Mark Twain's encomium to Tom Blankenship, the model for Huck: "He was the only really independent person—boy or man—in the community," Twain re-membered in his *Autobiography*, adding in *Tom Sawyer* that all the other children "wished they dared be like him."[5]

As *Casablanca*'s moral center, Laszlo was more ambiguous. While his principles were rationally acceptable, he represented too many of the things traditionally disparaged by the frontier mythology: marriage, political commitment, collective action, the denial of individualism. At moments, the movie allowed the im-plicit sense of Laszlo's coldness to surface in thin disguise: "We read five times that you were killed in five different places," a fellow underground fighter whispered. "As you see," Laszlo re-plied, seeming to acknowledge the cost of idealism to the human elements of his character, "it was true every single time."

In a cinematic tradition so dependent on audience identifica-tion, Laszlo's glacial perfection diminished his appeal. In con-trast to Rick's emotional drunk scene, his control suggested a less passionate attachment to Ilsa. As Rick observed, she seemed mostly another "part of his work, the thing that keeps him going"—the conventional western's low estimate of married love. Rick's love, the movie assured, was the genuine article.

Having established Rick and Laszlo as representatives of the two divergent strains of American mythology, *Casablanca* as-sumed the national ideology's basic project: their reconciliation. Characteristically, the movie began by blurring the differences between the two men, using their shared love for Ilsa as the most obvious device to suggest underlying similarities. Laszlo, in fact, made this love the basis of his final appeal to Rick:

LASZLO: It is perhaps a strange circumstance that we should both love the same woman. The first evening I came here to this café, I knew there was something between you and Ilsa. Since no one is to blame, I . . . , I demand no explanation. I ask only one thing. You won't give

me the letters of transit. All right. But I want my wife to be safe. I
ask you as a favor to use the letters to take her away from Casablanca.

The movie furthered this blurring process by revealing that Rick's
indifference to politics belied his former participation in anti-
Fascist fighting in Spain and Ethiopia, and that Laszlo's collective action involved his participation in the underground, an
outlaw movement.

In working to reconcile the competing values of Rick and Laszlo,
Casablanca systematically redistributed the audience's fundamental allegiance to the outlaw hero. While softening Laszlo's
idealism, the movie made Rick's moral detachment, normally
glamorized as essential to the outsider's independence, seem ni-
hilistically selfish. Thus, as the Gestapo dragged Ugarte away,
a customer chided, "When they come to get me, Rick, I hope
you'll be of more help." In this context, Rick's version of the
standard outlaw hero reply, "I stick my neck out for nobody,"
appeared simply inadequate, an implication that the frontiersman's flight from society derived from his sense of life's ultimate
futility. Rick's unconcern about the murdered German couriers
evinced a similar despondency: "They got a lucky break," he told
Ugarte coldly. "Yesterday they were just two German clerks. Today they're the honored dead." Worse still was his reply to Ilsa's
threat with a gun: "Go ahead and shoot. You'll be doing me a
favor." "If we stop fighting our enemies, the world will die," Laszlo
pleaded with him. "What of it?" came Rick's answer. "Then it'll
be out of its misery."

While the outlaw tradition had always contained a dark side
of purposelessness, *Casablanca* made Rick's suicidal tendencies
seem a betrayal of the ring-tailed roarer's enormous vitality. Indeed, one of the principal functions of the renegade tradition had
been to reverse the official standard's subordination of pleasure
to duty and responsibility. But what good was it to be an outlaw
if it wasn't any fun? *Casablanca*, too, suggested a possibly bleak
future for Rick, providing in the dissolute Ferrari a possible image of his eventual fate (as Huck's drunkard father loomed as
his destiny).

While undercutting Rick, *Casablanca* also went to some lengths to make the ascetic Laszlo more attractive. "Apparently you think of me only as the leader of a Cause," he told Rick. "Well, I'm also a human being." In contrast to Rick's cruel imputations of sexual promiscuity, Laszlo's refusal to press Ilsa for explanations about her relationship with Rick increased his appeal. Above all, the movie reduced Laszlo's potentially abstract ideals to the pragmatics acceptable in the frontier mythology: "Don't you sometimes wonder if it's worth all this?" Rick asked skeptically; "I mean what you're fighting for?" "We might as well question why we breathe," Laszlo assured him, insisting on the immediacy of the issue. "If we stop breathing, we'll die. If we stop fighting our enemies, the world will die."

Having transposed American anxiety regarding the intervention decision into Rick's reluctance to help Victor Laszlo, *Casablanca* set itself the task of demonstrating how Rick could act without sacrificing his separateness. The movie's solution involved moving Rick and Laszlo closer together until, if only for a moment, they could act in concert. Thus, the film progressed from one set of attitudes (isolation, independence, autonomy, self-sufficiency) to another (participation, interdependence, responsibility, collectivity). Rick's statements represented the two poles:

Autonomy	*Interdependence*
"Suppose you run your business and let me run mine."	"But I've got a job to do, too. . . . Ilsa, I'm no good at being noble, but it doesn't take much to see that the problems of three little people don't amount to a hill of beans in this crazy world. Someday you'll understand that."
"I stick my neck out for nobody."	
"Your business is politics, mine is running a saloon."	
"The problems of the world are not in my department. I'm a saloon keeper."	
"I'm the only cause I'm interested in."	

For a movie, however, that purported to champion the causes of commitment and collective action, the balance between these two poles was way off. Not only did the outlaw tradition of autonomy get more of the lines; the film's interest center gathered around Rick's solitude, self-sufficiency, and independence. How then did *Casablanca* achieve its solution?

Certainly, Rick's intervention did not derive from rational arguments, although *Casablanca* worked hard to suggest their importance, bombarding Rick with appeals to abandon his stubborn detachment:

FERRARI: My dear Rick, when will you realize that in this world today, isolationism is no longer a practical policy?

LASZLO: You must know it's very important that I get out of Casablanca. It's my privilege to be one of the leaders of a great movement. You know what I have been doing. You know what it means to the work, to the lives of thousands and thousands of people that I be free to reach America and continue my work.

ILSA: Well, I know how you feel about me, but I'm asking you to put aside your feelings for something more important.

LASZLO: I wonder if you know that you're trying to escape from yourself and that you'll never succeed.

None of these neat arguments, however, was the reason for Rick's change of heart. Indeed, their rationality only insured their ineffectiveness as appeals to an outlaw hero who wanted not logical motives for conduct, but instinctive ones. Presented with all of the above arguments, Rick ultimately behaved like Huck Finn:

She [the Widow Douglas] told me what she meant—I must help other people and look out for them all the time, and never think about myself. . . . I went out in the woods and turned it over in my mind a long time, but I couldn't see no advantage in it—except for the other people; so that at last I reckoned I wouldn't worry about it any more, but just let it go.

But, of course, what both Huck and Rick "let go" was not the deed (helping Jim and Laszlo to escape) but the elaborate reasons for it. "The less time to think, the easier for all of us," Rick advised Ilsa. "Trust me."

And the film assured its audience that Rick deserved such trust. In demonstrating his ultimate willingness to help Laszlo, *Casablanca* reaffirmed the frontier mythology's faith in the individual's instinct as the source of right conduct. As Tocqueville noted, this ideology portrayed selfishness as "based on misguided judgment rather than depraved feeling. It is due more to inadequate understanding than to perversity of heart."[6] Which was precisely what *Casablanca* confirmed, reassuring its audience that Rick's selfishness derived entirely from his misunderstanding of Ilsa's "faithlessness." With that explained, he could act.

In making Rick's love for Ilsa outweigh the politics of anti-Fascism as a motivation for Rick's helping Laszlo, *Casablanca* provided its American audience with a concretely manageable reason for intervention. Much earlier, Tocqueville had noted the American requirement of such specific incidents:

It is difficult [in America] to force a man out of himself and get him to take an interest in the affairs of the whole state, for he has little understanding of the way in which the fate of the state can influence his own lot. But if it is a question of taking a road past his property, he sees at once that this small public matter has a bearing on his greatest private interests. . . .[7]

In *Casablanca*, the "road" past Rick's property was Ilsa's reappearance in his life.

Throughout this discussion of *Casablanca*, I have made deliberate references to *Huckleberry Finn*. For part of the movie's authority derived from its reworking of many of the motifs of Twain's novel, which Hemingway referred to as the source for all American literature. Indeed, *Casablanca*'s particularly close connection to *Huck Finn* was merely one instance of Classic Hollywood's characteristic, and probably unconscious, repetitions of that literature's fundamental themes.

Casablanca not only made Rick a reincarnation of the renegade Huck; it also imitated basic elements of Twain's plot. The opening map sequence of *Casablanca*, with its dark, moving line representing "a tortuous, roundabout refugee trail," simulated a river, in the midst of which the city of Casablanca, and Rick's café, lay like a raft. Like Huck, Rick lived on this "raft" with a black companion (Sam), and this "river" (like the Mississippi) provided an escape route from oppression. *Casablanca* divided

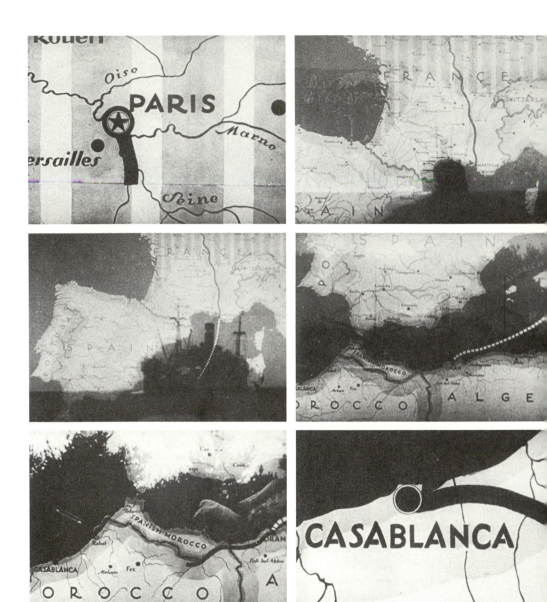

the character of Jim, the runaway slave, into two figures: the black friend, Sam, and the white man, Laszlo, who assumed Jim's problem, the need to escape.

Furthermore, Rick repeated Huck's pattern of being apolitical, of trying to avoid the entire issue of helping Laszlo with its complicated issues of right and wrong. Sam, who was more like Tom Sawyer than Jim, pleaded with his boss to get away from the dilemma. Sounding like Jake Barnes in *The Sun Also Rises* proposing the trip to Spain to Bill Gorton, Sam begged, "We'll take the car and drive all night. We'll get drunk. We'll go fishin' and stay away until she's gone."

But Rick, like Huck, ended up helping Laszlo, almost in spite of himself. His plan, which involved deceiving Ilsa and Laszlo until the last moment, repeated the kind of elaborate trickery that Tom and Huck had inflicted on Jim. Above all, *Casablanca* reaffirmed *Huck Finn*'s assurance that the outsider's freedom could survive the entanglements required by helping someone else. The movie depicted any such commitment as only temporary, an emergency measure without lasting implications. As Huck ended by "light [ing] out for the Territory," staying one step ahead of civilization, Rick told Louis, "I could use a trip," and set out for the mysterious "Free French garrison over at Brazzaville," a phrase whose exotic, Foreign Legion remoteness effectively converted French North Africa into another frontier.

Casablanca's ending was crucial to the success of the film's ideological project: the avoidance of choice between autonomy and commitment. Rick's intervention assumed the typical western form, the gunfight, as he outdrew the German officer trying to prevent Laszlo's escape. But as in all westerns, the crucial issue in *Casablanca* turned on the woman. Ingrid Bergman's well-known account of the scriptwriters' uncertainty about whether Ilsa would stay with Rick or leave with Laszlo misleadingly suggests the relative appropriateness of either conclusion. In fact, however, as a disguised western intent on demonstrating the impermanence of all interventions in society's affairs, *Casablanca* could not have conceivably allowed its outlaw hero to keep the girl. For the frontier mythology persistently portrayed the real danger to that hero's independence not as intervention for the good of others, but as marriage. *Casablanca* reassured its male audience (the source of the national anxiety regarding World War II intervention) that one could accept responsibilities without forfeiting autonomy, if one could evade the symbolic entanglements offered by the Good Good Girl.

The power of *Casablanca*'s ending, like *The Maltese Falcon*'s, derived from the coincidence of ideological need (to send the woman away) with official morality: in *The Maltese Falcon*, the woman had to be turned over to the police because she was the

murderer; in *Casablanca*, because she had to remain with her legal husband. The striking visual resemblances between the two conclusions merely suggested the frequency with which Classic Hollywood resorted to this basic western trope.

In both films, the woman played the sacrificial lamb which allowed the audience to avoid choosing between the outlaw code and the official morality. Freed of Ilsa, Rick could light out for the Territory with Renault, their banter encouraging the film's audience to consider such temporary commitments as fun.

Despite its achieved solution, however, *Casablanca* could not entirely conceal this ending's hint of sadness. Leslie Fiedler wrote about Huck, he does not know to *what* he is escaping, except into nothing: a mere anti-society, in which he is a cipher, a ghost without a real name. "All I wanted was to go somewheres," he tells Miss Watson, "all I wanted was a change, I warn't particular." Huck is heading for no utopia, since he has heard of none; and so he ends up making flight itself his goal. He flees from the impermanence of boyhood to that of continual change; and, of course, it is a vain evasion except as it leads him to understand that *no* society can fulfill his destiny.[8]

Certainly, this passage applied to Rick, who left with Renault for nowhere in particular. *Casablanca*'s richness depended on its willingness to suggest this counterposition, this dark side of an essentially optimistic belief. For Molly Haskell[9] to the contrary, Rick and Louis did not walk off into "the equivalent of the lovers' sunset," but rather into a swirling, thick fog that swallowed them up and slowly erased their outlines, until they seemed to lose substance and become, in the last frame, like ghosts—or, like the myths they were.

4. Classic Hollywood's Holding Pattern: The Combat Films of World War II

Casablanca's immense lasting popularity has obscured the film's decidedly topical origins. Indeed, the most neglected fact about *Casablanca* is that it was a war movie, one of a cycle of American films made between 1941 and 1945 with a definite propagandistic intent. Nevertheless, *Casablanca*'s simultaneous status as an explicit allegory of U.S. military intervention and as the culmination of Classic Hollywood's reconciliatory pattern indicates how little World War II affected the American Cinema. In fact, even the combat features made during the war adhered to the model of choice avoidance established as the norm for the commercial movie. If anything, this model merely became more obvious, rendered less subtle by the simplification procedures that Basil Wright has seen as typical of the wartime film:

> To the artist war brings—at least to begin with—instant simplification. Issues are no longer in doubt, or at any rate are not seen to be so. One knows what to do. Wartime films are therefore ideologically and emotionally very simple. Their value in later times tends to be historical rather than aesthetic.[1]

Far from prompting a new kind of popular film, therefore, World War II merely provided the American film industry and its audience with an occasion for reaffirming the traditional forms. For despite their reliance on realistic *mise en scènes*, the combat pictures were essentially romances that magically resolved the tensions created by contradictory needs.

The continuity between Hollywood's Classic movies and the wartime films derived at least partially from the influence of Howard Hawks's prewar *Only Angels Have Wings* (1939). As a model for the simplification process undertaken by the war movies, Hawks was the inevitable choice, for of the great Hollywood directors, he had most consistently reduced the reconciliatory pattern to its basic elements, producing broadly drawn optimistic films that sometimes resembled cartoons.

Hawks's movies, like the combat films, are often misunderstood as being simply about groups. In fact, his groups were very special, capable of accommodating individualism without devouring it, relying as much on personal acts of heroism as on teamwork. The members of these groups were carefully particularized: Hawks's ideal world was a melting pot full of distinctly different individuals. Thus, his films represented a mythic solution to the individual-community opposition central to American culture, and as such, were the inevitable model for the combat films whose propagandistic project was to reaffirm the American myth that, even in wartime, essential choices could be avoided.

Although *Only Angels Have Wings* was not a war film per se, it contained almost all of the motifs that became the basis of Hollywood's portrayal of World War II combat: the male group directed by a strong leader, the outsider who must prove himself by courageous individual action, the necessity for stoicism in the face of danger and death, the premium placed on professionalism, and the threat posed by women. So broad was *Angels'* use of these motifs that the movie functioned as an archetypal source for the World War II films that followed.

No one has ever topped Manny Farber's plot summary of *Only Angels Have Wings*:

This movie about a Zeta Beta Tau fraternity of fliers in a South American jungle is a ridiculous film of improbability and coincidence, the major one being that Bat McPherson, the blackest name in aviation, the man who betrayed Thomas Mitchell's kid brother and married Grant's old flame, should show up years later broke and in need of a job in Barranca, where buddies Grant and Mitchell are busting up planes on the strangest stalactite mountains. . . . *Only Angels*, a White Cargo melodrama that is often intricately silly, has a family unit living at the Dutchman's, a combination bar, restaurant, rooming house, and airport run by a benevolent Santa Claus (some airline: the planes take off right next to the kitchen, and some kitchen: a plane crashes, the wreck is cleared and the pilot buried in the time it takes them to cook a steak; and the chief control is a crazy mascot who lives with a pet donkey and serves as a lookout atop a buzzard-and-blizzard-infested mountain as sharp as a shark's tooth).[2]

Farber does neglect to mention some specifics: the reason given for the film's action (the men—some pilots, some investors—had signed a contract to deliver the mail to towns across a dangerous mountain range), the complications (the arrival of Bat, a woman, and chronic bad weather), and the solution (acts of individual heroism by Bat—Richard Barthelmess—and the group's leader, Jeff—Cary Grant). This fantastic, clichéd plot, full of hokey coincidences and stylized melodrama ("frankly terrible," Peter John Dyer called it[3]) was not nearly so important as what Hawks managed to do with it: on this story, he hung all the motifs that would dominate the wartime films.

1. *The isolated male group involved in a life-and-death task*: The group of flyers in *Angels* became the model for the patrols or platoons of the wartime movies—patrols cut off from the main body of the army (*Flying Tigers, Air Force, Wake Island, Guadalcanal Diary*) or assigned to a particularly dangerous mission behind enemy lines (*Destination Tokyo; Thirty Seconds Over Tokyo; Objective, Burma!*). The war movies employed these small, isolated groups as a device for viewing a world war that, without this focusing, would have seemed only an enormous, impersonal machine. The point of view of the single platoon was the movies' equivalent of Henry James's narrative consciousness—an organizing principle.

2. *The group, composed of distinct types, that relies on both teamwork and individual exploits*: The men in *Angels* were friends (especially Jeff and "The Kid," played by Thomas Mitchell), but more importantly, they worked as a team. In the opening scene, Jeff and "The Kid" operated together to "talk down" a pilot lost in the fog over the runway. As Robin Wood has noticed, the sequence showed "Mitchell using his ears and Grant his voice as if they were two aspects of the same human being."[4] The point was that the lost pilot, Grant, and Mitchell were a team of three— it took all three to save the plane. When the same pilot subsequently ignored the orders of his "teammate" Grant (hurrying to land despite orders, in order to keep a date), he crashed. The moral: you can't do it alone.

The men evinced their mutual dependency in other ways as well. The cook, Dutchy (Sig Ruman), did not fly but had financed the entire operation, buying the planes and paying the pilots' salaries. But his investment depended in turn on the flyers' willingness and ability to keep the mail moving, despite crackups and bad weather.

Although *Angels* overtly emphasized the values of the group, its detailed characterizations implicitly affirmed the American ideological insistence on the compatibility of individual and communitarian values. Each member of the *Angels* team embodied a distinct type: Dutchy, the comic butt with the heavy foreign accent; "The Kid," the aging flyer losing his eyesight; Jeff, the glamorous leader matter-of-factly executing the duties of command. Ultimately, too, the group's success depended on individual acts, especially on Jeff's final mission, undertaken in the worst possible weather.

3. *Professionalism and stoicism in the face of danger and death*: Faced with a task that required them to risk their lives on a daily basis, the flyers in *Angels* built up protective mechanisms either to deny the possibility of death or to deal with it, if it came, in a ritualized manner. Crucial was the belief in professionalism with its faith that death did not come by chance but as a result of someone's failure to do his job properly. By allowing the flyers to feel some control over their fates, this belief encouraged a respect for discipline, care, and skill. Thus Grant's blaming Joe's death on the fact that "he wasn't good enough" comforted the remaining flyers, each certain of his own ability.

The stoic, stiff-upper-lip response to disaster played an integral part in this code. By eating the steak prepared for the dead pilot, Grant asserted that life had to go on—and also that their situation was too precarious to stop and mourn the dead. Because he had died for a foolish reason (to keep a date on time), Joe had become a debilitating threat to the rest of the pilots' ability to perform. Therefore, he had to be dismissed. "That's Joe's steak you're eating," Jean Arthur said to Grant, shocked by his callousness. "Who's Joe?" Grant replied.

As a part of this stoic attitude toward danger, Hawks's characters spoke in oblique Hemingwayesque language, which Hawks himself called "three-cushion." ("In order to say something, you bounce around from one cushion to another and then you've said it and it doesn't become a rash statement"[5]). Part of this language was, in fact, nonverbal, particularly the Hawksian routines with cigarettes and matches. In *Angels*, Grant never had a match, and by having to ask others for one, particularly Mitchell, he suggested his dependence on them. As Mitchell was dying, Grant at least returned the favor by giving him a cigarette. Together, they used the ritual as a way of not talking about death: Joe crashed and Grant turned to Mitchell, asking "Got a match?" Women resisting this kind of refusal to express emotion openly could win acceptance only by playing the game—Arthur finally achieved entry into Grant's world by recognizing the proposal hidden in his offer, "Stay if it's heads, you leave if it's tails," made with a two-headed coin.

The combat films repeatedly used another basic element of the stoicism motif, the inventory of the dead pilot's belongings. Almost always, these men left little behind but a handful of loose change and a few pictures of someone back home. Nevertheless, serious inventory of even the meager possessions implied the community behind the individual, at once supporting and depending upon him.

Angels also confronted the possibility that stoicism could break down at the last: the dying Mitchell asked Grant to leave the room because he was not sure of his own courage. The war movies, borrowing this idea, continually stressed that really brave men admitted to fear (see especially the cave scene in *Guadalcanal Diary* and William Bendix's soliloquy about fear).

4. *Outsiders enter the group and become threats to it*: While *Angels'* outsiders did in fact come from remote, external sources, the war films' outsiders were typically malcontents within the group itself (e.g., the Garfield character in *Air Force*). The first outsider in *Angels* was Bonnie Lee (Jean Arthur), a wandering showgirl stranded in Barranca ("I quit a show at Valparaiso"). She disrupted the carefully established rituals and teamwork of the group: Joe's date was with her. Further, her grief for him was too explicit. By refusing to adopt the stoic, oblique-language game, by nagging at Grant and the men to pay attention to Joe's

death, she threatened to break down the protective barriers enabling them to avoid paralyzing fear. Bat's wife (Rita Hayworth)
posed a different kind of threat: voluptuous, seductive, she not
only prevented the men from concentrating on their work, but
also stirred up jealousy that eroded group teamwork. Bat himself, however, proved the greater threat, for as the pilot who had
let another man down, he sowed the seeds of doubt and fear in
the others.

5. *The outsiders must win admission into the group*: The women
in *Angels* could gain admission into the group only by accepting
the male world on its own terms. While Bat's wife made her
peace by tacitly supporting her husband, Bonnie Lee gained entrance by engaging Jeff in his own tongue-in-cheek banter. As a
male, however, Bat's route back to the group was arduous, requiring a suicide mission over the mountains in zero-visibility
weather and an aerial version of a no-man's-land rescue, his refusal to bail out of a damaged plane and leave a wounded Mitchell behind. (This motif reappeared in *Air Force*, where the "person" to be rescued was the plane itself, the *Mary Ann*.)

ALTHOUGH it was nominally an action/adventure picture, *Only
Angels Have Wings* had very few real action sequences—and they
were the worst thing in the movie, at times using weird, obviously fake mountains, giant condors, and recognizably miniature planes. In fact, like most of the combat films that copied it,
Angels was less about adventure itself than men's reactions to
it. Influential, too, was Hawks's simple, even stark, technique
based on invisible editing, simple sets, and a sparing use of close-
ups, a style whose reductiveness matched the broadness of the
film's reconciliatory pattern. (A convoluted technique would have
commented ironically on that pattern.) Invariably, the combat
movies employed similar techniques, emphasizing what appeared to be a casual, semi-documentary look that attempted to
portray war not as a strange distortion of the normal world, but
as something solvable by "business as usual."

But despite the superficial realism of the combat films, they
were in fact as stylized as *Only Angels Have Wings*. Even with
a self-effacing technique, Hawks made little effort toward veri-
similitude, preferring instead a melodramatic quality fueled by

the hothouse atmosphere of a frankly artificial staging. The dramatic opening sequence, the best few minutes in *Angels*, was typical. Working in the dark, Grant and Mitchell tried to "talk down" Joe, lost overhead in the fog. No background music accompanied this scene, only the drone of the invisible plane's props. The darkness and obvious artificiality of the studio set actually worked to increase the tension—without lights, without vistas of any kind, the *mise en scène* invoked an oppressive heat and a jungle world where pilots and ground crews lived on top of each other, growing irritable with the weather, the constant danger, and their own fear. The closed-in atmosphere of the set furthered the idea of the men's absolute mutual dependence, but also glamorized the individual leader. Against the black background of Dutchy's bar and the night, Grant stood out in his white suit.

Clearly, *Only Angels Have Wings* came from the world of the romance. As Farber put it, the film "isn't dated so much as removed from reality, like the land of Tolkien's Hobbits."[6] By using *Angels'* reductive version of the Classic Hollywood pattern as the model for its combat films, therefore, the industry proposed to its audience that reality be ignored for the duration of World War II. What was seen on the screen, as a result, was less a true image of combat than a special genre using the traditional Hollywood pattern. Made only a few weeks after Pearl Harbor, and released in early 1942, *Flying Tigers* established the trend. The movie was actually a remake of *Only Angels Have Wings*, with no credit given to Hawks. The plot was identical: Hawks's male group of South American mail pilots became General Chennault's volunteer irregulars, fighting the Japanese in China before American entry into the war. Although the men were adventurers of the *Angels* breed (they did not *have* to be there), the Japanese threat reduced the gratuitousness of their flying. As the group leader, John Wayne assumed Cary Grant's *Angels* role, even to the extent of being called "Pappy" (as Grant had been) by obviously older men. Like Grant, he stressed teamwork: a pilot who had foolhardily taken up an unarmed plane and been forced to crash-land received a lecture. "You're not the first ball carrier who didn't appreciate his blockers." The others joined in: "A few more flights like this and he'll qualify as a Jap ace."

Into this cozy setup came a pilot who had been a coward. Wayne turned him away, but as Rita Hayworth had done for her husband Barthelmess in *Angels*, the outcast's wife pleaded for another chance. Again, the film, for all of its talk about teamwork, stressed the importance of individual acts: to gain readmittance into the privileged group, the pariah had to prove himself by hiding on board a plane and subsequently saving an injured Wayne on a suicide mission. In the meantime, Wayne's own girlfriend began to cause trouble by taking up with a reckless flyer. When a date with her made the pilot too late for a mission, Wayne's best friend, grounded for bad vision like Mitchell in *Angels*, took his place and was killed—presumably, it was the woman's fault. New recruits were lectured on the policy of teamwork ("Don't try to win the war by yourself") while Wayne struggled to hold the men together. Hawks should have sued for plagiarism.

Flying Tigers was a sign of things to come. All of the major combat films were, in effect, remakes of *Only Angels Have Wings*. All sought in specific to reconcile the individual-group conflict by demonstrating that even the effort required by the war did not undermine the essential American myth that all such oppositions were ultimately resolvable. The symbolic affirmation of this myth, seized upon by the movies, was the Doolittle Raid on Tokyo in April 1942, a mission whose military purpose was subordinate to its possibilities as a morale-building gesture. "Of all the military operations in the first two years of the war," war-movie historian Lawrence H. Suid writes, "probably nothing so stimulated the imagination of the American people as Doolittle's mission against Japan."[7] At the time, the raid seemed important only as a demonstration of the American capability to strike at the Japanese mainland. In fact, it was the special character of the carefully staged event that established its appeal. In an enormously complicated, potentially abstract conflict, the Doolittle Raid was a simple, direct, understandable action, a western-style tactic easily dramatized. More important, with its reliance on interservice teamwork (the navy took the army pilots to within striking distance of the Japanese coastline) and individual heroism (of the men who flew the mission), the raid yielded an ideal image of America at war. It was inevitable that the Doolittle

Mission would become a subject for the movies, and, indeed, three wartime combat pictures told the story: *Destination Tokyo* (1943) concerned itself with a U.S. submarine stealing into Tokyo Bay to gather information for the raid; *Thirty Seconds Over Tokyo* (1944) recounted the preparations, the raid itself, and the subsequent rescue of the downed flyers; and *The Purple Heart* (1944) focused on the problems of those pilots shot down and captured by the Japanese. Because of its concentration and obvious capacity for romance, the Doolittle Raid, in thinly disguised form, provided the basis for the overtly unrealistic Errol Flynn movies *Desperate Journey* (1942) (RAF pilots shot down over Germany) and *Objective, Burma!* (1945) (paratroopers operating behind Japanese lines).

In addition to these movies' particular reliance on the Doolittle Raid as an image of American-style combat, almost all the major war movies developed around the motifs established by *Only Angels Have Wings* that I discussed above.

1. *The isolated male group involved in a dangerous situation*: Each of the wartime movies focused on a limited group as a vantage point for the wider theaters of war. Hawks's own *Air Force* (1943) centered on the crew of one B-17, en route to Pearl Harbor on December 7, 1941, and subsequently appearing at all of the principal battlegrounds of the Pacific War's first week—Wake Island, the Philippines, and the Coral Sea. The heroes of *Wake Island* (1942) were the few hundred marines and civilians who managed to hold off the vastly superior attacking Japanese for over a week before being overrun. *Guadalcanal Diary* (1943) portrayed the war for that island from the point of view of one of the first marine platoons to land there. *Thirty Seconds Over Tokyo* used the captain of one of Doolittle's planes as the narrative center of consciousness for an account of the Tokyo mission. In *Destination Tokyo*, the same story was told from the perspective of a submarine crew doing reconnaissance work for the flyers. *Objective, Burma!*, the most fanciful of the films, followed the adventures of one patrol parachuted behind enemy lines fighting its way back to safety. All of these groups were the combat equivalent of *Angels'* mail pilots.

2. *The group, composed of distinct types, that relies on both*

teamwork and individual exploits: All of the war films followed *Angels'* model of the Hawksian group composed of distinct types working together under an idealized leader. The racially mixed platoon or flight crew (foreshadowed by Hawks's Dutchy-Jeff-Kid team) became a stock device of these films: *Air Force* had a Winocki and a Weinberg; *Destination Tokyo*, a Greek (known as Tin Can because of his unpronounceable name) and a New Yorker; *Guadalcanal Diary*, a Brooklyn cab driver and an Indian; *Objective, Burma!*, an entire melting pot (except for a black)—a Hogan, a Nebraska Hooper, a Miggleori, a Hennessey, a Negulesco, a Brophy, a Higgins, and even a helpful Burmese.

In stressing the importance of cooperation, Hawks's own *Air Force* was unusually realistic. While most flight movies focused on the pilots, *Air Force* eagerly demonstrated the importance of each crew member. Even the navigator's success in locating Wake Island, "a tiny speck in this ocean," came to seem heroic. Similar sequences suggested how much the success or failure of a mission could depend on a tail gunner (John Garfield) or a bombardier. And, in the film's climactic scene, each member of the crew, supervised by the chief sergeant, worked feverishly to repair the plane as the Japanese approached. On this job, the normally glamorous pilots contributed the least: the mechanics (especially Harry Carey) were the heroes.

Thirty Seconds Over Tokyo portrayed an even broader kind of teamwork. Cooperation between crew members was, of course, still crucial: the navigator located Tokyo, the bombardier timed and released the weapons, the mechanics kept the plane running, and the pilots flew it. At another level, the movie showed the cooperation among the crews of the different planes, training together, learning from each other's mistakes as they adapted to the short takeoffs needed on a carrier, and the hedge-hopping flight patterns used over Tokyo. At a still higher level, the movie placed great emphasis on the army-navy teamwork necessary to produce the Doolittle Raid. On first boarding the carrier *Hornet*, the planes' crews displayed routine distrust for the navy—a distrust furthered by the sailors' ability at poker. But with the goal of the mission revealed, the mutual chauvinisms and distrust fell away, the new-found teamwork clinched by the symbolic gesture of giving the pilots the best beds. After the flyers crash-landed in China, *Thirty Seconds* took a new tack, celebrating cooperation between the Chinese and the Americans, as an underground network of Chinese villagers passed the wounded Americans from hand to hand, keeping them from being captured by the Japanese.

Destination Tokyo's portrayal of submariners' mutual dependence depended on a compendium of submarine picture clichés: the fresh recruit, who saved the ship by deactivating a live but unexploded torpedo, was subsequently operated on for appendicitis by the pharmacist's mate, tended to in turn by the cook. More important, the sub's task, gathering information for the Tokyo Raid, demanded systematic intraservice cooperation.

Even though the combat films overtly celebrated teamwork, they continued to glamorize the individual heroes on whom a mission's success utterly depended. "I'd go through hell for that man," a crew member said of submarine captain Grant in *Destination Tokyo*, and clearly Doolittle (Spencer Tracy) in *Thirty Seconds Over Tokyo*, Brian Donlevy in *Wake Island*, and Errol Flynn in *Objective, Burma!* were equally important to their platoons. Inevitably, these films turned on individual feats: Garfield's miraculous landing in *Air Force*, Grant's daring tactics that managed to sink a threatening Japanese destroyer, the courageous last stands of *Wake Island* and *Guadalcanal Diary*. The pattern was the traditional Hollywood reconciliation of contradictory values. Even in combat, these movies proposed, there was no need to choose between individual and group.

3. *Professionalism and stoicism in the face of danger and death*: All of the combat features followed *Angels'* model in suggesting stoicism as the proper way for dealing with danger and death. *Air Force* repeated *Angels'* inventory of a dead pilot's meager collection of belongings with the same litany, "Not much to show for twenty years." Again as in *Angels*, the film allowed no time for grieving: the crew of the *Mary Ann* had to ready her for take-off.

In *Guadalcanal Diary* and *Wake Island*, the stoic, professional attitude revealed itself through humor (William Bendix's jokes and worries about the Dodgers and his girlfriend back home) and the willingness to admit fear (Bendix asking the chaplain to pray). Both films portrayed the maturation of green platoons, who moved from naïve overconfidence to a grudging respect for the Japanese as an enemy.

The combat films often stressed that the inevitable dehumanization accompanying the assumed stoic attitude constituted only a temporary departure from the natural and proper pattern of civilian life. None of these movies followed the earlier, bleak suggestion of *All Quiet on the Western Front* (1930) that the emotional stunting occasioned by war had permanently debilitating effects. Instead, normal lifestyles were easily resumed. Submarine captain Grant's home-pier reunion with his wife proved typically uncomplicated. Less blithe homecomings (in *Thirty Seconds Over Tokyo* and *Pride of the Marines*) were explained away as special cases, resulting from crippling injuries that required radical readjustments.

4 & 5. Outsiders who are threats to the group but finally win admission into it: Almost all of the combat pictures had versions of *Angels'* Bat McPherson, a malcontented, disruptive outsider required to perform an individual act of heroism to be admitted into the group. *Air Force*, in fact, contained two such figures: tail-gunner Winocki, angry at not making pilot and eager to quit the service, and Lieutenant Raider, a flashy, devil-may-care fighter pilot who made fun of the slower, less maneuverable bombers. The assimilation of these two derived partially from the declaration of war. As Winocki saw what the Japanese had done to the Americans at Pearl Harbor, Wake, and the Philippines, his complaints vanished. Similarly, fighter-pilot Raider, at first only a hitchhiker on the B-17 (which was to fly him to a new assignment), eventually assumed the pilot's role after the regular captain's death. Winocki's peace, however, was less natural. Like Bat in *Angels*, he had to perform special tasks to prove himself: refusing to bail out and leave the wounded pilot behind (a sequence repeated exactly from *Angels*), and hurrying to rescue a parachuting flyer being attacked by Japanese planes.

Both *Objective, Burma!* and *Wake Island* depicted the outsider as a civilian (*Burma*'s war correspondent, *Wake*'s contractor). But the war correspondent's latent pacifism was only slightly threatening and easily corrected. More troubling was contractor Mc-Closky's initial refusal to obey air raid warnings, his disdain for the American servicemen on the island ("Just once, I'd like to see a marine do a good day's work"), and his general insubordination ("I've got my government contract, and there's not one word in it about taking orders from brass hats"). Inevitably, however, he changed his tune when the Japanese attacked, sharing a foxhole to the last with the island's marine commander, swapping football stories between grenade throws.

Hollywood's combat films, therefore, were merely a new and radically simplified version of the classic pattern of reconciliation established by the prewar commercial cinema. Above all, they reaffirmed the myth that proposed the compatibility of individual and community values. Only after the war, when the need for morale-boosting disappeared, did the real image of World War II and its effects on American culture begin to appear. The movies made between Pearl Harbor and VJ Day, then, were merely the last products of the Classic Hollywood whose enormous power could convert even a world war into another occasion for its exercise.

Part Two. The Postwar Period
(1946–1966)

5. The Dissolution of the Homogeneous Audience and Hollywood's Response: Cult Films, Problem Pictures, and Inflation

AT THE END of World War II, America and Hollywood arrived simultaneously at the summit of power and influence. It was not only that the United States had won the war. More important was the relatively minor suffering it had incurred in doing so. America, in fact, was the only major country in the world that had escaped fighting on its home ground. Thus, while most of Europe lay in ruins, the United States emerged from the war stronger than ever before, free of a decade-long depression, in the midst of an economic boom, and alone possessing the most powerful weapon on earth, the atom bomb. The talk of a new regnum, an "American Century," was not farfetched. "In the late 1940s America glittered on a solitary peak," William Manchester observes in retrospect. "No other nation could even come close to it."[1]

And no other segment of the entertainment business could come close to the movies. By any standard of measurement, the Hollywood of the immediate postwar period was immensely successful. In 1946, domestic films grossed $1.7 billion, the most profitable year since the beginning of the American film industry. Roughly ninety cents of every amusement dollar were spent at the movies. Even more staggering was the result of Hollywood's own research, which indicated that 1946's average weekly attendance of 90 million represented, as Robert Sklar puts it, "nearly three-fourths of their 'potential audience'—that is, the movie industry's estimate of all the people in the country capable of making their way to a box office, leaving out the very young and very old, the ill, those confined to institutions, and others without access to movie theaters."[2]

More than any economic indicator, however, the movies' ability to act as a unifying social force provided the best measure of their strength. World War II had been a glorious occasion for demonstrating the industry's collective myth-making power. Manchester describes the culminating effect of Hollywood's Classic Period:

Appealing as they did to all ages and slighting no class—except blacks, who remained unnoticed even by themselves—films had strengthened familial ties and reminded moviegoers of values they shared. . . . Moreover, to an extent unappreciated at the time, the generalized pretransition movies provided the country with a common lore. Even in the 1970s middle-aged strangers could relate to one another and find a meeting ground by references to *The Philadelphia Story, Mutiny on the Bounty,* or any other of a hundred films remembered and cherished, over thirty years later, by virtually an entire generation.[3]

Hollywood's enormous Classic Period success established its formal and thematic paradigms as the exclusive possibilities for commercial filmmaking. Indeed, Hollywood's dominance made its movies seem mere applications of some given definition of the cinema itself. The most immediate result of this preeminence was that, for the mass audience, a film departing from the Classic Hollywood model would not seem like a film at all. The whole structure of the American film industry, therefore, favored gradual, conservative evolution. No single other fact is more important for an understanding of the movies from 1946 to 1967.

As we have seen, however, far from being an application of fixed possibilities, the development of Classic Hollywood's formal and thematic procedures had resulted from an evolutionary process that had always been intrinsically sociological. The apparently inevitable nature of commercial American films had, in reality, developed primarily and over time from the interaction of three factors: Hollywood (with its own internal determinants), the audience (with its expectations and perceptions, shaped to a significant extent by the movies), and the objective situation of America (the least important factor, since Americans had learned to experience historical events of even World War II's magnitude by means of the traditional mythological categories adopted by Classic Hollywood). Any and all of these three controlling factors could change.

That the postwar era was the first period since the coming of sound to recognize this possibility for change makes it a most interesting time in Hollywood's history. For with that recognition came the implicit understanding, on the part of both filmmakers and filmgoers, that the Classic Hollywood film was no more than a provisional model, created by a special set of circumstances, and capable of being challenged or replaced by alternative forms, developed here or abroad. Thus, it was during this period, which film historian Gerald Mast calls "The Years of Transition," that the conservative inertia of both Hollywood and its audience was first tested. Indeed, the movies of the late forties and fifties can best be understood as a series of tentative, awkward compromises between the self-perpetuating nature of the Classic Hollywood movie on the one hand, and the pressures for change caused by a new set of facts on the other. For of the three principal components that had produced the Classic Hollywood movie—the industry, the audience, and the situation of America—none escaped severe alterations.

The shocks to Hollywood itself were particularly severe. In quick succession during the postwar period, the industry found itself victimized by one of the first and most vigorous of the congressional witch hunts (1947), stripped of its guaranteed markets by the *Paramount* antitrust ruling (1948), and deprived of its overseas markets by European import tariffs and freezes on the removal of revenues (1947-1950). Any of these factors alone would have encouraged a conservative approach to moviemaking. Together they were devastating. The fear of being labeled "un-American" encouraged the production of bland, politically neutral movies, particularly in safe genres like the musical or the biblical epic. It was impossible to be too cautious. The congressional committee's index, after all, included *The Best Years of Our Lives, Citizen Kane*, and *The Grapes of Wrath*. Similarly, without the built-in profits guaranteed by the studio-owned theater chains and the European markets, Hollywood turned more and more to the presold picture, a movie based on an already successful novel, story, Broadway play, fairy tale, or biblical legend.[4] In the first ten years after the war, the Top Twenty Box Office Lists contained the following adaptations:

From Novels or Stories

Forever Amber
Life with Father
The Yearling
The Razor's Edge
The Three Musketeers
Cass Timberlane
Gentleman's Agreement
Little Women
Cheaper by the Dozen
A Place in the Sun
The Snows of Kilimanjaro
The African Queen
From Here to Eternity
The Caine Mutiny
The High and the Mighty
Magnificent Obsession
Battle Cry
Not as a Stranger
East of Eden
The Bridges at Toko-Ri
War and Peace
Moby Dick
The Man in the Gray Flannel Suit

From Plays

Key Largo
Annie Get Your Gun
Show Boat
A Streetcar Named Desire
Born Yesterday
Come Back, Little Sheba
Mister Roberts
Guys and Dolls
The King and I
High Society
Picnic

From Epics/Fantasies/Fairy Tales

Joan of Arc
Samson and Delilah
David and Bathsheba
Quo Vadis
Ivanhoe
The Robe
Cinderella
Peter Pan
Hans Christian Andersen
The Egyptian
Knights of the Round Table
Demetrius and the Gladiators
Twenty Thousand Leagues Under the Sea

Almost without exception, these movies were stodgy, literal-minded, and "safe." All of them made money, and all of them hewed to the traditional model of the Hollywood movie.

But if the witch hunts, antitrust rulings, and foreign import duties all fostered a conservative evolution for the postwar popular cinema, the other shock to the studio seemed a mandate for innovation. In 1946, there were only 8,000 households in the United States with television sets; by 1956, there were 35 million.[5] In 1951, televisions outsold radios for the first time, and Samuel Goldwyn recognized the implications:

Even the most backward-looking of the top-most tycoons of our industry cannot now help seeing just around the corner a titanic struggle to retain audiences. The competition we feared in the past . . . will fade into insignificance by comparison with the fight we are going to have to keep people patronizing our theaters in preference to sitting home and watching a program of entertainment. It is a certainty that people will be unwilling to pay to see poor pictures when they can stay home and see something which is, at least, no worse.[6]

In fact, they could stay home to see an old Hollywood movie. By 1960, five times more movie footage appeared each year on television than was released annually by Hollywood.[7] If the industry wanted to attract people into the theaters, it appeared that it would have to offer something new.

Even without the damage caused by witch hunts, antitrust rulings, eroding foreign markets, and television, Hollywood would have had problems maintaining its enormous popularity. For as a result of the tacit agreement with its audience to ignore reality during wartime for the sake of national morale, the industry had allowed a gap to open between the movies' concerns and those of many Americans. The Classic Hollywood movie had been based on a pre-World War II America that now seemed remote. The problem was how to respond to the new situation with its strange mixture of continuity and change. That the industry managed to survive depended on an odd circumstance: caught between events that argued for conservative evolution and those that called for departures from tradition, Hollywood in the 1950s mirrored the state of America itself.

Certainly, the objective status of the country was different. After hearing the news of the atomic bombing of Nagasaki, Secretary of War Henry Stimson had said it plainly: "The world is changed." World War II, as Daniel Bell has pointed out, "was the fateful turning point for American society."

The United States, though isolationist after World War I, could not retreat to an insular role in 1945. The scope of America's economic reach was now worldwide. And if political power did not necessarily follow the contours of the expanding economic influence, it had a trajectory of its own—to fill the power vacuums created by the withdrawal of the British and French from Asia, to defend Europe itself against the pressures of Russian expansion.[8]

In effect, then, the great fear of *Casablanca* had come true: by fighting the war to preserve the American Dream, the United

States had been forced to forsake permanently the splendid isolationism on which that dream rested. More than any other issue, it was this paradox that haunted Americans in the late forties and fifties, causing widespread disillusionment and anxiety. America had won the war, but in doing so had lost some essential part of its self-definition, the freedom, perhaps, to lead a remote, unentangled existence, interrupted only occasionally by threats that could always be quickly defused. The enduring appeal of America's great myth—the reluctant outlaw hero, like Huck or *Casablanca*'s Rick, who briefly emerged from his solitude to help society before lighting out again for the territory—suggests how basic this image of an unencumbered life was to the American self-image. Now, ironically, by virtue of its success, America could no longer entertain that lifestyle as a possibility. As Godfrey Hodgson observes:

> Between 1941 and 1945, the United States emerged as the strongest power in the world. At the same time, and partly indeed for this very reason, isolation ceased to be either attractive or even possible as an option for American foreign policy. By the end of the 1940s, the United States had accepted the responsibility of becoming "the leader of the free world"; that is, of influencing the political evolution of as much of the world as its gigantic strength would allow. The effect, though not the intention, was that America became an imperial power; of a new kind, certainly, but nevertheless as committed to intervention as it had been so recently to isolation.

All the significant international events of the late forties and fifties not only confirmed the necessity of permanent American involvement in world affairs, but even worse, suggested, as Hodgson points out, that "the safety and even potentially the existence of the United States were threatened . . . for the first time since 1814."[9] If the signing of the U.N. Charter, the Berlin airlift, the Truman Doctrine, the Marshall Plan officially demonstrated America's willingness to become a permanent member of the community of nations, the widespread disillusionment with the Korean War and the popularity of "massive retaliation" as the means to effect containment signaled the desire of most Americans to retreat into an isolationist shell, leaving nuclear weapons (which did not demand the physical presence of soldiers overseas) to deal with the Soviet threat.

So abiding was America's love affair with isolationism that its leaders repeatedly found the need to preach the new lesson of involvement. Roosevelt made it the subject of his Fourth Inaugural Address, arguing bluntly, "We have learned that we cannot live alone, at peace, that we must live as men, and not as ostriches." Even Arthur Vandenberg, having survived a V-2 attack on London, reversed his former stance to advocate the new policy:

How can there be immunity or isolation when man can devise weapons like that? I have always been frankly one of those who believed in our own self-reliance. I still believe that we can never again—regardless of collaborations—allow our national defense to deteriorate to anything like a point of impotence. But I do not believe that any nation hereafter can immunize itself by its own exclusive action. . . . I want maximum American cooperation. . . . I want a new dignity and a new authority for international law. I think self-interest requires it.[10]

But still the new ideas of containment and coexistence did not catch on with the majority of Americans, representing, as Eric Goldman has suggested, too sharp a departure from deep-seated American tradition of temporary commitments.[11] If anything, most people seemed eager to continue living as ostriches, with bomb shelters to hide their heads in rather than sand. It took the Korean War to crystallize the debate.

The pervasive influence of the frontier mythology did not stop at Hollywood's malleable mass audience. At the outset, even the most hardheaded members of Truman's government thought of Korea as a temporary problem requiring only immediate, but short-range solutions. Thus, after months of fighting, MacArthur's public dispatches still announced "general offensives" that "should for all practical purposes end the war." The problem, however, was that Korea represented a new kind of war, impervious to the old strategies. As Manchester puts it:

Unfortunately, winning it was out of the question. The nature of hostilities had changed since 1945. Hiroshima and Nagasaki had changed it. . . . The mad solution, then, was war with neither triumph nor sub-jugation—a long, bloody stalemate which would end only when the ex-hausted participants agreed to a truce.[12]

This kind of endless, clinging entanglement was a nightmare to many Americans. In December 1950, Joseph P. Kennedy, echo-ing Rick's sentiments ("the problems of the world are not in my department"), called upon his countrymen to "mind our own business and interfere only when someone threatens . . . our homes." But the intensity of the American attachment to the old ways surfaced with the April 1951 firing of MacArthur, a deci-sive hero in the frontier tradition. As Goldman summarizes the implications:

. . . the impact of his dismissal was not lost. Here was an unquestionably skillful general, intimately associated with the victory in World War II, now cashiered because he insisted, regulations or no regulations, on advocating the old-fashioned American remedy of quick total victory. The MacArthur dismissal was one more event—and a tremendously jar-ring one—in the whole series of developments which was leaving so many Americans feeling confused, irritated, utterly frustrated.[13]

That the initially overwhelming support for MacArthur's po-sition eventually waned was an indication less of a grudging acceptance of America's new place in the world than of a tacit decision on the part of most Americans in the fifties to simply ignore the whole problem of world affairs: "How I Learned to Stop Worrying and Love the Bomb," as Kubrick's subtitle to *Dr. Strangelove* put it. And, indeed, many factors about the Ameri-can situation in the late forties and fifties argued for a continu-ance of the old ways. If the new realities of international politics discredited the stock American myth of the reluctant hero, able to act and then return to his self-sufficiency, the immense abun-dance of domestic America offered an apparent justification for the promise that even the most incompatible values could be reconciled. As Hodgson points out:

The war unleashed an economic leap forward, which gradually engen-dered a new social optimism. By 1945, the United States seemed to be the supremely successful society as well as the supremely victorious nation. Most Americans benefited from this new prosperity. . . . A few years earlier, capitalism had seemed to be on the defensive. Suddenly it seemed the wave of the future. In the rich humus of the wartime boom, a social ideology sprang up to match anti-communism in international politics. The heart of this new ideology of free enterprise was a faith in the harmony of interests: the promise of American capitalism seemed to be that it could produce abundance on such a scale that social problems would be drowned under a flood of resources. Social conflict would become an anachronism.[14]

The resulting American condition, therefore, manifested a curious mixture of new and old: a new sense of the necessity for permanent involvement in world affairs contradicted (or complemented) by a continued sense of unlimited opportunity at home. The conservative evolution of the American Cinema of the period indicates that for most Americans, domestic optimism outweighed any conscious recognition of how radically the country's situation had been altered by the atomic age. But the increasingly harsh and/or bleak portrayals of *Casablanca*-style reluctant heroes suggested both an unconscious awareness of the vanishing possibilities represented by such heroes, and an acute anxiety about the loss.

SINCE the commercial cinema in the United States had evolved by responding not only to the actual situation of America but also (and perhaps primarily) to the audience's perception of that situation, we need to ask how much of the new postwar world that audience had acknowledged. The matched conservatism of the period's politics and films suggests, as film historian Eric Rhode observes, that a great deal was being swept under the rug:

The revelations of the Second World War—the power of the atom bomb, in particular, and the obscenity of the concentration camps—had brought about a change in mankind that was, and still is, incalculable. The shock of this change had still to be assimilated; it was felt to be too overwhelming, perhaps, to be grieved; and the Cold War was one of its consequences. It was a little like the acrimony, or dullness, or sense of triumph that can occur when a family fails to mourn the death of someone in their midst.[15]

And yet there were signs that something was wrong. Hollywood's persistent use of its old formulas was greeted by a sharp and steady fall in attendance, an indication that the traditional patterns no longer neatly coincided with the audience's intuitive understanding of reality. By 1953, almost 45 million people had stopped going regularly to the movies. Certainly, part of this loss could be attributed to television, but the presence of a new phenomenon indicated that something more basic to the success of Classic Hollywood was at stake.

That new phenomenon was the fragmentation of the mass audience. The audience for films was not merely smaller; it was also sharply divided between what Pauline Kael came to call "the art-house crowd"[16] and old-fashioned, entertainment-seeking moviegoers. To an extent, one could have accounted for the rise of the art-house audience by certain practical facts: in the postwar period, there were more foreign films being imported into the United States than ever before and more theaters to show them in. Cut loose from the studios by antitrust decrees, small movie houses previously content to play fourth-runs now converted to foreign features in order to survive.

But it was the nature of the most successful of the foreign imports, particularly of the Italian neorealist films, that suggested the dividing lines between the art-house and the mass audiences. With their harsh frankness about postwar realities, movies like *Open City, Shoeshine, Paisan*, and *The Bicycle Thief* had no possibility of widespread acceptance. But the discovery that there was an audience sizable enough to make even these bleak movies profitable unsettled the American film industry, which had always thought of its potential market as a uniform mass sharing the same perception of the world. In fact, even European filmmakers had worked on the same principle. As Richard Schickel observes:

It is ... particularly important to remember that, until the post-war years, all films—the good and the bad, the most artistic and the most commercial—were all directed at the same audience. A Renoir, a Chaplin, an Eisenstein, or a Griffith aimed for the largest possible number of viewers, at a kind of universal communication. There was no great temptation to appeal to a small group of cognoscenti.[17]

The homogeneous mass audience, however, was disappearing. The rise of the art-house audience signaled that the old consensus, on which the Classic Hollywood movie in particular had depended, had come at least partially undone. Writing in the fifties, John Houseman recognized the issue: "The real problem with American films today is who you are making them for," he observed. "Most of us face this harassing dilemma that we are working in a mass medium that has lost its mass audience."[18]

Going beyond the simple fact of their increased availability, how can we account for the sudden development of an audience for overtly "serious," frequently pessimistic movies? The answer clearly lies in the divergence of responses to the changed situation of America. Because the implications of so many events of the late forties and fifties were abstract, only a sophisticated minority consciously recognized the damage done to the self-sufficient image of America on which Classic Hollywood had depended. World War II, the atom bomb, and the Cold War, by forcing the United States into permanently joining the community of nations, had, in effect, "Europeanized" America.[19] Inevitably, therefore, the European film became the new model for a coterie of intelligentsia who became the art-house patrons. To a degree, the foreign movies themselves had educated this elite to acknowledge the significance of recent events. As Charles Champlin points out, "*Open City* signaled the start of a revolution of rising expectations, among filmmakers and filmgoers alike, for the movies and what they might say or show about real life."[20] But this audience's receptiveness to Italian neorealism required a prior sympathy with the new assumptions of its films. In effect, the art-house crowd was reacting against Hollywood's formulaic genre pictures by breaking the agreement to ignore the new world created by the war. In Leo Braudy's terms, the declining popularity of standard Hollywood movies indicated that their simplicity no longer corresponded to the increasingly complex world views held by at least a part of the audience. By rejecting these movies, that group was saying, "That's too infantile a form of what we believe." By turning to the "serious" pictures, it was saying, "Show us something more complicated."[21]

This minority art-house crowd troubled Hollywood because it represented only one manifestation of the new widespread and growing audience awareness of alternative possibilities for the movies. Another sign of this awareness was the sudden emergence of the cult film and the cult star, phenomena unheard of before the late forties and fifties. Throughout Hollywood's Classic Period, the homogeneous audience had responded uniformly to the industry's products, with the result that there were no underestimated movies or actors supported by coteries. The hit movies, the great stars belonged to everyone in a way no longer true in the fifties. In the postwar period, while John Wayne, Rock Hudson, Martin and Lewis, and Doris Day ruled the box office, cults grew up around Marlon Brando, Montgomery Clift, and James Dean, even though Brando made the Top Ten Box Office Attractions list only three times, and Clift and Dean never. Similarly, if the Classic Period contained no unrecognized masterpieces, the postwar era seemed full of them, a difference made dramatic by cinematic history. For while the current estimate of the Classic Period's significant films largely coincides with the popular favorites of that time, what is remarkable about the late forties and fifties is the number of movies now regarded as important that were then only cult objects. None of the following movies, released between 1946 and 1958, made *Variety*'s Top Twenty Box-Office Lists:

1946: *My Darling Clementine, The Big Sleep*
1947: *Body and Soul, Monsieur Verdoux, Out of the Past*
1948: *Fort Apache, The Lady from Shanghai, Letter from an Unknown Woman, The Treasure of the Sierra Madre*
1949: *On the Town, White Heat, She Wore a Yellow Ribbon*
1950: *Sunset Boulevard, In a Lonely Place, The Third Man, Wagonmaster*
1951: *Strangers on a Train, The Steel Helmet*
1952: *Rancho Notorious, Pat and Mike*
1953: *The Wild One, The Big Heat, Pickup on South Street, The Naked Spur*
1954: *Johnny Guitar, Beat the Devil, Magnificent Obsession*
1955: *The Night of the Hunter, Kiss Me Deadly, The Big Knife*
1956: *Invasion of the Body Snatchers, The Wrong Man*
1957: *Sweet Smell of Success, Run of the Arrow*
1958: *Vertigo, Touch of Evil, Man of the West*

In contrast, the top three box-office successes for these years were the following:

1946: Only alphabetical listing of top twenty available

1947: *The Best Years of Our Lives, Duel in the Sun, The Jolson Story*
1948: *The Road to Rio, Easter Parade, Red River*
1949: *Jolson Sings Again, Pinky, I Was a Male War Bride*
1950: *Samson and Delilah, Battleground, King Solomon's Mines*
1951: *David and Bathsheba, Show Boat, An American in Paris*
1952: *The Greatest Show on Earth, Quo Vadis, Ivanhoe*
1953: *The Robe, From Here to Eternity, Shane*
1954: *White Christmas, The Caine Mutiny, The Glenn Miller Story*
1955: *Cinerama Holiday, Mister Roberts, Battle Cry*
1956: *Guys and Dolls, The King and I, Trapeze*
1957: *The Ten Commandments, Around the World in Eighty Days, Giant*
1958: *The Bridge on the River Kwai, Peyton Place, Sayonara*

In no other period in the history of the American popular film had there existed such an enormous discrepancy between the most commercially successful movies and those that have ultimately been seen as significant.[22] Indeed, that discrepancy constitutes the crucial, distinguishing characteristic of the late forties and fifties popular cinema. As such, it suggests several ways of approaching the period.

The first, and most obvious, point concerns the extent to which our sense of the postwar era's films has been decisively, and perhaps permanently, shaped by the auteurist critics. While almost all the popular movies on the second list were condemned or ignored by the auteurists (*Red River* and *An American in Paris* being the great exceptions), almost all those on the first were auteurist favorites. What is important is not whether the auteurists' judgments were correct (it seems to us now that they were), but the fact that the *auteur* theory, which was, in effect, an elaborate justification for cult films, could only have arisen in a period of audience fragmentation and industry confusion. The shock value of auteurist aesthetics depended on the existence of a gap between popular and critical tastes that originated in the fifties. During the Classic Period, there would have been no point in a virtuoso defense of something like *The Philadelphia Story*: the audience had known, perhaps even better than the critics, how to spot a good movie.

The disagreement, of course, lay not only between the auteurists and the popular audience, but also between the auteurists and the critical establishment. In January 1956, *Newsweek* offered a mid-decade appraisal of the American popular film occasioned by John Huston's about-to-be-released *Moby Dick*.[23] Including Huston, the article named "the top five directors in the industry" as William Wyler, George Stevens, Fred Zinnemann, and Billy Wilder—all *bêtes noires* of the auteurists, and all but Stevens eventually included in American auteurist Andrew Sarris's most damning category, "Less Than Meets the Eye." Predicting that "in 1956 Hollywood is scheduled to have its liveliest twelve months since it got the TV jitters four years ago," *Newsweek* went on to list twelve films that were "some of the coming year's best bets": *The Ten Commandments, War and Peace, Giant, Around the World in Eighty Days, The Spirit of St. Louis, The Man in the Gray Flannel Suit, The King and I, Picnic, The Benny Goodman Story, The Swan, The Conqueror*, and *Moby Dick*, which was the "one picture above all [that] seemed to promise that consummation of prestige and box-office draw for which the entertainment world always devoutly wishes." At the end of the year, only one of these twelve films (*Picnic*) was mentioned by any of the seventeen critics associated with the auteurist *Cahiers du cinéma* who each picked out the year's ten best films.[24] By contrast, four out of five of the Academy's nominees for both Best Picture of the Year and Best Director of the Year involved movies from *Newsweek*'s list (for Best Picture, *Giant, The King and I, The Ten Commandments*, and the winner *Around the World in Eighty Days*; for Best Director, *War and Peace, The King and I, Around the World in Eighty Days*, and the winner *Giant*—the one exception in both categories was Wyler's *Friendly Persuasion*).

The destruction of the critical consensus, coupled with the enormous discrepancy between box-office success and our retroactive sense of genuine worth, suggest how confused both Hollywood and the audience were in the postwar period. In fact, the implicit arrangement between the industry, audience, and objective situation of America—on which the Classic Hollywood movie had depended—was breaking down. That the studios willingly poured out huge amounts of money into inflated versions of stock genre pictures (e.g., *Duel in the Sun, Shane, Giant*), and that the audience willingly went to see the results, both indicated a reluctance on the part of industry and filmgoer alike to give up the model that had evolved for the popular American movie. But if the Classic Hollywood film had provided a way of experiencing the world, the anomalies created by World War II and the Cold War, revealed by the Italian neorealists, threatened to discredit it.

We should remember that of the postwar period's two distinct types of movie—the commercially successful, quickly outmoded blockbuster and the small-audience, retroactively applauded cult film—neither had flourished during the Studio Era. In retrospect, the blockbusters' rapid obsolescence tempts us to regard the cult films as more "realistic," more accurate "reflections" of the period's important material circumstances. Such an estimate, however, would merely repeat film criticism's traditional ploy of using the term "realistic" to valorize judgments based on altogether other (and altogether concealed) principles. Further, in making even good-faith appraisals of earlier movies' "realism," we inevitably read the past through the present, regarding as important those elements of the previous epoch that bear some marked relationship to our own—particularly one of similarity, cause, or precursor. Thus, a present distinguished by anxiety is apt to see in all past works displaying a similar mood a validating "realism." In other words, the current film audience's decided preference for the cult movies does not make them more "realistic" than the blockbusters.

In fact, *both* the blockbusters and the cult films were realistic—and in two senses. First, each reflected one of the postwar period's predominant moods: the blockbusters, the tendency to escapism; the cult films, the growing anxiety about America's fallen position. Taken together, they provided a barometer of the time. Second, the disparity between the two types accurately pointed to rapidly developing, crucial changes in the conditions of production and consumption—particularly the fragmentation of the previously homogenized mass audience.

The cult audience and the art-house crowd had discovered something that profoundly shook the industry: the Classic Hollywood movie was not the inviolable model for the commercial cinema. Other forms were not only possible; they were available, and apparently more capable of dealing with the serious matters of the time. If the fifties were a time when no one was sure what a good movie was, they were also the first period in Hollywood's history when people began to see what the movies could be.

Hollywood's task was somehow to satisfy the new art-house, cult audience (with its tolerance for franker portrayals of the American situation) without losing the majority of filmgoers who clearly wanted more of what the industry had always produced—entertainment films predicated on the assumption that hard choices could be avoided. As Penelope Houston observed in 1963, "New formulas had to be devised, and the question was how far they could accommodate such impulses toward realism as were clearly present."[25]

Hollywood's first attempt at a solution was to blend the serious social consciousness of the foreign movies with old-fashioned storytelling. The result was the "problem picture" that earnestly portrayed verterans' struggles to adapt to homecoming (*The Pride of the Marines, The Best Years of Our Lives, The Men*), cruelties caused by racial prejudice (*Crossfire, Gentleman's Agreement, Pinky, Intruder in the Dust*), or the sufferings of maltreated mental patients (*The Snake Pit*). These films had less importance as works of art than as indicators of the new sensibility. The industry, and especially Warner Brothers, had always produced, even during the homogeneous Classic Period, an occasional "social consciousness" movie. The difference was, however, that while films like *I Am a Fugitive from a Chain Gang* and *Wild Boys of the Road* never made thirties top box-office lists, the postwar "problem pictures" did big business. As a phenomenon, they were thus significant, signaling the audience's growing tolerance, and even demand, for movies that explored disturbing areas of American life previously ignored by the blithe sweep of Hollywood's reconciliatory pattern. Where Classic films like *The Philadelphia Story*, and the wartime melting-pot pictures like *Wake Island*, had assumed that social and racial distinctions were waived by Americans in the name of common interests, the postwar movies were less certain.

In retrospect, these films' commercial success obviously depended on their conservatism, thinly disguised by an outward display of social concern. All of them were solved in advance, "resolving" complications by converting social/political issues into aesthetic ones. Certainly, *The Best Years of Our Lives* worked in this way. Despite the divisive quarrels that developed among the three veterans from different services, who return home to their previous, and distinct, social standings, the film's opening sequence (where the three men crowded together in the nose of a B-29 to spot home-town landmarks) clearly implied the superficiality of all subsequent misunderstandings. The concluding wedding scene that united the pilot, the navy groom, and the army sergeant in one deep-focus shot blurred the probability that they were condemned to live in separate, and, to some extent, competing worlds.

The most enduring of the problem pictures, *On the Waterfront* (1954), demonstrated the frontier mythology's capacity to adapt itself to the serious subject matter and realistic *mise en scènes* derived from Italian neorealism. For despite the movie's reliance on location shooting and contemporary newspaper accounts, the narrative converted the social problem of union corruption into another reluctant hero story, centering on Terry Malloy (Marlon Brando), an outlaw hero unwilling to help the crime commission's investigation into union-related murders. Despite the pleas of official hero Father Barry (Karl Malden), Terry characteristically required a personal motive for acting—a motive supplied by the union's killing of his brother.

Clearly, *On the Waterfront* was another disguised western, the story of a gunfighter (here, boxer) who, putting away his guns (retiring from the ring), refused to intervene in the community's problems until they arrived at his door: in this case, they summoned Terry to an alley where he found his brother's body hung to the wall with a longshoreman's hook. Furthermore, the movie displayed the western's typical ambivalence toward the law. First, Terry's brother, the mob leader's right-hand man, was a lawyer, manipulating rules to cheat rank-and-file union members. Second, *Waterfront* reincarnated the weak sheriff in the fumbling, slow-moving crime commission, whose inability either to make or enforce laws represented society at its most ineffectual. Confronted by the stock inadequacy of the legal system, Terry could only take the standard outlaw hero course: individual action.

At first, however, Terry (like the standard frontiersman) simply wanted to be left alone, especially by the twin representatives of society, the nagging priest and the sister of a murdered man (Eva Marie Saint). As always, they needed him to defend the community, asking him (in a new variation) for his testimony rather than for his gun. The film's narrative turned on the conventional clash between the moral center's condemnation of individual violence and the interest center's obvious implication of violence as the only possible solution. Thus, at a crucial point, Father Barry talked Terry into putting away a pistol in order to fight mob leader Johnny Friendly (Lee J. Cobb) with an appearance before the commission. Despite the movie's overt sanctioning of this course, however, the story repeatedly confirmed Terry's sense of the futility of this way. In doing so, *Waterfront* restated the basic dichotomy of Classic Hollywood's thematic paradigm, the conflict between a rational allegiance to society's laws and procedures and an intuitive sense of their ultimate dependence on the individual hero.

Waterfront followed the fundamental western pattern to reconcile this opposition. Terry put away his gun, put on a coat and tie (always an ambivalent gesture for the outlaw hero), and reported to the crime commission. None of this, however, did any good. Ultimately, Terry had to confront Johnny Friendly in a fist-fight filmed as a gunfight. Characteristically, Terry rejected the abstract reasoning of the priest ("I don't know nothin' about that") for a private motive ("I was rattin' *on myself* all those years"), thereby reaffirming the American ideology's premise that benefit to the community could result from utterly private motives.

While *Waterfront*'s main project was simply to demonstrate the continued viability of the traditional American mythology, the movie also allowed to surface anxieties about the frontier tradition which *Casablanca* had kept tacit. For the film's most famous lines (Brando's "I could've been a contender. I could've been somebody, instead of a bum, which is what I am") unearthed the half-buried cultural fear that the American mythology's most treasured heroes—its self-images—were merely romanticized versions of the bum. While Fiedler has observed this anxiety even in *Huckleberry Finn* ("Huck's shadow is his own father . . . the town drunk—a vision of what he himself may become"),[26] Hollywood's sudden willingness to allow it to emerge suggests a new postwar uneasiness about the avoidance of commitment. All that had protected Huck from his father's fate was his youth, an excuse no longer available to Terry, and perhaps no longer available to America itself.

The box-office success of the first wave of "problem pictures" insured that they would be a staple genre throughout the fifties and early sixties. Hollywood eagerly provided the audience with pat stories about the problems of command (*Twelve O'Clock High, The Caine Mutiny*), racial prejudice (*Home of the Brave, The Defiant Ones, Imitation of Life, Guess Who's Coming to Dinner*), alcohol or drug addiction (*Come Back, Little Sheba; The Man with the Golden Arm*), teenage gangs (*Blackboard Jungle, Rebel Without a Cause*), and the atomic threat (*On the Beach, Fail Safe*). Surrounded by Hollywood's traditional mythology, these movies usually had happy endings that belied their "problems." As a result, they often seemed vaguely voyeuristic: protected by the certainty of an ultimate resolution, a viewer could devote himself to the 85 percent of a film that dramatized the horrors of heroin, incest, or madness. Robbe-Grillet has inadvertently described this phenomenon in other terms:

I don't know whether any of you has recently been to Copenhagen, but there is a kind of enormous space in the middle of Copenhagen which has been abandoned to marginal characters—down-and-outers—where one can take drugs or do whatever one wishes. While this goes on, the Danish bourgeoisie continues to function all around. And the Danish bourgeoisie on Sunday circulates around this terrain just to go and look at the marginal people of ideology.[27]

In spite of its commercial appeal, the problem picture provided, at best, a temporary solution to Hollywood's problem. The abiding issue for the industry lay in determining the extent to which serious subjects could be treated in genre films. As Robert Sklar observes:

What Hollywood had learned to do extremely well—comedy, musicals, genre westerns and crime pictures, melodramas, popularizations of classics—did not provide many lessons for a new era of seriousness and responsibility. Hollywood's triumph had been overwhelmingly a triumph of formula, and the novelty and freshness of American commercial movies had come from the inventive new ways in which formulas were reshaped to meet the times. Formulas worked beautifully in their place—and continue to do so—but formulas and significant social themes did not mix effectively. . . .[28]

Sklar's last point is highly disputable, but, in any case, Hollywood determinedly set out to make genres and serious themes mix. In effect, it had no choice. To ignore the modified American situation, reflected in the audience's new-found taste for "serious" films, would have risked reducing the American film industry from an enormously powerful, ongoing concern to an obsolete, commercially unacceptable enterprise. This terrifying possibility, in fact, was perfectly allegorized by 1950's *Sunset Boulevard*. As aging silent film star Norma Desmond, sealed off from the world in her mansion, surrounded by relics of the past (including her ex-director and former husband, now a butler, and a complete supply of her own pictures), Gloria Swanson represented Hollywood's worst fears about itself. Irony was thick. The story of Salome, rejected in the movie by DeMille (playing himself) as a comeback vehicle for Norma, and everywhere made to sound like a ridiculous possibility, actually became a movie (*Salome*) just three years later, one of 1953's biggest hits. In fact, Norma's proposal, subjected to so much scorn by *Sunset Boulevard*, was exactly the kind of epic project to which the industry resorted repeatedly throughout the fifties and early sixties (e.g., *The Robe, David and Bathsheba, Quo Vadis*, and as disastrously as *Sunset Boulevard* had predicted, *Cleopatra*).

Sunset Boulevard used Swanson, von Stroheim, and Buster Keaton disturbingly. For the members of the audience who had grown up with these stars, seeing them aged and outmoded provided a sudden intimation of mortality. Hollywood subsequently repeated this device of employing an actor's real age as a part of the film's story in movies like *The Barefoot Contessa, Love in the Afternoon*, and *Ride the High Country*, where it came to suggest the aging of America itself.

For Hollywood, however, the principal moral of *Sunset Boule-*

vard remained clear: all of Norma's carefully erected barriers could not keep the contemporary world (in the person of William Holden) from breaking in. Somehow, the movies would have to learn how to accommodate that new world and all its problems. To fail to do so would be to become like Norma—mad, pathetic, and worst of all, finished at the box office.

All during the postwar period, Hollywood groped, trying to develop ways of adding serious themes to entertainment films. The most superficial attempt at a merger was the epic, versions of which dominated the box-office lists in the fifties. Rather than developing their own concerns, these films merely relied on the mass audience's preexisting belief in the "seriousness" of biblical stories. Looked at closely, the epics, with their wide screens and full color, were only cosmetically elaborate reworkings of the old sentimentalities. Their main purpose was to show the television audience what Hollywood could still do technically.

A second attempt at mixing seriousness and entertainment, that seemed at the time to be a major departure from the tradition of the Classic movie, was in fact nearly as superficial as the epic. Most obviously represented by the "adult western" and the "integrated musical," this attempt involved the inflation of standard genres by means of either style or theme.

Both processes began in the late forties. The first of the stylistic inflations, disguised as a *deflation*, based itself mainly on a realistic look borrowed from the Italian neorealists. The result was the pseudodocumentary "street film" that typically dealt with big-city crime. But, in fact, movies like *The House on 92nd Street, Call Northside 777, The Asphalt Jungle*, and *Brute Force* were only old-fashioned melodramas filmed on locations in a low-key manner. The realist style, which for the Italians had been a moral point, was here nothing more than a kind of mannered primitivism.

The first of the amplified musicals, *On the Town*, was, in a sense, an extension of the "street films." Shot on location in New York, the movie had its protagonists dance on bridges, through subways, and on top of the Empire State Building. But a more significant indicator of the direction that the musical would take in the fifties was the abstract, vaguely surreal "Miss Turnstiles

Ballet" sequence performed by Gene Kelly. From then on, the clearest sign of the "serious musical" was a ballet number invariably performed against an abstract background, and almost always explained as the protagonist's "dream." *An American in Paris, Singin' in the Rain, The Band Wagon, Invitation to the Dance*—all used ballet, and all were recognized at the time as being a new and better kind of musical.

Stylistic inflations in the western were even more obvious. Beginning with 1947's *Duel in the Sun*, Hollywood filmmakers amplified stock western stories into epics: *The Gunfighter, High Noon, Shane, Giant, 3:10 to Yuma, Gunfight at the O.K. Corral, The Magnificent Seven, The Alamo, One-Eyed Jacks, How the West Was Won.* Almost invariably, these films used color and widescreen processes (*The Gunfighter* and *High Noon* were the exceptions). All (again excepting *The Gunfighter* and *High Noon*) were very long, often running three hours or more. Their action was elaborately stylized, slowed down, and weighted with portentousness. At times it seemed to take a protagonist five minutes to cross a room or nod his head. These movies located their characters in enormous, empty vistas, whose potential for picturesqueness seemed more important than their meaning in the story.

Shane, the most abidingly popular of these films, was, as we have seen, also the most typical. With its glacial perfection, it could have been either the first western or the last. What made its absolutely traditional story seem suddenly "important" was the meticulous care with which everything had been worked out. In the opening sequence, a deer in the picture's foreground turned his head slightly to reveal Shane riding into the valley, perfectly framed by the animal's antlers. In a later gunfight sequence, Jack Palance and Elisha Cook, Jr. circled each other warily, moving in and out of shadows cast by perfectly timed, drifting clouds. For a funeral on a hillside, director George Stevens slowly withdrew his camera until his characters took on the quality of a lovely abstraction.

Stylistic amplification of stock stories was not limited to musicals and westerns. Hollywood used this ploy repeatedly throughout the fifties and early sixties in an attempt to inject standard formulas with new importance. The blown-up quality of such films as *King Solomon's Mines, Mogambo, The High and the Mighty, Strategic Air Command, Raintree County, The Young Lions, The Guns of Navarone,* and *The Cardinal* was a means of hiding the fact that they contained nothing new.

The alternate process of inflation, the thematic, also centered on the western. Standard plots were overlaid with pseudopsychology (*Duel in the Sun, The Left-Handed Gun, The Misfits*), pat lessons about racial prejudice (*Broken Arrow, Bad Day at Black Rock, Giant*), critiques of moral passivity (*High Noon*), pride (*The Gunfighter*), and selfishness (*Hud*). In almost every case, the thematic issues seemed extraneous to the principal appeal of the story, grafted on and in no way essential. The inevitable result was a marked split between the moral and interest centers of these films. *Giant,* for instance, displayed overt moralizing about the evils of class divisiveness, pride, and racial prejudice (even to the point of ending with a shot of a white and a black lamb standing beside the hero's two grandchildren, one of whom was very white, the other very Mexican). But, in fact, almost everything that was exciting about the movie implicitly recognized the realities of class and racial distinctions, and the enormous pleasure and power to be gained through pride. James Dean's best scenes all turned on the sense of distance between his character (sharecropper Jett Rink) and the landowner Bick Benedict, transforming this divisiveness into a source of glamorous possibilities for freedom, pride, and revolt. Similarly, as Benedict, Rock Hudson used his most moving scenes to suggest a deep-rooted incompatibility between the West and the East, symbolized by Benedict's awkwardness in his in-laws' Maryland home.

This thematic inflation, developed most fully in the western, spilled over into other standard stories like *Key Largo, The Treasure of the Sierra Madre, Twelve Angry Men, Not as a Stranger,* and *The Apartment* (a kind of pretentious screwball comedy). It even found a place in the musical, turning *South Pacific* and *The King and I* into pleas for racial understanding.

Both kinds of inflation seemed to play themselves out in the mid-sixties. Stylistic inflation became camp in the James Bond films, stock spy/adventure tales enlarged into cartoons, while thematic inflation culminated in *Guess Who's Coming to Dinner* and *The Sound of Music* (where there were so many "serious" issues that there was barely time for the music). Having begun as an answer to the Italian neorealists, this amplification may have also been ended by Italian filmmakers. For if Antonioni's *L'Avventura, La Notte,* and *L'Eclisse,* with their unrelieved seriousness and constant talk, seemed like parodies of thematically inflated American movies, Leone's spaghetti westerns, where the action slowed to a snail's pace amidst enormously enlarged landscapes, seemed like spoofs of the stylistically inflated ones. In any case, whether seen as parodies or not, the Italian movies clearly trumped the Americans at their own game, and in doing so, freed Hollywood to take a different direction.

6. The Discrepancy between Intent and Effect: *Film Noir*, Youth Rebellion Pictures, Musicals, and Westerns

THE AMERICAN film industry's postwar attempts to revitalize its product had ironic results. For by subjecting its formal and thematic paradigms to inflation, Hollywood initiated the unraveling of the very models it sought to preserve. Intrinsically, the stylistic aggrandizements of movies like *Shane* or *Duel in the Sun* violated the continuity system's basic goal, the effacement of style. Indeed, compared to Classic Hollywood's pictures, with their laconic, invisible forms, many postwar films, eager to distinguish themselves from television, advertised themselves openly as movies. Thus, 1955's leading box-office success, *Cinerama Holiday*, offered a version of Mélièsian trickster cinema that lay well outside Classic Hollywood's tradition.

Similarly, Hollywood's efforts to extend its thematic paradigm to a broader range of subjects often succeeded only in revealing that paradigm's ideological basis. In fact, the more realistically the problem pictures portrayed postwar America's sociological crises, the more they enabled the audience to recognize the transparently mythological status of their reconciliations. Having sat through sustained and graphic depictions of anti-Semitism, class divisiveness, and drug abuse, a viewer could hardly accede to the abrupt resolution of these matters offered by the problem pictures' traditionally optimistic conclusions.

Both of these results—stylistic conspicuousness and unsettling resolutions—had appeared earlier in the work of Orson Welles, whose most prominent films were proto-problem pictures. In particular, *Citizen Kane*, a study of yellow journalism and the corrupting effects of wealth, couched in a baroque, highly visible style, had an enormous, if late-developing, influence on the postwar period's movies. As we will see, *film noir* borrowed *Kane*'s tactic of using a thoroughly subjective style to call into question a purportedly conventional conclusion. For Welles's oblique angles, forced perspectives, expressionist lighting, and wittily rhymed transitions had made the psychological explanation proposed by "Rosebud" (Kane as unloved child) appear inadequate.

In partially (and unconsciously) adopting Welles's methods, postwar Hollywood unknowingly employed an idiosyncratic, highly personal, internally contradictory filmmaking as a model for traditional, unsurprising, supposedly commercial movies. Inevitably, therefore, the period's most powerful films displayed marked contradictions between intent and effect. Indeed, the most noticeable feature of the best postwar movies was their eagerness to convey a moral that the films' interest centers systematically undermined.

The split between intent and effect appeared only occasionally in the problem picture, epic, and inflated genre film. As representatives of the industry's attempts to create a new model for the commercial movie, these three types signaled a tacit acknowledgment that Classic Hollywood's reconciliatory pattern had been thrown into question by postwar developments. These "serious" movies revealed very little about postwar developments, or about the concerns generated by them. Instead, they limited themselves to a few domestic issues (particularly race), dealt with along the safe, official lines encouraged by a studied ideological optimism. These movies almost never portrayed the central American anxiety of the time—the fear that World War II had permanently altered the conditions of American life on which so much of the culture's mythology depended.

With its explicit message about the impracticality of isolationism, *Casablanca* had been a kind of prototype of the postwar "serious" film. But the percentage of moralizing in *Casablanca* remained so small that the movie's intent was very different from its effect. The result was less a stirring call to arms than a portrayal of the anxieties felt by many Americans that the war could cost America its independence. One could ignore the message for the unconscious expression of the message's opposite: the glamorizing of isolationist self-sufficiency. With the postwar problem pictures, however, the official moral devoured the movie, leaving no part of the story untouched. Intent and effect merged, to the movies' detriment: there was nothing to respond to except the overt theme.

With their explicit encapsulations of the public attitudes of the time, the "serious" movies provided only the most superficial reflections of the real American mood, which harbored a genuine and pervasive apprehensiveness. Because the gap between official optimism and hidden fears was especially great during the postwar period, it was inevitable that the true image of America would be expressed in the movies by indirect, and at times unconscious, means. It was the auteurists, with their emphasis on the point of intersection between individual filmmakers and their formula subjects, who drew attention to the locus of interest in the period's popular movies. "Interior meaning," Andrew Sarris wrote, "is extrapolated from the tension between a director's personality and his material."[1]

The auteurists studied this tension for its ability to reveal personal (and presumably idiosyncratic) styles. But this tension also indicated a general shift in the American popular cinema far more fundamental than that effected by the "serious" pictures. For with their strained attempts to reaffirm the traditional mythology of choice avoidance, the period's genre movies suggested how much the collective American imagination had been changed by World War II and the Cold War.

These movies' makers worked with what Manny Farber called "termite art,"[2] tunneling under the stock story line to reveal more urgent anxieties through the holes in the pattern. The typical result was a tour de force of duplicity, whereby the superficial marks of the old pattern were maintained while the pattern itself was implicitly discredited.

Hitchcock's *Shadow of a Doubt* (1943) provided the model for this tunneling procedure. The movie's duplicity worked on two levels. Uncle Charlie's disruption of his niece Charlie's sunny, small-town reveries paralleled Hitchcock's own subversion of the blithe happy ending written by Thornton Wilder and Sally Benson, who had previously created the small-town, nostalgic optimism of *Our Town* and the stories adapted in *Meet Me in St. Louis*. "You live in a dream world," Uncle Charlie told his niece, "and I have brought you nightmares," a lesson that the film's conclusion, despite its formal closure, could not completely contain. It was no answer to hear from the detective that the world was fundamentally sound, that "It just has to be carefully watched." By filming this speech in front of a church, and over the background sound of a minister's glowing eulogy of Uncle Charlie, Hitchcock suggested that such reconciliations rested on hypocrisy.

In an age marked by an extreme unwillingness to face the inconsistencies threatening for the first time to discredit traditional American attitudes, institutions, and values, it was inevitable that Hitchcock would become the great filmmaker. His theme, as Andrew Sarris pointed out, was complacency;[3] his method, duplicitous and voyeuristic. Working in the thriller form, he could satisfy the most pressing commercial requirements of a Hollywood fearful of leaving its audience behind. But to the conventions of the formula picture, he brought strong doses of anxiety and dread, like some filmmaking Uncle Charlie bent on disrupting the cheery dreams of his audience. His plots generally turned on the conflict between order (usually some traditional form of self-imposed blindness) and chaos (the true nature of the world). In Hitchcock's films, the irrational, with all its Dionysian powers to unsettle, disrupt, and destroy, seethed just on the other side of the flimsy protective dikes his characters erected. Hitchcock's pessimism about the effectiveness of ruling principles made for the truly disturbing element in his films: invariably the means of avoidance, of denial, became the instrument for unlocking chaos. The dominant "humor" or idea of the protagonist got him into trouble, whatever quality or notion it may have been: adventurousness and energy (*The 39 Steps*: inviting the woman up to his room, pursuing her clues); love of music and naïveté about danger (*The Lady Vanishes*); affability and health (*Strangers on a Train*: Guy's easy willingness to chat with Bruno on the train, his healthy dismissal, or underestimation, of Bruno's sick plan); blandness and routine (*The Wrong Man* and *Shadow of a Doubt*: the blandness that would not fight false accusations, the routine that could not recognize aberrations like Uncle Charlie); wealthy smugness (*North by Northwest*: where Roger Thornhill explains that the O in his monogram ROT stood for nothing); supercilious curiosity (*Rear Window*); love and marriage (*Rebecca, Suspicion*); love and duty (*Notorious*); love and family (*The Man Who Knew Too Much*); love and money (*Psycho*); and love that becomes obsession (*Vertigo*). In each of these films, the method used by the hero to maintain order became the very means by which that order was undone.

Hitchcock's view of the world was more profoundly pessimistic than that of the "serious" films, whose outward bleakness hid an optimistic faith in the possibilities of reform. This distinction becomes clear when one compares Hitchcock's *The Wrong Man* (1957) to the similar *Call Northside 777* (1948), a "serious" street film made by Henry Hathaway. Obvious points of comparison suggested themselves. Both centered on innocent men accused (*Wrong Man*) or convicted (*Northside*) of crime. Both drew on true stories. (Hitchcock told Truffaut that he found the incident in a 1952 *Life* magazine.) Both used a dogged, semi-documentary style shot on location (*Northside*: Chicago; *Wrong Man*: New York), with the photographers employing portable lights and fast film to suggest the grainy quality of newsreel footage. In *The Wrong Man*, Hitchcock went to extreme lengths of realism, choosing to film in the real-life hero's house, the courtroom of his arraignment, the jail where he had waited for bail, and even the mental institution where his wife had been taken after her complete collapse.

But despite these similarities, the differences between the two films proved more suggestive. While *Northside*'s semi-documentary attributed the fate of Frank Wiecek (Richard Conte) to police corruption, *The Wrong Man*'s metaphysical anxiety could blame what happened to Manny (Henry Fonda) only on chance.

Northside gradually made clear that Frank had been set up by the police, framed to provide impatient superiors with a victim. Deliberately provided with an inept lawyer (a drunk), positively identified by a lying female witness, Wiecek had to depend on the efforts of an investigative reporter, McNeal (James Stewart) who overcame all police obstructions to uncover the truth.

In *The Wrong Man*, by contrast, Manny's troubles depended solely on absurd coincidences that piled up one after another. By coincidence, Manny looked like the real criminal. Bad luck caused him to misspell the same word in a duplicate of the holdup note that the police required him to write. While in *Northside*, the police had intentionally assigned Wiecek an incompetent lawyer, in *The Wrong Man* Manny's lawyer's inadequate trial tactics derived solely from his lack of experience—he had, in fact, been recommended by Manny's brother-in-law. In *Northside*, the key witness had been deliberately hiding. In *The Wrong Man*, all the witnesses who could have verified Manny's alibi were, by chance, dead.

Even Manny's salvation depended utterly on accident, the miraculous discovery of the real thief. In *Northside*, not accident, but McNeal's insistent pursuit of new facts had freed Wiecek. Thus, despite its bleak exterior, *Northside* held to the traditional mythological dependence on individual solutions. Indeed, the film's blithe moral reassured that hard work could correct societal injustices—the basic assertion of the official rhetoric. *The Wrong Man*'s outlook, however, suggested that against the casual cruelty of accident, only another accident might preserve us.

The Wrong Man, with its unrelieved bleakness, represented an extreme even for Hitchcock. But in distilled form, it embodied his view of the world. Significantly, Hitchcock's pessimism, a constant throughout his career, deepened noticeably in the postwar era, almost as a response to the blandly confident face of fifties America. His crowning achievements, *North by Northwest* and *Psycho*, specifically dealt with the anxieties hidden by American culture, its obsession with money, mothers, and movement. Of all his films' great sequences, the most memorable was the crop-dusting sequence in *North by Northwest*, an image that took the very basis of the American dream, open space, and revealed its hidden capacities for danger and claustrophobia.

For the postwar popular movie, Hitchcock's chief significance was his ability to mix his personal sense of Cold War realities with entertainment movies. *Shadow of a Doubt*, with its disingenuous nod in the direction of formula concealing its harsher truths, was perhaps the period's model film, for it suggested a means of combining seriousness and tradition that would satisfy both the art-house crowd and the mass audience. Most Hollywood filmmakers, however, proved less skillful at playing this double game. Increasingly, the period's most affecting movies displayed inconsistencies that Classic Hollywood's traditional thematic paradigm could not entirely conceal. Most often, these inconsistencies revealed themselves in an unprecedented discrepancy between a movie's obvious intent and its actual effect. Frequently, as in Orson Welles's films, this contradiction appeared as a disjunction between content and style. Thus, the flat, unexpressive visuals of the problem pictures belied the purported seriousness of their dilemmas. This arrangement, however, was exactly reversed in the genre ultimately designated as *film noir*. To an extent, the *noir* films represented an eruption into the American cinema's main tradition of values, emotions, anxieties, and behavior systematically suppressed by Classic Hollywood. Almost every Classic Hollywood genre had its *noir* version, which at once parodied and subverted the ideological basis of the original. *Noir* "screwball comedies" (*The Postman Always Rings Twice, Double Indemnity, The Lady From Shanghai*) exposed the standard love triangle as the obvious occasion for murder. *Noir* westerns (*Johnny Guitar, The Far Country*) suggested that the outlaw hero's reluctance derived from the fear of his own capacity for violence. *Noir* problem pictures (*Crossfire*) located racial prejudice in private madness, untreatable by normal means. *Noir* musicals (*It's Always Fair Weather*) flirted with portraying song and dance as inappropriate to postwar America, or (*A Star Is Born*) went backstage to reveal the costs of success.

At times, the resemblances between a *film noir* and a Classic Hollywood film could prove unnerving. *Gilda* (1946), for example, reproduced *Casablanca*'s basic donnée (American expatriate casino operator encounters ex-lover, now another man's wife) only to expose that story's previously repressed sadomasochism. "I hate you," Glenn Ford told Rita Hayworth, only to hear her answer that precipitated the film's most passionate embrace: "I hate you, too. Oh, how I hate you."

Despite these *noir* thematic reversals, the genre's unsettling quality depended primarily on a pronounced discrepancy between the ordinariness of its plots (which nearly all had happy endings) and the baroque radicalization of its style. This disjunction derived from an odd coincidence: while most of the *noir* scriptwriters were American, many of the most prominent *noir* directors were European, often with roots in German expressionism (Wilder, Curtiz, Lang, Dmytryk, Siodmak, Tourneur, Ulmer). As a result of this odd pairing, a *film noir*'s visuals often seemed to operate at an entirely different level of intensity, conveying anxieties not suggested by the stories themselves. Individual moments, irrelevant to the plot, stood out as abstract symbols of menace: typical was the frenetic chiaroscuro of Elisha Cook, Jr.'s drum sequence in *Phantom Lady*. The *noir* movie that has received the most critical attention, Orson Welles's *Touch of Evil* (1958), used a tawdry melodrama, like a parody of the racially conscious problem pictures, as an occasion to create a stylistic universe whose deep shadows, looming close-ups, oblique camera angles, prowling camera, and crowded compositions intimated a sense of entrapment and loss that went far beyond the mere events of the plot.

The *noir* films had difficulties telling their stories straight. Many relied on voice-over narrations and/or flashbacks (e.g., *Double Indemnity, Laura, The Lady from Shanghai, Out of the Past, The Postman Always Rings Twice*). Together, these narrative methods implied a concern with the past as a source of present trouble. The *noir* protagonists' relentless search for the moment where things had begun to go bad was an image of the American postwar mood—vaguely disillusioned, convinced that somewhere along the line the wrong turn had been taken, intuitively aware of the power of historical determinism for perhaps the first time in the nation's history. So prevalent was this looking-backward that the flashback became increasingly common, spilling over from *noir* films into even mainstream Hollywood movies like Crosby and Hope's *Road to Utopia* (1945). The *noir* pictures, in the meantime, resorted to increasingly mannered versions of the device: Hitchcock's *Stage Fright* (1950) contained a lying flashback; *Sunset Boulevard* (1950) was told entirely by a dead man whose body was seen in the opening scene floating face down in a swimming pool.

If the stylistic independence of *film noir* represented the postwar period's characteristic discrepancy between intent and effect, the more typical disjunction operated at the thematic level. There, the project often involved acknowledging the existence of sharply incompatible attitudes, which could then be surrounded and contained by the traditional pattern of reconciliation.

Influenced heavily by *film noir*, the "youth rebellion" movies (*The Wild One, East of Eden, Blackboard Jungle, Rebel Without a Cause*) were obvious examples of this project. All had protagonists whose alienation, nihilism, and impulses toward violence and rebellion were profoundly antisocial. In effect, they were extreme versions of the outlaw hero, with cars and motorcycles instead of horses. These movies exaggerated the traditional outlaw hero's reluctance to acknowledge society's demands: "What are you rebelling against?" a naïve girl asked Brando in *The Wild One*. "Whadda ya got?" was the answer that became famous.

Inevitably, the young, with less invested in the traditional attitudes and values, were among the first to detect the damage done by World War II and the Cold War to the most basic American assumptions. In fact, the "youth rebellion" movies reflected an actual spirit of disillusionment among the period's adolescents, which figured in the tiny Beat movement of the fifties before becoming pervasive in the mid-sixties. The movies, however, sought to deny these intuitive protesters any reasons for revolt. Each of them eagerly demonstrated that the hero was a rebel *without* a cause, explaining that the problem lay with either a few troublemakers (*The Wild One, Blackboard Jungle*) or with psychological traumas of adjustment to adulthood (*The Wild One, East of Eden, Rebel Without a Cause*). *Rebel Without a Cause* characteristically accounted for its protagonist's (James Dean) behavior as resulting from the absence of a strong father. "If he had the guts to knock Mom cold once," Dean complained, "maybe she'd be happy and stop picking on him. I don't ever want to be like him. . . . How can a guy grow up in a circus like that?" The film's conclusion, as the father promised, "I'll try to be as strong as you want me to be," swept under the rug two deaths (one in a chicken race, the other by a police sniper), a knife fight, and above all, the movie's most disturbing image of the real cause for rebellion—the lesson of the planetarium's lecturer that so small was earth (and by implication, America) that it could be easily destroyed by a solar accident, and having disappeared, "would not be missed" by the universe.

The broken-backed nature of these movies resulted from the struggle to reconfirm the old values in the face of a new, and different, kind of opposition. Attempts to portray these violent heroes as softened Good Bad Boys rang obviously false: Brando's becoming gentle with the local girl, and defending her against Lee Marvin, in *The Wild One*, and Poitier's last-minute conversion to teacher Glenn Ford's cause in *Blackboard Jungle* were patent sentimentalities. The previous indifference of these outlaw heroes seemed too authentic, and, more important, too attractive. The appeal of a life lived solely in terms of the self was never greater than in these movies, and their interest center clearly lay entirely with the very acts of rebellion that the films' endings sought to discredit as a passing "stage." No cult in the history of Hollywood equaled the fervor of James Dean's. It survived even *Giant*, a kind of elaborate "youth rebellion" picture that offered the cautionary tale that someone who did not mature out of his youthful revolt doomed himself to failure, disgrace, and unhappiness. The audience ignored the moral, attending instead to Dean's early scenes of protest against the blank selfishness of the cattle baron Benedicts. The effect of *Giant*, therefore, was exactly the same as that of the "youth rebellion" movies. As Joan Mellen puts it:

Marlon Brando and James Dean seemed to be pure and total rebels in those fifties films—an impression that is less than accurate, for by the end of many of the films that offered alienated, tormented heroes, traditional values were reasserted. The hero was brought around and forced to conform, or he saw the desirability of acceptance. But these "resolutions" fooled no one, and audiences responded to Brando, Dean, and Montgomery Clift because people cherished their independence and the irrepressible energy they exuded.[4]

In many ways, Hollywood's difficulties with accommodating these rebel heroes in its traditional patterns crystallized around the overtly antitraditional figure of Elvis Presley. The rock-and-roll sound that Presley unleashed in early 1956 gave musical

expression to the adolescent mood portrayed in *The Wild One,
Blackboard Jungle*, and *Rebel Without a Cause*, and Presley, with
his long sideburns, motorcycles, and explicit sexuality was clearly
rock's equivalent of Brando and Dean. Ultimately, he proved to
be more important than either. For young people, disillusioned
or not, rock and roll replaced the movies as a social unifier, providing both stimulation and release for rebellious emotions. The
student movements that ultimately developed in the sixties would
have been unthinkable without it.

From 1956 through 1958, Presley was at the center of the storm
of controversy created by rock and roll, eliciting reactions whose
emotional frenzy, pro and con, far surpassed those produced by
Brando or Dean. Girls in his audiences fainted or fought to touch
him, religious leaders proclaimed his wickedness, businessmen
courting customers offered to break copies of his records, and
television producers agreed to film him from the waist up to avoid
showing his erotic dancing. In the meantime, Presley, without
ever becoming a genuine movie star, did enormous business at
the box office. In 1957, three of his films made the Top Twenty
Box-Office list (*Love Me Tender, Jailhouse Rock*, and *Loving You*),
and from 1957 through 1966, he made *Variety*'s roster of Top Ten
Box-Office Stars seven times, missing only during the years when
he was in the army (1958-1960).

Hollywood began by treating Presley as the successor to James
Dean, giving him parts as sensitive outsiders: a Confederate soldier in *Love Me Tender*, a farm-boy-turned-pop-singer in *Loving
You*, a convict in *Jailhouse Rock*, and a street-tough, New Or-
leans punk in *King Creole*, a kind of musical *Blackboard Jungle*
directed by *Casablanca*'s Michael Curtiz. Inevitably, Presley's
characters were Good Bad Boys whose outward rebelliousness
hid an allegiance to traditional values. The songs allowed him
almost never touched the raw excitement with which his career
had begun. When he did get a good song, as with *King Creole*'s
"Trouble," the result was shocking: "If you're looking for trouble," he sang, "You've come to the right place. If you're looking
for trouble, look right in my face." Although moments like this
drew the audience to Presley's films, they remained rare. More

typically, he could be found singing bland, safe pop like "Teddy Bear," "Love Me Tender," or "Dixieland Rock," some adult's idea of rock and roll.

The basic problem with Presley's films was clear from the start: with their semi-serious, linearly developed plots, highly choreographed dance numbers, and stylized backgrounds, they represented updated versions of the old-fashioned Hollywood musical whose form had evolved around exactly that kind of Tin Pan Alley song against which Presley's rock and roll was in revolt. The two forms had nothing in common. Where Tin Pan Alley songs were sophisticated, witty, coolly detached, urbane, polished, and vaguely asexual, rock was primitive, direct, involving, rural, amateurish, and overtly erotic. By introducing rock's leading figure into one of Tin Pan Alley's favorite forms, Hollywood insured that one party would lose.

Of course, it was Presley. His movies were even more divided than Brando's or Dean's, the glimpses of genuine rebellion fewer, the traditional, "safe" values quicker to assert themselves. In no single group of films in Hollywood's history had the gap between the moral and interest centers been so wide. The audience waited for the songs and spent the rest of the time at the concession stands. After 1961, even the faintest vestiges of a genuine interest center had been snuffed out, with Presley reduced to singing songs like "There's No Room to Rhumba in a Sports Car," "Do the Clam," and "Yoga Is as Yoga Does." But the movies continued to make money, almost up to the end, perhaps drawing on the memory of the way Presley had once been. Not until Richard Lester's film, *A Hard Day's Night* (1964), would the movies figure out a form for rock and roll.

In many respects, the shape of Presley's Hollywood career paralleled Brando's: early success in compromised "youth rebellion" movies, followed by a steady decline and softening. Both ended up in formulaic "products," Presley in endless versions of *Blue Hawaii*, Brando in stock movies like *Desirée, Guys and Dolls, The Young Lions,* and *The Appaloosa* or the camp of *The Teahouse of the August Moon, Mutiny on the Bounty,* and *Candy*. In retrospect, Hollywood's ability to assimilate the threats to its traditional pattern posed by Brando and Presley indicates the enormous emotional and economic power of the assumptions on which that pattern rested. To have accepted Brando and Presley on their original terms would have been to explicitly discredit at least part of those assumptions, particularly those that gave equal support to the interests of the community. For Brando and Presley embodied the most extreme versions of the outlaw hero with which the movies had had to deal; the bad movies dealt to them were a kind of punishment for that extremity.

THE PRESLEY movies were, of course, musicals, a genre important to Hollywood since Jolson's *The Jazz Singer* introduced sound in 1927. But the musical had never been so dominant as in the postwar period. Between 1946 and 1965, at least one musical found the Top Twenty Box-Office list in every year but 1959 and 1961:

1946: *Blue Skies; I Wonder Who's Kissing Her Now; The Time, the Place, and the Girl*
1947: *The Jolson Story, Till the Clouds Roll By*
1948: *Easter Parade, When My Baby Smiles at Me, The Emperor Waltz*
1949: *Jolson Sings Again, Words and Music, In the Good Old Summertime, Take Me Out to the Ball Game, The Barkleys of Broadway*
1950: *Annie Get Your Gun, Three Little Words*
1951: *An American in Paris, Show Boat, The Great Caruso, On Moonlight Bay*
1952: *Singin' in the Rain, With a Song in My Heart, I'll See You in My Dreams*
1953: *Peter Pan*
1954: *Seven Brides for Seven Brothers, White Christmas, The Glenn Miller Story*
1955: *A Star Is Born, There's No Business Like Show Business*
1956: *Guys and Dolls, The King and I, The Eddy Duchin Story, High Society, I'll Cry Tomorrow*
1957: *Pal Joey, April Love, Love Me Tender, Loving You, Jailhouse Rock*
1958: *South Pacific*
1960: *Can-Can*
1962: *West Side Story, The Music Man, Flower Drum Song, Blue Hawaii, Babes in Toyland*
1963: *Bye Bye Birdie, Gypsy*
1964: *A Hard Day's Night*
1965: *My Fair Lady, The Sound of Music, Mary Poppins, Help!*

As it had developed in the thirties around the figure of Fred
Astaire, the musical had proved another means of demonstrating
how the apparently incompatible impulses of the individual and
the community could be reconciled. Typically, this pattern had
taken shape as a struggle between spontaneity and pretentiousness, with Astaire representing a sublime naturalness expressed
by the effortless way his walk stretched into dance, and his speech
into song. No situation could contain him for long. A stuffy men's
club, whose members demanded silence, became the occasion for
a blithe (and noisy) tap dance (*Top Hat*). His conversation tended
to lift into singing at the slightest pretext ("Let's Call the Whole
Thing Off" in *Shall We Dance*, "A Fine Romance" in *Swing Time*,
"No Strings" in *Top Hat*).

The project was to merge this exuberant private energy with
a wider community.[5] The reconciliatory pattern depended on two
devices. The first involved the conceit of casting Astaire and Ginger Rogers in roles that were opposites of their screen personae.
Thus, while the aristocratic, urbane Astaire was frequently called
on to play musical versions of the outlaw hero (Huckleberry [Huck]
Haines in *Roberta*, gambler "Lucky" Garnett in *Swing Time*),
the saucy, down-to-earth Rogers appeared in parts that called
for her to assume airs (Countess Scharwenka in *Roberta*, the
prim divorcée in *The Gay Divorcée*). But the screen personalities
of Astaire and Rogers made sure that the audience would recognize their fictional differences as temporary: it was clear that
down deep, Astaire could be as dignified, and Rogers as natural,
as they needed to be. The plots that kept them apart, therefore,
nearly always turned on mistaken identities, and it gradually
became clear that the two were perfectly compatible.

The second device worked a variation on the western. Although he was frequently pursuing Rogers, Astaire was also very
much the lone wolf, reluctant to give up his freedom. Advised by
Edward Everett Horton in *Top Hat* that it was time to get married and settle down, he protested: "No thanks. In me you see a
youth who is completely on the loose. No yens. No yearnings. No
strings. No connections. No ties to my affections. . . ." and into
the song "No Strings." In *A Damsel in Distress*, he was as isolationist as *Casablanca*'s Rick, singing

Bad news, go 'way!
Call 'round some day
In March or May—
I can't be bothered now.

My bonds and shares
May fall downstairs—
Who cares, who cares?
I'm dancing and I can't be bothered now.[6]

He kept saying no: "I Won't Dance" in *Roberta*, "Never Gonna Dance" in *Swing Time*. Eventually, of course, he yielded to join Rogers. But because these movies gave Astaire the prime association with dance and music (he nearly always had the first song), this union, consummated in a dance, seemed undertaken on his terms. That their dance sequences frequently developed spontaneously (*Shall We Dance*'s roller skate number—"Let's Call the Whole Thing Off"—was the obvious example) linked them more to Astaire's previously established naturalness than to Rogers's propriety. The result was a kind of community that embraced the best of individualism, and waived the necessity for choosing between them.

Almost all postwar musicals sought to maintain the pattern developed in the Astaire-Rogers series. The three best—*An American in Paris, Singin' in the Rain*, and *The Band Wagon*—explicitly dealt with the clash between naturalness and cultured affectation. In *An American in Paris*, Gene Kelly struggled to escape the designs of a millionairess, preferring instead a naïve, simple girl. *Singin' in the Rain*'s story turned on transforming an artsy operetta into a brash, energetic song-and-dance picture. *The Band Wagon* was virtually identical: a pretentious director, attempting to make a musical *Faust*, was finally convinced to yield to the audience's demands for "just entertainment."

But as with so many fifties movies, the intent of these films was obviously different from their effect. Where in the Astaire-Rogers series the resolution had seemed utterly natural, here everyone appeared to be trying so hard to show that unstuffy communities were possible that the films were, in fact, pretentious. All contained elaborate ballet sequences against stylized, surreal backdrops. All were highly self-conscious. In the Astaire-

Rogers films, Continental characters like Eric Blore and Erik Rhodes had been the butt of jokes; in the fifties movies, the tiresome, European-styled wit of Oscar Levant became the jokes' source.

Above all, there was the screen persona of Gene Kelly, whose clenched-teeth grin seemed to express, in Michael Wood's phrase, "a frantic *will* to be happy." Kelly's obvious need to work so hard implied a growing weakness in the reconciliatory pattern. If the resolutions in the Astaire-Rogers movies had been natural and inevitable, in Kelly's they were the result of unconcealed effort. As Wood has described him,

> Gene Kelly has plenty of skill, but ease is the last thing we associate with him. He does all kinds of difficult numbers, but we are meant to see how difficult they are. His stock-in-trade is drive and buoyancy, an expense of energy and steam which often seems awkward beside Astaire's restraint, but which also makes far more ambitious claims for itself. Fred Astaire is a style, but Gene Kelly is a state of mind, almost an ideology. . . . It urges not confidence in yourself, or in America, but confidence in confidence.[7]

Kelly displayed a kind of desperation that one had never sensed in Astaire, and in that desperation, an image of a loss of faith in the American Dream. In the black-and-white sanctuary of the Astaire-Rogers movies, that dream had seemed invulnerable; the color and wide screens of the fifties worked to reveal its flaws. *Peter Pan, Seven Brides for Seven Brothers, April Love*, and *Mary Poppins* even portrayed it as a child's way of experiencing the world.

The effect of the fifties musicals, therefore, contradicted their intent. Far from confirming the continued validity of the old myth of reconciliation, they implied a bleak image of America where only effort and willed self-confidence could maintain the traditional ways. Their pretentiousness was the most obvious sign of that effort, and the most visible contradiction of the Classic Hollywood musical's faith that individual energy and community cooperation were not incompatible.

The implication of the fifties musicals' pretentiousness was a new-found preference for the values of the official hero. This preference was confirmed in the period's westerns, where it often appeared in converse form—as a new distaste for the outlaw hero's values. It seems clear, as Leo Braudy points out, that "the attack against destructive individualism . . . developed . . . as a result of World War II," which had emphasized the necessity of cooperation.[8] More important, the rise of the western, the one American genre with a historical sense, reflected an emerging American awareness that the passage of time might have discredited certain values and attitudes previously assumed immutable. That a disproportionately high percentage of the westerns now regarded as significant were made between 1946 and 1967 suggests how pervasive that awareness had become in the postwar period. One has only to see a list to feel how important the western was for the time:

1946: *My Darling Clementine*
1947: *Duel in the Sun*
1948: *Fort Apache, Red River*
1949: *She Wore a Yellow Ribbon*
1950: *Broken Arrow, Winchester '73, The Gunfighter, Rio Grande, Wagonmaster*
1951: *Across the Wide Missouri*
1952: *High Noon, Bend of the River, The Big Sky, Rancho Notorious*
1953: *Shane, The Naked Spur*
1954: *Hondo, Johnny Guitar, The Far Country*
1955: *Vera Cruz, Bad Day at Black Rock, The Tall Men, The Man from Laramie, Wichita*
1956: *The Searchers, Run of the Arrow*
1957: *Gunfight at the O.K. Corral, 3:10 to Yuma, The Tin Star, The Tall T*
1958: *The Big Country, Man of the West, The Left-Handed Gun, From Hell to Texas*
1959: *Rio Bravo, The Horse Soldiers*
1960: *The Magnificent Seven, Comanche Station*
1961: *One-Eyed Jacks, Two Rode Together, The Misfits, North to Alaska, The Alamo*
1962: *The Man Who Shot Liberty Valance, Ride the High Country*
1963: *How the West Was Won, Hud*
1964: *Major Dundee*
1965: *Cat Ballou, The Sons of Katie Elder, Shenandoah*
1966: *The Professionals, Nevada Smith*
1967: *El Dorado, Hombre, Hour of the Gun, Will Penny*

These westerns were different from their predecessors in that they were almost always located in a specific period of American history. The prewar films' deliberate vagueness about dates had conveyed a sense of the western myth's permanence. (*Stagecoach* and *Destry Rides Again* were obvious examples of this effect.) The new movies, in contrast, confirmed the westerner's dependence on a certain set of conditions that were disappearing.

Howard Hawks's *Red River* (1948) was a prototype for this new, more pessimistic western. Its story of the first cattle drive along the Chisholm Trail was specifically set in 1865. In the film's first half, Hawks and scriptwriter Borden Chase seemed intent on reaffirming the pattern of *Casablanca* by portraying the mutual dependence of outlaw hero Tom Dunson (John Wayne) and official hero Matthew Garth (Montgomery Clift), symbolized by the growth of the herd from the original mating of Dunson's bull with Matthew's cow. But as it progressed, the film transferred its emotional allegiance from Dunson to Matthew. There had been early indications of Dunson's ruthlessness and selfishness: his fiancée had died in an Indian raid after he refused to take her with him to Texas; he had stolen his land from Mexicans and Indians. Now those indications were confirmed. Dunson savagely drove his men on the trail, pushing them past convenient stopping places. He shot deserters, whipped slackers. He insisted on taking the long trip to Missouri rather than the shorter one to the new railhead in Abilene, Kansas. And after each such wrongheaded action, he was told by the cook, Groot (Walter Brennan), "You was wrong, Mr. Dunson," a phrase that began to sound like a Greek chorus. Finally, when Dunson tried to hang two deserters, Matthew intervened and took over leadership of the drive. Preparing to leave, Dunson swore, "I'll kill you, Matt."

At the end of the drive, Dunson reappeared for a showdown in Abilene. When Matthew refused his challenge to draw, Dunson began to beat him savagely. The younger man fought back, until the brawl was interrupted by Matthew's girl, who pronounced the movie's overt moral: "Anyone with half a mind would see you love each other." Smiles. Handshakes. The End. The reversal required less than a minute.

Superficially, then, *Red River* reaffirmed the reconciliation of the outlaw and official hero. The audience was intended to regard the cattle drive as a joint achievement, requiring both Dunson's tough-minded strength and Matthew's more temperate leadership. But, in fact, as with so many of the period's films, the movie's effect completely contradicted its intent. Few endings in the history of American popular cinema have been so often criticized as being emotionally inconsistent with what preceded it. For the concluding reconciliation simply ignored the fact that the rest of *Red River* had fully discredited Dunson's values. As Robin Wood saw,

the film traces the way in which Dunson's ruthlessness, necessary for survival in the primitive conditions in which the film begins, becomes obsolete as civilization develops, so that the more liberal outlook of Matthew Garth . . . gains him the men's allegiance as Dunson alienates it.[9]

As distinguished from its intent, the effect of *Red River*, in other words, was to make Dunson (and by implication, *Casablanca*'s Rick) seem an impossible alternative.

John Ford's *The Searchers* (1956) was similarly divided. Here, the outlaw hero, Ethan Edwards (John Wayne)—ex-Confederate soldier, probable bank-robber—had become, as Lindsay Anderson felt, a full-blown neurotic,[10] obsessively trailing Indians who had abducted his niece long after it was evident that she had been fully assimilated into their culture. Again, the film's sudden reversal at the end (as Ethan lifted the girl in his arms and said, "Let's go home, Debbie") could not contain what had previously taken place, particularly Ethan's earlier attempt to kill the girl. The effect of the movie was again to discredit the outlaw hero.

Anthony Mann's *The Far Country* (1955) resembled *Red River* and *The Searchers*, but was subtler than either. At first glance, the movie turned on merely another version of *Casablanca*'s story of a reluctant hero who ultimately recognizes his responsibility to a larger community. James Stewart played Jeff Webster, a cattleman who, with pal Ben (Walter Brennan), had taken their herd to Alaska to sell to the highest bidder. When asked by the struggling community of Dawson to serve as a temporary sheriff to frighten off a local boss, Webster refused with a flat "I ain't interested." Ben, who liked the town, pleaded with Jeff to stay on, but Webster remained adamant: "We got ours and we're gettin' out," he shouted at the old man; "leastways, I'm gettin' out."

But en route down-country, the two were ambushed, with Ben killed and Webster seriously wounded. Only then did he act, riding into town to a showdown with the villain who muttered cynically, "We *knew* he'd turn into a public citizen."

Although *The Far Country* seemed like a simple reaffirmation of the Classic Hollywood pattern, the character of Jeff made it an implicit repudiation of that myth. The movie revealed the stock outlaw hero's self-sufficiency as a ruthless indifference to others' needs. Webster, in effect, was an even more brutal version of *Red River*'s Dunson. In the film's opening sequence, Ben greeted Webster at the end of his cattle drive with the accusation, "You started with four men." "Two of them *tried* to turn back," Webster answered coldly, handing back guns to the remaining two, one of whom swore, "I'll live to see you hanged." Further on, Jeff's selfishness became explicit. "Ben told me that you don't like any place very much, that you don't even like people," a girl asked him, and Jeff nodded. "I don't need other people. I don't need help. I can take care of me," he protested to Ben. "You've got to help people, don't you?" the girl tried again. "I don't know," was the answer, "I help me."

Even more unsettling was what it took to involve the hero in the needs of the community—the murder of his one friend, and being shot and beaten himself. The violence of this impetus to action so far exceeded what it had taken to move *Casablanca*'s Rick that it seemed to express a different kind of anxiety or resentment altogether. As Jim Kitses points out about *The Far Country*:

> ... the central character moves through conflict until at the end he is ostensibly a part of the community. But the paradox here is that his movement is resolutely *away* from the community, and we rarely witness a process we could call *growth* in the character. If there is a strong didactic tone often present ... it is the result of the hero being literally *beaten* into line; we feel that "he's learned his lesson." His old partner shot in the back and he himself nearly shot to pieces, Jeff Webster "chooses" a revenge that also saves the community. ... Entry into the community can thus feel like *defeat*, the hero not so much integrated as exhausted by his compulsion to pursue an unnatural course, not educated so much as beaten by a struggle against profound forces that operate as a kind of immutable law.[11]

It is not stretching it to see *The Far Country*'s reluctant, battered hero as the postwar audience's image of America itself, forced by the terrible losses at Pearl Harbor into an acknowledgment of international interdependence that at best seemed involuntary, and at worst, a defeat.

The postwar period's emerging preference for the values of the official hero could be felt in even those films whose story seemed to criticize them. John Ford's *Fort Apache* (1948) was a notorious example of the era's common attempts to sell these new values to an audience whose sympathies clearly remained with the outlaws. As Col. Owen Thursday, Henry Fonda was an archetype of the official hero. He came to his western cavalry post from the East (Boston). He had been in Europe. He was a stickler for all codes, military or social, refusing a sergeant's son permission to court his daughter. He was obsessed with details of dress and etiquette. Worse, he devoted himself to personal glory, sought in by-the-book combat with the Apaches. In battle, his utter lack of flexibility proved disastrous. Ignoring the obvious warning signals, he led his men into an ambush where all were killed.

But the film's conclusions contained a surprising reversal. Presented with a romanticized painting of "Thursday's Charge," the fort's new commander (John Wayne) refused the chance to correct the legend of Thursday's heroism. "No one died with more honor or courage," Wayne pronounced. "Thursday made it a command to be proud of." In an interview with Peter Bogdanovich, Ford affirmed his agreement with Wayne's lie:

Yes—because I think it's good for the country. We've had a lot of people who were supposed to be great heroes, and you know damn well they weren't. But it's good for the country to have heroes to look up to.[12]

This kind of whitewashing of obviously wrongheaded official heroes spilled over into nonwesterns like *The Caine Mutiny* and *The Bridge on the River Kwai*, whose protagonists' utter obsessions with rules and army codes clearly signaled madness. Both Captain Queeg and Colonel Nicholson were incompetent in military terms. Queeg botched landing operations through cowardice, destroyed morale, and panicked in the midst of a typhoon. Nicholson, on the other hand, endangered the lives of his officers with his unilateral protest against their being required to do manual labor (which he ultimately ordered himself). Furthermore, as his medical attaché adjudged, he collaborated with the Japanese by building them a better bridge than they could have built themselves.

Both movies, however, were compromised. Where *Kwai*'s attempts to gain sympathy for Nicholson spread throughout the film, *The Caine Mutiny*'s shift in attitude toward Queeg occurred abruptly at the end, when the mutineers' defense attorney denounced their insensitivity to Queeg's tacit pleas for help. Because of its suddenness, *The Caine Mutiny*'s conclusion rang as false as *Fort Apache*'s. In both cases, they were contradicted by the main body of the film.

In effect, then, movies like *Fort Apache, The Caine Mutiny*, and *The Bridge on the River Kwai* were mirror images of *Red River, The Searchers*, and *The Far Country*. Both sets of films were typical of the postwar period's marked split between intent and effect. The latter group overtly reaffirmed the need for the outlaw hero in stories that implicitly revealed him as inhumanly selfish, brutal, and indifferent to communal needs. The former group overtly praised the official hero in stories that discredited him as dangerously inflexible. Both sets of heroes were ultimately neurotic extremes of the traditional alternatives. As such, they suggested the period's emerging anxiety that if before, both had been possible, now neither was. Outwardly, the old pattern of reconciliation was being maintained. But in the crevasses of these films, one could sense that some things had changed.

7. *It's a Wonderful Life* and *The Man Who Shot Liberty Valance*

THE SPLIT between the intent and effect of the best postwar movies was not new to the American Cinema. In fact, many of Classic Hollywood's most exciting films had manifested the same disjuncture, resulting from the inability of their displacement mechanisms to efface completely the anxieties occasioning their surface melodramas. Typically, such a disjuncture required both an anxiety powerful enough to resist complete transposition (e.g., the fear regarding World War II's threat to American separateness: *Casablanca*) and a movie's willingness, however minimal, to refer to that anxiety by name ("My dear Rick, when will you realize that in this world today, isolationism is no longer a practical policy?"). An anxiety neither pervasive nor powerful usually proved incapable of generating the period's most affecting films. Thus, in the 1930s, despite the Depression, apprehensions about laissez-faire capitalism had not become critical enough to make the gangster movie a major commercial genre.[1] By the 1970s, and *The Godfather*, they had. Similarly, movies that completely concealed their motivating fears diffused their own energy source. With their avoidance of internal contradictions, for example, the seamless Errol Flynn vehicles (*Captain Blood, The Charge of the Light Brigade, The Adventures of Robin Hood, Dodge City, Virginia City, The Sea Hawk, Santa Fe Trail*) lacked the urgency of Bogart's and Gable's best movies. That the seven Flynn movies were all directed by *Casablanca*'s Michael Curtiz suggests that the *auteur* theory cannot fully account for the differences among Classic Hollywood's movies.

Since the power of whole films frequently derived from this phenomenon of acknowledgment, it is not surprising that Classic Hollywood's most affecting scenes often developed from explicit references to the very concerns their movies sought to allay. *Casablanca*'s drunk scene, that began with Bogart's thinly veiled reference to Pearl Harbor, was this pattern's great example. But other famous sequences worked similarly. *The Philadelphia Story*'s *après soirée* between Stewart and Hepburn (that won Stewart an Oscar) grew out of their opening sallies regarding class divisiveness and snobbery; the poignancy of *Meet Me in St. Louis*'s "Have Yourself a Merry Little Christmas" depended on the openly stated conflict between the values of stable family life and restless careerism.

By attempting to extend its mythology to more areas of contemporary life, postwar Hollywood widened the gap between intent and effect in its most powerful films. For such extensions invariably involved the kind of explicit acknowledgment of anxiety from which a movie seemed incapable of fully recovering. Thus, *On the Waterfront*'s realistic *mise en scène* and overt allusions to the outlaw hero's identity with the bum made the stock western showdown, grafted onto a topical problem, appear inadequate as an ending. Similarly, *Rebel Without a Cause*'s final father-son reconciliation could not entirely contain the purposeless desperation conveyed by James Dean's typical fifties adolescent.

As the contradictory nature of Classic Hollywood's thematic paradigm became increasingly apparent (with its traditional dichotomies developing a new resistance to standard resolutions), the formal paradigm also began to unravel. In particular, the *noir* movies (the heirs of *Citizen Kane*) replaced the continuity system's transparent forms with conspicuous devices that called attention to the filming process: cameras tilted wildly, shadows fell expressively. The stylistic inflation of even the non-*noir* films further subverted the thematic paradigm's invisibility, substituting the grand and picturesque for the familiar and matter of fact.

Stylistic exceptions to the continuity conventions were not entirely a postwar invention. Classic Hollywood's most celebrated director, John Ford, had occasionally crossed the sacrosanct 180° axis during chase scenes, a tactic that momentarily made a fleeing stagecoach and pursuing Indians seem to be going in opposite

directions. But while Ford's deviations from the formal paradigm remained inexpressive stylistic accidents, postwar departures often reinforced the anxious, irresolvable quality of crucial sequences. Thus, when the first signs of strain began to show in Classic Hollywood's dominant pattern, the cracks appeared simultaneously in the form and content of the movies, with thematic breaks often occurring in departures from continuity conventions. In *Rebel Without a Cause*'s knife fight, for example, Nicholas Ray's unmotivated oblique angles and 180° violations further suggested Jim's (James Dean) irreconcilable feelings of superiority and inconsequentiality, and his contradictory impulses toward solitude and belonging—contradictions set loose during the immediately preceding planetarium lecture:

[*Medium close-up of Plato* (Sal Mineo) *and Jim*]
PLATO: It's hard to make friends with these guys.
JIM [Having just tried to banter with Buzz (Corey Allen) and Judy (Natalie Wood)]: I don't want to make friends.
[*Close-up of Plato*]
LECTURER: We will disappear into the blackness of the space from which we came. [*Shot of planetarium screen*] Destroyed as we began, in a burst of gas and fire.
[*Medium shot of Buzz's gang*] [*Close-up of Judy*] [*Close-up of Plato*] [*Close-up of Jim*] [*Close-up of Buzz and Judy*] [*Shot of planetarium screen*]
LECTURER: The heavens are still and cold once more. [*Shot of lecturer*] In all the immensity of our universe and the galaxies beyond, the earth will not be missed. [*Close-up of Buzz and Judy*] To the infinite

reaches of space, the problems of man seem trivial and naïve indeed. [*Close-up of Jim*] And man, existing alone, seems himself an episode of little consequence. [*Shot of planetarium screen*] That's all.

In the following fight, Ray's overhead shot (freed from any character's point of view) imitated the insignificance implied by the lecturer, while the low-angle shots swelled his adolescents to heroic size. Further, the repeated 180° crossings during the fight itself not only conveyed the participants' confusion, but also set Jim against opposed backdrops: the group that promised an answer to loneliness and the empty city landscape that resembled an abandoned planet. *Rebel*'s conventional happy ending, filmed in standard continuity and proposing a solution to Jim's emotional impasse, could not overcome the power of the planetarium sequence and thus left implicitly unresolved the contradictions that Ray's style had conveyed.

Two MOVIES in particular represented the postwar American mood and Hollywood's responses to it. Frank Capra's *It's a Wonderful Life* (1946) appeared early in the period, and John Ford's *The Man Who Shot Liberty Valance* (1962) toward the end, but both signaled the partial erosion of the once-unassailable formal and thematic paradigms. Both films manifested the period's characteristic split between intent and effect, as each struggled to reaffirm the Classic Hollywood pattern of reconciliation while simultaneously dramatizing the growing incompatibility of traditional American values. In both, moments that most strained Classic Hollywood's thematic paradigm occurred in cinematic language that challenged the underlying premises of American Cinema's formal conventions. Specifically, *It's a Wonderful Life* made the invisible style visible while *Liberty Valance* ignored the formal paradigm's most fundamental guarantee—that shot selection and editing would always provide the audience with the optimum vantage point on any unfolding action.

IT'S A WONDERFUL LIFE

Capra's *It's a Wonderful Life* told the story of George Bailey (Jimmy Stewart, in his favorite role) from age twelve to thirty-eight. By spanning the years from 1919 (just after World War I) to Christmas Eve 1945 (the first Christmas after World War II), the movie effectively summed up a generation. Superficially, however, Capra appeared to ignore the results of historical change, setting his story in the small town of Bedford Falls, a nostalgic, unchanging place existing outside of time. On the surface, in fact, Bedford Falls was another version of the Andy Hardy world (Carvel) that Charles Champlin has identified as the epitome of the old Hollywood, "a world not as it was but as it ought to have been, with virtues intact, pieties unfeigned, commandments unbroken, good rewarded, evil foiled."[2] Indeed, the movie's beginning seemed intent on evoking memories of the Andy Hardy stories, picturing young George and his friends at play, and

structuring the early drama around the simultaneous, and yet solvable crises of father and son. Amidst these allusions to the popular Mickey Rooney series lay one portentous reversal: Lionel Barrymore, the original Judge Hardy (in 1937's *A Family Affair*) had now become the Dickensian villain, arriving by horse-drawn coach outside the soda shop where George worked.

For an Andy Hardy-style movie, however, *It's a Wonderful Life* began ominously. After the credits and two opening establishing shots of Bedford Falls, Capra introduced six consecutive shots of buildings accompanied by voice-overs retroactively identifiable as Mr. Gower (the pharmacist), Martini (the bartender), George's mother, Bert the cop, Ernie the cabdriver, and Mary and Zuzu (George's wife and younger daughter). The desperation of these voices, and their concerted resort to prayer, suggested a further departure from the Andy Hardy world where, as Champlin puts it, "There were problems and crises, but none that could not be tidily solved, usually by the generous application of good sense and fatherly advice." That George Bailey's problem, on the other hand, required God's intervention implied a graveness out of place in Carvel. Indeed, *It's a Wonderful Life* promptly discredited the standard Andy Hardy answer to a boy's troubles. Discovering the grieving Mr. Gower drunkenly filling a prescription with poison, George ran to his father for advice, only to find him occupied with his own unsolvable crisis. Capra's ironic juxtaposition of the

MR. GOWER: I owe everything to George Bailey. Help him, dear Father.

MARTINI: Joseph, Jesus, and Mary, help my friend Mr. Bailey.

GEORGE'S MOTHER: Help my son George tonight.

BERT: He never thinks about himself, God; that's why he's in trouble.

ERNIE: George is a good guy. Give him a break, God.

MARY: Dear Lord, watch over him tonight.
ZUZU: Please God, something's the matter with Daddy. Please bring Daddy back. Please bring Daddy home.

pharmacy's poster ("Ask Dad, *he* knows") with the image of the weary, harassed Mr. Bailey dispelled the Andy Hardy myth of the omniscient father, and, in so doing, implicitly questioned the ideological pattern that figure had served.

This juxtaposition, typical of the movie, suggested that surface similarities only concealed the enormous differences between George Bailey's Bedford Falls and Andy Hardy's Carvel. In repeatedly exposing those differences, *It's a Wonderful Life* implicitly (and unintentionally) acknowledged the damage done by historical change to the Classic Hollywood mythology that Andy Hardy movies had embodied. Capra's film, in fact, drew much of its power from the contradiction between the sunny, small-town world of its surface and the deaths, anxieties, frustration, and near-madness shown to exist here. And, despite Capra's intent, *It's a Wonderful Life*'s complications, like those of so many postwar movies, stubbornly resisted the consolation of its nominal happy ending.

The movie's apparently simple plot hid reversals and twisted chronologies typical of postwar films. It began like a fairy tale, with Capra swinging upward from the opening shots of buildings and their chorus of prayers to a luminous heaven where the voices of God and Chief Angel Joseph issued from pulsating stars. Summoning a smaller star (Angel Second Class Clarence Oddbody, yet to earn his wings after 200 years), the voices explained that George Bailey was about to commit suicide. Clarence (Henry

Travers) would have one hour to learn about George before descending to earth to help him. What followed was a long, *film noir*-like flashback, covering George's life up to the present. (The film did not quite live up to its promised time limit; George's story required not an hour, but nearly 100 minutes.)

George, it appeared, was a good man, married, with four children. He had dreamed of great things but had ended up spending his entire life in Bedford Falls, managing the Bailey Building and Loan which lent money to small homeowners too poor to get credit from the bank, owned (like everything else in town) by Mr. Potter (Lionel Barrymore). On Christmas Eve, George's Uncle Billy (Thomas Mitchell), a warmhearted, but slightly addled man, absentmindedly misplaced $8,000 intended for deposit. Inevitably, the money fell into Potter's hands. With the bank examiner paying an unexpected visit, and without the funds to balance the books, George faced ruin. With no solutions in sight, he decided to drown himself to leave his family with the proceeds from his meager life insurance policy. Just as he was about to jump off a bridge, however, Clarence materialized, jumped in first, and called for help. George instinctively jumped in to save him but refused to accept Clarence's subsequent explanation: "I'm your guardian angel. I've come here to help you." Unable to rid George of his despair, Clarence determined to answer his wish: "I wish I had never been born." The ensuing sequence took George on a tour of Bedford Falls (now "Pottersville") to show him the "results" of his never having lived. Terrified by this vision, George prayed to be allowed to live again. The wish granted, he returned home to find that his wife and friends had raised the money to meet the bank shortfall and to learn that he had, after all, lived a wonderful life.

Summarized in this way, *It's a Wonderful Life* would appear mawkishly sentimental. In fact, it was almost frighteningly bleak for most of its 129 minutes. The movie turned on three basic oppositions central to American culture in general, and to the American postwar mood in particular: adventure/domesticity, individual/community, and worldly success/ordinary life. Although Capra obviously intended to demonstrate the illusoriness of these oppositions, the film's emotional weight derived from his own, evidently unconscious, sense of their reality.

The movie's principle narrative tactic was juxtaposition. Throughout, it alternated sharply between optimism and despair, following scenes appealing to one set of values with others appealing to their opposite. Transitions occurred abruptly. An Andy Hardy-style sequence in the drugstore, with the boy George boasting happily to Mary about his future exploring plans, slid alarmingly into the nightmare of Mr. Gower's drunkenly filling a prescription with poison. Similarly, later in the film, George's date with Mary, on the point of concluding giddily, broke off suddenly with the news of Mr. Bailey's death.

It's a Wonderful Life's large narrative segments contained smaller units structured around contradictory imagery. "Who's that?" Clarence asked, seeing a fine carriage stopping in front of the Bailey Building and Loan. Joseph's answer, "That's Henry S. Potter, the richest and meanest man in the county," implied the inseparability of the two adjectives. But the movie's next shot showed young George running into the pharmacy, pressing the good-luck lighter, and announcing brightly, "Wish I had a million dollars!"

At certain points, even individual shots included conflicting codes. Returning to his makeshift house on his wedding night, George looked around in amazement, his glance (accompanied by Hawaiian music subsequently revealed as diagetic) cueing a series of shots that showed 1) a bouquet of chrysanthemums and

daisies (ordinary life, domesticity) and a South Seas travel poster (worldly success, adventure); 2) a poster bathing beauty (adventurous sex), a bottle of champagne (worldly success, adventure), and a wedding cake surrounded by candles and plain china (ordinary life, domesticity); 3) chickens turning over an open fire (domesticity, but also hinting at an adventurous frontier life of camping out) and an old victrola (ordinary life, domesticity). By bracketing this series with a medium shot of a befuddled George and a soft-focus close-up of Mary (Donna Reed), Capra implied a closed world in which George's dreams would permanently exist side by side with their opposites.

The violent effect of these juxtapositions suggested the inescapable contradictions inherent in all of one's most felt desires. Indeed, so stark and rigorous was *It's a Wonderful Life*'s logic that when George reached the point of suicide, crying (at the time, a very rare act for a male star) and praying ("God, dear Father in Heaven, I'm not a praying man, but if you're up there and you can hear me, show me the way. I'm at the end of my rope. Show me the way."), the scene was the nadir of hopelessness in the American Cinema.

The three oppositions in *It's a Wonderful Life* (adventure/domesticity, individual/community, worldly success/ordinary life) have been frequently identified as the fundamental polarities of American mythology and literature.[3] The traditional ideology officially celebrated both halves of each dichotomy. But despite American culture's apparent impartiality, the successful, individual adventurer had clearly won the competition for the American imagination—at the expense of the man who did the quiet work at home. *It's a Wonderful Life* attempted to correct this imbalance. Its project was to summon support for the common life lived by the ordinary citizen, whose respresentative was George Bailey, "a local boy," in James Agee's words, "who stays home, doesn't make good, and becomes at length so unhappy that he wishes he had never been born."[4]

Indeed, George's problem resulted directly from the latent American preference for values, lifestyles, and attitudes that had no place in ordinary life. In sociologist Robert K. Merton's terms, he was a victim of anomie, "the disassociation between culturally prescribed aspirations and socially structured avenues for realizing those aspirations."[5] George was a Victor Laszlo who wanted to be a Rick Blaine, a Good Good Boy desperately trying to be a Good Bad Boy, who seemed to get most of the glory and most of the fun. The goal of *It's a Wonderful Life* was to liberate George, and the audience, from the frustrations caused by this desire, which the film identified as mistaken. To measure the movie's success, we need to look first at its three basic oppositions. Because many of the film's sequences (such as the wedding night scene) employed two or three of these oppositions simultaneously, separating them for discussion is partially misleading. Each opposition, however, embodied a different set of concerns; thus, each required a different solution.

Adventure versus Domesticity: That America's discovery, exploration, and settling depended on what Daniel Boorstin has called "the exploring spirit"[6] insured that the traditional American mythology would reserve its special affection for the adventurer. Following Columbus's suggestion, "The farther one goes, the more one learns," the culture relied heavily on its individual pioneers to make the necessary discoveries (both geographic and scientific) and even to do the living for those left behind. The domestic life, embraced too willingly, was a betrayal of the American spirit.

But American culture also preserved a strong instinct for adventure's opposite, countering the glorification of the wandering hero with a sanctification of family and home. Erik Erikson has argued that the mythology of domesticity developed as a reaction to the cult of adventure:

The frontier, of course, remained the decisive influence which served to establish in the American identity the extreme polarization which characterizes it. The original polarity was the cultivation of the sedentary and migratory poles. Towns, too, developed their sedentary existence and oriented their inward life to work bench and writing desk, fireplace and altar, while through them, on the roads and rails, strangers passed bragging of God knows what greener pastures. You had either to follow—or stay behind and brag louder. The point is that the call of the frontier, the temptation to move on, forced those who stayed on to become defensively sedentary, and defensively proud.[7]

Or, as in *It's a Wonderful Life*, to become increasingly frustrated and melancholy about being left behind. For the movie, despite

MARY: I don't *like* coconuts. GEORGE: You don't like *coconuts*? Say, brainless, don't you know where coconuts come from? Lookit here. From Tahiti, the Fiji Islands, the Coral Sea. MARY: A new magazine! I never saw it before. GEORGE: Of course you never. Only us *explorers* can get it. *I've* been nominated for membership in the National Geographic Society.

MARY: Is this the ear you can't hear on?

MARY: George Bailey, I'll love you 'til the day I die.

GEORGE: *I'm* going out exploring some day—you watch. And I'm gonna have a couple of harems and maybe three or four wives.

GEORGE: Wait and see.

its intent, repeatedly demonstrated the incompatibility of the dream of exploring and the fact of settling down. George Bailey stayed home while Sam Wainwright and Harry Bailey passed through, bragging of greener pastures in Florida, upstate New York, and the plastics business. And rather than becoming defensively proud about his own accomplishments, George became another in the long line of melancholy American figures first noted by Tocqueville in his prescient chapter "Why the Americans Are Often So Restless in the Midst of Their Prosperity": "In America I have seen the freest and best educated of men in circumstances the happiest to be found in the world; yet it seemed to me that a cloud habitually hung on their brow, and they seemed serious and almost sad even in their pleasures."[8]

What made George melancholy—the contradiction between the appeals of adventure and domesticity—became apparent in one of *It's a Wonderful Life*'s first scenes. Still a boy working at the soda fountain, George waited on a girl named Mary. She ordered a chocolate sundae; he asked if she wanted coconut topping. "Did he ever marry the girl? Did he go exploring?" Clarence asked, watching this scene. The point was that he could not do both, but that both were attractive. On the word "wives," Capra cut to a soft-focus close-up of the girl, prefiguring the similar shot that closed the equally contradictory wedding night sequence. The soda fountain scene's irony, of course, was that George would ultimately marry Mary rather than go exploring, and despite his general happiness, would be continually frustrated by having to have made the choice. Ideally, the movie made clear, he would have preferred having things both ways.

But that was what George could not do. He spent his life trying to leave town, dreaming of adventures he would never have. Every attempt to get away was frustrated by a sudden crisis demanding his continued presence in Bedford Falls. On the eve of his trip to Europe, his father died. Three months later, on his way to the train for college, he was appointed head of the Bailey Building and Loan, with the stipulation that without his acceptance, the firm would either close or fall into Potter's hands. Having waited four years for brother Harry to return from college to take over, George was frustrated again: Harry in the meantime

had married and taken a position with his father-in-law's glass factory. In these last two cases, Capra, normally very sparing with close-ups, drew his camera in tightly on George's face to intimate his sense of entrapment as he learned the news.

Because it confirmed the incompatibility of adventure and domesticity, the sequence that followed was one of the most moving in *It's a Wonderful Life*. During his brother's homecoming party, George sat sadly on the front porch, leafing through suddenly useless travel folders as a train whistle reminded him of what he was missing. Finally, at his mother's prompting, he ended up at Mary's house, where he rudely expressed incredulity that she could have come back home after college because she was homesick for Bedford Falls. Mary's beau, Sam Wainwright, called from

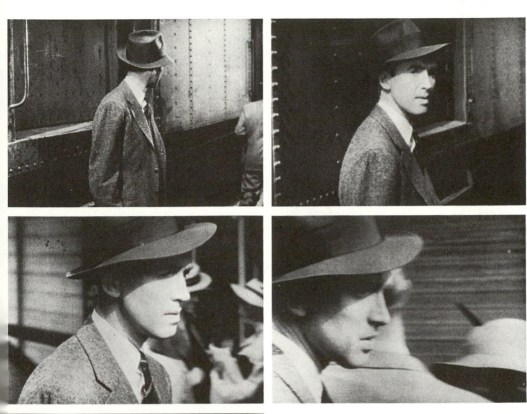

New York. George left in a huff, returned to get his hat, and was invited to speak to Sam, who offered him a job "on the ground floor" of the plastics business. Holding the phone together, he and Mary looked longingly at each other. He held her, she dropped the phone, and sobbing, he began to kiss her, saying brokenly, "Now you listen to me. . . . I don't want to get married . . . ever . . . to anyone . . . you understand that? I want to do what *I* want to do. . . ." The movie's next scene was their wedding.

George's frustrations continued. The planned honeymoon trip to New York and Bermuda (an attempt to have the best of both worlds: travel *and* marriage) was blocked on the way to the train by a run on the Building and Loan, and George spent his wedding night in an abandoned old house that he had previously told Mary "I wouldn't live in as a ghost." Sadly, Joseph told Clarence, "Now you've probably already guessed that George never left Bedford Falls." Even the war offered no escape: he was 4-F because of his bad ear, reduced to fighting the battle of Bedford Falls (scrap drives, air raid drills, etc.) while other men got away. As Joseph summarized it, the war was a big adventure:

Bert the cop was wounded in North Africa, got the Silver Star. Ernie the taxidriver parachuted into France. Martini helped capture the Remagen Bridge. Harry—Harry Bailey topped them all—a navy flyer, he shot down fifteen planes, two of them as they were about to crash into a transport full of soldiers.

Nothing glamorous happened to George. Far from being an adventurer, he had become a settled man whose domesticity, albeit reluctant, was symbolized by his job: he built homes.

Of course, characters before George Bailey had been unhappy in American movies, but typically, their unhappiness had resulted from being unable to have exactly the kind of life George led. The goal in films like *I Am a Fugitive from a Chain Gang*, *Fury*, or *The Grapes of Wrath* had been the very normal domesticity that made George chafe. The truly subversive point about *It's a Wonderful Life*, then, was its recognition that a man could have so many of the things promised by the American Dream (wife, children, job, friends, house, car) and still be unhappy. For the movie acknowledged that having one thing (domesticity) required giving up its opposite (adventure). George had chosen, and was unhappy that he had had to do so—after all, the American myth had suggested that he could have it all.

George's problem, too, derived from his susceptibility to myths of adventure that had long outlived their usefulness in American culture. The frontier period, as Erikson saw, had made the exploratory-sedentary contradiction a real one: townspeople saw pioneers passing through on the way to unknown places and romanticized the figure of the homeless adventurer. To an extent this phenomenon was repeated after World War II by those who stayed behind and saw others go off to combat. To the vast majority of Americans who did not actually serve overseas, the war, rightly or wrongly, seemed like the last great adventure in a world where the possibilities for such exploits were increasingly diminishing.

It's a Wonderful Life, however, demonstrated that myths that had outlived their basis could in fact become pernicious. It was clear that dreams of adventure only caused George frustration, because he lived in a world to which they did not apply. Clearly, too, his ideas about adventure were entirely secondhand. It was no accident that Clarence carried *Tom Sawyer*, for George was another version of Twain's hero, his head stuffed full of romance borrowed from the *National Geographic* and the library. The promiscuous Vi taunted him, "Georgie, don't you ever get tired of just reading about things?" Trying to pick a suitcase for a European trip that never happened, George referred to Tom Sawyer's favorite sourcebook and Huck's preferred means of travel:

I don't want this for *one* night, I want this for 1,001 nights, with plenty of room here for labels from Cathay and Baghdad, and Italy. . . . [Handed a bigger suitcase] Now you're talkin'. Gee whiz! I could use this for a raft in case the boat sunk.

If Tom Sawyer had daydreamed about being a pirate, or hunting buffaloes with the Indians "in the mountain ranges and the trackless great plains of the Far West," or of disappearing mysteriously and going away, "ever so far away, into unknown countries beyond the seas,"[9] George Bailey was no different. His dreams seemed prompted by boys' books, his targets, all the picturesque sights prescribed by Richard Halliburton. "I'm shakin' the dust of this crummy little town off my feet," he told Mary, "and I'm gonna see the world—Italy, Greece, the Parthenon, the Coliseum." He could give only the vaguest answers to his father's questions about what he intended to do: "Oh, well, you know . . . what I've always talked about . . . build things, design new buildings, plan modern cities—all that stuff I've been talking about."

The connections between *It's a Wonderful Life* and Mark Twain were important to the movie's meaning. Like George, Twain had been personally obsessed with having missed a basic part of the American experience. His books betrayed a sense of lateness and his own painful awareness that he had never been the Wild West roughneck that he had wanted, and claimed to have been, having settled instead for a Gilded Age, Connecticut domesticity remarkably like George's life in Bedford Falls. Furthermore, *It's a Wonderful Life* shared Twain's acute recognition of an outworn romantic myth's capacity to disparage normal life. If the sound of a train whistle made George unhappy with what he had, the steamboat had done the same for Twain:

> When I was a boy [he wrote in *Life on the Mississippi*] there was but one permanent ambition among my comrades in our village on the west bank of the Mississippi River. That was to be a steamboatman. . . .
> Once a day a cheap, gaudy packet arrived upward from St. Louis, and another downward from Keokuk. Before these events, the day was glorious with expectation; after them, the day was a dead and empty thing.[10]

Twain knew too well that he was more like Tom Sawyer, the boy who lived on his imagination, than like Huck, the genuine outlaw hero. George Bailey was Tom Sawyer grown up. Like Tom, he considered drowning himself as a way out of his problems, a vaguely romantic solution that Huck would never have considered. In fact, the scene in Twain's novel, where Tom considers ending it all, was like a parody of *It's a Wonderful Life*, including even the flower petals:

He wandered far from the accustomed haunts of boys, and sought desolate places that were in harmony with his spirit. A log raft in the river invited him, and he seated himself on its outer edge and contemplated the dreary vastness of the stream, wishing, the while, that he could only be drowned, all at once and unconsciously, without undergoing the uncomfortable routine devised by nature. Then he thought of his flower. He got it out, rumpled and wilted, and it mightily increased his dismal felicity. (p. 27)

Tom's real wish resembled George's: "Ah, if he could only die *temporarily!*"

Both Twain and *It's a Wonderful Life* dealt with the power of myth to shape lives. In doing so, both were modern. With its hero frustrated by dreams of adventure that had no outlet, *It's a Wonderful Life* prefigured *Taxi Driver*, whose protagonist sought to impose his romantic experience of events (steeped in cowboy tales) on a world in which it no longer applied.

Individual versus Community: It's a Wonderful Life directly attacked the Classic Hollywood myth that a person could involve himself in the affairs of the community without losing his own individuality. In fact, the film repeatedly dramatized the costs of helping others. As an official hero, too unselfish to become the outlaw hero he wanted to be, George Bailey was forever coming to the rescue and paying for it. He jumped into an icy river to save his brother and lost his hearing in one ear. He stopped the pharmacist, Mr. Gower, from accidentally putting poison in a prescription and was beaten. (This rescue also caused him to hear Mr. Potter calling his father a failure.) His commitment to the Building and Loan cost him, in succession, his European trip, college, his honeymoon, and the glamorous careers offered him by Sam Wainwright and Mr. Potter. "I want to do what *I* want to do," he told Mary, but whatever that was, his sense of community clearly kept him from doing it.

As a way out of the impasse between the attractiveness of the outlaw hero's life, lived solely in terms of the self, and the need for community responsibility, the Classic Hollywood movie had proposed the archetypal American solution: the individual hero whose willingness to help society was pictured as a temporary departure from the natural and proper pattern of his life, which remained free of abiding entanglements. Involvement, then, represented only a momentary concession to emergency and not a genuine acknowledgment of society's claims. As Leo Marx has pointed out, such a view discredited politics in America; to make a *career* out of involvement was somehow suspect.[11]

It was also threatening. For George's series of commitments, originally conceived of as temporary, became a permanent trap. He would waive the Europe trip and stay home for three months to tide things over after his father's death. He would wait four years for Harry to come home from college. But his dreams of getting away never materialized. Mr. Potter recognized George's feelings exactly:

> Now if this young man of twenty-eight was a common, ordinary yokel, I'd say he was doing fine. But George Bailey is not a common, ordinary yokel. He is an intelligent, smart, ambitious young man who hates his job, who hates the Building and Loan almost as much as I do. A young man who has been dying to get out on his own ever since he was born. A young man—the smartest one of the crowd, mind you—who has to sit by and watch his friends go places because he's trapped, yes sir, trapped into frittering his life away, playing housemaid to a lot of garlic-eaters.

In George's frustration at being unable to extricate himself, there was an image of the central American anxiety of the postwar period—the fear that the crisis of World War II, to which the country had only committed itself at the last possible moment, had led to permanent international entanglements from which there would be no escape. Joseph's sad comment, "George never did leave Bedford Falls," was ominous: it seemed to mark the end of an era in American history. From now on, one could no longer solve a problem and light out again for the territory. America, like George, was trapped.

Similarly, George's feelings of futility, his sense that all of his sacrifices had accomplished nothing, mirrored the pervasive postwar disillusionment resulting from seeing the Nazis swiftly replaced by the Soviets. Neither George nor the American public had learned to think in terms of long-term problems requiring permanent responses, whose results could not be immediately measured. George's endless struggle with Potter, where the small gains and losses could be felt only over a period of years, represented a miniature Cold War, less clear-cut, more consuming, but ultimately as important as the glamorous war that Harry Bailey went off to fight. George's problem was America's: because so much of American culture supported the myth of the outlaw hero, whose commitments were only temporary and his results quick and sure, little support had developed for the idea that a permanently involved individual (or nation) could have a measurable impact on society. In Bedford Falls, Harry Bailey seemed the hero, not George.

Worldly Success versus Ordinary Life: It's a Wonderful Life frequently turned on the American attitudes toward success, whose inherent contradiction Robert Warshow called "our intolerable dilemma: that failure is a kind of death and success is evil and dangerous."[12] If ambition and striving signaled worth, the wealth and power those traits led to seemed inevitably associated in the American mythology with baseness. It was fine, in other words, to be on the make; it was somehow less fine to have made it.

Capra's juxtapositions repeatedly exposed this contradiction. We have seen that Joseph's description of Potter as "the richest and meanest man in the county" directly preceded George's "Wish I had a million dollars!" a wish repeated later in the movie. Further, George, as Potter recognized, was ambitious, but the film made clear that his decency precluded the kind of success associated with Potter's ruthlessness and Sam Wainwright's fast-talking opportunism. George, in fact, rejected offers from both. "Confound it, man," Potter shouted at George, "are you *afraid* of success?"

Sam Wainwright was the more ambiguous figure, a childhood friend of George, and ultimately to come to his aid. But he was also loud, unfaithful to Mary (being kissed by another girl as he telephoned Mary from New York), and an implied wartime profiteer. His products, plastics (not coincidentally, to become *The Graduate*'s code word for the inauthentic), were vaguely distasteful, unromantic (because inorganic) goods antithetical to the simple traditionalism of George's Bedford Falls.

Potter, however, was a pure, nineteenth-century, melodramatic villain obviously derived from Dickens's Scrooge. He tempted George with a devil's offer significantly couched entirely in worldly terms: a $20,000 per year job, the finest house in town, trips to New York, "maybe once in a while to Europe," fine clothes for Mary. Again, Capra's juxtaposition suggested the conflict between success and ordinary, decent life. Having rejected Potter's offer, recognizing it as a trick to destroy the Building and Loan,

George returned home to find that Mary was pregnant with the first of their four children. The soft-focus, peaceful lighting of George and Mary's bedroom noticeably contrasted with the harsh, direct tones of Potter's office.

It's a Wonderful Life's obvious efforts to associate wordly success with baseness could not overcome its simultaneous intimation that ordinary, unsuccessful life barely hid an almost constant desperation. In fact, the Baileys made little progress. The boy George, who had seen his father beg Potter for another month to raise $5,000 while Uncle Billy worried about the bank examiner, became the man who begged Potter for time to raise $8,000 to head off another audit. From the first, George had recognized the despair in ordinary life, becoming depressed by even the idea of returning to the Building and Loan:

I couldn't. . . . I couldn't face being cooped up the rest of my life in a shabby little office—I'm sorry, Pop. I didn't mean it, but . . . this business in nickels and dimes, spending all the rest of your life trying to figure out how to save three cents on a length of pipe—I'd go crazy.

Tocqueville had noticed this constant fear of poverty as characteristic of the American middle class:

. . . men whose comfortable existence is equally far from wealth and poverty set immense value on their possessions. As they are still very close to poverty, they see its privations in detail and are afraid of them; nothing but a scanty fortune, the cynosure of all their hopes and fears, keeps them from it. (p. 636)

It's a Wonderful Life repeatedly demonstrated the paradoxical nature of democracy noted by Tocqueville, its double potentiality for a freedom that was liberating and an anonymity that was terrifying.[13] For in a radically egalitarian society, only the thinnest edge separated an individual from submergence in the faceless mass. Potter, in fact, spoke constantly of the worthless "rabble," but the movie more graphically expressed ordinary life's anxieties in the recurring images, both real and metaphorical, of going under. Drowning was a crucial, overdetermined motif; George saved Harry who had fallen through the ice; Harry in turn saved a troop ship from being sunk by enemy planes; George contemplated drowning himself. In a comic variant, the gym floor opened to swallow up the dancers in the swimming pool below. The movie's plot turned on the Building and Loan's constant near-failures (an economic going under), and a bank run took place in a driving rain. The panic in George's voice, when he realized that Uncle Billy had lost the money, told what it was like to live an inch away from anonymity, and disgrace, and the ruin of total poverty. "Where's that money, you silly stupid old fool?" he shouted desperately. "Don't you know what this means?—it means bank-ruptcy, and scandal, and prison. One of us is going to jail and it isn't going to be me."

George Bailey, then, was caught between these contradictory attitudes toward success. He could not, it seemed, be both pros-perous and decent. Nor, however, could he choose comfortably between prosperity and ordinary life, for success carried with it the inevitability of meanness and ordinary life the terrible anx-iety of anonymity—a fear particularly powerful in a postwar American society suddenly stripped of the built-in sense of pur-pose provided by the war. George, *It's a Wonderful Life* sug-gested, had to choose, but he had nothing to choose between.

THE juxtapositional structure of *It's a Wonderful Life* implied that the irreconcilable contradictions inherent in American life had driven George Bailey to the point of suicide. The misplaced $8,000 was only the final breaking point that revealed George's half-hidden frustrations. Again, it was Mr. Potter who saw the truth, that George had never fulfilled his own lofty ambitions, had become trapped rather than free, and neither rich nor happy:

You used to be so cocky. You were going to go out and conquer the world. You once called me a "warped, frustrated old man." What are you but a warped, frustrated young man, a miserable little clerk beg-ging for help, no securities, no stocks, no bonds, nothing but a miserable little $500 equity in a life insurance policy. You're worth more dead than alive. Why don't you go to the riffraff you love so much and ask them to let you have your $8,000? You know why, because they'd run you out of town on a rail. . . . Go ahead, George, you can't hide in a town like this.

The overt intent of *It's a Wonderful Life* was to acknowledge George's dilemma and then solve it, to reaffirm the American

Dream by showing that the conflicts between opposed values were illusory. To succeed, the film had to demonstrate that a domestic, responsible, ordinary life contained possibilities for adventure, heroism, and success.

The means of that affirmation were implicit throughout the film. Mary's wedding-night surprise, a kind of makeshift campsite in the old, abandoned house, with chickens roasting over a fire, mixed adventure and domesticity, evoking a pilgrim couple's first night ashore, but undercutting it with the irony of travel posters and the atmosphere of decay. Similarly, George's ability to prevent a crippling run on the Building and Loan allowed him a moment of heroism comparable to the climax of John Ford's *Young Mr. Lincoln* (1939) where Lincoln had turned away a lynch mob. Finally, on some subconscious level, *It's a Wonderful Life* denied the contradiction between prosperity and a decent life: George, in fact, never looked too poor. His house may have had a loose knob on the bannister, but it had more of the solid comforts of Classic Hollywood houses, as in *Meet Me in St. Louis*, than it lacked.

But these subtle reconciliations could not entirely resolve the film's basic oppositions. Instead, the success of *It's a Wonderful Life* depended utterly on George's vision, provided him by Clarence: the chance to see what Bedford Falls would have been like if he had never been born. That vision was the movie's great trick. Without it, the film would have been unbearably bleak; with it, the movie managed to reaffirm the American Dream.

First, the vision set at rest the fear that a permanently involved individual, as opposed to the outlaw hero, could have no measurable impact on society. George, the vision showed, was not merely a hero; he was the center of the world on whom everything depended. Without him, Bedford Falls had become Pottersville, a *film noir* landscape of human wrecks and neon signs. Because George had not been born, Harry had died (and all the men on the troop transport as well, since there was no Harry to save them), the pharmacist Mr. Gower had gone to prison and become an alcoholic, Uncle Billy had gone mad, Martini had disappeared, Ernie the taxidriver was divorced, and Mary had become an old maid. Only George, the movie suggested, had prevented these things from happening. The vision also suggested that the individual-community contradiction rested on a misunderstanding, that true wisdom involved obeying the dictates of a generous conscience. For the nightmare of George's one-wish-come-true suggested that to give in to the desires of the self was to live in a world ruled by Mr. Potters.

It's a Wonderful Life also sought to resolve the incompatibility between success and ordinary life by asserting that the nagging fear of anonymity was to be associated not with the decent man in the bosom of society, but with the loner who had gone his own way. As Barbara Deming has pointed out, George had difficulty attending to Clarence's moral.[14] He seemed less concerned with what had happened to Bedford Falls without him than to the terrifying fact that no one recognized him. "This is George Bailey, don't you know me?" he pleaded to Mr. Gower, his mother, Ernie, Bert, and Mary. It was as if the haunting anxiety about being swallowed up in the void had come to pass:

GEORGE: If I wasn't born, who am I?
CLARENCE: You're nobody—you have no identity.
GEORGE: What do you mean, no identity? My name's George Bailey. [Looking for ID's]
CLARENCE: There is no George Bailey—you have no papers, no cards, no driver's license, no 4-F card, no insurance policy . . .

The movie taught that having friends was true success. As Harry Bailey toasted, "To my brother, George, the richest man in Bedford Falls."

Above all, the vision resolved *It's a Wonderful Life*'s crucial dichotomy, the apparent incompatibility of adventure and domesticity. By allowing George to see what the world would have been like without him, Clarence gave him an adventure greater than even he had ever imagined. Not surprisingly, because of George's kinship with Tom Sawyer, that adventure resembled Tom's trip to his own funeral, "the proudest moment of his life." The movie's lesson, in Clarence's words, was that "You see, George, you really had a wonderful life." The film's conclusion was nearly irresistible, with George restored to his life, standing beside the Christmas tree, little girl clinging around his neck, surrounded

by friends who had rallied to his need with more than enough money to cover the missing $8,000.

But like so many of the best postwar films, *It's a Wonderful Life* could not entirely allay the anxieties it had invoked. Troubling points resisted resolution. First, Potter, clearly the film's device for displacing its profound conflicts into the solvable realm of melodrama, escaped his anticipated comeuppance, even presumably keeping Uncle Billy's lost $8,000. To the extent that the movie isolated Potter as the cause of George's problems, the failure to call him to account constituted a serious weakness in the displacement mechanism—as if *Casablanca*'s Major Strasser had avoided Rick's retribution. Second, for a movie that sought to demonstrate the nobility of ordinary lives, *It's a Wonderful Life* implicitly discredited every common man but George, without whom average citizens became drunkards, poisoners, old maids, prostitutes, bullies, madmen, and embittered old women. Indeed, the movie's intended celebration of George's ordinary, and yet wonderful, life inadvertently demonstrated that life's necessarily extraordinary quality. Third, the film's desire to illustrate money's inferiority to friendship ended ironically in a sequence whose imagery implied that the extent of friendship could best be measured in terms of money.

More tellingly, *It's a Wonderful Life*'s style undercut Capra's intent to sweep away the pessimism of the movie's first three-

quarters. First, the interpenetration of the *noir* and Andy Hardy worlds (Pottersville versus Bedford Falls) intimated an unsettling sense of their proximity typical of the postwar period. *Kiss of Death* (1947), for example, a classic *film noir*, evoked sympathy for its working-class gangster hero (Victor Mature) by granting him a momentary haven whose imagery (children roller-skating, fences with swinging gates, a mother cooking in the kitchen) derived from the middle-class Andy Hardy world.

In Capra's film, the natural evolution of the movie's early street scenes into the Pottersville vision retroactively revealed the barely controlled *noir* elements existing just beneath the surface of Classic Hollywood's stock imagery. George, Bert, and Ernie ogling humorously at the passing Vi (played, significantly, by the actress subsequently to become one of the queens of *noir*, Gloria Grahame), the prowling George eyeing a strange woman and proposing a night on the mountain to Vi—these scenes invoked a thinly repressed sexuality that erupted explicitly in Pottersville where Vi had become a prostitute. The middle scene was obviously transitional, its nighttime setting and more overt sexual play prefiguring George's frightening vision. Further, the remarkable similarities between all of *It's a Wonderful Life*'s street sequences (all depended primarily on tracking and point-of-view shots) made formally explicit how easily an Andy Hardy setting could be converted to the *noir* world through slightly tilted cameras, more rapid (and thus dizzying) tracking shots, and the addition of neon signs and a jazz soundtrack. More than anything, this formal demonstration irretrievably confirmed the presence of the previously repressed *noir* world in the body of the Classic Hollywood mythology.

Significantly, *It's a Wonderful Life*'s challenge to Classic Hollywood's thematic paradigm occurred most obviously in Capra's frame (Joseph explaining George's life to Clarence), where the normally invisible ideological mechanism became apparent, and a viewer could become aware of the cinematic apparatus. Thus, as Joseph introduced George to Clarence, Capra imitated a focusing projector, gradually allowing the blurred picture of the boys to become clear. A few minutes later, as Clarence watched George ask for a suitcase worthy of an Arabian Nights' adventure, Capra ironically froze the image. While a few Hollywood films had previously used freeze frames in opening credits (*The Palm Beach Story*, 1942) or as a final shot (*The Philadelphia Story*, 1940), their introduction into the body of a film was more startling and signaled a more overt departure from the formal paradigm's traditional invisibility.

The obviously nostalgic and fanciful quality of Capra's devices further subverted his intended resolution. The Currier and Ives styled titles, the opening "You Are Now in Bedford Falls" sign, the talking stars, the literal *deus ex machina* solution all implied failed beliefs desperately retained, an awareness that conflicting desires could now be resolved only in obvious fantasy. Indeed, the whole last part of the movie seemed to exist in a kind of

GEORGE: Hey, I . . . I'm a rich tourist today. How 'bout driving me home in style? BERT: Well! . . . Yes, sir! ERNIE: Hop in, your highness, hop in. And for the carriage trade . . . I put on my hat.

VI: Good afternoon, Mr. Bailey. GEORGE: *Hello,* Violet.

GEORGE: Hey, you look *good.* That's some dress you got on there.

: What? This old thing? Why I only wear it hen I don't care how I look.

ERNIE: How would you like to . . . GEORGE:
Yessss . . .

VI: *Excuse* me . . . MAN ON RIGHT: Now wait a minute . . . VI: I think I gotta date. But, uh, stick around, fellas, just in case, huh? MAN ON LEFT: We'll wait for you, baby.

VI: Hello, Georgy Porgy. GEORGE: Hullo, Vi . . . VI: Hey, what gives? GEORGE: Uh . . . nothing.

VI: Where're you going? GEORGE: I'm . . . probably end up down at the library. VI: Georgie, don't you ever get tired of just reading about things? GEORGE: Yes—what're you doing tonight? VI: Not a thing. GEORGE: Are you game, Vi? Let's make a night of it? VI: Oh, I'd love it, Georgie. What'll we do? GEORGE: Let's go out in the fields and take off our shoes and walk through the grass. VI: Huh? GEORGE: Then we can go up the falls—it's beautiful up there in the moonlight. And there's a green pool up there, and we can . . . uh, swim in it. And then we can climb Mt. Bedford and smell the pines and watch the sunrise against the peaks, and we'll stay up there the whole night, and everybody'll be talking, and there'll be a terrific scandal—what about it? VI: Georgie, have you gone crazy? GEORGE: No, now listen, Vi . . . VI: Walk in the grass in my bare feet?

VI: Why it's ten miles up to Mt. Bedford.

GEORGE: Shh, shh, shh—oh, oh, OK. Just forget about the whole thing.

GEORGE: Hey! Hey!

GEORGE: Hey! Where'd the Building and Loan move to?

POLICEMAN: The Building and *what*? GEORGE: The Bailey Building and Loan. It was up there. POLICEMAN: That went out of business years ago.

VI: And I say he's a liar! I know every big shot in this town! I know Potter and I'll have you kicked off the . . . every big shot in this town.

GEORGE: Violet! Hey! Hey! Listen, that's Violet Bick! POLICEMAN: I know. GEORGE: I *know* that girl. POLICEMAN: Take a walk. Beat it.

conditional syntax, as if to say, "This *could* be so if you are willing to believe it." The evident strain involved in achieving the film's happy ending implied that what had once been guaranteed as a part of the American landscape itself, now rested only on the most precarious faith. What had once been manifest had become a matter of belief.

More than any other character of the movie, George Bailey recognized that the American Dream was no longer a given, that it depended on the will of its adherents. "We can get through this thing all right," he pleaded with the Building and Loan customers during a run on the bank. "We've got to stick together, though; we've got to have faith in each other." George's problem was that he was the most prone to doubt, most aware of the

inherent contradictions in the fabric of American life. It was no
accident that in the movie's most obviously overdetermined image, George, as another character observed, was "standing right
over that crack" that opened under the feet of the dancers in the
high school gym, no accident that he was the first to fall into the
water below—a comic image of the abyss that was eerily disturbing.

George experienced the movie's most pessimistic truth, that
the value attached to even our most cherished objects—Christmas, home, marriage, family, life itself—rested on the thinnest
tissue of sustaining faith that could be torn by the most random
of accidents (such as Uncle Billy's loss of the deposit funds).
Without that faith, even these cherished things became night-
marish. "It's this drafty old house," George exploded in frustration. "Why did we have to live here in the first place and stay
around this measly, crummy old town? Who says this is such a
happy family? Why do we have to have all these kids?"

It was this glimpse of the utter emptiness of American life that
remained despite the film's happy ending. In fact, only the barest
difference existed between 1946's *It's a Wonderful Life* (whose
hero had learned to give up his dreams of adventure to settle for
Clarence's maxim that "*no* man is a failure who has *friends*")
and Arthur Miller's 1947 *Death of a Salesman* (whose hero had
missed the chance to go to Alaska and settled for being "well-

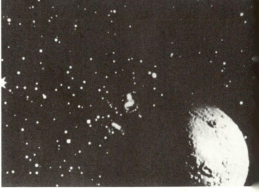

liked"). Only the will to keep on believing in the traditional pattern of reconciliation made *It's a Wonderful Life* into at least a superficially optimistic story. That almost everyone cried at the end suggested the audience's sense of how narrow the escape had been for that pattern and for the faith behind it.

THE MAN WHO SHOT LIBERTY VALANCE

Made toward the end of the postwar period by Classic Hollywood's most decorated filmmaker (six Academy Awards),[15] John Ford's *The Man Who Shot Liberty Valance* (1962) provided both a summary of and a eulogy for the traditional reconciliatory pattern. As William Pechter wrote, in the best essay on the movie (and on Ford in general), "the uniqueness of *The Man Who Shot Liberty Valance* consists in its bringing into explicitness what has for so long lain beneath the surface." The effect, Pechter observed, "is of a lecture-demonstration . . . a summing-up."[16] In fact, *Valance* used almost all of the classic oppositions central to American literature's and popular cinema's traditional mythology (West-East, individual-community, wilderness-civilization), but, unlike *Red River*, traced the implications of these conflicts to their logical conclusions.

Not surprisingly, the movie's plot was another version of the outlaw hero-official hero story. It opened with a shot of a train steaming through a western landscape, evoking the fundamental wilderness-civilization polarity described by Leo Marx in *The Machine in the Garden*. The train arrived at the small, but obviously bustling town of Shinbone where an old man, Link Appleyard (Andy Devine), waited on the platform for two visitors, Senator Ransom Stoddard (James Stewart) and his wife Hallie (Vera Miles), both also visibly aged. Link apparently had been the town marshal, but not for some time: "I reckon the only one of us from the old days still working steady is the Senator," he explained to Hallie, who remarked almost sadly, "Place sure has changed—churches, high schools, shops." "The railroad done that," Link replied, confirming Leo Marx's point that "the locomotive . . . is the leading symbol of the new industrial power . . . a power that does not remain confined to the traditional boundaries of the city."[17]

While Stoddard gave a rather pompous interview to a gathering of newspapermen, Link drove Hallie by buckboard to the ruins of a burned-out house where he sat in silence while she picked a cactus rose. Back at the platform, Stoddard, under questioning, admitted that he had returned to Shinbone for the funeral of one Tom Doniphon, a name not recognized by even the local reporters. Stoddard volunteered nothing further, but went instead to the undertaker's where he became angry that Doniphon's body had apparently been stripped of boots, spurs, and gunbelt. Link, however, corrected him on one point: "He didn't carry no handgun, Ranse," he said quietly; "he didn't for years." The undertaker had taken the boots, trying to recoup his losses for what would be a pauper's funeral. "The county's gonna bury him," he told Stoddard. "Gosh, I ain't gonna make a nickel out of it."

Pressed by the local editor to account for his presence at the funeral of a complete unknown, Stoddard finally gave in and began his story which, in yet another postwar-period flashback, became the body of the film. Describing himself as "a youngster, fresh out of law school" who "had taken Horace Greeley's advice literally—'Go West, young man, go West, and seek fame, fortune, and adventure,'" Stoddard told about his arrival in Shinbone (from this point until the film's end, the voice-over narration disappeared). The flashback's first shot showed a stagecoach whose direction and movement exactly matched that of the train in the movie's opening scene. Oddly, however, the action was now occurring on what was obviously a set. Civilization's precarious hold in the West abruptly became evident as the stage was ambushed by Liberty Valance's gang, and Stoddard brutally whipped and beaten for trying to protect a woman. "What kind of man *are* you?" he shouted at Valance (Lee Marvin). "*This* kind, Dude," Valance answered, hitting him across the face; "now, what kind of man are *you*?" Told by Stoddard that he was a lawyer, Valance became angrier still, ripping up the young man's lawbooks while he beat him: "Lawyer, huh? Well, I'll teach you law—*western* Law."

The film cut from this scene to show Stoddard being brought into town in the back of Tom Doniphon's (John Wayne) buckboard—the first of many sequences in the movie's first half in which Ranse's horizontal posture suggested his weakness when compared to Tom's dominant verticality (a contrast reversed in the frame story).[18] In town, Ranse was treated by Tom's girl, Hallie, and his black servant, Pompey. Reviving, Ranse spoke determinedly of putting Valance in jail, but Tom, standing over him, and patronizingly referring to him as "Pilgrim," let him know how things were in the West. "I know those lawbooks mean a lot to you," Tom said, making the classic distinction, "but not out here. Out here, a man settles his own problems." Stoddard was flabbergasted by this frankly extralegal code: "Do you know what you're saying to me? You're saying just exactly what Liberty Valance said. What kind of community have I come to?" Only Hallie was sympathetic, admitting that "a little law and order around Shinbone wouldn't hurt anyone." Tom, however, was practical, warning Stoddard that "Liberty Valance is the toughest man south of the Picketwire—next to me."

Without clients for his would-be law practice, Stoddard found work as a dishwasher in Hallie's restaurant, where he was humiliated further by having to wear an apron. Clearly, however, he had begun to provoke Tom's jealousy by teaching Hallie to read and write, and by describing to her the attractions of civilization, represented throughout the film by the image of the rose, opposed to its wilderness counterpart, the desert-flowering cactus rose. Tom, however, appeared in no hurry to commit himself to marriage: "Don't rush me, don't rush me," he told his friend, newspaper editor Dutton Peabody (Edmund O'Brien).

The film's first showdown took place in the restaurant, as Valance tripped up Ranse as he waited tables. Only the presence of Tom (once again standing over the horizontal Stoddard) kept Valance away, a fact quickly pointed out to the lawyer:

TOM: Now I wonder what scared him off?

PEABODY: You know what scared him off: The spectacle of law and order here, risin' up out of the gravy and mashed potatoes.

RANSE: All right, all right, You made your point. It was the gun that scared him off—Pompey's gun, your gun, Tom.

But Stoddard was adamant: "I'm staying, and I'm not buying a gun."

Instead, he became Shinbone's schoolteacher, thereby taking on yet another role normally assumed by women, working in a classroom with portraits of Washington and Lincoln, and with a motto on the blackboard: "Education is the basis of law and order." The lessons were interrupted, however, by the returning Tom, who announced angrily the imminent arrival of Liberty Valance, hired by the cattle interests to take by force the town's seat at the statehood convention and to cast his vote for keeping the territory an open range. Confronted with this new threat, Ranse yielded ("When force threatens, talk's no good anymore"), taking shooting lessons from Tom, whose principal interest appeared to lie in establishing that "Hallie's *my* girl."

At the town meeting, Tom's own refusal of the nomination ("I got other plans, *personal* plans") and his help in securing it for Ranse inadvertently led to a second showdown between Ranse and Valance, conducted after dark on the main street of town. Despite a wounded arm and his own poor gunmanship, Stoddard somehow managed to kill Valance. Tom arrived at Hallie's to find her lovingly caring for Ranse. Aware now that she had transferred her affection to Stoddard, Tom said very little: "Sorry I got here too late. . . . I'll be around." His stoicism, however, was only a mask. Back in the saloon, he began drinking heavily, and, in a rage, drove Valance's remaining two henchmen out of town. Then, in the film's starkest scene, Tom returned home, and still drunk, deliberately set fire to the house he had been building for Hallie. Pompey appeared at the last moment to drag him to safety.

The scene shifted suddenly to the territorial convention, the placards, windy speechmaking, and general festiveness contrasting sharply with the grimness of what had just transpired. This world now belonged recognizably to Stoddard, but once again Tom was needed. Having heard his name placed in nomination to become the Territory's representative to Washington to plead the cause of statehood, Ranse suddenly left the hall, appalled at hearing himself described as "the man who shot Liberty Valance." ("Isn't it enough to kill a man without trying to build a life on it?") At this moment, Tom reappeared, looking haggard, unshaven, and out of place. In a flashback-within-a-flashback, Tom revealed that *he* had killed Liberty Valance, firing with a rifle from an alley across the street when it became obvious that Ranse had no chance—"Cold-blooded murder," he admitted to Stoddard, "but I can live with it." His reasons, he explained, were utterly personal: "Hallie's happy; she wanted you alive." "But you saved my life," Ranse protested. "I wish I hadn't," Tom answered roughly. "Hallie's your girl now. Go on back in there and take that nomination. You've taught her to read and write. Now give her something to read and write about."

And, of course, he did, becoming the state's first governor, and in the list reeled off by the listening editor (as the movie returned to the present), "three terms a governor, two terms in the Senate, ambassador to the Court of St. James, back again in the Senate, and a man who, with the snap of his fingers, could be the next Vice President of the United States." "You're not going to use the story?" Stoddard asked. "No, sir. This is the West, sir; when the legend becomes fact, print the legend."

Leaving town on the train, Stoddard asked Hallie if she would like to come back to Shinbone to live. "If you knew how often I'd dreamed of it," she said simply. "My roots are here. . . . Look at it—it was once a wilderness, now it's a garden. Aren't you proud?" Then as the train wound out into the countryside, reversing the direction of the film's opening shot, Ranse thanked the railroad conductor for the fine treatment, only to hear the final irony, "Nothing's too good for the man who shot Liberty Valance."

Like *Casablanca, The Man Who Shot Liberty Valance* organized itself around certain schematic oppositions that revealed themselves as the story progressed:

East	West
Ranse	Tom
train/stagecoach	buckboard/horse
lawbook	gun/whip
weakness	strength
legal system	private justice
idealism	pragmatism
coffee	whiskey
apron	gunbelt
shoes	boots
words	action
mental	physical
rose	cactus rose
law office/schoolroom	saloon
literacy	illiteracy
fences	open range
statehood	territory
community	individual
politician	private man
conscience	pride
married	unmarried
fame	anonymity
prosperity	poverty
life	death
civilization	wilderness

Clearly, too, the film made some attempts at reconciling these divisions, showing the interpenetration of the two sets of values, postures, and lifestyles. Thus, the westerner, Tom Doniphon, was not entirely a man of the open range, living instead just outside town on a small spread surrounded by fences. Also significantly, his own unwillingness to serve as the town's representative did not prevent his taking an active role in local meetings and intervening against Liberty Valance on Ranse's behalf. If Doniphon was not the utterly private man he seemed to be, neither was Stoddard a pure representative of law and order. Challenged by Valance, he went to meet him with a gun. With its opposing heroes taking on each other's traits, *The Man Who Shot Liberty Valance* adopted Classical Hollywood's standard means for further demonstrating their complementariness: both loved the same woman, and both were necessary to defeat Valance, for although it was Tom who did the actual shooting, it was Ranse who brought the issue to a head.

With its two strong, complementary heroes situated in a love triangle, *The Man Who Shot Liberty Valance* had much in common with Ford's 1946 western *My Darling Clementine*. (Joseph McBride and Michael Wilmington have even called *Valance* the "remake" of *Clementine*.)[19] More important, however, was the extent to which both *Clementine* and *Valance* reworked the non-western *Casablanca*'s version of Classic Hollywood's thematic paradigm. All three stories dramatized the cooperation between an outlaw hero (Rick Blaine, Doc Holliday, Tom Doniphon) and an official hero (Victor Laszlo, Wyatt Earp, Ransom Stoddard), working together against a common enemy (Nazis, Clantons, cattle interests) who provided a displacing focus for larger anxieties. All these stories pictured both heroes in love with the same woman (Ilsa, Clementine, Hallie) who eventually transferred her allegiance from the outlaw to the official hero. All three stories portrayed the outlaw hero's initial reluctance to get involved as overcome, not by new-found idealism, but by personal motivations (Rick and Tom acting to insure the happiness of the woman they were losing, Doc seeking revenge for his murdered dance-hall girl).

At several points, the three movies bore startling similarities, repeating specific motifs and incidents almost exactly. *My Darling Clementine*'s early scenes, for example, which prepared the way for, and then introduced, the outlaw hero Doc Holliday, contained obvious echoes of *Casablanca*'s early sequences. Significantly, both Rick and Doc preferred the saloon as their natural terrain, and both treated women with an identical callousness. The first mutually respectful meetings between Wyatt and Doc and Rick and Laszlo both occurred in saloons and both prompted similar shot-reverse shot sequences (although Ford's violated the 180° rule). (See p. 90 for *Casablanca* scene.) Further, Rick's an-

YVONNE: Where were you last night? RICK: That's so long ago I don't remember. YVONNE: Will I see you tonight? RICK: I never make plans that far in advance.

CHIHUAHUA: Say, Mac, I . . . I hear Doc's comin' back tonight. MAC: Maybe he is and maybe he ain't; I ain't heard. CHIHUAHUA: Well . . . do you know where he's been? MAC: Tucson? over the border? . . . who knows where Doc goes.

DOC: Why don't you go away and squawl your stupid little songs and leave me alone.

WYATT: Howdy. DOC: Good evening. WYATT: I'm . . . DOC: Wyatt Earp— I know. I know all about you . . .

DOC: . . . and your reason for being here. WYATT: I've heard a lot about you, too. Doc. You left your mark around in Deadwood, Denver, and places.

SAM: Boss, ain't you goin' to bed? RICK: Not right now. SAM: Ain't you plannin' on goin' to bed in the near future? RICK: No. SAM: Well, I ain't sleepy neither. RICK: Good, then have a drink. SAM: No, not me, boss. RICK: Don't have a drink. SAM: Boss, let's get out of here.

TOM: Pour yourself a drink, Pompey. POMPEY: You know I don't drink no drams, Mister Tom. TOM: I said take a drink. POMPEY: No, sir. We got a mare in foal and horses to feed and water. Come on home. TOM: Home sweet home. You're right, Pompey. We got plenty to do at home.

tisocial "the problems of the world are not in my department" matched Doc's challenge to Wyatt, "I hope you haven't taken it into your head to deliver us from evil," and his frank recognition, "I see we're in opposite camps, Marshal."

In *Casablanca, Clementine,* and *Valance,* the outlaw hero's drunk scene (prompted in each case by a woman) provided the most affecting moment. The emotional power of these sequences, particularly those in *Casblanca* and *Valance,* betrayed their obvious overdetermination. In each, the ideological mechanism momentarily surfaced, showing the strain now involved in effecting the traditional reconciliation between a vanishing individualism and an ascendant community. *Valance*'s Pompey and Tom even repeated the black man-white man motif of *Casablanca*'s Sam and Rick.

Despite the cracks in the once-seamless thematic paradigm, however, *Valance* ultimately employed a reconciliatory pattern identical to those of *Casablanca* and *Clementine,* using the woman as the occasion for Tom and Ranse to work together (as had Rick and Laszlo, Doc and Wyatt) to achieve what neither could have done alone.

THE STRIKING resemblances among *Casablanca, My Darling Clementine*, and *The Man Who Shot Liberty Valance* suggested that Hollywood's repetition of certain tropes resulted from something more profound than conscious decisions to rework particular stories. Clearly, American movies drew on a store of motifs that had become coded, detachable units, capable of migrating from film to film.[20] Their recurring appearances in widely dissimilar genres indicated the extent to which each Hollywood movie, far from being created from scratch, was mediated through an inherited mythology and structured around a received thematic paradigm. This fundamentally intertextual nature of American movies transformed Classic Hollywood's entire product into a kind of large, single genre to which Robert Warshow's remarks on the western equally applied: "It is an art form for connoisseurs, where the spectator derives his pleasure from the appreciation of minor variations within the working-out of a pre-established order."[21]

In the American Cinema, these "minor variations," far from being insignificant, typically accounted for the extraordinarily different effects produced by two superficially identical movies. *Valance*, for example, despite its apparent resemblances to *Casablanca* and *Clementine* and its adherence to the traditional reconciliatory pattern, was disturbing in a way that the other two were not. *Valance*, in fact, replaced *Casablanca*'s and *Clementine*'s optimistic reaffirmations of the thematic paradigm with an elegiac acknowledgment of loss. Robin Wood described *Clementine* in terms equally applicable to *Casablanca*: "Its complexities are experienced as resolvable in a constructive way, the different values embodied in East and West, in civilization and wilderness felt to be ultimately reconcilable and mutually fertilizing."[22]

Certainly, *Clementine* achieved much of that feeling by blurring the lines between outlaw and official hero so that their surface disagreements would only emphasize their essential similarity. Thus, while Wyatt was obviously part outlaw (a skilled gambler and gunman, initially reluctant to take the job as marshal, and finally leaving town without Clementine), Doc was just as clearly part official hero (with Boston origins, a medical de-

gree, and the ability to recite speeches from *Hamlet*). Their ultimate reconciliation, therefore, came as no surprise.

Because of its simple optimism, Ford thought of *Clementine*, "as essentially a film for children."[23] *The Man Who Shot Liberty Valance* was stronger medicine. That Ranse's rise came at Tom's expense suggested the historical incompatibility of outlaw and official values. Even more pessimistically, the film suggested Tom's fall had been inevitable and, in fact, accomplished by his own hands. For in killing Valance, Doniphon destroyed the very conditions that made him, rather than Stoddard, a hero. In a more civilized community, rid of outlaws and on its way to statehood, the power shifted from the private man with a gun to the public man with a lawbook. Tom's bitter admission to Ranse, "Hallie's *your* girl now," indicated that he knew, if Ranse did not, what an immense change had taken place.

Significantly, *Liberty Valance*'s crucial revelation of Tom's role in Valance's death discredited the most basic figure in Classic Hollywood's formal paradigm—the shot-reverse shot. The audience's acceptance of this figure had always depended on the tacit guarantee that nothing narratively important lay outside the seam of significance isolated from the larger space by shot-reverse shot patterns. Sustained shot-reverse shot sequences repeatedly confirmed that guarantee. In *The Man Who Shot Liberty Valance*, Ranse's showdown with Valance occurred in such

a sequence, with twenty-four shots conclusively reducing the viewer's area of concern to the thin strip of space between the two men. Only a later flashback revealed that Tom had shot Valance from a position that the twenty-four-shot sequence had systematically kept offscreen. In demonstrating that crucial narrative developments could take place outside the seam established by such a classically rigorous sequence, Doniphon's confession undermined the invisible style itself, exposing the guarantee on which its most fundamental figure rested as a mere cinematic convention. Most important, by implying that every camera setup and editing pattern resulted from exclusionary choices, this formal rupture expressed the flashback's thematic insistence that Ranse had triumphed at Tom's expense.

In earlier movies, Ford had similarly denied his audience the optimum vantage point on critical actions. *Young Mr. Lincoln* used a cutaway reaction shot (to the Clay brothers' mother) and a long shot of the fight to conceal the actual murder of Scrub White. In *Stagecoach*'s final shootout, Ford withheld the concluding reverse shot to postpone revealing the results until Luke staggered into the bar fatally wounded. Neither of these sequences, however, matched *Valance*'s fundamental challenge to the formal paradigm. Ford's suppression of *Stagecoach*'s final reverse shot amounted to only an undisguised storytelling ploy immediately resolved two shots later. *Young Mr. Lincoln*'s trickery,

more problematic, had precedents in detective stories (as in *The Maltese Falcon*'s scene that showed only the shoes of Miles Archer's murderer), where the audience consented to a less-than-optimum vantage point for the sake of the narrative game. With their handful of shots, neither sequence achieved the finality that made *Valance*'s twenty-four-shot series seem so complete and its subsequent retraction so shattering.

In an earlier café confrontation between Stoddard and Valance, Ford had formally prefigured this ruptured shot-reverse shot, allowing Tom to move from offscreen-right (his identical position during the critical showdown) into a narrow seam previously isolated by five reverse shots of Ranse and Liberty. Here, however, Doniphon's intervention ("That's *my* steak, Valance") was less formally disturbing. By directly preceding the reverse series with a shot of Tom, Ford had established his proximity to the subsequently developing action and had made his offscreen presence felt throughout the Ranse-Liberty exchange.

The Man Who Shot Liberty Valance's discredited shot-reverse shot sequence represented one of its "minor variations" on Classic Hollywood's basic paradigms. What also made *Valance* different from *Casablanca* and *My Darling Clementine* was the frame story, which revealed the effects of history on the traditional American mythology. *Casablanca* and *Clementine*, by ending with the moment of victorious collaboration, had avoided confronting the threat of time. Both films had assumed the continued viability of the outlaw hero's lifestyle, with Rick bound for the Free French garrison at Brazzaville, and Wyatt (who after Doc's heroic death had assumed at least a quasi-outlaw role) for California. But in *Valance*, the dark side of the outlaw hero life appeared: anonymity, poverty, and a pauper's funeral in a town where no one knew Doniphon's name. This end was Terry Malloy's (*On the Waterfront*) fear come true, without even a glamorous last stand to go out on. To imagine how much had been lost between *Casablanca* and *Valance*, one must imagine a different *Casablanca*, with an opening frame in which Victor Laszlo, secretary-general of the United Nations, appears in Casablanca for the funeral of an unknown Rick Blaine.

The impossibility of determining Ford's preference between *Valance*'s two heroes and two sets of values made the film simultaneously powerful and bleak. Throughout, the movie implied their incompatibility and the necessity for choosing between them. (Indeed, history *had* chosen.) Still more troublingly, *Valance* suggested that the inherent equivocalness of both sets of values made any choice treacherous. For as it progressed, the story disclosed the intrinsic ambiguity of almost every image, issue, action, and character. The railroad that ran straight to Washington and brought progress to Shinbone also filled the sky with black smoke (an effect deliberately exaggerated in the opening sequence). Violence was both ugly and necessary, and even statehood a mixed blessing. The film's attitude toward Ranse's civilizing efforts seemed taken from Freud's *Civilization and Its Discontents*: education, however attractive, involved repression (Ranse ordered hats off in the classroom, corrected grammar, ordered children to be quiet), marriage, a loss of spontaneous vitality (the loud, cheerful Hallie was transformed into a sober, stern woman). The outlaw values were no less equivocal. Tom's strength and self-sufficiency made him attractive but also too much like Liberty Valance for comfort. As Ranse pointed out, both lived by the same private, violent code ("Out here a man settles his own problems"). To dramatize their similarity, Ford had Tom and Valance play the same trick on Ranse, shooting holes in a container to splatter him with liquid. Neither called Ranse by his name, Tom using the patronizing "Pilgrim," Valance the equally disrespectful "Dude."[24]

The film's ambiguity was furthered by having the conflict played out between John Wayne and James Stewart, the two biggest box office stars of the period from 1946 to 1966. In both *Casablanca* (with official hero Paul Henreid) and *My Darling Clementine* (with outlaw hero Victor Mature), one of the poles had been emotionally weaker, overmatched by the presence of a bigger, more affecting star. But *Valance* kept the struggle on an equal footing, between two men with markedly contrasting personae, Wayne's implacably anachronistic, Stewart's uncertainly contemporary. That both were attractive was the film's point. Which was more beautiful, the cultivated or the cactus rose?

The movie, then, refused to idealize either possibility: if the wilderness condition was dangerous and brutal, civilization was drab and uniform. The tacit criticism of civilization was particularly unsettling coming from Ford, who, in movies like *Drums Along the Mohawk* (1939), *Young Mr. Lincoln* (1939), and *Wagonmaster* (1950), had been Hollywood's greatest advocate of community and progress. *Valance*, in effect, not only reversed Ford's previous confidence in the results of history, but also overturned the basic pattern of the western, and in doing so, suggested a growing American disillusionment. The classical western had never relied on any suspense as to the outcome of the wilderness-civilization struggle—we always knew how that had turned out. But the almost total absence of sadness associated with the passing of the frontier (and the attitudes that went with it) had depended on our sense that it had turned out well—that the victorious civilization was what we had hoped it would be. To begin to see that victory in an ambiguous light, however, implied a new awareness of contemporary difficulties. Similarly, by redirecting the western's focus from the present to the past, *Valance* implied an erosion of the progressive vision that Americans had historically assumed as their birthright. Replacing this vision was a new nostalgia, not merely for the precivilized state, but for the brief moment when *both* were possible, the power and freedom of Tom, the decency and wisdom of Ranse.

An awareness of the tragedy involved in the loss of the American wilderness was a postwar innovation in the western, a form whose previous optimism had rested on the assumption of an unendingly progressive future whose merit would justify the historical sacrifice. The equivocal nature of that sacrifice, however, was an established theme in American literature, particularly in the work of William Faulkner. Significantly, Faulkner's reputation rose only after World War II, when his suspicion of civilization became a pervasive element of even the popular cinema. It was no accident that Ford did his greatest work in the same period, for, in fact, there were remarkable similarities between Ford and Faulkner. Both were romantic, rhetorical regionalists, given to low comedy and celebrations of traditional authority (military, family, conventions, etiquette). Both worked from a pronounced historical sense that frequently prompted an acute examination of the narrative process itself, and the discrepancy between truth and legend (e.g., *Absalom, Absalom!; Fort Apache; The Man Who Shot Liberty Valance*). Above all, both were preoccupied with the wilderness-civilization struggle.

In fact, *Valance* repeated the pattern and motifs of Faulkner's greatest story, "The Bear." Tom and Ranse's cooperative war against the unrestrained Valance, Tom's fall, and the railroad's destruction of the wilderness all had their analogues in "The Bear." The great bear himself, an "apotheosis of the old wild life," resembled Liberty Valance, free and untamed, but terribly destructive. Faulkner's description of him suggested a roughneck's Saturday night spree:

... the long legend of corn-cribs broken down and rifled, of shoats and grown pigs and even calves carried bodily into the woods and devoured and traps and deadfalls over-thrown and dogs mangled and slain and shotgun and rifle shots delivered at point-blank range yet with no more effect than so many peas blown through a tube by a child—a corridor of wreckage and destruction beginning back before the boy was born. . . .[25]

Valance invoked the identical paradox: to destroy this dangerous, anarchic wildness was to destroy the wilderness itself, and with it, some better part of American life. Thus, despite the necessity of the hunt, "there was a fatality in it. . . . It was like the last act on a set stage. It was the beginning of the end of something." (p. 226) Specifically, it was the beginning of the end for Boon, who in killing the bear, as with Tom's killing Valance, destroyed the very conditions of his own lifestyle. Boon in Memphis was like Tom at the convention:

But in Memphis it was not all right. It was as if the high buildings and the hard pavements, the fine carriages and the horse cars and the men in starched collars and neckties made their [Boon's and Ike's] boots and khaki look a little rougher and a little muddier and made Boon's beard look worse and unshaven and his face look more and more like he should never have brought it out of the woods at all. . . . (p. 231)

The bear's death, then, like Liberty Valance's, initiated the death of the frontier and the freedom it had supported. In fact, both *The Man Who Shot Liberty Valance* and "The Bear" were set in the same decade of American history (1873-1883),[26] and both used the locomotive as the image of advancing civilization. That Faulkner regarded this advance as a fall from Eden was indicated by his comparison of the train to a snake. Returning to the woods a few years after the hunt, Ike was amazed by the changes— the new planing mill, the miles of stacked steel rails, the tents for the workers:

Then the little locomotive shrieked and began to move: a rapid churning of exhaust, a lethargic deliberate clashing of slack couplings traveling backward along the train. . . . and from the cupola he watched the train's head complete the first and only curve in the entire line's length and vanish into the wilderness, dragging its length of train behind it so

that it resembled a small dingy harmless snake vanishing into weeds.
. . . (p. 318)

. . . yet this time it was as though the train (and not only the train but
himself. . . .) had brought with it into the doomed wilderness even before
the actual axe the shadow and the portent of the new mill not even
finished yet and the rails and ties which were not even laid. . . . (p. 321)

In contrast to *The Man Who Shot Liberty Valance*, however,
"The Bear," with its pronounced hostility toward civilization and
its nostalgic vision of the wilderness as an idyllic retreat, remained a straightforward, relatively uncomplicated pastoral.
Unlike Faulkner, Ford refused to idealize either of the poles:
Valance implied that Tom was a tragic figure *and* that Ranse
was right.

Ford's more complicated pastoralism resembled that of James
Fenimore Cooper. Like *The Leatherstocking Tales, Liberty Valance* worked from an inverted chronology, beginning with the
end of the outlaw hero's era (*Valance*'s frame matching Cooper's
device of starting with *The Pioneers*' image of Natty Bumppo as
an old man, and working backwards to the glorious youth of *The
Deerslayer*). By showing the results of an action before its causes,
both *Valance* and *The Leatherstocking Tales* established a double
time-consciousness that determined that our perception of earlier events would be shaped by our knowledge of their ultimate
outcome. A loss of innocence was implicit in this method, a com-
plication of the simple idea of heroism. One could no longer take
the exploits of Tom Doniphon and Natty Bumppo at face value
knowing what they had become—poor, old, and anachronistic.
Similarly, the inverted chronology of *Valance* and *The Leatherstocking Tales* discredited the optimistic American assumption
that history and myth were, if not identical, at least compatible.
Instead, in these stories, as A. N. Kaul has pointed out about
Cooper, "history and myth function in a mutual critique":[27] subsequent events not only disproved the original myths, but also
revealed how far short of the promise of those myths our history
had fallen.

Of all Cooper's novels, *Valance* most resembled the first of *The
Leatherstocking Tales, The Pioneers*. The simultaneously flawed
and compelling quality of Ford's movies and Cooper's books de-

rived from the paradox that in both authors, an overt allegiance to civilization was continually opposed by an intuitive sense of its destructiveness—a sense conveyed in Cooper by the character of Natty Bumppo, a figure who seemed to have risen almost against his author's will. Like *Valance*, *The Pioneers* depicted the clash between an outlaw hero (Natty) and an official hero (Judge Temple). The two stories began identically, with a frame, taking place thirty years after the main events, that described a return to a former wilderness, now transformed into a civilized garden. In *Valance*, Hattie noted the "churches, high schools, shops." In *The Pioneers*, Cooper described the "cultured" values, "beautiful and thriving villages," "manufacturing," "neat and comfortable farms," "academies and minor edifices of learning," and "places for the worship of God" that all stood for progress.[28]

Cooper's story then reverted to a flashback whose opening scene was remarkably similar to *Valance*'s: a sleigh (rather than a western stagecoach) moving through the woods, bringing Judge Temple home to the valley, was stopped by Natty Bumppo. Although no violence occurred (Natty, unlike Valance, was not malevolent), the issue was the same: western law versus civilized law, or, in specific terms, whether Temple had the right to impose a hunting season on the wilderness. Natty took the classic outlaw hero's position:

There's them living who say Nathaniel Bumppo's right to shoot on these hills is of older date than Marmaduke Temple's right to forbid him. . . . But if there's a law about it at all, though who ever heard of a law that a man shouldn't kill where he pleased!—but if there is a law at all, it should be to keep people from the use of smoothbores. (p. 23)

Ultimately, this quarrel over hunting seasons became the key to the story's development. Judge Temple, an arch-official hero, with a house filled with busts of Homer, Shakespeare, Franklin, and Washington (like Stoddard's schoolroom), insisted that "the sanctity of the laws must be respected." Natty, on the other hand, was only disgusted. "This comes of settling a country," he pouted, after seeing an organized hunt.

Natty and Temple, however, like Tom and Ranse, were bound together by experience. In fact, as Cooper's outlaw hero, Natty was a remarkable prefiguration of Ford's Tom Doniphon. Like Tom and Pompey, Natty and his Indian companion Chingachgook lived in a cabin outside of town. Like Tom with Ranse, Natty continually found himself in the position of having to rescue Temple or Temple's daughter Elizabeth. On his first night in the wilderness, alone and lost, Temple had been found and saved by Natty (just as Ranse had been rescued by Tom after his beating by Valance). More crucially, Natty violated the hunting laws by killing a panther about to attack Elizabeth. For Natty, as for Tom with his shooting of Valance, this heroic act was the beginning of his own downfall. Prosecuted for hunting illegally, he, like Tom, burned his house as if to signal his own recognition of his world's destruction. He saved Elizabeth again (from a forest fire), but decided to leave the valley, saying simply to Temple, "your ways isn't my ways," thereby admitting the incompatibility of their two lifestyles. When he reappeared as a dying old man in Cooper's *The Prairie*, his last words, advice to a young man to marry and give up the wilderness, were remarkably similar to Tom's speech to Ranse at the statehood convention ("Hallie's your girl now. Go on back in there and take that nomination. You've taught her how to read and write—now give her something to read and write about"):

... much has passed atween us [Natty said] on the pleasures and respectableness of a life in the woods or on the borders. I do not mean to say that all you have heard is true, but different tempers call for different employments. You have taken to your bosom there a good and kind child, and it has become your duty to consider her as well as yourself in setting forth in life. You are a little given to skirting the settlements, but to my poor judgment the girl would be more like a flourishing flower in the sun of a clearing than in the winds of a prairie. Therefore forget everything you may have heard from me, which is nevertheless true, and turn your mind on the ways of the inner country.[29]

The phrase "which is nevertheless true" perfectly captures the divided nature of Cooper's and Ford's allegiance. Both acknowledged (Ford only at the end of his career) the tragic paradox that wilderness freedom and civilized progress were equally attractive and mutually contradictory.

How they had become so was of concern to both Cooper and Ford. Both suggested that something had gone wrong, perhaps at the very starting point of civilization. *Valance* and *The Pioneers* specifically indicated, in fact, that the civilizing process rested on a lie at its beginnings: the legend that Ranse had killed Liberty Valance, Judge Temple's unlawful claim to his property. The postwar sense that some past wrong was responsible for present troubles was new to American cinema. It was, of course, a frequent theme of *film noir*, expressing perhaps the specific guilt about having initiated the atomic age. In the western, however, the idea, which frequently took shape as a questioning of the right of property, seemed to implicate American institutions in general. Several of the period's most popular films revealed a greed and rapacity at the root of civilization. Dunson in *Red River* simply stole his land from Indians and Mexicans, and then watched his graveyard fill up with men who tried to take it back. In *Shane*, the principal cattleman's boast that "we make this country" turned into an admission that they had killed in doing so. In *Giant*, Jett Rink (James Dean) explained to Leslie Benedict (Elizabeth Taylor) the facts about her new family: "How did they get this land if they didn't take it off someone else? . . . They took it off Mexicans for five cents an acre."

For the first time in the history of the popular cinema, therefore, American viewers were confronted with challenges to the myths of their civilization's origins. (Cooper had made the same challenges, but his readership amounted to a small fraction of the audience for popular movies.) That audience's willingness to attend to these indictments implied an increased disillusionment with postwar American society. The figure of Tom Doniphon, the outlaw hero who, acting in the name of civilization, had unintentionally destroyed the conditions that made his own freedom possible, was especially disturbing, representing America's image of itself after the potentially self-destructive effort of World War II. Above all, *The Man Who Shot Liberty Valance*, despite its superficial adherence to the Classic Hollywood pattern of reconciliation, suggested that the progress of history resulted ultimately from a choice. It had once been possible to have either the wilderness and its freedom or the community and its security, but, except for a brief moment that had really existed only in American mythology, it had never been possible to have both.

Part Three. The Contemporary Period (1967–1980)

8. The 1960s: Frontier Metaphors, Developing Self-Consciousness, and New Waves

IN 1968, MEMBERS of the National Society of Film Critics responded to a series of questions "designed to shed light on a few of the most important issues currently confronting both filmmakers and critics." Among the questions were the following:

2. Are we standing on the brink of a radically different film age? . . .
3. What of the American commercial movie? Can it go on as it is? If not, how much restructuring—and of what sort specifically—will be required artistically and economically if it is to remain a significant force on the world film scene?

The critics' answers were surprising. On the whole, they did not anticipate a radically different film age, and although a few agreed with Stanley Kauffmann that "the best American commercial films seem to be 'growing up,'" most sided with John Simon's opinion:

Seeing that the American commercial movie has gone on more or less unchanged for—is it decades? centuries?—there is no reason to assume it will have to mend its ways in the foreseeable future.[1]

At the time, the apparent freshness of American movies made these answers seem stubborn or snobbish. In 1967, Hollywood had produced *Bonnie and Clyde* and *The Graduate*, films that, as Robert Sklar put it, not only "brought movies once again to the center of national attention," but also appeared to be genuinely different from their predecessors. *Bonnie and Clyde* in particular became what Sklar called "a cultural phenomenon";[2] more importantly, its appeal derived from its ostensible break with Classic Hollywood Cinema.

In refusing to acknowledge a New Hollywood movie, however, the critics could have cited the 1946-1966 period, when the industry had successfully persisted with its Classic paradigms in the face of events damaging to the American "exceptionalism"[3] that those paradigms repeatedly invoked. If Hollywood could ignore the changes in America effected by the atom bomb, television, jet planes, and permanent international commitments, it could ignore the developments of the sixties as well—in Simon's words, Hollywood could avoid "growing up."

Such condemnations of Hollywood's "immaturity" tacitly rested on a naïve reflection theory: according to this argument, the movies refused to grow up when they failed to mirror historical anomalies that challenged their basic conventions. In fact, however, Classic Hollywood's ability to withstand postwar "anomalies" demonstrated again that the movies reflected not historical events, but the audience's *relationship* to those events, a relationship decisively shaped by the traditional mythological categories perpetuated by the movies themselves. Indeed, these perceptual categories had become a kind of "knowledge," communally reinforced by the shared examples Hollywood provided.[4] In Althusser's terms, therefore, what the movies reflected was "ideology," "a system of mass representation" ("images, myths, ideas, or concepts") internalized unconsciously by the American audience.[5]

In this context, historical events alone could not discredit Classic Hollywood's traditional forms; only the audience's perception of events as anomalous could raise that challenge, and in the postwar period, the traditional categories had forestalled such perceptions from developing. Certainly the events of the 1946-1966 period eroded the America that the reconciliatory myth invoked. But the mass audience, trained by the movies to think in terms of direct confrontations resolvable by decisive action, failed to recognize the implications of events that remained more abstract. For this audience, the traditional mythology reduced the Cold War (requiring permanent U.S. involvement in international affairs) to a series of unconnected, ad hoc showdowns between clearly defined interests.

The durability of Classic Hollywood's thematic paradigm also suggested its richness. If, to invert Thomas Kuhn's proposition about science, a mythology's power increases with the number of specific incarnations its practitioners have at their disposal,[6] Classic Hollywood's paradigms remained the most compelling component of the traditional American ideological projection. Although the western was its typical expression, the reconciliatory pattern could take many shapes and the outlaw hero many forms. Particular variants, long dormant, could reappear, and, once mobilized, initiate a new cycle of movies. Thus, the outlaw-hero-as-rebel-youth, a standard Warner Brothers figure in the 1930s (*Angels with Dirty Faces, Wild Boys of the Road*), could resurface in the 1950s (*The Wild One, Rebel Without a Cause*) and prove adaptable to the audience's new needs. The reluctant hero story's ability to accommodate itself to different historical circumstances suggested Classic Hollywood's characteristic "repression-by-toleration":[7] the most potentially destructive events (e.g., World War II) could be assimilated by the paradigm (e.g., *Casablanca*) and defused.

The postwar period, therefore, reconfirmed two basic facts about the American Cinema: first, the movies responded less to historical events than to the audience's culturally mediated perceptions of such events; second, Hollywood's adopted mythology had proved extraordinarily adaptable. In specific terms, the thematic and formal paradigms were remarkably durable and the audience remarkably attached to them. The movies were inherently conservative, perpetuating a mythological representation of the world that Hollywood had borrowed from traditional American culture. Inevitably, both the industry and its audience clung to the established conventions, which had managed to transform every American crisis—the Depression, class divisiveness, widespread crime, World War II, the Cold War—into new occasions for the reconciliatory pattern that avoided final choices. An intuition of irreconcilable contradictions, normally suppressed by this pattern, appeared only in the odd moments of Hollywood's most emotionally arresting films: in Rick's drunk scene in *Casablanca*, in *It's a Wonderful Life*'s Pottersville vision, in the desperation of *Liberty Valance*'s Tom Doniphon, setting fire to his own house to mark the passing of the wilderness and the coming of civilization.

Equipped by their mythology with an effective means of naturalizing any new developments, Americans in 1959 were, according to Hadley Cantril (a pioneer in public opinion studies), "the most confident people in the world." This confidence, Cantril predicted, would remain the dominant American mood

until some major event or crisis transpires which creates major and widespread frustrations. Only then are people likely to become awakened to the inadequacy of the assumptions they have come to take for granted.[8]

The history of the sixties is largely a record of such major events or crises that *did* transpire, beginning in 1963 with the fall of the Vietnamese Diem regime, the Birmingham race riots, and the Kennedy assassination. As the decade progressed, similar crises followed: racial unrest (1964-1967), increased U.S. participation in Vietnam (beginning with the 1965 commitment of American ground troups), student and counterculture dissent (peaking at Columbia in 1968), the assassinations of Robert Kennedy and Martin Luther King (1968), the Altamont rock festival deaths (1969), the Cambodian invasion (1970), and the right-wing reaction to protest (Chicago Democratic Convention—1968, Kent State—1970).

Writing in 1959, Cantril had forecast that a single major event or crisis would discredit the assumptions on which American culture depended. From the vantage point of 1976, Godfrey Hodgson confirmed Cantril's prediction:

What happened in the age of Kennedy and Nixon was something more than an acceleration in the pace of change. *There was a real break in the continuity of American experience* ... the great conflicts of the age of Kennedy and Nixon challenged the central premise of American life as it was not challenged by a shortage of jobs in the 1930s, or by war in the 1940s and Cold War in the 1950s.[9]

Historian Eric Goldman agreed, calling the sixties "a watershed as important as the American Revolution or the Civil War in causing changes in the U.S."[10]

Certain developments seemed to bear out Hodgson and Goldman. The decade's events polarized American society more acutely than any crisis since the Civil War, and the rise of issue politics indicated that individuals and groups had grown less tolerant and more ready to insist stridently on their own needs. At times, both poles resorted to violence hitherto unknown to twentieth-century American politics. While Abbie Hoffman offered the advice, "I think kids should kill their parents," the Right responded with bumper stickers reading, "WE SUPPORT MAYOR DALEY AND HIS CHICAGO POLICE." As the decade progressed, polarization itself replaced the old consensus as the prevailing assumption, and in doing so, seemed to challenge Hollywood's thematic basis, the reconciliatory pattern.

Certainly the sixties abounded in incidents capable of discrediting the traditional American mythology which that pattern had deployed. Whether these incidents did, in fact, undermine that mythology, however, is a far more vexed question. Because this mythology represented not American experience (historical, social, or geographic) but the culture's collective means of dealing with that experience, it could not be overthrown by events alone. Only the advent of a decisively new, and widely accepted, way of perceiving events could accomplish that revolution. A "break" in the continuity of Hollywood Cinema, to use Hodgson's term, could, therefore, only follow a "break" in the American ideological projection.

It is still too soon to know whether the 1960s marked such a "break." Recent historians have warned that major shifts in perceptual patterns occur rarely, and that what seem like pronounced departures generally develop into variations on the established mode.[11] Similarly, philosophers have noted the impossibility of disowning a system of thinking while using that system's language.[12] As a result, we should be wary of the decade's announcements of a New American Culture and an attendant New American Cinema.

In fact, the language most often used to describe the suspected mythological break indicated that a truly decisive rupture had not yet occurred. For despite their annunciatory tone, commentators inevitably read sixties developments through the traditional mythology's own most representative explanation of American life: Frederick Jackson Turner's frontier thesis, with its vision of American culture's abiding dependence on the openness once available in the American West.[13]

The frontier thesis's compelling status in American thought, like that of the mythology it purported to explain, derived from its malleability. Historians following Turner had repeatedly transformed his specific, geographic space into metaphorical El Dorados, of which Kennedy's "New Frontier" was only the most obvious. Dixon Ryan Fox, for example, had reincarnated Turner's open land in "the edge of the unused," and Harvard economist Joseph Schumpeter had argued explicitly that "we must not confuse geographical frontiers with economic ones. Technological possibilities are an uncharted sea."[14] These figurative definitions flowered in the 1950s when, as "New Frontiers of boundless economic growth," they supported the domestic consensus's premise that choices could be avoided. President Johnson's economic advisor, Walter Heller, became this assumption's official spokesman, asserting that issues of redistribution found their answers in growth: "When the cost of fulfilling a people's aspirations can be met out of a growing horn of plenty—without robbing Peter to pay Paul—ideological roadblocks melt away and consensus replaces conflict."[15]

To this chorus of uniformly optimistic applications of the frontier thesis, only Texas historian Walter Prescott Webb dissented. Pointing out that Turner's American West had represented only a small part of "The Great Frontier" opened to European civilization during the Renaissance, Webb maintained that modern institutions had evolved to meet the needs of societies confronted by open spaces of rich land. Specifically, democracy and capitalism, both stressing the individual, had arisen to deal with this "Great Frontier," which Webb described as "basically a vast body of wealth without proprietors." As a Turner fundamentalist, Webb insisted that these institutions retained their validity only so long as an actual, geographic frontier existed. To the extent that the metaphorical frontiers had no connection with an actual physical space, they had become literally ungrounded. "They are all fallacies, these new frontiers," Webb wrote, "and they are pernicious in proportion to their plausibility and respectability."[16]

All the commentators who proclaimed the demise of the traditional American mythology implicitly built on Webb's literal interpretation of Turner. Economist Kenneth Boulding declared a "crisis of closure," and similarly titled books returned again and again to the received language of confinement and the concomitant need for difficult choices: *The Closing Circle, The Limits to Growth, The End of Affluence, Business Civilization in Decline, Small Is Beautiful, Social Limits to Growth, The End of the American Future, Awakening from the American Dream: The Social and Political Limits to Growth,* and *Tragic Choices.*[17]

Read through Turner's traditional explanation, the critical events of the 1960s became demonstrations of the shrinkage suffered by the physical and metaphorical space on which American institutions had presumably depended. In particular, the naggingly interminable Vietnam War, following World War II and Korea, and conducted on the brink of either side's potential nuclear intervention, came to suggest a contraction in worldwide space. Even more important, steadily escalating internal dissent, symbolized by the ease with which thousands of protestors could appear in Washington, was interpreted as signaling the disappearance of what Daniel Bell called "insulated space,"[18] the figurative "room" that supposedly had enabled American culture's conflicting values to coexist without violence. Under the aegis of the frontier theory, even one of the period's triumphs, the Apollo space program, seemed to dramatize with its photographs of the earth how limited the world's space actually was.

The unique authority of Turner's account of American history insured that the sixties' polarization would take shape around the frontier imagery that both sides shared. Both the Left and Right adopted Webb's generalized sense of "lateness," which threatened to retract the great American promise of space and time for every aspiration. At its most extreme, the Left's vision explicitly challenged the traditional mythology's most basic archetype, the reluctant hero story, with its image of short-lived crises solvable by decisive action. "The frontier, any frontier," Peter Schrag wrote, "was the American answer to Marx." Backed by this sense of space,

liberal policy grew from the belief that if men were free from artificial restraints (or if they received temporary assistance to overcome obstacles), then progress would inevitably follow. Every problem in America was an aberration—depressions, unemployment, disease, perhaps even death—and every program was temporary.[19]

Closed frontiers, the Left argued, made such ad hoc decision-making disingenuous; in a limited space, the necessity for choice became inevitable.

To the Left's vision of geographic and figurative closure, the Right responded with the insistence that new frontiers could still be found. Economic growth, as always, remained the stock metaphorical frontier. But as Richard Schickel noted, the Vietnam War could be seen as representing the Right's attempt to "externalize" the frontier no longer available in America itself.[20] (Indeed, the word "frontier" could have replaced "war" without losing the meaning of the marine general's notorious "It's not a good war, but it's the only war we've got.") By positing a now-static America, the Left pictured societal problems as complex and interlocking. By contrast, the Right persisted with the traditional mythology: problems were regarded as isolated and circumscribed, solvable by the kind of direct action represented by the Cambodian raids, conceived of as a large-scale cavalry rescue.

How these attitudes toward the frontier got translated into responses to particular issues could be observed in the different reactions to the event that had precipitated the polarization—the assassination of John Kennedy. For the Left, the assassination signaled that the old assumptions had failed, that there was something deeply wrong with American institutions and culture. The Right, on the other hand, regarded the assassination as an individual act of evil whose source could be located and eliminated. Frequently, the two positions merged. Thus, while President Johnson saw the assassination as symptomatic of deep-rooted problems, his response ("We have to do something about that") came in terms of the direct, simple solutions favored by the Right.

Johnson's confused rhetoric reflected the sixties' tendency to blur the differences between the opposed positions. Superficially, the Left (or counterculture, as it came to be known) represented a revolt in the name of values historically associated with individualism (or the outlaw hero): freedom from restraint, a preference for intuition as the source of conduct, a distrust of the law, a prolonging of adolescence, and a bias against technology, bureaucracies, and urban life. The Right countered with the values of the community (or the official hero): law and order, international peace-keeping, and respect for the middle-class family. But to the nominally individualistic values of the counterculture, the Left also brought a new sense of community, stressing ecology, cooperation, and anticompetitiveness. On the other side, to implement its values of law and order, the Right advocated the kind of temporary, direct, ad hoc action normally associated with the outlaw hero—the avatar of the Left.

The counterculture response to an America without frontiers complicated matters further. Although the Left's mature branches proposed sophisticated, permanent institutional changes designed to deal with an increasingly complex society, the counterculture's most visible members imprisoned themselves in the very mythology they had attacked. Thus, despite their insistence that the frontier's closing had rendered traditional lifestyles and institutions obsolete, their ideals were blatantly mythical: a passive dropping out that resembled the wandering outlaw life, and the small communal farms that seemed parodies of the yeoman husbandry that Jefferson himself had declared outmoded as a basis for American life. Both responses, Leslie Fiedler saw, represented a "reactionary nostalgia" whose individualistic hedonism undercut the Left's programmatic calls for cooperative sacrifice.

In fact, the counterculture's strident pronouncements of the old America's death barely concealed the obvious: at the heart of their vision lay yet another metaphorical frontier, an image of new possibilities derived from drugs, sexual freedom, and a vague spirituality. The counterculture's style betrayed its members' obsession with the West. Clothes (jeans, boots, buckskins) and hairstyles (long and unkempt, moustaches) derived from daguerreotypes of nineteenth-century gunfighters; and pop music returned repeatedly to frontier images: The Buffalo Springfield's "Broken Arrow," The Grateful Dead's "Casey Jones," The Band's "Across the Great Divide," James Taylor's "Sweet Baby James,"

Neil Young's "Cowgirl in the Sand," Creedence Clearwater Revival's "Proud Mary," The Byrds' *Sweetheart of the Rodeo*, and the Eagles' *Desperado*. Above all, drugs stood for the new uncharted territory, as dangerous as the real frontier and, for the adventurous, equally tempting.

The Left's confused self-image resulted from its experience as the first real media generation. Faced with the need to find suitable lifestyles, its members often appeared to be acting out a grab bag of movie myths, including even those which the counterculture's own rational premises had disowned. Godard's *Weekend* (1967), with its young revolutionaries radioing back and forth in the code names "Arizona Jules" and "Johnny Guitar," caught the problem exactly. The Right's vocabulary also drew on film clichés, but it was at least internally consistent. The retained faith in new frontiers made its western metaphors natural: police precincts in the South Bronx became "Fort Apache," Vietnam helicopter squads became "the cavalry."

The Left and Right's shared preoccupation with the frontier account of American history indicates that the potentially convulsive events of 1963-1974 did not cause a complete "break" in the traditional American mythology. Without a mythology of its own, the Left could only mount its challenges in terms of the traditional mythology's most well-established imagery. Thus, even the most polarized arguments developed around notions of the frontier, suggesting that the culture's relationship to events had not fundamentally altered.

But if the traditional American mythology had not entirely succeeded in healing itself, it had perhaps taken the first steps in that direction. Recent historians have shown that major perceptual shifts can only occur after a preliminary period during which the existing way of experiencing the world has been subjected to intense scrutiny.[21] To the extent that such scrutiny first reveals itself in a culture's growing self-consciousness about its own mythology, the 1960s represented the beginnings of the transition period. For while the traditional stories, heroes, and genres persisted, the movies subjected these thematic conventions to increasingly heavy doses of irony, parody, and camp. If one wished to locate the exact moment when this mythological self-consciousness began to appear prominently in American popular culture, one might point to the fall of 1957, when into the midst of dozens of straight television westerns (e.g., "Gunsmoke," "Tales of Wells Fargo," "Have Gun Will Travel," "The Life and Legend of Wyatt Earp," "Cheyenne," "Zane Grey Theater," "Wagon Train," "Sugarfoot"), ABC introduced a new series that eventually parodied them all: "Maverick." For the next three years (until its star, James Garner, left in 1960), "Maverick" managed to spoof every western convention: its hero always preferred gambling, women, and con games to a fair fight, which he avoided at all costs. He treated ladies, even those in distress, without the slightest hint of favor, and was not above cheating at cards. As the series progressed, its parodies became increasingly sophisticated, often mocking the narrative forms of other hit shows. Thus, one takeoff of "Dragnet" used Jack Webb-style voice-over, exposing the ridiculousness of that series's claim to "complete documentary authenticity."

By the spring of 1966, on the eve of the self-proclaimed New Hollywood Cinema, parodic versions of traditional genres had become television and movie staples. Premiering in January 1966, ABC's hugely popular "Batman" (a top-five series) provided most Americans with their first introduction to unadulterated camp, while NBC's "Get Smart," a spoof of the already tongue-in-cheek James Bond films, demonstrated that even parodies could be still further mocked. In the movies, *Thunderball*, the fourth in the increasingly campy Bond series, led the box office, earning nearly twice as much as any other release. And in the most significant event of all, that April's Oscar for Best Actor went to Lee Marvin for his starring role in 1965's *Cat Ballou*, the first outright parody of a traditional genre to receive the Academy's cachet.

Between 1966 and 1980, an enormous number of films depended on their audiences' ability to recognize them as overt parodies, "corrected" genre pictures, or exaggerated camp versions of Hollywood's traditional mythology. Even a partial listing will suggest the extent of this sudden wave of self-consciousness:

1967
You Only Live Twice (James Bond)
Casino Royale (James Bond)
In Like Flint (Bond parody)

1968
Bonnie and Clyde (revisionist gangster movie)
McCabe and Mrs. Miller (revisionist western)

1969
Butch Cassidy and the Sundance Kid (revisionist western parody)
True Grit (parodic western)
Support Your Local Sheriff (western parody)
Take the Money and Run (Woody Allen, slapstick gangster story)
On Her Majesty's Secret Service (James Bond)
The Maltese Bippy (horror movie parody)

1970
M*A*S*H (slapstick war movie)

1971
Bananas (Woody Allen adventure parody)
Little Big Man (revisionist western)
Diamonds Are Forever (James Bond)

1972
Sleuth (dectective parody)
Play It Again, Sam (*Casablanca* parody)

1973
Live and Let Die (James Bond)
The Long Goodbye (revisionist *noir*)

1974
Blazing Saddles (western parody)
The Three Musketeers (adventure parody)
Young Frankenstein (horror parody)
Monty Python and the Holy Grail (King Arthur parody)
Phantom of the Paradise (camp version of *Phantom of the Opera*)

1975
The Return of the Pink Panther (detective story parody)
Nashville (revisionist musical)
Rooster Cogburn (western parody)
Hearts of the West (movie about moviemaking)
Rancho Deluxe (western parody)
The Adventure of Sherlock Holmes' Smarter Brother (Holmes parody)
The Rocky Horror Picture Show (camp horror musical)
The Black Bird (*Maltese Falcon* parody)

1976
Silent Movie (parody of silent screen days)
Murder by Death (detective parody)
The Shootist (revisionist western)

Robin and Marian (revisionist Robin Hood)
Bugsy Malone (camp gangster movie with all-child cast)
Buffalo Bill and the Indians, or Sitting Bull's History Lesson
  (western parody)
King Kong (camp version of original classic)
Silver Streak (Hitchcock parody)
The Pink Panther Strikes Again (detective parody)
Nickelodeon (silent screen days)
The Big Bus (disaster movie parody)

1977
Star Wars (camp, cartoonish version of *Casablanca*)
Smokey and the Bandit (car chase spoof)
The Spy Who Loved Me (James Bond)
High Anxiety (Hitchcock parody)
New York, New York (revisionist MGM musical)
The Late Show (revisionist *noir*)
Kentucky Fried Movie (TV parodies)

1978
The Cheap Dectective (*Maltese Falcon* parody)
Hooper (revisionist stuntman movie)
Death on the Nile (detective parody)
Movie Movie (parodies within parodies)
Superman (camp incarnation of comic strip)
Grease (parody of fifties teenage lifestyles)

1979
The Electric Horseman (revisionist western)
Apocalypse Now (revisionist war movie)
All That Jazz (campy backstage musical)
1941 (war movie parody)
Star Trek (campy, cartoonish version of TV series)
The Jerk (Horatio Alger parody)
Dracula (camp version of classic)
The Life of Brian (parody of the *Greatest Story Ever Told*)
Love at First Bite (camp *Dracula*)

1980
Willie and Phil (two men and a woman imitate *Jules and Jim*)
The Man with Bogart's Face (camp *noir*)
Flash Gordon (camp cartoon characters incarnated)
Popeye (camp cartoon characters incarnated)
Airplane! (parody of *Airport* series)
The Empire Strikes Back (campy, cartoonish *Star Wars* sequel)
Bronco Billy (revisionist western)

The Blues Brothers (musical parody)
Wholly Moses! (Biblical parody)
Fade to Black (psychotic murderer assumes various movie identities)

No other period in Hollywood history had produced so many overtly satiric movies. While not all of these films were popular, the sheer number of them suggested American culture's increasingly ironic attitude toward its own traditional mythology. And, in fact, many of these films became enormous hits, while the rare earlier attempts at spoofing stock genre conventions (e.g., John Huston's *Beat the Devil*—1954) had almost uniformly failed at the box office.

The movies' new self-consciousness also flourished on television, where "Rowan and Martin's Laugh-In" (1968-1973), "The Carol Burnett Show" (1967-1978), and NBC's "Saturday Night Live" (1975-) all featured irreverent media parodies, particularly of movies and TV news. Other regular series clearly could not be taken straight: "All in the Family" (1971-1979), "The Rockford Files" (1974-1979), "Happy Days" (1974-1984), "Mary Hartman, Mary Hartman" (1976), and "Soap" (1977-1981) all traded on obviously ironic uses of standard television formulas.

The period's growing self-consciousness about the received American myths also promoted a new kind of star, who in Classic Hollywood might have operated only in the margins of straight genre movies. Elliott Gould, Walter Matthau, Dustin Hoffman, Al Pacino, Robert DeNiro, Woody Allen, Gene Wilder, Gene Hackman, Mel Brooks, Jack Nicholson, Jane Fonda, Goldie Hawn, and Jill Clayburgh were all essentially character actors whose self-reflexive, self-doubting personae contrasted sharply with the confident, natural imperturbability of Cooper, Grant, Gable, and Wayne. While the Classic stars had depended on the cumulative power of typecasting and genre conventions, these new performers specialized in playing against the expectations created either by a film's nominal genre or by their own previous roles. Their model for this iconoclasm was clearly Marlon Brando, whose desire to avoid typecasting had frequently led him to adopt a mannered, campy style as a defense against overly conventional material (e.g., *Teahouse of the August Moon*—1956, *The Young*

Lions—1958, and most notoriously, *Mutiny on the Bounty*—1962, and *The Missouri Breaks*—1976).

That traditional performers (Wayne, Eastwood, Newman, Redford, McQueen, Bronson, and Streisand) still dominated the box office, however, indicates the period's schizophrenic alternation between a developing irony and a reactionary nostalgia. That same alternation began to appear in Hollywood's curious new patterns of release. For despite the wave of parodies and revisionist genre films, 1967-1977's annual money-winners typically represented the most conservative kind of filmmaking: *The Dirty Dozen* (1967), *The Love Bug* (1969), *Airport* (1970), *Love Story* (1971), *The Poseidon Adventure* (1973), *The Sting* (1974), *Jaws* (1975), and *One Flew Over the Cuckoo's Nest* (1976). During these years, only *The Graduate* (1968) and *The Godfather* (1972) managed to achieve both minimal freshness and enormous commercial success.

The almost annual appearance of re-releases among the years' Top Twenty Box-Office Films also suggested the ambivalence of both the industry and its audience. Never before in its history had Hollywood reissued so many movies with so much success: *Gone With the Wind* (1967-1968), *Swiss Family Robinson* (1969), *101 Dalmatians* (1970), *Song of the South* (1972), *The Sound of Music* (1973), *Mary Poppins* (1973), *Robin Hood* (1974). These reissues' formal and thematic conservatism implied the existence of a longing for traditional modes and the established mythology they represented. Hollywood further attempted to satisfy that longing with a new genre, the nostalgia film: *Summer of '42* (1971), *The Last Picture Show* (1971), *Paper Moon* (1973), *American Graffiti* (1973), *The Way We Were* (1973), *The Great Gatsby* (1974), and *National Lampoon's Animal House* (1978), all offered their audiences the chance to relive a particular period in the past. Some of them demonstrated how startlingly soon the recent past had become remote from the new sensibility. By the times of their release, the early 1960s of *American Graffiti* and *Animal House* seemed as quaint as the 1920s.

Hollywood's unprecedented reliance on sequels confirmed the industry's growing uncertainty about its inherited patterns and also testified to a sudden loss of resourcefulness. While Classic

Hollywood had relegated outright sequels to the B-movie ranks, preferring to build on major hits by casting the same performers as similar, but different, characters (1942's *Casablanca* became 1944's *Passage to Marseilles*, 1944's *To Have and Have Not* became 1946's *The Big Sleep*), the New Hollywood appeared far less flexible, depending to an extraordinary extent on "continuations" of successful films. Thus, between 1967 and 1977, nearly one-third of the 220 leading money-makers were either sequels themselves or films that prompted sequels.

SEQUELS OR FILMS THAT PROMPTED SEQUELS AMONG EACH YEAR'S TOP TWENTY MONEY-EARNERS

1967
You Only Live Twice
Casino Royale
In Like Flint
A Guide for the Married Man

1968
The Valley of the Dolls
Planet of the Apes

1969
The Love Bug
Funny Girl
Butch Cassidy and the Sundance Kid
True Grit
Support Your Local Sheriff

1970
Airport
On Her Majesty's Secret Service
Beneath the Planet of the Apes
A Boy Named Charlie Brown
A Man Called Horse

1971
Love Story
Summer of '42
Willard

The Stewardesses
Shaft
The French Connection

1972
The Godfather
Diamonds Are Forever
Dirty Harry
Escape from the Planet of the Apes

1973
Live and Let Die
American Graffiti
Sounder
Walking Tall
Billy Jack

1974
The Exorcist
Magnum Force
Herbie Rides Again
The Trial of Billy Jack
Butch Cassidy and the Sundance Kid (reissue)
Billy Jack (reissue)
Airport 1975
That's Entertainment
The Three Musketeers

1975
Jaws
Benji
The Godfather, Part II
Funny Lady
Return of the Pink Panther
The Man with the Golden Arm
Escape to Witch Mountain
The Other Side of the Mountain

1976
The Omen
The Bad News Bears
Jaws (reissue)
Lucky Lady
The Exorcist (reissue)

1977
Star Wars
Rocky
Smokey and the Bandit
Silver Streak
The Enforcer
The Spy Who Loved Me

Oh, God!
The Pink Panther Strikes Again
Airport 77
Herbie Goes to Monte Carlo

1978
Grease
Jaws 2
Star Wars (reissue)
Revenge of the Pink Panther
The Gauntlet
Omen II: Damien

1979
Superman
Every Which Way But Loose
Rocky II
Star Trek
The Muppet Movie

1980
The Empire Strikes Back
Smokey and the Bandit II
Urban Cowboy
Friday the 13th

Paradoxically, Hollywood's conservative sequel strategy further radicalized its audience, fostering the kind of ironic relationship to the movies that results from an increased awareness of an art's intertextuality. Having seen Dirty Harry or Shaft or Billy Jack migrate from film to film, the audience inevitably became aware of these characters' artificiality, and of the manipulations inherent in constructing new plots for them. To the extent that Classic Hollywood's movies had depended on the audience's accepting its characters and situations as "real" and spontaneously generated, this new widespread sense of film's "made" quality represented a major departure in the direction of self-consciousness.

The single most important factor in the traditional mythology's growing self-consciousness, however, was television. In 1955 and 1956, all the major Hollywood studios (except MGM) had sold the bulk of their pre-1948 films to distributors who promptly rechanneled them to local stations.²² In the early 1960s, the major networks followed their affiliates' lead, increasing the number of prime time hours devoted to movies. "NBC Saturday Night Movie" launched this move in 1961, and by 1968, television also had an "ABC Sunday Night Movie," an "NBC Monday Night Movie," an "NBC Tuesday Night Movie," an "ABC Wednesday Night Movie," a "CBS Thursday Night Movie," and a "CBS Friday Night Movie." When coupled with the local stations' combined use of old movies and syndicated TV series, the networks' new commitment to Hollywood's product turned every household into a private film museum. The effect on how Americans watched movies was enormous. By plundering Hollywood's archives, television encouraged a new attitude toward the popular cinema and the traditional mythology it embodied.

The American mythology's survival had always depended on two things: its adherents' ability to continually regenerate it in fresh, topical examples, and its audience's ability to forget the weakest, most mutable of those examples. Hollywood had proved a particularly fertile source of affecting new variants, transforming *Huck Finn* into *Casablanca*, and thereby bequeathing the mythology to another generation. But the movie industry, and the nature of film itself, complicated the necessary forgetting process by flooding the audience with examples that were at once disposable and permanent. Indeed, the economic constraints that forced Hollywood to reproduce the traditional American mythology 300-500 times a year inherently undermined that mythology by fostering too many trivial incarnations. But those same constraints, by encouraging a planned obsolescence, kept that undermining slow and subtle, and prevented its effect from being felt. All but the most exceptional movies (e.g., *Gone With the Wind*) vanished after short runs, replaced by the steady stream of new versions designed to keep the traditional mythology afloat.

The result, to change the analogy, was like a high-wire act that depended on the ability to keep moving and not look back. In the 1960s, however, Hollywood's movement slowed dangerously, with the industry releasing only an average of 154 new movies a year, compared to 1937's Sound Era high of 538. Deprived of the Classic Period's rich array of annual mythological reinforcements, much of Hollywood's audience turned to television, which had simultaneously begun to scour Hollywood's past. Television, however, by indiscriminately reviving old movies (including many clearly intended as disposable), exposed the weakest versions of the standard myths and damaged even passable examples by resurrecting them into a new, inhospitable environment. Television's film revivals not only spawned camp; they also implicitly threatened the entire American ideology. For with a mythology so protean, even isolated damage menaced the whole fabric. Weak, forgotten versions of Hollywood's reconciliatory pattern, when revived, contaminated the best: thus, *Casablanca*'s successors, *Action in the North Atlantic* (1943) and *Passage to Marseilles* (1944), revealed the ideological mechanism of the original. Revived in the early 1970s, television's "Father Knows Best," with its simplified version of family life, subtly implicated the far more sophisticated *Meet Me in St. Louis.*

Even when new, most of television's regular series effected the same tacit sabotage. To satisfy their insatiable need for programming, the networks had reproduced all of Classic Hollywood's standard genres: western, gangster, screwball comedy, musical, detective, horror. Made cheaply and rapidly, however, these shows were debased, less inventive versions of the original formulas. To see "Cheyenne," "The Untouchables," "I Love Lucy," "The Perry Como Show," NBC's "The Thin Man," and even "Alfred Hitchcock Presents" was the equivalent of coming upon a nearly identical twin whose features revealed the hidden flaws in the familiar one.

Television programming and viewing habits further exposed the traditional mythology. Late afternoons, a viewer could switch channels freely between straight news broadcasts and syndicated reruns of "Superman," "Lassie," "Captain Midnight," "Highway Patrol," and "Hopalong Cassidy." Similarly, the sudden transition from the networks' news shows to each evening's first regular series eliminated all buffer space between actual events and mythological representations. The implicit critique afforded by such juxtapositions was new to the television age. Hollywood had effectively protected its product from such potentially damaging contrasts by isolating the moviegoer in a theater where the perfunctory newsreel rehearsed only weeks-old events already digested by the audience. But in the spring of 1963, for example, a television viewer could watch as network videotapes of the Birmingham race riots led directly into "Cheyenne," "Laramie," "Mr. Ed," "Ozzie and Harriet," or "Wagon Train," depending on the network and the night.[23] Inevitably, that viewer's attitude toward conventional versions of America's mythology became increasingly ironic.

In the 1960s, other developments furthered the movie audience's growing sense of the American Cinema's dense intertextuality. Revival houses, spurred by Harvard Square's Brattle Theater and its Bogart cult, gave young filmgoers (most of these houses were in college towns) chances to see a star's persona or a genre's conventions mature from film to film. In addition, increasingly serious film criticism (appearing in national, large-circulation magazines like *Time, Newsweek, The New Yorker, Life, Saturday Review*, and *Esquire*) spread the *auteur* theory's cross-referenced picture of Hollywood's history. Such criticism inescapably implied that the movies, far from being "real," were artifacts, the product of particular individuals working in particular eras.

With television revivals, and the new film criticism, therefore, the movie audience of the early 1960s had ample occasion to develop an incipiently ironic posture toward Hollywood's traditional thematic paradigm. Not surprisingly, the industry itself had its own stimuli encouraging self-consciousness. First, the demise of the old guard stimulated experimentation: of Andrew Sarris's "Pantheon" of American directors (Chaplin, Flaherty, Ford, Griffith, Hawks, Hitchcock, Keaton, Lang, Lubitsch, Murnau, Ophuls, Renoir, von Sternberg, and Welles), only Hawks, Hitchcock, and Welles made films after 1967—and none was major. At Sarris's second rank (that included Aldrich, Capra, De Mille, Losey, Mann, McCarey, Minnelli, Preminger, Ray, Stevens, Sturges, Vidor, and Walsh), only Robert Aldrich and Joseph Losey remained active, the former typically making stock formula pictures, the latter working in England. When added to the death or retirement of the old guard, the breakup of the studios (effected by television and antitrust rulings) made possible not only the rise of new young filmmakers, but their relative independence as well.

These new directors had varying backgrounds: film criticism (Bogdanovich, Schrader), photojournalism (Kubrick), theater (Nichols), film schools (Forman, Coppola, Lucas, Polanski, Malick, Scorsese, Milius), television (Altman, Penn, Spielberg, Mazursky, Peckinpah), and acting (Beatty, Hopper). Having for the most part escaped the long apprenticeships required during the Studio Years, these new directors felt less bound by the industry's institutionalized conventions. In effect, they began as obsessive buffs who learned about filmmaking by going to the movies. Having seen most of Hollywood's Studio Years product, they were now prepared, if not to disassemble it, at least to show its paradigms less respect. Not coincidentally, the director of the period's breakthrough film (Mike Nichols, *The Graduate*) duplicated the early career of Orson Welles, coming to Hollywood from Broadway, undertaking a private crash course to learn standard filmmaking procedures, many of which he then took apart.

The new directors' iconoclasm, however, clashed with the industry's inherent conservatism, intensified by the late sixties' conglomeratization of Hollywood. Between 1966 and 1969, Paramount, United Artists, Warners, and MGM all followed Universal's 1959 move, transferring ownership to corporate groups who imposed new systems of bookkeeping and accountability on a business previously run largely on instinct. The resulting internal conflicts both determined and reproduced the period's simultaneous impulses toward irony and nostalgia. What came out of this split was the period's representative form, the "corrected" genre movie (e.g., *Butch Cassidy and the Sundance Kid, Smokey and the Bandit*) that satisfied both the new directors and their new bosses, and that could be taken as either a traditional action picture or a spoof, depending on a viewer's predisposition. Robert Altman made a whole career out of such films, working almost exclusively within standard genres whose conventions he discredited: *M*A*S*H* (1970: war movie), *McCabe and Mrs. Miller* (1971: western), *The Long Goodbye* (1973: hard-boiled detective story), *Thieves like Us* (1974: gangster movie), *California Split* (1974: caper film), *Nashville* (1975: musical), *Buffalo Bill and the*

Indians, or Sitting Bull's History Lesson (1976: western, myths in general), *Three Women* (1977: soap opera), *A Wedding* (1978: screwball comedy), *Popeye* (1980: cartoons).

Above all, the period's defining self-consciousness arose from a new awareness of the inescapable interrelationship of media, audience, and historical events. Where cameras, tapes, and commentators had once seemed only to record the news, they now clearly helped determine it, with many of the period's most crucial incidents becoming inconceivable without the guaranteed media presence. More than any other event, the 1960 Nixon-Kennedy Debates prompted a recognition of the media's power to shape compelling images. Henceforth, the Left and Right competed to control such images, orchestrating events for public display. Jonathan Schell's *The Time of Illusion* describes the Vietnam War as the Right's staged demonstration of the United States' willingness to confront Communist encroachments:

now all hope of *doing* anything was abandoned. . . . What remained was proving something, to friends and foes alike: America's will and determination. The tangible objectives of limited war had been completely eclipsed by the psychological objective. The war had become an effort directed entirely toward building up a certain image by force of arms. It had become a piece of pure theatre. The purpose of the enterprise now was to put on a performance for what [Assistant Secretary of Defense] John McNaughton called "audiences."[24]

Intuiting the war's theatricality, the Left responded with its own carefully designed counterimages, the protests, demonstrations, and rallies conducted under the slogan, "The whole world is watching."[25]

In retrospect, even the period's apparently spontaneous events appear excessively determined by media considerations. Madly intended as symbolic gestures, assassinations (especially those of nonpoliticians Martin Luther King and John Lennon) rose numerically in direct proportion to the increase in media-created celebrity. Even the unprecedented grief provoked by John Kennedy's death derived in part from the prior media-manufactured Camelot imagery associated with his administration. Nixon's Watergate fall, another event concerned less with substance than appearances, resulted from his colleagues' criminal attempts to suppress the Left's image-making and from his own self-destructive eagerness to provide future commentators with exact transcripts of his most private conversations. The records of these calamities, the Zapruder Kennedy assassination film and Nixon's White House tapes, inevitably became the period's representative documents.

The counterculture's inability to invent a fresh mythology, its self-contradictory preoccupation with received frontier emblems, suggested the age's discovery: experience was no longer pure; indeed, it never had been. In every transaction between the self and the world, cultural images perpetuated by the media intervened. This recognition irrevocably altered the relationship of American Cinema's determinants. If Classic Hollywood's movies had resulted from a triangular configuration of industry, audience, and the culture's collective perception of historical developments, the new arrangement had become utterly circular.

FACED with declining profits and its audience's developing irony about the Classic Period's conventions, Hollywood by 1967 was ready at last to experiment. What presented itself as a possibility was the European art film. As early as 1965, Dennis Hopper had wondered about the potential for American imitations:

> Five years ago [in 1960] there were fifty art theaters in the United States; now there are six thousand. . . .
> "Hey how can we get into their [the Europeans'] market? We cannot compete on their level of film. Hey! I've got a great idea! Let's make art films. That's something they'll never think of!"
> And of course we haven't yet.
> Fifty theaters to six thousand in five years.
> No American films for six thousand theaters.[26]

The industry's most conservative faction had always objected that foreign films were not profitable. In the early 1960s, however, exceptions appeared, as more and more foreign movies worked their way to the top of the box-office lists. The sexually explicit *Never on Sunday* (1961) came first and made a star of Melina Mercouri. In 1963, the Academy gave its Best Picture Oscar to the British-made *Tom Jones*, slightly less explicit, but infinitely more brash cinematically. *Blow-Up* (1967) became the biggest surprise of all, a puzzling, unresolved movie by one of world cinema's most uncompromising modernists (Antonioni) that placed fourteenth on *Variety*'s annual money-making chart.

By far the most significant of the foreign movies, however, were the Beatles' *A Hard Day's Night* (1964) and *Help!* (1965), commercial hits directed by an American, Richard Lester, working in England. With their witty blend of anarchy and communality, the Beatles represented the counterculture's own best image of itself. As a group, they suggested whole new possibilities for lifestyles, particularly those that simultaneously used and mocked existing conventions. The Beatles wore suits and ties, played music recognizably derived from traditional rock and roll, and showed an obvious interest in success. At the same time, however, they kept their hair shockingly long, dismantled conventional pop chord structures, and poked fun at their own celebrity. Thus, they provided an ideal symbol for an American audience developing an ironic attitude toward an ideology it wished to retain. Writing from hindsight, Godfrey Hodgson remarked that "it would be hard to exaggerate the influence of the Beatles on the generation of Americans who grew up in the sixties."[27] It would be harder still to exaggerate the impact that *A Hard Day's Night* had on the American film industry.

Even Beatles fans expected a typical exploitation movie, designed to trade on a current fad. What appeared, however, was, in Andrew Sarris's words, a "cataclysmic cultural event" insuring that for the popular American movie, "an era had ended, for better or worse, and another had begun."[28] *A Hard Day's Night* differed in every way from Hollywood's idea of a popular movie. It was in black and white. It had no plot to speak of, consisting rather of "a day in the life of the Beatles," incidents and short takes connected only by the energy of Lester's editing. The Beatles did not assume roles, as Elvis had done, but merely played versions, albeit caricatured, of themselves. Much of the dialogue was obviously improvised. And throughout, the movie and its stars displayed a witty irony toward the film's ostensible subject, Beatlemania.

But the movie's most important influence was its visual style. Lester seemed to have worked out a perfect commercial synthesis of all the new formal elements in recent European films: *cinéma-vérité*, jump cutting, hand-held cameras, delirious tracking shots, rapid kaleidoscopic editing. An early train sequence typified the dizzying suspension of normal conventions. Trapped in a compartment with a stuffy businessman, the Beatles began to quarrel with him about their right to have the window open and the radio on. Lester began the scene, whose dialogue parodied an American western's standard debate over the law, by straightforwardly, but artfully, cutting back and forth between the parties. In many ways, in fact, the scene resembled a similar one early in Hitchcock's *The 39 Steps*.

JOHN: Yeah, but there are four of us, like, and we like it open, if it's all the same to you, that is.

MAN: Well, it isn't. I travel on this train regularly twice a week, so I suppose I've some rights.

RINGO: Aye, well, so have we.

MAN (turning off radio): And we'll have that thing off as well, thank you.

RINGO: But I . . .

MAN: An elementary knowledge of the Railway Acts would tell you I'm perfectly within my rights.

PAUL: Yeah, but we want to hear it and there's more of us than you. We're a community, like, a majority vote. Up the workers and all that stuff!

MAN: Then I suggest you take that damned thing into the corridor or some other part of the train where you obviously belong.

JOHN (leaning forward): Give us a kiss.

PAUL: Look, Mister, we've paid for our seats too, you know.

MAN: I travel on this train regularly, twice a week.

JOHN: Knock it off, Paul, you can't win with his sort. After all, it's his train, isn't it, Mister?

MAN: And don't you take that tone with me, young man! I fought the war for your sort.

RINGO: Bet you're sorry you won.

If this exchange failed to establish the Beatles' unthreatening antitraditionalism, the visual riffs that followed did the trick. Forced to leave the compartment, the Beatles appeared at the window, standing in the aisle making hideous faces. Suddenly, without either preparation or explanation, they were *outside* the train, running alongside, still shouting at the same man. They retreated to the baggage car where they began to play cards as the music for "I Should Have Known Better" began on the sound track. In mid-song, Lester jump cut to the group, still sitting around the same makeshift card table, but now playing their instruments. As the music began to fade, another jump cut returned them to the card game. By thus freely moving back and forth between nondiegetic and diegetic sound, Lester exposed the manipulations inherent in image-sound juxtapositions, and thereby violated the formal paradigm's essential quest for invisibility.

In the movie's most spectacular sequence, the Beatles escaped from manager and rehearsals to an empty playground, where Lester created a modernist version of Busby Berkeley, freely intercutting between ground-level shots (often close-ups) and extreme long shots (often speeded up) taken from a helicopter. The film's end was equally dazzling: titles superimposed over a montage of facial close-ups of the Beatles, flashed rapidly to produce a cubist effect.

By demonstrating that at least one aspect of the contemporary sensibility could be portrayed in a widely popular movie, *A Hard Day's Night* helped to break the cinematic impasse of the 1950s: here at last was a film where intent and effect merged. By convulsing the British "kitchen sink realist" tradition with Mélièsian tricks, Lester also showed Hollywood a way of spoofing established modes. Most importantly, *A Hard Day's Night* finally made available to the American audience the stylistic innovations of the French New Wave.

Succeeding Italian neorealism as the second major foreign influence on postwar Hollywood, the French New Wave had begun several years before *A Hard Day's Night* translated its style into a popular idiom. Between 1958 and 1963, when the movies everywhere were losing their audience to television, 170 French directors had made their first feature-length films. The *annus mirabilis* was 1959, which saw the premieres of Godard's *Breathless*, Truffaut's *The 400 Blows*, and Resnais's *Hiroshima, mon amour*. Confronted by this explosion of energy that ultimately revived (and transformed) world cinema, Françoise Giroud in

L'Express dubbed the movement *La Nouvelle Vague*—The New Wave.

From the start, the most apparent quality of the New Wave films was their youthfulness. The New Wave directors—Truffaut, Godard, Chabrol, Resnais, Rozier, Rohmer, Marker, Rivette, and others—seemed to be reinventing cinema with each new movie, frequently invoking older Hollywood forms and stories only for the pleasure of exposing the assumptions on which they rested. "What I wanted," Godard said of his first movie, *Breathless*, "was to take a conventional story and remake, but differently, everything the cinema had done. I also wanted to give the feeling that the techniques of filmmaking had just been discovered for the first time."[29]

The playfulness of the early New Wave films belied the movement's complex origins. Its most prominent directors were former film critics, sponsored by the *Cahiers du Cinéma*'s André Bazin, educated by the superlative film archives of the Cinémathèque Française, a museum often playing six different features a day. As formulators of the *auteur* theory, they had praised Hollywood directors (Hawks, Hitchcock, Nicholas Ray) whose fast-paced, unpretentious action movies opposed what Truffaut denounced as the French "tradition of quality"—stagy, heavy adaptations of classics controlled by *littérateurs*-turned-scriptwriters.

In making their own films, the New Wave directors preferred speed or lyricism. They replaced Balzac and Zola with gangsters and molls, studio-bound costume dramas with genre plots filmed on location, all the while remaining careful to credit their sources: Godard dedicated *Breathless* to Monogram Pictures, Hollywood's principal B-movie producer, and Truffaut offered *The Bride Wore Black* as an homage to Hitchcock. Influenced by Jean Renoir's *Rules of the Game*, however, the New Wave directors refused the implicit limitations of stock subjects, choosing instead to shift moods constantly to unsettle their audiences. In any New Wave film, slapstick villains had the potential to kill, and comedy always threatened to develop into tragedy. In *Shoot the Piano Player*, Truffaut shifted so abruptly from gangsters to Chaplinesque comedy to romantic melodrama that he hardly needed to explain that "every film must contain some degree of 'planned violence' upon its audience."[30]

Although the New Wave directors, unlike the Italian neorealists, issued no manifestos, they shared the preoccupations of modernism: a recognition that the aesthetics of representation were inherently problematic, an increased concentration on art's means of production, a dense allusiveness, a new awareness of the political implications of matters previously assumed to be aesthetic, a distrust of coherent narrative, and a preference for the mundane as perhaps the one area of life unsullied by previous artistic or philosophical assumptions.

Like most modernists, the New Wave directors were formalists, concerned with the capacity of apparently neutral techniques to determine perception. Departing from Hollywood's institutionalized subordination of style to content, they repeatedly called attention to cinema's inherent properties by exaggerating them beyond what a complacent audience, accustomed to Hollywood's "zero point of cinematic style," had come to expect. Recognizing the movies' twin origins, they pointed to both cinema's basic reality (using the *cinéma vérité* style of long takes, handheld cameras, available lighting, improvised dialogue, and fast film stock) and its irreality (with freeze frames, jump cuts, nondiegetic titles, and slow motion). The result was a paradox: films that were at once extraordinarily realistic and extraordinarily stylized. Or, as Godard defined cinema, "Life, in other words, fills the screen as a tap fills a bath which is simultaneously emptying at the same rate at the same time."[31]

Godard's subsequent radicalization insured that, for American filmmakers, his most suggestive film would remain his first feature, *Breathless*, the most influential movie of the 1960s. There, Godard's dialectical procedures still operated on a situation recognizably derived from Hollywood's own thrillers. Starting with what resembled an odd mix of gangster movie and screwball comedy, however, Godard proceeded to expose the arbitrariness of Classic Hollywood's continuity rules and to unravel the closed world of its genre conventions. In *Breathless*, a gun pointed screen-right could kill a policeman previously "established" as being offscreen-left. In *Breathless*, a cops-chase-killer story frequently paused for long interviews or conversations that did not advance the plot.

The movie's plot clearly evoked the stock Hollywood formula (the outlaw hero's collision with society represented, as always, by a woman) only to shun the traditional reconciliation (marriage). In fact, by betraying her lover to the police, *Breathless*'s heroine, Patricia Franchini (Jean Seberg), destroyed the values that the American mythology regarded as her necessary complement. For despite the Parisian setting, Godard's allusions identified the car thief hero, Michel Poiccard (Jean-Paul Belmondo), as a downbeat, existentialist version of the American archetype, the Good Bad Boy. One shot-reverse shot sequence sealed this identification by using eyeline matches to cut back and forth between a worshipful Michel and a promotional picture of Bogart on an ad for his last film, *The Harder They Fall*.

Even without this obvious clue, an American audience might have spotted Michel as an outlaw hero from his other characteristics: his studied childishness (manifested by his consistently capricious behavior, that included responding to Patricia's dare by jumping out of a taxi to flip up the skirts of passing girls); his general disdain for women (he visited an ex-lover only to steal her money); his anti-intellectualism ("Who's [William Faulkner]?" he asked Patricia, "some guy you slept with?"); his scorn of abstract, tangled metaphysics (responding to Patricia's Faulkner quotation, "Between grief and nothing, I will take grief," he said quickly, "Grief's a waste of time—I'd take nothing"). Typical of the outlaw hero was his refusal to answer Patricia's constant "pourquoi's" and "qu'est-ce que c'est's" with reasoned explanations for his behavior. "Why do you want to sleep with me?" she asked. "Because you're beautiful." Her reply was literal: "No, I'm not." "Well, then, because you're ugly." Preferring action, like all outlaw heroes, he refused to speculate about motives: "Squealers squeal," he told Patricia "robbers rob, lovers love."

With her culture-mongering and part-time enrollment at the Sorbonne, Patricia became the stock female representative of civilization and its entanglements. She lectured Michel in the spirit of the Widow Douglas's dealings with Huck: "Do you like

this poster?" she asked, pointing to a Renoir print. "Not bad," he replied disinterestedly. "Renoir is a very great painter," she chided, provoking only an impatient, "I said not bad." Inevitably, Patricia threatened Michel with domestication, even using her unplanned pregnancy menacingly.

In *Breathless*, Godard employed the traditional American outlaw hero-civilizing woman conflict. Disturbingly, however, he radicalized the two positions until no possibility for reconciliation survived. "When we look into each other's eyes," Patricia told Michel, in the movie's most pessimistic line, "we get nowhere." Far from being an isolated instance of failed resolution, this polarized relationship became the model for future movie couples. In a 1964 *Esquire* article, David Newman and Robert Benton (*Bonnie and Clyde*'s scriptwriters) pointed to Patricia and Michel as one of the "Key Couples of the New Sentimentality"[32] (the other was Mr. and Mrs. John Kennedy), and versions of their conversation-at-cross-purposes ("Do you know William Faulkner?" "No, who's he? Some guy you slept with?") appeared again and again in American movies of the 1960s and 1970s, most obviously in *Bonnie and Clyde, Butch Cassidy and the Sundance Kid, The Way We Were, Taxi Driver, Smokey and the Bandit*, and *Saturday Night Fever*.[33]

Formally, *Breathless* proved even more influential, demonstrating that departures from Hollywood's sacrosanct formal par-

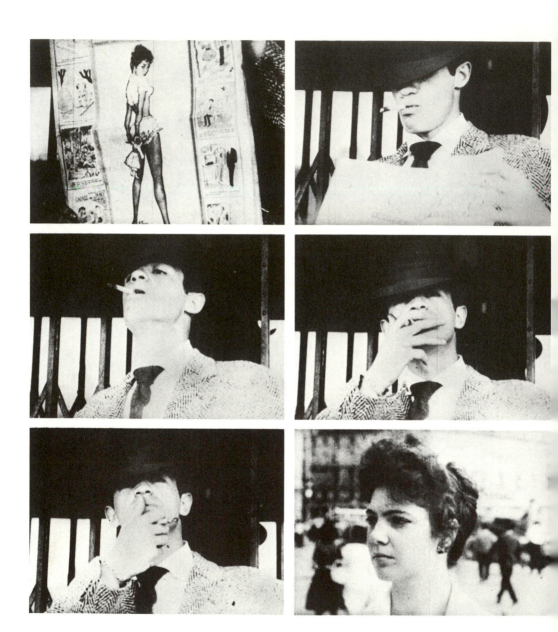

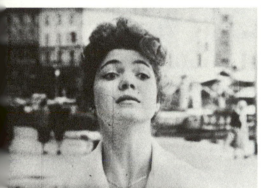

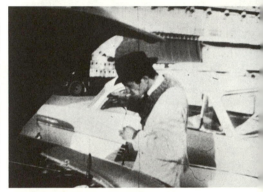
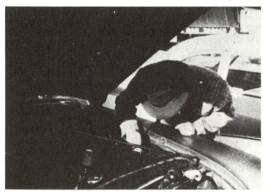

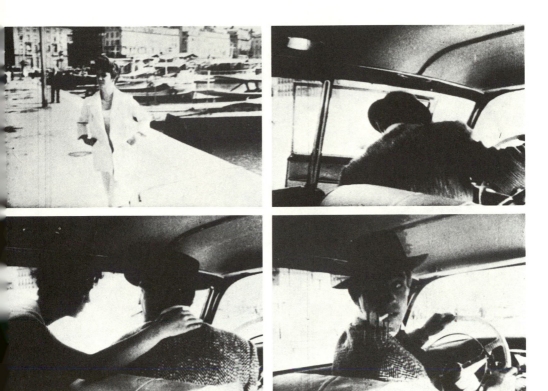

adigm could generate unanticipated excitement. The movie's initial sequence broke nearly all the continuity rules. Suppressing establishing shots, Godard fragmented the opening car theft into isolated components (Michel, the female lookout, the car) held together only by a convention (eyeline matches) whose spatial guarantees Godard violated in the shootout two minutes later.

With his hero on the road, Godard filmed from inside the car (a rare shot in 1959), broke Michel's discovery of the gun into two "mismatched" shots with a jump cut, and had him address the camera directly ("If you don't like the ocean . . ."), thereby temporarily rupturing the illusion that Classic Hollywood had so diligently pursued. The comic tone associated with this last tactic (Groucho Marx had often spoken directly to the audience)

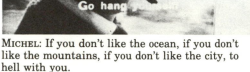

MICHEL: If you don't like the ocean, if you don't like the mountains, if you don't like the city, to hell with you.

deceived the audience about what was to follow. Prepared for slapstick, the audience now encountered what seemed to be a developing thriller. As the motorcycle cops began their pursuit, however, Godard repeatedly crossed the 180° axis (designed to maintain continuous screen direction) so that the police seemed not to be chasing Michel at all. With Michel trapped on a side road, Godard apparently set up a standard shootout. Instead, the killing occurred in a kind of cartoon, with a series of close-ups atomizing the incident into barely related units. Having tacitly used the movie's opening sequence to remind the viewer of his dependence on spatial continuity conventions, Godard suddenly

"My goose is cooked!"

violated them, crossing the 180° axis to make Michel appear to be firing off into empty space, and to make the concluding jump cut to the dead policeman all the more shocking because of its illogic.

In such sequences, Godard's jump cuts and 180° violations implicitly exposed what Hollywood's continuity rules sought to conceal—the inherent discontinuity between any two shots. The apparent inevitability of Hollywood's transitions, in fact utterly dependent on conventions, hid the very process of cinematic choice, which Godard increasingly made his subject. By *A Woman Is a Woman* (1961), Godard was repeatedly ignoring the customary matching rules, having his heroine flip an egg into the air, go to the telephone, and return to catch the egg. By 1965, he was writing that "the only great problem with cinema seems to me more and more with each film when and why to start a shot and when and why to end it. . . . two shots which follow each other do not necessarily follow each other."[34] Finally, in *2 or 3 Things I Know about Her* (1966), Godard made explicit the necessity for choice that had persistently obsessed him. Showing his heroine arrive at her husband's garage, Godard whispered an anguished voice-over:

For example . . . for example, how can you describe an event? What way do you show how or explain how, that afternoon, at about ten past four, Juliette and Marianne went to a garage near the Porte des Ternes where Juliette's husband worked?
Sense and nonsense.
Yes, how do you describe exactly what happened? Of course, there's Juliette, there's her husband, there's the garage. But do you really have to use these very words and those images? Are they the only possible ones? Are there no others? Am I talking too loud? Am I looking too close or from too far away? . . .
It is 4:45 p.m. Should I have described Juliette or the leaves? It was really impossible to describe both, so let us simply say that both were trembling gently at the beginning of the end of an October afternoon.

Throughout the early 1960s, Godard had tacitly demonstrated what this sequence openly acknowledged: that every camera setup and every transition revealed one thing at the expense of everything else. In *Masculine-Feminine* (1966), he withheld normal reverse shots to convert boy-girl conversations into "interviews" in which the questioner remained offscreen. Similarly, that film's opening sequence kept the central character at the edge of the frame where he was barely visible. *Vivre sa vie* (1962) experimented with inopportune camera setups, with one sequence showing the principal characters only from the rear. One dialogue scene in *A Woman Is a Woman* came accompanied with shots of unidentified Parisians walking in various parts of the city.

The conspicuous arbitrariness of these cinematic choices reflected the fitful decisiveness of Godard's characters, all of whom recognized the urgent need for selecting a defined lifestyle. His movies bristled with texts and images that his heroes mixed indiscriminately in their search for roles. *Breathless*'s Michel played at being Bogart, while *A Woman Is a Woman*'s Angela first announced, "I would like to be in a musical, with Cyd Charisse and Gene Kelly, choreography by Bob Fosse," and then proceeded to behave as capriciously as an MGM heroine. *Vivre sa vie*'s Nana, having failed at becoming a movie star or a respectable bourgeoise, settled for a prostitute's life, romanticized by her identification with Falconetti's Joan of Arc. *Masculine-Feminine*'s Paul moved emphatically between sterotypical student Marxism and utterly conventional careerism, while the willful plot of *Pierrot le fou* (1965) seemed derived from scrambled versions of its hero's constant reading.

In all of these films, Godard thematically and formally repudiated Classic Hollywood's concealment of choice. The implications of this attack, however, went unassimilated by the American Cinema. Indeed, throughout the early 1960s, Hollywood had persisted in regarding the New Wave in general as too radical a break with America's traditional commercial forms. But *A Hard Day's Night*'s simultaneous commercial success and obvious reliance on French influences (particularly Louis Malle's 1960 *Zazie dans le Métro*) sponsored the movement as a new possibility for the flagging American Cinema. The new American directors, however, adopted only the New Wave's superficial stylistic exuberance, leaving Classic Hollywood's paradigms fundamentally untouched.

At first, the changes seemed more profound. Looking back at 1967 (the year of *Bonnie and Clyde* and *The Graduate*), Andrew Sarris remembered a heady sense of something new: "Hollywood, we were told, had turned a corner, with *The Graduate* supposedly marking the end of an era, and the beginning of a new age."[35] Attendance rose significantly for the first time since 1945-1946, indicating that the industry had apparently succeeded in creating a new film for its new audience.

Certainly the movies *looked* different, bursting with stylistic devices usually reserved for comedies. *Bonnie and Clyde* alone assaulted its audience with fast motion (after one of the robberies), slow motion (the final massacre), scenes shot through oddly distorting filters (Bonnie's reunion with her mother), black-and-white photographs as titles for a color film, extreme close-ups (the opening shot of Bonnie's lips), music that commented ironically on the action (Flatt and Scruggs's banjo bluegrass), montages freely moving through time and space (as Bonnie read her poem, the scene shifted from Clyde's car, to the police station where Hamer read it in a newspaper, then back to a field with Clyde reading another newspaper).

All these spectacular formal devices had been lifted directly from individual New Wave films. As early as 1965, *The Pawnbroker* had assimilated *Hiroshima, mon amour*'s unannounced, incomplete, out-of-sequence flashbacks that promptly became the staple of such commercial movies as *Two for the Road* (1967), *Point Blank* (1968), and *Petulia* (1968). *Butch Cassidy*'s repetition of *The 400 Blows*' freeze-frame ending sponsored its adoption on American television, where it quickly developed into the stock device for concluding a show or for leading into an advertisement. After Truffaut himself had suggested it, Arthur Penn stitched together the montage of Bonnie's poem by copying the exchange of letters between Jim and Catherine in *Jules and Jim* (1961). *Butch Cassidy*'s lyrical bicycling interlude came directly from a similar passage in *Jules and Jim*, and both films used nondiegetic music, syncopated editing, filters, and slow motion to suggest the fairy tale quality of memory. The slow motion used repeatedly for violent scenes in the new American movies (*Bonnie and Clyde, The Wild Bunch, Easy Rider*) derived both from Catherine's suicidal plunge in *Jules and Jim*, and from the pillow fight in Jean Vigo's *Zero for Conduct* (1933), one of the few classic French films openly admired by the New Wave directors. *Shoot the Piano Player*'s (1962) final gunfight in the snow, with its absence of establishing shots, frequent 180° crossings, long shots, and fizzy off-center compositions, became the climax of Altman's *McCabe and Mrs. Miller* (1971). The 360° pans of *Breathless* and *Weekend* (1967) (both accompanied by Mozart) were repeated in *Five Easy Pieces* (1970) (accompanied by Chopin). *Carnal Knowledge*'s (1971) flat-background, long-take conversations between Art Garfunkle and Jack Nicholson imitated *Masculine-Feminine*'s mock "interviews." *Breathless*'s free use of jump cutting became an almost standard device, best used by Martin Scorsese in *Mean Streets* (1973) and *Taxi Driver* (1976).

The most important of the new American movies, *Bonnie and Clyde*, resembled a pastiche of New Wave effects. Its scriptwriters, David Newman and Robert Benton, freely acknowledging their debt to *Breathless, Jules and Jim*, and *Shoot the Piano Player*, had even approached both Truffaut and Godard with offers to direct their film (settling for Arthur Penn only because Truffaut was making *Farenheit 451* and Godard was rejected as too experimental by American producers).[36] Although *Shoot the Piano Player* had clearly provided the model for *Bonnie and Clyde*'s abrupt shifts from comedy into violence, Penn's movie borrowed most obviously from *Breathless*. Both were "corrected" genre films that manipulated expectations created by previous versions of gangster stories. Like Michel in Godard's movie, Bonnie and Clyde drifted casually into crime. Both movies portrayed their heroes as self-conscious role-players, intent on celebrity, forever reading newspaper accounts of their own activities. Both films used the motif of constantly exchanged stolen cars. Both sets of outlaws took refuge in movie theaters, where the film within the film (in *Breathless*, Budd Boetticher's *Westbound*; in *Bonnie and Clyde*, the "We're in the Money" sequence from *Gold Diggers of 1933*) commented ironically on the main narrative. Both films depended for their pacing on an alternation between extremes of movement (when the editing became "breathless") and stasis (when both Penn and Godard resorted to long takes to film Michel and Patricia and Bonnie and Clyde hiding out in bedrooms, debating their relationships). Godard's sexually reluctant heroine became Penn's impotent Clyde ("I told you I was no lover boy"). Both movies eschewed psychology, treating their childlike, affectless characters as cartoons. *Breathless*'s opening shot of the comic page (with Michel hiding behind it) explicitly referred to the tactics of both films. As Penn explained:

In *Bonnie and Clyde*, we don't have a story of very strong characters. They're relatively shallow, rather empty people as far as we know. . . . Consequently, we had to deal more at the level of the outer side, like the cartoon, more the outline. I thought in terms of cartoons—each frame

changing. Here we laugh, here we cry, here we laugh again, and so we cut the film like that and the images were made up like that instead of long, fluid ones.[37]

By implicitly exposing his movie as a composite of discrete fragments transferred from other films, Penn's allusiveness (itself a tactic borrowed from Godard) further reduced his characters to pop images. Some of *Bonnie and Clyde*'s quotations were merely playful jokes intended for the buff: thus, Clyde's broken dark glasses referred to Michel's. At other points, *Bonnie and Clyde*'s quotations became more complex. Imitating *Breathless*, Penn opened with a distorting succession of fragments, withholding the customary establishing shot until the sequence's tenth take. Not coincidentally, the narrative also borrowed *Breathless*'s *in medias res* beginning: Clyde, like Michel, was stealing a car. This sequence, however, contained allusions within allusions: the film's opening shot, an enormous close-up of Bonnie's lips, duplicated the audience's first view of Charles Foster Kane as he whispered his dying word "Rosebud." In one of *Bonnie and Clyde*'s first violent moments, Penn's allusions served expressive purposes. The close-up of the bank teller, shot after jumping on the escaping gang's running board, invoked a similar shot from *Potemkin*'s Odessa Steps slaughter. The sequence as a whole, with its odd match between Shots 1 and 3 that appeared to reverse Clyde's position in the car, made the teller's death as star-

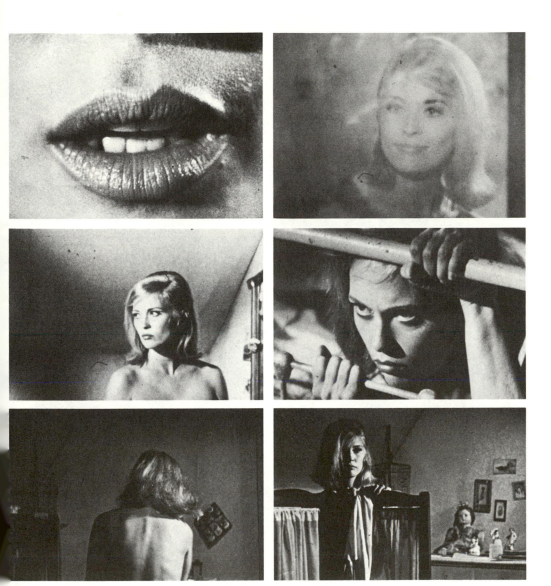

tling and cinematically illogical as *Breathless*'s spatially confusing shootout.

FOR A BRIEF period, perhaps lasting only a few months, the New Wave style seemed to have radicalized the American Cinema and effected at last a genuine "break" in Hollywood's paradigms. Close inspection, however, would have revealed that Hollywood's procedures remained intact. First, the new movies' explicit sex and violence and odd, off-key endings were still contained within formally closed narratives. Thus, most of these films could be appreciated as genre pictures: *The Graduate* as a kind of kinky screwball comedy, *Bonnie and Clyde* as a combination gangster-western (derived from numerous, and therefore comforting, predecessors, including Lang's 1937 *You Only Live Once* and Nicholas Ray's 1949 *They Live by Night*).

Nor had Hollywood disowned the use of stars. The new movies did everything possible to exploit the personalities of Warren Beatty (*Bonnie and Clyde*), Dustin Hoffman (*The Graduate, Midnight Cowboy*), Robert Redford and Paul Newman (*Butch Cassidy, Cool Hand Luke*), William Holden (*The Wild Bunch*), Jack Nicholson (*Easy Rider, Five Easy Pieces, Carnal Knowledge*), and even the low-budget, drive-in-movie persona of Peter Fonda (*Easy Rider*).

Despite its obvious stylistic pyrotechnics, the American Cinema also remained formally conservative, surrounding the borrowed New Wave devices with long stretches that completely conformed to traditional continuity rules. More important, in the 1960s, the increasingly rapid dissemination of every cinematic innovation quickly co-opted the power of all but the most radical departures, converting the New Wave's revelatory defamiliarizations (e.g., freeze framing, slow motion) into mere cosmetic flourishes assimilable by Hollywood's conventional forms. In the less media-fluent postwar period, *It's a Wonderful Life*'s freeze frame had amounted to a significant deconstruction. By the date of *Bonnie and Clyde*, however, even in the commercial cinema, slow motion and photographs-as-credits were already three years old: *A Hard Day's Night* had employed most of the New Wave tricks in 1964, and its formal imitator, television's "The Monkees," had been running for nine months.[38] In effect, the critics who proclaimed the New American movie (and who avoided TV) overestimated the impact of formal departures that the television viewer had largely digested. Not surprisingly, the same critics underestimated the television-spawned irony which that viewer now brought to Hollywood's products.

9. The Left and Right Cycles

THE RADICAL fashions of the 1960s and 1970s concealed the obvious: the traditional American mythology had survived as the generally accepted account of America's history and future. Thus, the "New" American Cinema—superficially radical, internally conservative—perfectly represented its audience's ambivalent relationship to the period's developments. Like the counterculture with its western imagery, Hollywood mobilized renovated versions of its traditional genres and heroes to satisfy the audience's schizophrenic impulses toward irony and nostalgia. Most crucially, because the thematic paradigm's myth of reconciliation had defined the popular audience's unconscious expectation of what an American movie should be, Hollywood determined to retain it, using it to structure even its seemingly most subversive films.

At times, Hollywood's new tendency to sentimentalize irreconcilability made the operations of the traditional thematic paradigm hard to direct. *The Way We Were* (1973), for example, appeared to glamorize the incompatibility of Robert Redford's Waspish diffidence and Barbra Streisand's Jewish moral earnestness, building to a romantic unhappy ending, as Redford refused to try the marriage one more time: "No, Katie, that would be wrong for both of us," he intoned. "We'd both lose." But the starkness of the film's dichotomies was undercut by the personae of its two stars. With a background in American Cinema's most conservative form (remakes of big Broadway musicals), Streisand never seemed as radical as the movie pretended. Redford's indecisiveness, on the other hand, was continually contradicted by his associations with previous action parts. Thus, the two characters' incompatibility appeared more a plot device than a genuine expression of new pessimism.

The traditionalism of *Five Easy Pieces* (1970), one of the period's best films, also remained tacit. Superficially, the movie dramatized the gulf between an intellectual upper class (the hero's musical family) and a physical lower class (the hero's girlfriend, Rayette), polarizing the opposition in schematic North-South imagery. Thus, the spiritual aridity of Bobby Dupea's (Jack Nicholson) adopted proletarian life found its visual correlative in the hot, dusty oil fields of California, where he worked as a day laborer, lived with the pregnant Rayette, and hung out with a pal, drinking beer, going bowling, and chasing girls. His family's emotional sterility, on the other hand, suggested itself in the rainy, cold remoteness of a Puget Sound island life, and in their own physical unhealthiness (sister Tita, fat and neurotic; brother Carl in a neck brace; the father mute and immobilized by a stroke).

By making this division appear unnatural, however, *Five Easy Pieces* reconfirmed the desirability of reconciliation. Its hero was another version of Huck and Holden, surrounded by phonies whose snobbery and obtuseness had betrayed the American promise. Indeed, Bobby's own ideal blend of toughness and sensitivity merely revived a 1940s variant of the outlaw hero, the roughneck classical musician (*Golden Boy, Humoresque*). Inevitably, the conclusion, with Bobby abandoning Rayette and hitching a ride to Alaska, proved utterly traditional, another lighting out for the territory.

The surface pessimism of *The Way We Were* and *Five Easy Pieces* constituted the crucial element in Hollywood's refurbished displacement strategy. To retain its popularity with an increasingly younger audience, the industry needed to find ways of acknowledging the shocks of the 1960s in forms still recognizable as entertainment. Since the reconciliatory pattern had come to define movies for most Americans, it would be retained. Around it, however, would be embroidered reworkings of traditional genres, spiced with apparently irresolvable conflicts and nominally unhappy endings, all designed to allow the audience to assuage its conscience about cinema's inherent "escapism." For these new movies, in other words, Hollywood self-consciously reversed the unconsciously developed pattern of the postwar period. Where the external optimism of *It's a Wonderful Life* had struggled to contain an unintentionally subversive view of American life, the blatant, self-congratulatory gloom of *Five Easy Pieces* merely re-affirmed the traditional mythology's abiding validity.

The extent of intentional manipulation in Hollywood's revised tactics is ultimately irrelevant. While Classic Hollywood's use of the traditional American mythology had certainly not been in-nocent, its "sincerity" (to use Godard's description) had reflected the culture's own naïve relationship to the world. By contrast, the contemporary period's self-conscious reworkings accurately mirrored the audience's increasingly ironic attempts to deal with historical events in the traditional terms.

To express those attempts, the popular American Cinema of the late 1960s and early 1970s divided conspicuously into a Left and a Right. At the outset, this development appeared radical, for it involved the externalization of choice, which ceased to be an explicit subject of individual films, becoming instead an issue between the movies and their audience.

The Left cycle began first. After the 1967 success of *The Graduate* and *Bonnie and Clyde*, the industry followed with a series of movies intended to appeal to the counterculture's most visible elements. Nixon's election, and the surprising popularity of the old-fashioned *Airport* (1970), however, demonstrated the exist-ence of a large conservative audience and set off a wave of right-wing films. The two categories' most popular films were the fol-lowing:

Left	Right
The Graduate (1967)	*Bullitt* (1968)
Bonnie and Clyde (1967)	*Coogan's Bluff* (1968)
Cool Hand Luke (1967)	*Patton* (1970)
2001: A Space Odyssey (1968)	*Dirty Harry* (1971)
Midnight Cowboy (1969)	*The French Connection* (1971)
Easy Rider (1969)	*Walking Tall* (1973)
Butch Cassidy and the Sundance Kid (1969)	*Death Wish* (1974)
The Wild Bunch (1969)	
Little Big Man (1970)	

McCabe and Mrs. Miller (1971)
Billy Jack (1972)
A Clockwork Orange (1972)
One Flew Over the Cuckoo's Nest
   (1975)

Superficially, these films separated the outlaw hero from the official hero, making the former the subject of the Left films and the latter the hero of the Right. Almost all the Left movies, in fact, used outlaws or outsiders to represent the counterculture's own image of itself as in flight from a repressive society. The Right films, in contrast, typically centered on cops or vigilantes engaged in war against criminals. Choice as a subject seemed to have disappeared from these films: rarely was a character forced to decide between opposed values. But in their self-righteousness and refusal to admit competing possibilities, both sets of films appeared to be arguing that a choice had been made *before* each film began, with the action that followed only the logical results of having settled on a particular set of values. Presumably, a viewer would decide which set he preferred and then attend that cycle of films. As a result, the American cinema lost its Classic Period richness: the new Left movies were *Casablanca*s without a Victor Laszlo; the new Right movies were *Liberty Valance*s without a Ranse Stoddard.

The newly polarized films elicited unusually strong reactions from audiences. Pauline Kael reported that those who saw *Walking Tall* frequently cheered "Get 'em, get 'em!" as Sheriff Pusser wielded his club in the name of law and order,[1] while hippies shouted at the end of *Joe*, "Next time we'll have guns! We'll get you first, Joe."[2] Indeed, the movies' polarization often seemed to duplicate a contemporary cultural phenomenon described by Hodgson:

It was as if, from 1967 on, for several years, two different tribes of Americans experienced the same outward events but experienced them as two quite different realities. A writer in *The Atlantic* put the point well after the October 1967 demonstrations at the Pentagon. Accounts of that happening in the conventional press and in the underground press, he pointed out, simply didn't intersect at any point. It was as if they had been reporting two different events. "The older reporters, who were behind the soldiers' lines, or on the Pentagon roof, or inside the temporary war room, wrote about hippies and Maoists; the kids, on the other side of the line, wrote about the awful brutality of the U.S. marshals. Each wrote with enough half truth to feel justified in excluding the other."[3]

The movies, too, appeared to be describing the same events from different perspectives. The vicious southern cops of the Left's *Easy Rider, Bonnie and Clyde,* and *Cool Hand Luke* were transformed into the heroic Buford Pusser of the Right's *Walking Tall*; the sympathetic hippies of *Easy Rider* became the psychopathic killer of *Dirty Harry*, equipped with a peace symbol for a belt buckle. Both sets of films even managed to use the Kennedy assassination for their own purpose: the final sequence of *Bonnie and Clyde*, as Arthur Penn pointed out, intentionally invoked the assassination films, to the extent of having part of Warren Beatty's head fly off when struck by a bullet. Not to be outdone by the Left's appropriation of the Kennedy martyrdom, *Walking Tall* deliberately evoked memories of John Kennedy, Jr., with its funeral sequence and its long takes of Pusser's son walking the length of a hospital corridor, carrying his father's rifle.

In retrospect, as a guide to American culture's relationship to contemporary events, these movies reveal persisting similarities between the apparently polarized Left and Right. Ultimately, of course, both shared the same mythology, with its predisposition to regard events in terms of the reconciliatory pattern's abiding advocacy of individualism. Thus, both groups tended to think of material problems as temporary crises solvable by short-term interventions. Inevitably, therefore, the Left and Right movies maintained Hollywood's stock tactical blurring of apparent differences. The wide popularity of both sets of movies (suggesting that, far from choosing between them, most filmgoers went to both) indicated that tactic's continued success.

In the Left and Right movies, the blurring process typically involved the three factors that superficially divided them: the response to the frontier's closing, the characteristics of the hero, and the willingness to acknowledge self-consciousness.

RESPONSES TO THE FRONTIER'S CLOSING

The movies of the late 1960s and early 1970s returned again and again, explicitly or implicitly, to the frontier's continuing significance in American life. In the postwar period, Hollywood's westerns had tentatively raised doubts about the mythology of space that Classic Hollywood had so often invoked. In the late sixties, those doubts grew more widespread. Politically, the willingness to concede the frontier's closing became the bedrock issue dividing the Left and Right. Ironically, the frontier, historically the figurative means for solving potential divisiveness, now proved a source of polarization. With the Right refusing to grant that anything had changed, the Left (at least in its rational mood) insisted that all frontiers, geographical and metaphorical, had disappeared, and with them, the basis for certain lifestyles, institutions, and values premised on the existence of unlimited space.

The Left's position, of course, derived from Turner's thesis, whose tacit Darwinism had linked cultural institutions to a geographic condition. The general acceptance of Turner's logic enabled the Left to see clearly outmoded institutions as symbols of the frontier's close. The Right, in contrast, sought to deny the connection. Even its faint recognitions of closure carried with them no sense of invalidation of the traditional behavior.

Inevitably, the Left movies of the late sixties and early seventies consistently suggested that America was no longer living in a frontier age. This theme's most explicit treatment occurred in the western, increasingly relocated from its traditional period in the 1880s to the decades just before World War I, a time long after the Bureau of the Census's official announcement of the frontier's passing. Thus, *McCabe and Mrs. Miller* took place in 1901, and *The Wild Bunch* and *Butch Cassidy and the Sundance Kid* on the eve of the war itself. The latter movie even used a New York interlude to suggest progressive urbanization, and a bicycle to represent the quainter aspects of modernity. *The Wild Bunch*'s images of the new age were more vicious. One member of the gang was killed by being dragged behind a car, and the others were slaughtered by Mexican bandits armed with machine guns by a German "military advisor." *Little Big Man*, the one major western of the decade not set in the twentieth century, nevertheless implied the West's closing by making the defeated Indians the film's heroes. Forced into more and more circumscribed areas, and eventually into reservations, the Indians became, for the first time, an image of America.

The Left's nonwesterns translated this developing sense of "lateness" into physical settings of intense claustrophobia. *Cool Hand Luke* began with tight close-ups of its hero destroying a parking meter, an urban symbol of crowding, while the main story concerned life on a chain gang. Similarly, *One Flew Over the Cuckoo's Nest* was set in a crowded psychiatric ward, where patients (read "prisoners") had little space or privacy. The action of *Midnight Cowboy*, despite its title, took place in a teeming New York City that symbolized closed possibilities. *A Clockwork Orange*'s hallucinatory, Skinnerian laboratory, with its looming walls and ceilings, offered a view of a world where even mental freedom had become impossible. Finally, the cramped space capsules, cloistered living quarters, and claustrophobic spacesuits of *2001* belied the new promise of outer-space-as-frontier. Instead, the film corroborated Kenneth Boulding's image of "spaceship Earth," a frequent metaphor of the counterculture:

There is no room for "great societies" in the spaceship. It implies conservationism to the point of conservatism rather than expansionism. . . . There is no room in the spaceship for men on white horses, and very little room for horsing around.[4]

Even in movies without obviously circumscribed physical locales, Left filmmakers used other means to suggest contraction. *McCabe and Mrs. Miller*'s exceptionally low-ceilinged sets made its characters appear to be living on top of each other in a crowded, Breughelian world. Similarly, *The Wild Bunch* eschewed the Fordian vistas associated with the genre in favor of tightly composed mid-shots and zooming close-ups. In *Easy Rider*, even the exhilarating openness of the landscapes was undercut by the film's West to East movement, a reversal of the traditional westward direction, that suggested the West had run out of room.

The Graduate was a special case. Like other Left directors, Nichols used extreme close-ups to suggest confinement (particularly subjective shots from behind a scuba mask). But for the frontier issue, the most important aspect of the film was its location in California, the origin of the counterculture. With unending promise its raison d'être and the Pacific coastline its physical fact, California dramatized the polarization between Left and Right on the frontier issue. As Joan Didion wrote:

California is a place where boom mentality and a sense of Chekhovian loss meet in uneasy suspension; in which the mind is troubled by some buried but ineradicable suspicion that things had better work here, because here, beneath that immense bleached sky, is where we run out of continent.[5]

Trying to find a career, struggling to reconcile the casual sexual impulses of Mrs. Robinson with the sternly rational advice of her contemporaries ("Plastics!"), *The Graduate*'s hero represented California, which, for the Left, represented America itself. As Left historian Peter Schrag argued, "In California . . . we ran out of time, and were thus forced to confront the unresolved ambiguities of the national imagination itself."[6]

To suggest the frontier's closing, the Left movies typically opposed their heroes (inevitably outlaws or extreme individualists) with depersonalized villains who came to represent the incessant advance of modernity. In this motif's most obvious rendering, the nameless, faceless Pinkerton men relentlessly pursuing Butch Cassidy and the Sundance Kid resembled a force of nature. Never seen in close-ups, they were remote but always there, and the heroes' question (at first humorous, but increasingly uneasy),"Who *are* those guys?" caught on as a counterculture tagline that summed up the Left's anxiety about the Europeanizing of America. *The Wild Bunch*, another version of the same story, allowed the audience to see the trailing bounty hunters. But by associating them with jackals, the movie made clear that, without help, they could not have caught the Bunch: the U.S. Army supporting force, deployed from trains, added the modern note of bureaucratic relentlessness.

Other Left movies worked similarly, using villains whose impersonality seemed to stand for an historical process. *Bonnie and Clyde* used the emotionless Texas Ranger Frank Hamer, doggedly willing to cross state lines to kill his prey. *McCabe and Mrs. Miller* showed its hero, a small-time would-be entrepreneur, murdered by agents of a mysterious "Corporation" who had tried unsuccessfully to buy McCabe's interests. The principal antagonist in *Cool Hand Luke* was "The Man with No Eyes," a rifleman guard on the chain gang, whose enormous mirrored glasses permanently hid his features. (This figure clearly derived from *Psycho's* highway patrolman, looming at the window of Janet Leigh's car.) In *One Flew Over the Cuckoo's Nest*, Milos Forman's inappropriate naturalism softened Kesey's allegorical Nurse Ratched. But Nicholson's pronunciation of the name (to sound like "rat shit") and Louise Fletcher's unsettling imperturbability restored Ken Kesey's image of her as an agent of the repressive "Combine," his metaphor for a pernicious modern society impinging on his western heroes' freedom. This counterculture paranoia peaked in *Easy Rider*, where straight society appeared as unrelievedly (and anonymously) vicious; in *2001*, where the most dangerous enemies of all were the computer HAL and (perhaps) the mysterious monoliths; and in *A Clockwork Orange*, where medical technicians controlled even the impulses of the individual brain. All these films appealed to the Left's sense of societal problems as complex, impersonal, and pervasive. In no case did its heroes oppose an individual enemy.

The Left films' implicit reliance on Turner's frontier thesis determined that the theme of confinement would find its most explicit treatment in the western. Since *Red River* (1948), the western as a form had been preoccupied with the dying out of radically individualistic lifestyles. This preoccupation intensified in the sixties (*The Man Who Shot Liberty Valance, Ride the High Country, Hud, Hombre*) until by the end of the decade, it had become almost the genre's *only* theme. *The Wild Bunch* expressed it most overtly: its ageing heroes, gunfighters on the eve of World War I, were obvious anachronisms. "You boys ain't getting any younger," a companion advised, and arguing against another bank robbery, the leader, Pike (William Holden), admitted, "We gotta start thinking beyond our guns. Them days is closing fast." Their opponent, Mexican bandit Mapache, equipped with a car, machine guns, and an accountant, seemed more able to adapt to modern times. Like the Wild Bunch, Butch Cassidy and the Sundance Kid attempted to buy time by transferring operations to a more primitive country (Bolivia) where, presumably, conditions would still permit lifestyles that had become impossible in the United States. But the promise of Latin America as a frontier proved illusory. The only safe course, as *Pat Garrett and Billy the Kid* (1973) showed, involved abandoning the old ways. Asked how it felt to be on the side of the law, former outlaw Garrett could only say, "It feels different, but times are changing. I aim to get old—along with the country."

Although the outlaw remained the Left films' most common image of outmoded lifestyles, these movies sometimes pictured individualism itself as outdated. McCabe's methods, despite his whorehouse, were not illegal, but merely idiosyncratic, while Cool Hand Luke's crime was only getting drunk and chopping down a single parking meter. "Luke," his mother asked, "what went wrong?" He answered for all the Left's heroes: "I just can't seem to find no elbow room." *Midnight Cowboy* made the attempt to maintain the old order's trappings seem pathetic. Decked out in his western hat, shirt, and boots, Joe Buck was brought down to earth by Ratso: "That cowboy stuff," he sneered, "is strictly for fags." Even *Easy Rider*, with its warning "The time's running out," and its apocalyptic ending (the two bikers' random murder), suggested that certain ways of behaving had become not only impossible, but dangerous. As the small-town, ACLU lawyer George, Jack Nicholson explained how times had changed:

GEORGE: Oh, they're [people who had refused Wyatt and Billy motel rooms] not scared of you. They're scared of what you represent to them.

BILLY: Hey, man. All we represent to them, man, is somebody needs a haircut.

GEORGE: What you represent to them is freedom.

BILLY: What the hell's wrong with freedom, man. That's what it's all about.

GEORGE: Oh, yeah; that's right—that's what it's all about, all right. But talking about it and being it—that's two different things. I mean, it's real hard to be free when you are bought and sold in the marketplace. 'Course don't ever tell anybody that they're not free, 'cause then they're gonna get real busy killin' and maimin' to prove to you that they are.

> Oh, yeah—they're gonna talk to you, and talk to you, and talk to you about individual freedom, but they see a free individual, it's gonna scare 'em.
>
> BILLY: Mmmm, well, that don't make 'em runnin' scared.
>
> GEORGE: No. It makes 'em dangerous.

This speech perfectly represented the counterculture's contradictoriness, its paradoxical glamorization of the one value (individualism) most discredited by the phenomenon it persistently invoked—the frontier's closing.

In sum, the Left films of the late sixties and early seventies used four means to suggest the passing of frontier conditions: 1) a sense of "lateness," generated by relocating westerns in the twentieth century; 2) settings that dramatically emphasized confinement; 3) anonymous, relentless forces opposing the movies' heroes; and 4) demonstrations of the anachronous quality of certain lifestyles.

Surprisingly, the Right films also used the first two motifs. With the exception of *Patton*, all employed contemporary settings, and even *Patton* explicitly evoked a sense of "lateness" by portraying its hero as the last of a certain kind of military leader. The typical Right movie, however, took place in a metropolis, especially the two with the most radical images: San Francisco (*Bullitt, Dirty Harry*) and New York (*Coogan's Bluff, The French Connection, Death Wish*). Even *Walking Tall* determinedly made its small town the symbolic equivalent of the urban landscape. "We're a big city now," the hero was told at his homecoming. "We got our own crime, vice, and lust."

The crowded, decaying cities of the Right movies implicitly acknowledged the frontier's closing. Pauline Kael, in fact, could say that *The French Connection*, like other movies made in New York, "provided a permanent record of the city in breakdown."[7] But the Right films sought to ignore Turner's logic: in them, changed conditions did not demand changed institutions, attitudes, or lifestyles. Welcoming her son home, the hero's mother in *Walking Tall* summed up the consistent Right viewpoint: "If you look around town, you might see some changes. Pay them no mind, they got nothing to do with us."

Apparently, therefore, the Left and Right films disagreed over the third and fourth motifs. The Left cycle used its villains' anonymity as a metaphor for the complexity of modern society's problems. In *Easy Rider*, George (Nicholson) expressed the Left's sense that identifying contemporary malaise had become a baffling task: "You know, this used to be a helluva good country. I can't understand what's gone wrong with it." The Right, on the other hand, claimed to understand perfectly. In the Right films, problems had sources in particular individuals with names and faces, who could be located, tracked down, and eliminated so that society could return to normal. In the Right's view, difficulties required only an individual hero strong enough to stand up to the villain for the sake of ineffective communities.

The Right movies, of course, were urban westerns, briefs for the continued applicability of the reluctant hero story to contemporary life. Like the Classic Hollywood films they imitated, the Right movies reduced enormous social issues (war, crime, urbanization) to localized emergencies solvable by simple, direct action involving no long-term commitment to reform. Thus, the Right's plots inevitably built to man-to-man showdowns, frequently played as modern versions of gunfights.

Some Right films made the western mythology explicit. *Coogan's Bluff*'s main character (Clint Eastwood) was an Arizona sheriff trailing his enemy (a psychopathic, drug-taking hippie) to New York. The film's first half, which poked fun at Eastwood's awkwardness in the city, seemed to duplicate the Left's image of older lifestyles' new inappropriateness. "This isn't the O.K. Corral around here, you know," a reluctant witness warned Coogan; and baffled by the Arizonian's bull-in-a-china-shop act, a NYC police lieutenant asked wonderingly: "What gives with you people out there—too much sun?" But the movie's second half vindicated its hero's western-style tactics, and reaffirmed that legal niceties merely obstructed the practice of law and order.

Death Wish was another overt evocation of the western's values. With his wife murdered and his daughter driven into catatonia by three vaguely hippie attackers, the principal character (Charles Bronson) converted from his pacifist liberalism while on a trip to Arizona. Watching a staged gunfight in the streets of Old Tucson (where *Rio Bravo* had been filmed), Bronson decided to use the old methods against New York's criminals. The rest of the movie involved a series of showdowns, as Bronson invited and then fought off attacks in subways, Central Park, and deserted alleys, becoming a newspaper hero in the process, and causing assaults in the city to drop by one-third. Although the grudgingly admiring police eventually asked him to leave town, the movie never portrayed him as unsympathetic or wrongheaded. In fact, he had succeeded where the police had not.

Although *Dirty Harry* kept its western references less explicit, it clearly operated from the same assumptions. By making its villain (the Scorpio killer) a lone sniper, the movie implied the stock Right position that the JFK assassination, far from representing American society's general problems, was the work of a single aberrant individual. To the role of the tough cop Harry, Clint Eastwood brought his associations with western heroes, particularly those from the Sergio Leone Italian westerns where he had played "The Man with No Name," a relentless, silent, efficient gunfighter, who merely happened to be on society's side. *Dirty Harry's* plot mainly concerned Eastwood's attempts to ignore constraining legal proprieties (explained by a Berkeley law professor) and to deal straightforwardly with the killer. Dealing straightforwardly principally meant using an enormous revolver, which Eastwood proudly described as "just about the most powerful handgun on earth and would blow your head clean off." At the end, having ignored official orders to stay out of the case, Eastwood tracked and killed the assassin, and in a gesture of contempt for the weakness of liberal society, reprised *High Noon* by throwing away his badge.

Walking Tall was no different. Indeed, it contained, in faint disguise, nearly every standard western convention. Returning home after army duty and an aborted wrestling career, Buford Pusser discovered that his small town had become the seat of a local crime ring operating crooked gambling, whorehouses, and moonshine stills. Pusser imitated the reluctant hero's traditional unwillingness to involve himself in what he saw around him. A terrible beating, however, quickly converted him to a crusader, wielding an enormous club and hindered only by the corrupt legal system (whose corruption often involved upholding suspects' rights). To his worried wife, he repeated Shane's explanation to Mrs. Starrett: "There's nothing wrong with guns in the right hands." Inevitably, his example roused the townspeople from their indifference and fear, so that after he had been wounded, they finished the job he had started. The film's conclusion, in fact, with the community rising up to burn the villains' headquarters, borrowed directly from *The Far Country*.

Even the subtler Right movies converted complicated situations into occasions for western tactics. With his ivory-handled pistols and his habit of shooting at enemy planes, Patton reduced the enormous complexity of World War II to a series of personal, western-style encounters: Patton versus Rommel, even Patton versus Montgomery. Like Dirty Harry, Sheriff Pusser, and Coogan, Patton found his chief difficulty not with the Germans, but the Allied leaders who imposed political constraints on his operations. Although the film portrayed Patton as an anachronism, it also celebrated him as the war's most effective general.

Superficially, then, their opposed attitudes toward the closing of the frontier and the validity of the values associated with it made the Left and Right films appear very different. In fact, however, they were remarkably similar. Both cycles carefully blurred the lines of division to enable them to straddle the frontier issue. Thus, although the Right argued for the continued applicability of western tactics, it did so in urban crime movies that constantly implied the permanent loss of the frontier conditions on which those tactics were premised. And, too, the alienated, obsessive quality of the Right's principal characters suggested the emotional and human cost of holding on to old lifestyles in a modern world. "I'm gonna take and take and take until all they've got left is blood," Sheriff Pusser said in *Walking Tall*, "and then I'm gonna take that." The Right hero rarely maintained normal human relationships, sexual or otherwise. Coogan merely used people to find his prey. Bullitt's girlfriend didn't understand his work. Patton's wife never appeared in the movie. Dirty Harry's wife was dead, and his partner quit after being wounded (Harry made it clear he preferred to work alone anyway). *The French Connection*'s Popeye had a kinky fetish for girls in boots, but no normal heterosexual dealings. *Death Wish*'s

Bronson was utterly alone. Only *Walking Tall* attempted to show its hero as a family man, but plot developments deprived him of his wife midway through the film. The traditional western had portrayed its hero as a natural man; the new western hero of the Right movies was a borderline psychotic, obviously strained by his attempt to keep up the old ways. Occasionally the Right films acknowledged their heroes' inability to solve modern society's increasingly complicated problems with direct solutions. *The French Connection*'s unresolved ending was a Left motif, as was Dirty Harry's tossing his badge away, a sign that he recognized his own out-of-dateness (a gesture ignored by the sequels *Magnum Force* and *The Enforcer*).

If the Right's position was carefully hedged, the Left's ironic stance was even more compromising. First, the Left typically dramatized the frontier's closure in westerns, or disguised westerns, whose landscapes belied the supposed loss of open space (*The Wild Bunch, Butch Cassidy, Easy Rider, Little Big Man, Bonnie and Clyde*). Indeed, these stories of confinement contained far more physical space than the Right's city pictures.

Second, and more important, the Left movies that superficially acknowledged the invalidation of western lifestyles and values typically glorified the very myths they appeared to disown. Although Bonnie and Clyde, the Wild Bunch, Butch Cassidy and the Sundance Kid, *Easy Rider*'s Wyatt and Billy, McCabe, *Midnight Cowboy*'s Joe Buck were all in one sense anachronisms with no place in a modern world, they were also naïfs, glorious throwbacks to better times, people who refused to give in to changed conditions. Peckinpah's admiration for his heroes, Pat Garrett and Billy the Kid, expressed the viewpoint of the entire cycle: "These are cats who ran out of territory and know it. But they don't bend, refuse to be diminished by it. They play their string out to the end."[8] Thus, despite their overt intent to discredit frontier values, the Left movies affirmed such values more convincingly than the Right films, with their affectless cops.

The Left cycle glamorized its heroes in several ways. First, the Left heroes, almost always played by the films' only stars, never encountered appealing characters with opposed points of view. None of these movies offered the corrective to the outlaw-hero values represented by *Casablanca*'s Victor Laszlo, *Red River*'s Matthew Garth, or *Liberty Valance*'s Ranse Stoddard. Instead, Bonnie and Clyde, the Wild Bunch, Butch Cassidy and the Sundance Kid, and the others seemed to exist in worlds mysteriously emptied of alternatives. Noble outlawry confronted the impersonal villainy of nameless pursuers and invisible "Corporations" and "Combines"—no middle ground existed. Unlike the traditional western loner, who had been tempered by the communities he passed through (as Wyatt Earp had been in *My Darling Clementine*), these heroes lived in a world to themselves. Those that they encountered from normal society were inevitably caricatures—silly, lifeless people (e.g., the undertaker and his fiancée kidnapped by Bonnie and Clyde), never as likable as the witty, energetic outlaws.

The Left cycle even regarded sympathetically its heroes' violence, portraying it as the last possible expression of individual freedom. This romanticization, implicit in *The Wild Bunch*'s ending, became *A Clockwork Orange*'s explicit argument, and lay behind the willingness to tolerate Wyatt and Billy's drug-dealing in *Easy Rider*, and McMurphy's whoring, boozing, and brawling in *One Flew Over the Cuckoo's Nest*. In *Bonnie and Clyde*, where the outlaws' violence was clearly not self-expression (although perhaps compensation for sexual inadequacy), it appeared accidental, more the fault of victims who failed to "understand" than of the criminal who was only trying "to be free." "He tried to kill me," Clyde said in amazement after shooting a butcher who had defended himself from a holdup. "Why'd he try to kill me? I didn't want to hurt him. Try to get something to eat round here and some son-of-a-bitch comes up on you with a meat cleaver. I ain't against him. I ain't against him."

Even the Left films' violent endings glorified supposedly invalidated values. Ironically, once-radical New Wave devices became the means to apotheosize heroes who clearly embodied the traditional mythology: a freeze frame in *Butch Cassidy*; slow-motion slaughters in *The Wild Bunch* and *Bonnie and Clyde*; a soft-focus, fractured shootout in the snow in *McCabe and Mrs. Miller*; counterpointing music from Beethoven's *Ninth Symphony* ("I was cured all right") in *A Clockwork Orange*; and a slow upwardly spiraling helicopter shot in *Easy Rider*. In aes-theticizing its heroes' deaths, the Left cycle perpetuated the val-ues it had nominally discredited: individualism, self-sufficiency, and escapism. In doing so, it further blurred the distinctions be-tween itself and the Right.

To see how excessive sympathy for its heroes compromised the Left's films, one had only to look at *Chinatown*, a movie that employed all the Left's images of contraction without glamoriz-ing its hero. The film's plot, involving a water-rights swindle in 1930s Los Angeles, expressed a rudimentary ecological sense—the days of abundant natural resources had evidently passed. To imply this loss, Roman Polanski made the movie unrelentingly claustrophobic, filled with close-ups and tight compositions. Sig-nificantly, too, the source of evil was not individual, but a byzan-tine network of corruption resisting the detective's flip, overly confident explanations, continually revised, and just as contin-ually proved false. By clearly overmatching the detective, *Chi-natown* exposed his individualistic modus operandi as obsolete. But unlike the standard Left movie, *Chinatown* refused to dig-nify its anachronistic hero. In fact, Nicholson (as the detective) played the film's entire second half equipped with an enormous bandage on his nose (to protect a knife wound) that rendered him always slightly ludicrous, the unknowing butt of a black joke. Interestingly, *Chinatown*, despite being nominated for Best Pic-ture of the Year, failed to make *Variety*'s Top Twenty Box-Office Attractions.

The widely popular movies of the Left and Right cycles *did* make *Variety*'s list. They did so by continuing to allow the au-dience to have things both ways. The Right provided old-style western stories in contemporary urban settings, thus paying lip service to the frontier's passing. The Left provided glorifications of attitudes that its stories of closed frontiers implicitly discred-ited. The popular audience could go to either series—or both—and remain comfortable.

HEROES OF THE LEFT AND RIGHT

The Left and Right films of the late sixties and early seventies superficially polarized into outlaw-hero movies and official-hero movies. The Left's principal characters clearly stood outside the law, while the Right's were nominally its representatives: cops, vigilantes, and a general. But as with the frontier issue, the films blurred this point of distinction to confirm the fundamental similarities between the two cycles.

The Left films appeared to celebrate the values and attitudes traditionally associated with individualism: a dislike of institutions, a need for freedom from restraints, a preference for intuition and spontaneity as a source of conduct, a reluctance to settle down, a distrust of marriage, and a playfulness that suggested a resistance to growing up. All the Left movies had heroes who embodied these attitudes. *The Graduate*, the cycle's first film, was clearly an "us-against-them" story, designed for the youth audience revolting against its parents. Benjamin's indecisiveness indicated not his feckless immaturity, but his grace. *Bonnie and Clyde* portrayed charming young people who drifted casually into crime, perhaps to impress a girl, perhaps to get a ride in a fast car. Even decisive actions sprang from whim. The Wild Bunch had no plan to rescue Angel from Mapache; its leader, Pike, merely shrugged his shoulders and said, "What the hell, let's go." *Easy Rider*'s two heroes (whose names, Wyatt and Billy, linked them to the western tradition of Earp and The Kid) refused an invitation to remain at a commune:

COMMUNE MEMBER: You know, this could be the right place. The time's running out.
BILLY: Hey, man. Hey! If we're goin', we're goin'. Let's go.
WYATT: Yeah, I'm—I'm hip about time. But I just gotta go.

None of the Left's heroes was married or had a settled home. Cool Hand Luke, it seemed, had been married, but his mother approved of his divorce: "The idea of marrying got you all bollixed up," she told him. "Tryin' to be respectable. You was boring the hell out of all of us." The other Left figures were generally sexist, resorting to whores (*The Wild Bunch, Easy Rider, McCabe and Mrs. Miller, One Flew Over the Cuckoo's Nest*), or rape (*One Flew Over the Cuckoo's Nest, A Clockwork Orange*), or at times, complete disinterest (*Midnight Cowboy*). Even the *ménage à trois* of *Butch Cassidy and the Sundance Kid* concerned itself mainly with the two males. (Sundance: "What're you doing?" Butch: "Stealin' your girl." Sundance: "Take her, take her.")

The Left films clearly intended their outlaw heroes to represent the counterculture's own romanticized image of itself. As Robin Wood wrote about *Bonnie and Clyde*:

> Penn romanticizes Bonnie and Clyde. . . . uses them . . . as representatives of a spontaneous-intuitive aliveness that society even at its best can contain with difficulty or not at all: an aliveness that expresses itself in the overthrowing of restrictions, in asocial, amoral freedom and irresponsibility.[9]

Penn frankly admitted his intentional use of western mythology (with cars substituted for horses) and his efforts to identify Bonnie and Clyde with Robin Hood. Scriptwriters Benton and Newman made the counterculture connection explicit:

> What we now call "the underground," what the hip people do and feel, stems in great part from that "underworld" [of 1930s gangs].
> If Bonnie and Clyde were here today, they would be hip. Their values would have become assimilated in much of our culture—not robbing banks and killing people, of course, but their style, their sexuality, their bravado, their delicacy, their cultivated arrogance, their narcissistic insecurity, their curious ambition have relevance to the way we live now.
> . . .
> They are not crooks. They are people, and this film is, in many ways, about what's going on now.[10]

The heroes of the Right movies were, by contrast, mostly policemen, the counterculture's archvillains. Only Patton and *Death Wish*'s hero were not cops, but Patton was worse, a hawkish general, and *Death Wish*'s avenger won the respect of the police themselves.

In practice, the two cycles' free exchange of plots and motifs minimized their apparent differences. Thus, like the counterculture itself (which had cavalierly mixed individual and communal values), the Left films established a new variation by employing an element traditionally basic to official attitudes: a sense of community. The standard western hero (e.g., Shane) had been a loner. The new outlaws came in groups: Bonnie and Clyde, Butch and Sundance, Wyatt and Billy, Alex and his gang (*A Clockwork Orange*). "Partners is what I came up here to get away from,"

McCabe said, and promptly took a partner, Mrs. Miller. Asked whether they were associated with the U.S. Army, the Wild Bunch's Dutch shot back, "We're not associated with anybody," but the movie specified a particular code that bound the group together. "We're gonna stick together, all of us," Pike ordered. "When you side with a man you stick with him till he's finished or else you're nothing but some kind of animal." The Barrow Gang made up a small, traveling family, a fact the movie humorously acknowledged with its scenes of bickering and nagging. Similarly, the alternative to road life in *Easy Rider* was the extended family of the commune, romanticized and filmed in soft focus.

If the Left's outlaws were unusually community-oriented, the Right's characters, nominally official heroes, were extraordinarily alone. Like their Left counterparts, none had real homes, none had real friends, and none (except in *Walking Tall*) had real relationships with women. Even more significantly, all of them displayed the outlaw hero's abiding distrust of the law. As cops, Coogan, Dirty Harry, Sheriff Pusser, Popeye, and Bullitt were hampered by superiors who continually raised issues of legality. In *Death Wish*, the law appeared helpless in the face of the rampant Manhattan street crime. Patton's nemesis was a kind of international decorum that allowed the British to win some of the glory (and thus to move ahead of Patton's own army), but prevented a postwar attack on the Russians (a move favored by Patton). The evident calculation behind this blurring of distinctions between Left and Right heroes appeared explicitly in the advertisements for *Patton*. "*Patton*: A Salute to a Rebel," the posters read, and in the not-so-fine print below:

Patton was a rebel. Long before it became fashionable. He rebelled against the biggest. Eisenhower. Marshall. Montgomery. Against the establishment—and its ideas of warfare.[11]

Evidently the sales pitch, designed to capture both halves of the audience, worked: *Patton* became the third-leading money-earner of 1970.

In effect, both the Left and Right cycles reaffirmed the traditional reconciliatory pattern by reinvoking Classic Hollywood's most abiding myth: the reluctant hero story. The Right's films made the continuity obvious: solo cops solved society's problems. The Left, however, provided more imaginative reinventions. *Cool Hand Luke* and *One Flew Over the Cuckoo's Nest* kept the disguise thin, both employing a nearly identically camouflaged version of the stock western plot. Both heroes, Luke and McMurphy, were radical individualists (existentially modernized outlaw figures) brought into a demoralized community (prison, asylum) beset by villains who used rules to oppress its members. Both were at first reluctant to get involved: Luke kept to himself on his cot; McMurphy insisted on thinking he would soon be out. Like the standard western figure, both were initially defeated: Luke beaten by Dragline, McMurphy by guards. Both allied themselves with characters who resemble Huck's Jim or *Casablanca*'s Sam. Neither character was black, but *Cool Hand Luke*'s Dragline spoke with obviously black inflection, and *Cuckoo's Nest*'s Chief was the next best thing: an Indian.[12] Both films contained an early showdown that parodied a gunfight, but lifted the spirits of the community and converted it to the hero's side: *Cool Hand Luke*'s elaborate egg-eating contest, *Cuckoo's Nest*'s imaginary World Series game. After more showdowns, and attempts to escape, both heroes were ultimately killed, but their examples revitalized their communities, which continued to circulate rumors of their being alive. *Cuckoo's Nest* even borrowed a symbol from *Shane*. McMurphy's early, failed attempt to lift single-handedly a water fountain was ultimately completed by the Chief, who hurled it through the barred window to make his escape—an image of lifting and metaphorical teamwork that *Shane* had developed in the motif of Starrett and Shane working together to uproot an enormous stump.

Other Left movies seemed to add the reluctant hero pattern as an afterthought. Thus the utterly selfish *Wild Bunch* became unwitting revolutionaries when their deaths provided Mexican farmers with weapons to wage war against their corrupt government. While *McCabe and Mrs. Miller* clearly implied the town of Presbyterian Church's debt to McCabe's enterprise, it did not at first suggest that his death would preserve the community from the "Corporation" that sought to buy it. But the film's final sequence, a sustained parallel montage between McCabe's duel with the "Corporation's" agents and the townspeople's saving their church from fire, suggested a new communal spirit inspired by the individual hero.

Bonnie and Clyde kept the pattern more subtle, barely alluding to it in the narrative's margins. The movie sought to redeem its heroes by implying that they provided psychological inspiration to dispirited Depression victims. Thus, Clyde discovered his role ("We rob banks") after meeting a man who had lost his farm to a bank; in subsequent robberies, he carefully avoided taking money from private citizens, who later proudly posed beside bullet holes, apparently cheered by the excitement. Penn admitted his intention:

Socially, the people were paralysed by the Depression; for example, the scene in the camp near the end is nearly stylized in its immobility. I was trying to say that everybody else was still frozen by the atmosphere, by the Depression. At least Bonnie and Clyde were mobile and functioning—sometimes on behalf of foolish things, sometimes self-destructively—but at least they functioned.[13]

Far from being polarized opposites, therefore, the heroes of the Left and Right both reincarnated the same mythic hero—the westerner. Underlying both cycles of films lay a deep-rooted distrust of institutions that translated into a preference for individual solutions. Although the new, complex problems increasingly called for elaborate, permanent, cooperative reform, Hollywood (and thus by implication Americans), as Robert Warshow pointed out, had "always been uneasy with a situation that cannot be solved by personal virtue."[14] Hence both Left and Right films clung to the individual hero as the means by which the spoilers of the American Dream would be outfought. Like the traditional westerner, these heroes relied only on their own intuition: McCabe's boast, "I got the poetry in me," matched Patton's sixth sense, "I feel I am destined to achieve some great thing." Neither the Left nor Right movies ever questioned this private sense of right and wrong: the poetic martyrdoms of the Left and the victories of the Right justified their hunches. Often, too, these films drastically simplified the situations confronting their heroes so that more subtle, institutional responses seemed unnecessary. *Dirty Harry* suggested the sufficiency of Harry's own explicit version of the stock western phrase, "I don't know what the law says, but I do know what's right and wrong": "When I see an adult male chasing a female down an alley with nothing but a butcher knife and a hard-on, I don't figure he's out collecting for the Red Cross. I shoot the bastard. That's my policy." The Left hero's judgment was portrayed as equally infallible. "They're gonna make it," Wyatt solemnly announced about the struggling farm commune built in the dry sand hills. "Dig, man. They're gonna make it." And the viewer was left to assume he was right.

MYTHIC SELF-CONSCIOUSNESS

As opposed to the Right cycle, which told its stories relatively straightforwardly in transparent modes, Left movies displayed a marked self-consciousness about myths and conventions. At one level of self-consciousness, these films merely manipulated or reversed standard genre expectations. Thus, for example, *The Wild Bunch*'s opening shots (children watching fascinated as ants killed a scorpion) undercut the essential premise of the western—the innocence of "natural man." *Little Big Man* furthered the attack on the traditional western by making the Indians the heroes, and Wyatt's and Billy's deaths in *Easy Rider* denied the optimistic conventions of the road movie.

More significantly, the Left films borrowed an obviously self-conscious device from the New Wave (particularly from *Breathless*) in offering heroes who derived their behavior, and ultimately their sense of self, from the ready-made myths that surrounded them. Joe Buck in *Midnight Cowboy* had his Paul Newman *Hud* poster and was impressed by a radio program on which a woman revealed that Gary Cooper was the ideal man. On the first night camping out, *Easy Rider*'s Billy eagerly affirmed his participation in the western tradition: "Out here in the wilderness," he bragged to Wyatt, "fighting Indians and cowboys on every side." McCabe, as David Denby observed, was a faker, "a man who adopts the manner of some famous or legendary character of the Old West, but who actually has the imagination and humor of a second-rate traveling salesman."[15] Most of the movie's first part, in fact, treated McCabe's reputation as if it were genuine: had he actually killed the gunman Bill Roundtree? (the viewer never found out, but it seemed unlikely), and, as one character asked, "Why the hell would they call him Pudgy McCabe?" (the film gave no answer to that one, either). Butch and Sundance, like Bonnie and Clyde, obsessively photographed themselves, a motif also used in *Cool Hand Luke*, where a picture Luke had made of himself with two women (during his short-lived freedom) became a fetish object for the inmates left behind, a source of inspiration and wonder. Kesey's novel explicitly identified *One Flew Over the Cuckoo's Nest*'s McMurphy with pop iconography, particularly in describing the hero's final assault on Big Nurse:

> It was us that had been making him go on for weeks, keeping him standing long after his feet and legs had given out, weeks of making him wink and grin and laugh and go on with his act long after his humor had been parched dry between two electrodes.
>
> We made him stand and hitch up his black shorts like they were horsehide chaps, and push back his cap with one finger like it was a ten-gallon Stetson, slow, mechanical gestures—and when he walked across the floor you could hear the iron in his bare heels ring sparks out of the tile.[16]

With its naturalistic style, the movie largely ignored these references, but it did suggest that McMurphy had feigned madness to escape the work details of normal prison life, and thus, that he was acting out his own conception of what a mad person would be like. When the head doctor expressed doubt as to his insanity, McMurphy asked willingly, "What do you want me to do, Doc, take a shit on the floor?"

Godard used his heroes' self-conscious myth-making as a Brechtian device that revealed the received elements in all behavior. A viewer could observe the growing discrepancy between reality and the role or myth assumed, and, as a result, gradually withdraw his identification with the hero. *2 or 3 Things I Know about Her*, for example, clearly suggested the illusoriness of the bourgeois dreams of fine clothes and an apartment that had prompted a married woman to take up part-time prostitution. At times, the device worked similarly in the Left movies, but more often the films used the discrepancy between the hero's self-image and reality simply for comedy. Thus, most of the Left's characters were at times bunglers whose botches were funny. The Graduate couldn't remember what name to use in a hotel where he met Mrs. Robinson. Clyde held up a bank that folded; the Wild Bunch shot up a town for a sack of lead washers; and Butch and Sundance couldn't remember the Spanish orders for a holdup in Bolivia. McCabe, in particular, was far from his self-projection. The movie's opening sequence, with McCabe mysteriously arriving, barely visible under an enormous fur coat, ominous, projected, as Diane Jacobs observed, an image of McCabe "as he would like to be seen."[17] But the rest of the film moved steadily away from that idealization. McCabe lost consistently at cards and failed in his advances to Mrs. Miller, who punctured his balloon: "Hey, you know if you wanna make out you're such a fancy dude, you might wear something besides that cheap jockey club cologne." And more tauntingly, "You think small because you're afraid of thinking big."

Occasionally these disillusionments slid past comedy into scenes that raised more explicitly the implications of the gap between myth and fact. In *Cool Hand Luke*, for example, Luke's buddies tried to cheer up the recaptured hero with his own mythic photograph, only to hear the real story:

KOKO: Luke? . . . We got the picture! See?
DICK: A pair of beauties [the women with Luke in picture]. Best I ever seen.
TATOO: You really know how to pick 'em.
STEVE: Tell us about 'em. What were they like?
LUKE: Picture's a phony. . . . I had it made up for you guys.
KOKO: A phony! Whatta you mean, a phony?
GAMBLER: We saw the broads.
DICK: Yeah. Did you have them both at once or—
LUKE: It's a phony. Made it just for you guys.
STEVE: Aw, come on. We saw it all.
TATOO: The champagne.
TRAMP: Some life.
FIXER: You really had it made.
LUKE: Nothin'. I had nothin', made nothin'. Couple towns, couple bosses. Laughed out loud one day and got turned in.

Koko: But ... but. ...
Luke: Stop beatin' on it! That's all there was. Listen. Open your eyes. Stop beatin' it. And stop feedin' off me. Now get out of the way. Give me some air.

In general, however, the Left films did not try for a Godardian alienation. They rarely encouraged (or allowed) the audience to withdraw its sympathy from the protagonists. Instead, they celebrated the outlaw heroes' lifestyle—supposedly outmoded by the frontier's closure, supposedly revealed as a role assumed by otherwise empty people—as an analogously possible response to the events of the late sixties. This pattern held true even in *Bonnie and Clyde*, superficially the most Godardian of the popular Left films. Certainly Penn repeatedly demonstrated his heroes' self-consciousness, their overt theatricality, their uses of ready-made roles and styles. The movie began on a note of artificiality, with actual Depression snapshots giving way to pictures of Warren Beatty and Faye Dunaway as Bonnie and Clyde, a transition that established the underlying discrepancy between the film's mythologizing and the true story. The couple's first meeting produced references to films ("I bet you're a movie star," Clyde told Bonnie, having recognized her as a waitress), to Hollywood dreams ("Now, how you like to go walkin' in the dining room of the Aldophus Hotel in Dallas wearin' a nice silk dress and having everybody waiting on you?"), and to movie-magazine-influenced notions of style (about Bonnie's spit curl: "Change that. I don't like it."). With the arrival of Buck and his Kodak, the group posed constantly, with Bonnie assuming mock-tough stances borrowed from gangster movies, cigar and all. On bank robberies, Clyde announced himself like a master of ceremonies: "Good afternoon. This is the Barrow Gang." For her part, Bonnie worked, to Clyde's delight, on her poem, "The Story of Bonnie and Clyde":

Clyde: You know what you done there? You told my story. You told my whole story right there. Right there! One time I told you I was gonna make you somebody. That's what you done for me. You made me somebody they're gonna remember.

Although clearly himself part of the fictionalizing process, C. W. Moss was captivated by Clyde's legend. "You think laws is gonna

catch Bonnie and Clyde in town?" he asked his father in disbe-
lief. "Clyde's got a sense. Don't you know, Daddy? Nobody catches
Clyde. Never. Never."

Certainly the movie, with its mixture of comedy and gunplay,
and its steadily escalating violence, pointed to the discrepancy
between myth and fact, and to the corruption inherent from the
start in the Barrow Gang's self-image. At points, the film became
terribly painful (especially in the scene with Buck's death), certainly more so than *The Wild Bunch*, a film that for all its violence, contained little suffering.[18] Clearly, Penn intended for his
movie to work along Godardian (or Hitchcockian) principles: initial identification with the heroes, gradual withdrawal of sympathy, and final recognition of their errors and one's own complicity in them:

Very often we would lead the audience to believe one thing, and then
in the next sequence we turn around. . . . We used laughter to get the
audience to feel like a member of the gang, to have the feeling of adventure, a feeling of playing together. Then, near the end of the film,
we begin to turn a little bit. . . . We hope by then that you're already
trapped, that you're caught in the film as a member of the gang and
now you have to go along.[19]

To a certain extent, the film worked on this model, but never
entirely. Richard Schickel's insistence that the self-satirizing
elements so distanced the film's material that "no one—except
an adolescent—could mistake it for reality"[20] missed the movie's
reaffirmation of the outlaw-hero life as a viable sixties mode. For
Penn never fully undercut his heroes, allowing Clyde, for example, despite the evident demythologizing, to shoot a gun out
of Hamer's hand like an old-fashioned western hero, and to make
a series of incredible getaways. Robin Wood better understood
the film's effect:

For all the blood and pain, for all that we see the protagonists meet
peculiarly horrifying deaths and are shown quite unequivocally that
"Crime does not pay," the film is far more likely to encourage spectators
to be like Bonnie and Clyde than to encourage them to be conforming,
"responsible" citizens in society as it exists. The Bonnie and Clyde of
Penn's film, however many banks they rob, however many men they
kill, remain attractive and sympathetic characters: plainly the most at-

tractive and sympathetic in the film. Obviously, the intense identification audiences feel with the characters is a major factor—*the* major factor—in the film's immense box-office success.[21]

Significantly, *Badlands*, a movie that *never* allowed the audience
to identify with its protagonist, a James Dean-imitating killer,
had no success whatsoever with the mass audience. The constant
distancing devices, specifically the confession-magazine-style voice-
over narration and the remote, obviously stylized compositions,
made the film seem cold and lifeless. *Bonnie and Clyde*, on the
other hand, even in its conclusion, encouraged identification (the
heroes' white clothes and car and the sudden flight of birds made
the massacre seem to violate nature itself). In effect, therefore,
despite the presence of self-conscious references to myth-making,
Bonnie and Clyde, and the other Left films like it, resembled
their straighter, less self-conscious Right counterparts in continuing to glorify the old myths.

In sum, the Left cycle adopted the New Wave *topos* of self-
conscious heroes only to defuse it; in doing so, it reconfirmed the
American Cinema's voraciously assimilative power. Indeed, as it
appeared in the Left movies, the *topos* of self-consciousness was
so depoliticized that it was promptly appropriated by the Right
cycle as well. The key to this maneuver, whereby a device conceived as a critique of prevailing ideology could become a prop
for that same ideology, lay in converting Godard's insight about
the media age into an old-fashioned existentialism. Thus, while
Godard repeatedly depicted his protagonists' embrace of media-
given roles as the inevitable modern inauthenticity, the American Cinema typically represented such role-assumptions as glorious recognitions—those climactic moments when a character
"found himself" and came into his "true nature." The scene in
which Clyde Barrow responded to the foreclosed farmer by discovering the role of an avenging Robin Hood provided the *locus
classicus* of this figure, which increasingly appeared in the Right
films of the early 1970s as well.

Jacques Lacan's notion of "the mirror stage" and "the decentered ego" offers a way of reading such scenes ideologically.[22]
Lacan's entire psychoanalytic project turned on his denial of the

whole, autonomous self, and his counterinsistence that the individual ego always results from the succession of images that it introjects. This process, Lacan argued, begins with "the mirror stage": somewhere between the age of six and eighteen months, the infant becomes able to recognize his own image in a mirror. In doing so, he replaces his fragmented sense of self (in which even his various limbs seem separate and unconnected) with the full, autonomous image in the mirror. Thus, he begins his own ego-formation with a misrecognition: the mirror-image, after all, is only an image.

Those who use Lacan often ignore his warning that the mirror stage is itself only the most literal instance of these misrecognitions from which the individual constructs himself out of external images. Thus, the mother is the first "mirror," the parents together the second, and an individual's culture the third. A particular ideology, therefore, contributes overwhelmingly to the formation of even the most apparently "original" selves. Hence, the Left and Right cycles' self-advertised individualists inevitably represented only the sum of the misrecognitions that we call American culture. In this light, Bonnie and Clyde, The Wild Bunch, Butch Cassidy and the Sundance Kid, Buford Pusser, Dirty Harry, et al. seem not so much characters as "chords" of refracted, superimposed mirror images held together by the audience's complicity in their formation and recognition.

Althusser authorizes such a materialist reading of Lacan, observing how Lacan merely confirmed the inherent subversiveness of Freud's message:

Freud has discovered for us that the real subject, the individual in his unique essence, has not the form of an ego, centered on the "ego," on "consciousness" or on "existence"—whether this is the existence of the for-itself, of the body-proper, or of "behavior"—that the human subject is decentered, constituted by a structure which has no "centre" either, *except in the ideological formations in which it "recognizes" itself.*[23]

"The ideological formations in which it 'recognizes' itself"—what better description of the American Cinema and the popular audience's reaction to it? Certainly, in the immediate case, the Left and Right cycles' recognition scenes, in which a hero apparently comes into his own true nature, derived utterly from American mythology. Furthermore, while seeming to criticize those "ideological formations," the Left and Right movies perpetuated them by themselves becoming panoramic, powerful mirrors in which the mass audience could continually "find itself."

The most revealing version of such a (mis)recognition occurred in the Right film *Death Wish*. After the rape-murder of his wife and daughter, pacifist Charles Bronson temporarily left New York for an architectural project in Arizona. There, a friend took him to a reconstructed frontier town where actors played out for tourists movie versions of attempted robberies foiled by a gunfighting sheriff. Watching such a scene unfold (which becomes a movie-within-a-movie), Bronson "recognized" himself and his "destiny." In effect, this staged scene in a movie-set town became his and his audience's mirror, the image (of course ideological) of the true hero and the genuine, right conduct. By extrapolation, *Death Wish* itself became a still larger mirror, even more powerful for having disarmed its audience by means of the film's own internal disavowal.[24]

10. *The Godfather* and *Taxi Driver*

DESPITE their external extravagances, the Left and Right films' underlying traditionalism reconfirmed the New American Cinema's dependence on the paradigms established by Classic Hollywood. Almost entirely faithful to the continuity conventions, both sets of movies quickly neutralized (through stereotyping[1] and overuse) the few New Wave innovations they had borrowed. To maintain the reconciliatory pattern, the industry blurred the two groups' differences until each cycle contained ingredients of the other. Most obviously, the Left's outlaw heroes now appeared in self-contained "families," while the Right translated its formerly domestic official heroes into loners more isolated than the outlaws themselves.

By covertly minimizing the distinctions between the Left and Right films, Hollywood encouraged its audience to attend both cycles. This strategy involved a new, self-consciously intertextual means of avoiding choice, for it counted on a reconciliation occurring, not in individual movies, but in the mind of the filmgoer, who, despite taking seriously the superficial polarization, went to both groups. Thus, *Patton*'s glorification of an eccentric general found its complement in *Little Big Man*'s damning caricature of Custer, and *Easy Rider*'s paranoid view of policemen, in the sympathetic naturalism of *The French Connection*.

With single films, the industry relied not only on its blurring tactics, but also on the divided audience's increasing willingness to use a movie to confirm its own predispositions. For the Left, *Bonnie and Clyde* was a story of martyrdom; for the Right, it was a cautionary tale. The Right saw Dirty Harry as the ideal cop; for the Left, he merely verified the counterculture's worst fears. Counting on these opposed responses, Hollywood engaged in the calculated ambiguities Pauline Kael decried in *The French Connection*:

The movie presents [Popeye] as the most ruthless of characters and yet— here is where the basic amorality comes through—shows that this is the kind of man it takes to get the job done. It's the vicious bastard who gets the results. Popeye, the lowlifer who makes Joe or Archie sound like Daniel Ellsberg, is a cop the way the movie Patton was a general. When Popeye walks into a bar and harasses blacks, part of the audience can say, "That's a real pig," and another part of the audience can say, "That's the only way to deal with those people. Waltz around with them and you get nowhere."

I imagine that the people who put this movie together just naturally think in this commercially convenient double way. This right-wing, left-wing, take-your-choice cynicism is total commercial opportunism passing itself off as an Existential view.[2]

As the political divisiveness of the sixties subsided, a more profound distinction arose between naïve and ironic filmgoers. Preferring unselfconscious forms, the naïve moviegoer retained his affection for traditional genre pictures straightforwardly told. The ironist, by contrast, bored with conventional movies, favored art films and revisionist reworkings of Classic Hollywood formulas. While the ironic audience had always existed, the increasing popularity of foreign movies, cult films, and television parodies suggested that its numbers had grown markedly in the early 1960s.

The industry's solution to this new division was the "corrected" genre movie, a film like *Butch Cassidy*, which could provide enough straight action to appease the traditionalists and enough self-consciousness to satisfy the iconoclasts. In effect, the wide appeal of both the Left and Right films derived from their double nature: all, in fact, were "corrected" genre pictures, capable of being taken two ways. Where the Left used its westerns, gangster movies, prison stories, and science fiction movies to imply a pop ecological seriousness, the Right romantically humanized authority figures largely neglected by the American Cinema. Significantly, however, heavily "corrected" films, which systematically frustrated expectations promoted by their genres, almost uniformly failed at the box office: neither *Badlands* (a *Bonnie and Clyde* variant), *New York, New York* (musical), *The Conversation* (private eye), *Mean Streets* (gangster), *Payday* (musical bio), *The King of Marvin Gardens* (*noir* romance), nor even the widely promoted *Nashville* (musical) made the Top Twenty lists. Their lack of success reconfirmed the audience's fundamental conservatism, its persisting reluctance to part with the mythological categories that these films challenged.

The most important of the "corrected" genre movies were two films that managed to identify themselves with the preeminent modes of the late sixties and early seventies—the Left and Right films. Each of these series, in effect, came to an end in a corrective movie which, while appearing to be only another member of the class, opened up the cycle's basic story to admit previously suppressed, incompatible values. The film that completed the Left cycle was *The Godfather* (1972, 1974); the film that completed the Right cycle was *Taxi Driver* (1976).

THE GODFATHER

Through 1974, *The Godfather I* had earned more money than any film in the history of the cinema.[3] The movie's extraordinary commercial success depended, among other things, on its ability to perfect the contemporary period's two most popular forms: first, as part of the Left-Right cycle, it blurred completely those distinctions that had separated the cycles; second, as a "corrected" genre picture, it balanced ideally between reassuring conventionality and disquieting revisionism. As a result, *The Godfather I* appealed to both the Left and Right, and to both naïve and ironic filmgoers.

By using all the cycle's basic elements, and then intensifying and extending them to their logical conclusions, Francis Ford Coppola made *The Godfather I* the ultimate Left film. Its protagonists, like all those of the Left movies, were outlaws. Typically, the movie encouraged its audience to identify with these outlaws, to regard their refusal to pursue ordinary careers as the metaphorical equivalent of the counterculture's rejection of the

establishment. "I refused to be a fool, dancing on a string for all those big guys," Don Corleone (Marlon Brando) explained to Michael (Al Pacino), a boast that approximated the Wild Bunch's "We're not associated with anybody."

The Godfather I employed standard means to maintain audience sympathy for its heroes. Formally, Coppola's subjective point-of-view shots (often reserved for key moments) narrowed the viewer's perspective to that of the protagonists. Typical was the film's dramatic opening shot of the Undertaker ("I believe in America"), a highly restricted long take (circumscribed by tight framing and a totally dark background) that a pullback dolly gradually revealed as issuing from Don Corleone's point of view.

The film began, therefore, by firmly planting the viewer in Don Corleone's shoes, and confining him there (or with the Don's family) for most of the initial wedding sequence. Forty minutes into the movie, however, Coppola abruptly disengaged his audience's identification with the Don, gradually relocating it in Michael (a move suggested perhaps by Psycho's exemplary transferal from Marion Crane to Norman Bates). As Hitchcock had done, Coppola marked this break with a sudden transition from a shot of the attackers taken from the victim's point of view to an objective shot of the attack itself filmed from an unmotivated overhead angle.

Subsequently, Michael so fully monopolized the audience's sympathy that a hospital shot-reverse shot sequence between the Don and his son ("I'm with you now") allowed the camera to assume Michael's position while denying it Don Corleone's. Thus, although Brando's eyes looked directly into the camera, the reverse shot of Pacino originated from a more neutral position.

Thematically, The Godfather I, like all the Left films, controlled the identification process by isolating its heroes in a moral vacuum in which they could appear as forces of justice. Thus, the movie carefully limited the Corleones' victims to those who deserved punishment (a venal Hollywood producer, a crooked cop, family traitors, other gangsters wanting to sell drugs), thereby insuring that the audience's sympathy for the family would not be undermined by the sight of innocent blood. The Godfather's image of a corrupt establishment (with its hypocritical police and politicians) derived directly from the Left cycle's standard justification for its protagonists' outlawry, made explicit in Dennis Hopper's rationale for Wyatt and Billy's dope-dealing in Easy

Rider: "They peddle dope," he wrote, "because that seems no worse to them than the Wall Street tycoon spending eighty percent of his time cheating the government."⁴ *The Godfather*'s refusal to admit strong characters with competing values prevented this facile analogy from being scrutinized. Kay, normal society's only representative, remained too diffident (especially as played by Diane Keaton) to provide a challenge to the Corleones' values, which thus became the movie's moral norm. As with most of the Left and Right films, any opposition to the protagonists' standards occurred not within the film itself, but between the film and its audience. Although a viewer could take issue with the family's morality, no one in the movie (except Kay) did so.

At key junctures, *The Godfather*'s thematic and formal identification controls merged. One sequence, for example, which used Corleone's refusal to deal narcotics ("Drugs is a dirty business") as a sign of his relative probity, concluded with a completely subjective shot of the fearsome Luca Brasi taken from the Don's point of view. "I'm a little worried about this Sollozzo fellow," Corleone advised his hitman; "I want you to find out what he's got under his fingernails."

The hero with which *The Godfather I* urged its audience to identify was the perfect mixture of the Left and Right prototypes. On the one hand, Don Corleone represented the ideal outlaw, free of restrictions, able to intervene unilaterally to help family or friends. To a large extent, therefore, the movie, like all

the Left films, appealed to the American Dream (increasingly frustrated in contemporary society) of being able to do exactly what one liked. But having written the script for *Patton*, Coppola certainly recognized that with his power, Corleone also satisfied the Right's ideal of efficient authority. In the most perceptive review of the film, Arthur Schlesinger, Jr., implicitly described this connection:

The film shrewdly touches contemporary nerves. Our society is pervaded by a conviction of powerlessness. *The Godfather* makes it possible for all of us, in the darkness of the movie house, to become powerful. It plays upon our inner fantasies, not only on the criminal inside each of us but on our secret admiration for men who get what they want, whose propositions no one dares turn down.[5]

To the Don's image of uncompromising independence, however, *The Godfather I* added the Left's motif of the family, here deepened into a basic narrative device that often opposed Corleone's autonomy. Thus, the Don's fears for Michael forced him into a humiliating reconciliation with archenemies Barzini and Tattaglia. Within their own circle, however, and within the movie's closed world, the Corleone family resemble a romanticized, self-supporting commune.

The Godfather I adopted another standard Left motif by implicitly acknowledging the frontier's closing. Repeatedly, significant scenes took place in darkened, sealed, claustrophobic rooms.

More important, the movie represented Walter Prescott Webb's postfrontier world where limited resources required the family's explicitly competitive ethic. Predatory capitalism, Webb had argued, could only operate nonviolently at a time "when wealth existed in such abundance—and so out of proportion to the number of people who could share it—that everyone could engage in the scramble for it without creating social disaster."[6] In advising the Don to move into narcotics, Tom Hagen tacitly argued that this grace period had passed:

TOM HAGEN: There's more potential in narcotics than anything else we're looking at. And if we don't get into it, somebody else will—maybe one of the Five Families, maybe all of them. Now, with the money they earn, they can buy more police and political power. Then they come after us. Now we have the unions, we have the gambling, and they're the best things to have, but narcotics is a thing of the future. Now, if we don't get a piece of that action, we risk everything we have—I mean, not now, but ten years from now.

Hagen's warning was *The Godfather*'s equivalent of Pike's challenge to the Wild Bunch ("We've got to start thinking beyond our guns, them days is closin' fast") or *Butch Cassidy*'s "Who *are* those guys?"—an image of the inexorability of scarcity.

Unlike many Left films, *The Godfather I* did not contain protagonists who explicitly modeled themselves on pop myths. But the movie repeatedly emphasized the power of corrupt dreams to determine behavior: in the film's terms, Don Corleone was merely a capitalist extended, someone who had taken literally the American success myth and done everything in his power to achieve it. Characteristically, his last conversation with Michael took on Horatio Alger tones:

DON CORLEONE: I never . . . never wanted this [the gangster life] for you. I worked my whole life, and I don't apologize, to take care of my family. And I *refused* to be a fool, dancing on a string held by all those big shots. I don't apologize—that's my life. But I thought that . . . that when it was your time, that . . . *you* would be the one to hold the strings: Senator Corleone, Governor Corleone, something. Well, there just wasn't enough time, Michael. There wasn't enough time.

Michael's reply ("We'll get there, Pop, we'll get there") indicated that he had inherited his father's goal. Indeed, *The Godfather I* made clear that in preparing to avenge his father, Michael had rehearsed and adopted a role created by the Don. "That's not what Pop would do," he cautioned during Sonny's brief reign as family head. As the new Don, Michael adopted his father's idiom to scold family members. After the Sollozzo meeting, Vito had admonished Sonny, "*Never* tell anybody outside the family what you're thinking again." Having seen Fredo defend Moe Green, Michael warned, "Fredo, you're my brother, and I love you, but don't ever take sides with anyone against the family again, *ever*." Michael's self-consciousness, however, lacked the playfulness normally associated with the Left heroes' use of ready-made images: Clyde had enjoyed his theatricality; Michael saw his part as a burden.

With Brando's Don Corleone absent, *The Godfather II* further complicated the stock Left motif of role-playing. First, Michael's imitation of his father now required that he refer to behavior primarily existing in another film. Second, DeNiro's conception of the young Vito clearly derived from Brando's original, including the raspy voice and trademark gesture of resting his head on one hand's outstretched fingers. Both these borrowings, the character Michael's and the actor DeNiro's, clearly revealed the sequel's overt intertextuality, and thus, by implication, the inherent artificiality of the cinema itself, a world where characters grew not from "life," but from other fictions.

By MAKING the ruthlessly powerful Vito and Michael a father and son devoted to their family, *The Godfather I* skillfully drew on the crucial imagery of both the Left and Right cycles. Not surprisingly, the violence-family coupling also constituted the key to the movie's ideal balance between traditional and revisionist filmmaking. *The Godfather I* was the perfect "corrected" genre picture. On the one hand, it demonstrated the persisting power of the traditional mythology; on the other, it suggested that such mythology rested on irreconcilable contradictions, previously concealed. If it offered enough action to attract the naïve filmgoer, it also offered enough ideological criticism of that action to please the ironists. "We had been sure of the square audience," co-scriptwriter Mario Puzo observed of the movie's huge success, "and now it looked as if we were going to get the hip avant-garde too."[7]

As a "corrected" genre picture, *The Godfather I* achieved its exquisite balance by confining its critique to tacit references in an otherwise compelling story. In making its subversions thematic rather than formal, the movie reversed the *noir* strategy of convulsing conventional plots with radical style. Formally, in fact, *The Godfather* was more conservative than any of its Left predecessors; it eschewed New Wave pyrotechnics, relying instead on Classic Hollywood's continuity rules. Significantly, the movie's few stylistic distantiations satisfied both the ironic audience's desire for critical perspective and the naïve audience's desire for involving excitement. Thus, while *The Godfather*'s key formal device, parallel editing, provided a means for exposing hypocrisy, it was also cinema's most traditional way of generating narrative suspense. Indeed, D. W. Griffith had recognized this device's double potential as early as 1909's *A Corner on Wheat*, where his crosscuts between an evil grain speculator and a bread line achieved both a dialectical critique and a narratively compelling sequence. In juxtaposing Connie's wedding party with Don Corleone's murder plans, a christening with Michael's gangland killings, a First Communion party with Michael's scheming, a religious festival with Vito's first murder, *The Godfather* implicitly demonstrated, to those predisposed to think about such things, that American society functioned on two levels: an ideologically whitewashed exterior and a foundation of predatory violence. For those not so predisposed, these sequences merely represented particularly gripping instances of Classic American narrative cinema.

The Godfather I's ideal balance of traditional filmmaking and revisionist critique found its perfect expression in the film's crucial sequence, Michael's murder of Sollozzo and his hired cop, McCluskey. To satisfy both the naïve and ironic audiences, this scene had to be simultaneously involving and repellent, a mechanism for making the viewer want the murder to happen and for making him feel appalled when it did. The sequence's final thirteen shots accommodated both needs by alternating between point-

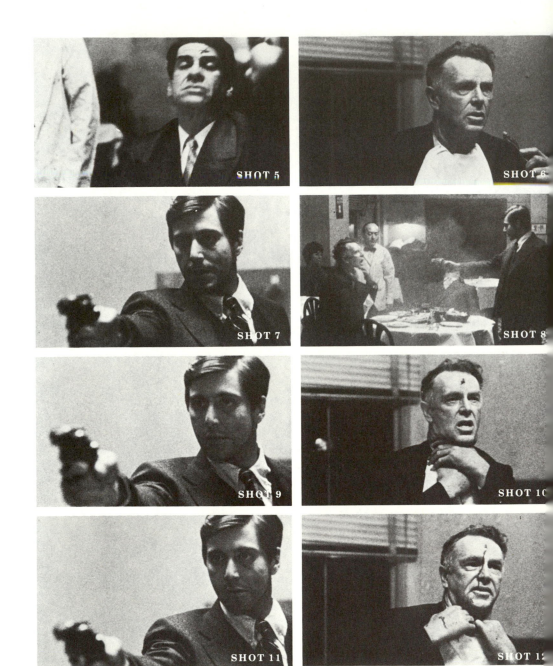

SHOT 13

of-view shots, that identified the viewer with Michael, and objective long shots, whose frozen tableaux encouraged estrangement.

Shot 1 reestablished the positions of Sollozzo and McCluskey by filming them from Michael's vantage point as he emerged covertly armed from the bathroom. Indeed, only Michael's own entry into the frame modified what at first appeared a purely subjective view. Shots 2 and 3, a simple reverse figure completed by Michael's walk to the table, narrowed the focus to the spatial seam between Michael and Sollozzo. In 4, by zooming in on Pacino's face from a neutral position, Coppola intensified the sequence's involvement with Michael while avoiding identifying the camera with Sollozzo's point of view. The nearly full subjectivity of Shot 5, with the gun jutting into the frame, placed the viewer in Michael's position as he fired on Sollozzo. Shots 6 and 7, another reverse figure, shifted the seam of significance to the space connecting Michael and McCluskey and further implicated the spectator in the developing action.

The carefully restricted perspectives of Shots 1-7 set up the shock of Shot 8's sudden objectivity. Shots 1-7 had unmistakably suggested, "This is what it feels like to commit a murder" (exciting); Shot 8 replied, "This is what a murder looks like from a bystander's position" (appalling). Shots 9-12 immediately retracted this newly acquired distance by plunging the viewer back into the space between Michael and McCluskey. With Shot 13, however, Coppola once again withdrew from the action, alienating the viewer with a long shot that took in the entire space of the room and the customers in it. Like Shot 8, Shot 13's sudden remoteness broke the absorbing spell created by the previous shot-reverse shots' restricted perspectives.

This sequence illustrated *The Godfather I*'s optimum commercial balance between compelling narrative and modernist critique. As a scene, the murder was at once utterly absorbing and incipiently alienating, with Shots 8 and 13 working to "correct" the involvement promoted by the classical reverse figures. Significantly, Coppola limited this "correction" to two shots, never imitating Godard's long stretches of formal rupture. As a result, *The Godfather I* could appease the growing ironic audience without losing the still more sizable naïve audience.

Coppola's basic strategy to retain the naïve audience, however, lay in primarily confining his "corrections" to tacit thematic analogies between the Corleones and capitalist America. In interviews, Coppola repeatedly made these analogies explicit, as if they alone had legitimized what he regarded as essentially trashy material. "I was desperate to give the film a kind of class," he said in another context; "I felt the book was cheap and sensational." He had taken on the project, he admitted, only because his independent Zoetrope Productions had put him $300,000 in debt, but rereading the novel had generated a different reaction: "I thought it was a terrific story, if you cut out all the other stuff. I decided it could be not only a successful movie but also a *good* movie."[8]

From the start, therefore, Coppola had intended to make a "corrected" film. His remarks, however, suggested a crucial departure for the American Cinema: where Classic Hollywood's great directors (Walsh, Hawks, Ford, Curtiz, Capra) had measured themselves by their ability to use the inherited paradigms, the new ambitious filmmakers equated quality with "corrections" of those paradigms. (Significantly, the same equation obtained in post-*Sgt. Pepper* popular music.) Almost certainly, their model for this new vision was *Citizen Kane*, the first major American commercial movie to subvert Classic Hollywood's standard patterns. Not surprisingly, therefore, Coppola's ambitions for *The Godfather* involved him in replicating *Kane*'s displacement of a latent social critique onto the story of one rich and powerful man's failure to find happiness.

The Godfather I's enormous commercial success indicated that, in fact, Coppola's intended anticapitalist critique operated at most as a subtext, readable by those predisposed to do so. Only the constant references to "business," a loose pragmatic that superseded all personal ties, brought the critique into the open. "Tell Michael it was only business," Tessio said matter-of-factly, having been discovered as the family traitor; "I always liked him." While this confession implied that the rudimentary outlaw ethic of brotherhood, so common to the Left films (especially *The Wild Bunch*), had given way to an extreme, every-man-for-himself individualism, the movie never made this message overtly political.

Despite this reticence, however, *The Godfather I* went further with its "corrections" than the standard "New" American movies, which Stanley Kauffmann described as "entertainment films on which 'meaning' is either grossly impasted or is clung to only as long as convenient."[9] In fact, although Coppola insisted that the popular audience had missed his point,[10] the movie's primary critique lay in more subtle exposures, whose power depended on that very audience's intertextual sophistication. Thus, real disenchantment with Michael resulted less from his murders (which the film's own logic justified) than from his betrayal of Classic Hollywood's basic myth. For only a filmgoer who recognized Michael as a reluctant hero (conceiving of his intervention as temporary) could experience the full shock caused by his subsequent development into a grotesque parody of the official values. Similarly, only someone intuitively familiar with the Andy Hardy image of the family could respond completely to *The Godfather I*'s disquieting mixture of paternalism and violence, best captured in Don Corleone's last conversation with Michael. As father and son sat together in the garden, a child's bicycle standing in the background, their talk resembled scenes between Judge Hardy and Andy, while confounding two worlds that Classic Hollywood had kept apart:

DON CORLEONE: So . . . Barzini won't move against you first. He'll set up a meeting with someone that you absolutely trust guaranteeing your safety, and at that meeting you'll be assassinated. I like to drink more wine than I used to. Anyway, I'm drinking more.
MICHAEL: It's good for you, Pop.

DON CORLEONE: Your wife and children, are you happy with them?

MICHAEL: Very happy.

DON CORLEONE: That's good. I hope you don't mind the way I . . . keep going over this Barzini business.

MICHAEL: No, not at all.

DON CORLEONE: It's an old habit. I spent my life trying not to be careless. Women and children can be careless, but not men. How's your boy?

MICHAEL: He's good.

DON CORLEONE: You know he looks more like you every day.

MICHAEL: He's smarter than I am—three years old and he can read the funny papers.

DON CORLEONE: The funny papers! . . . Look, uh . . . I want you to arrange to have a telephone man check all the calls that go in and out here because . . .

MICHAEL: I did it already, Pop.

DON CORLEONE: It could be anyone . . .

MICHAEL: Pop, I took care of that.

In occasional westerns (e.g., *Shane, High Noon*), Hollywood had managed to reconcile the conflicting claims of violence and family by justifying force used against a community's enemies. *The Godfather I*'s most moving scene—Michael's reunion with his near-fatally wounded father—appeared to reconfirm that reconciliation by foreshadowing the son's revenge. As the movie developed, however, it punished the audience for its complicity in this myth. Indeed, by *The Godfather II*, Michael himself had recognized the myth's falsity: "By being strong for his family," he asked his mother, "could a man lose it?"

The reversal had begun in *The Godfather I* with a scene that startlingly frustrated audience expectations. Having had brother-in-law Carlo killed, Michael was confronted by his own hysterical, accusing sister ("And you stood godfather to our baby!") and by his wife, Kay. "Michael, is it true?" she asked incredulously. "Don't ask me about my business, Kay," he replied coldly.

KAY: Is it true?

MICHAEL: Don't ask me about my business.

KAY: No . . .

MICHAEL: *ENOUGH!* . . . All right. This one time . . . this one time, I'll let you ask me about my affairs.

KAY: Is it true?

MICHAEL: [utterly sincere] No.

For all Coppola's talk about capitalist analogies, this scene was *The Godfather*'s most telling departure from Classic Hollywood's forms. Typically, its startling quality depended on implicit references to other movies, where violent men admitted their acts but explained their necessity to women who forgave them. The audience's memory of those movies made Michael's lie come as a shock and prove more damning than any of his crimes.

The Godfather I quietly reversed other stock conventions inherited from the Left films. While the Don displayed the outlaw hero's flawless sixth sense (anticipating Barzini's assassination plans for Michael), the movie elsewhere took care to undercut Hollywood's traditional portrayal of anti-intellectual intuition as infallible. Indeed, *The Godfather I* repeatedly demonstrated that the most intuitive, emotional character, Sonny, was not only the most vicious, but also the most stupid, continually allowing his temper to damage himself and his family. Even more significantly, survival now rested on organization and legal manipulation, previously depicted as the means of the enemy (as in *Butch Cassidy*'s railroad-Pinkerton team, or *The Wild Bunch*'s banker-bounty hunter coalition). Where the Left's heroes had remained individual entrepreneurs, the Corleones had become a corporation, equipped with lawyers and given to rational planning that even involved debates on potential "acquisitions" like narcotics. Where the Left's heroes had struggled to escape from carefully conceived ambushes, the Corleones themselves set the traps, planned the assassinations, and used the law to escape punishment. In *The Godfather I*, in other words, the outlaw heroes had corrupted themselves with the most debased of society's institutions.

By fully integrating these "corrections" into a compelling narrative, however, *The Godfather I* maintained its coveted balance between tradition and revision. Indeed, for all of Coppola's talk of anticapitalist analogies, the movie demonstrated the durability of Classic Hollywood's paradigms. In effect, *The Godfather I* was the *Casablanca* of the 1970s. Not surprisingly, the film's conventional style, period setting, attention to detail, devotion to storytelling, abundance of stars, big budget, and enormous length together provided the model for the wave of conservative movies that followed it: *The Way We Were* (1973), *The Day of the*

Jackal (1973), *The Sting* (1973), *The Great Gatsby* (1974), *The Towering Inferno* (1974), *Jaws* (1975), *Shampoo* (1975), *Three Days of the Condor* (1975), *The Great Waldo Pepper* (1975), *Marathon Man* (1976), *Rocky* (1976), *A Star Is Born* (1976), *The Other Side of Midnight* (1977). Not only did *The Godfather I* fail to radicalize the American Cinema, it ultimately made it more reactionary, spawning the blockbuster complex that reduced the industry's flexibility by fixating its attention on a very few presold, lavishly produced, heavily promoted films.

Without its sequel, *The Godfather I*'s Marxist critique of American success myths would have remained tacit. *The Godfather II*, however, made its "corrections" far more overt, and in doing so, upset the original's ideal commercial balance. (While still a sizable hit, the far more costly sequel earned only one-third as much as *The Godfather I*.) "This time," Coppola confessed, "I really set out to destroy the family. And I wanted to punish Michael."[11] Nevertheless, despite these claims, *The Godfather II*'s "corrections" operated squarely within the traditional American mythology, working variants on frontier imagery and the ideologically determined platitude, "It's lonely at the top." Compared to Godardian cinema, these "corrections" remained mild indeed. That they nonetheless cost the film two-thirds of *The Godfather I*'s audience suggested that American filmgoers had become only marginally more receptive to revisionism than in *Citizen Kane*'s day.

The Godfather II's chief commercial handicap lay in its strategy of alternating between scenes of Vito's youth and Michael's maturity. The parallel montages that *The Godfather I* had used primarily to generate excitement thus became the sequel's basic structuring principle, dialectically indicating the discrepancy between auspicious beginnings and their sterile issue, but also retarding narrative development. Clearly, however, this schema provided *The Godfather II* with the means to "correct" the Left cycle's mythology. First, the expanded chronology that resulted from the juxtapositions spelled out the analogy linking the history of the Corleones to the history of America. As a whole, in fact, *The Godfather* managed to represent all the stages of American development: the immigrant arrival (the child Vito sitting alone in an Ellis Island room, under the Statue of Liberty's shadow); the wilderness struggle for material comforts and status (Vito's early activities in New York's Little Italy); the Robin Hood phase of frontier individualism (Vito's early criminality); the robber baron period (the mature Don Corleone of *The Godfather I*); and finally, the entrenched, organized corporate state (represented by Michael, to whom fellow syndicate operator Hyman Roth boasted, "We're bigger than U.S. Steel").

More thoroughly than most Left films, *The Godfather II* also sketched the trail of America's receding frontiers. The Corleone family movements—from Sicily to America, from New York to the West (Las Vegas and Lake Tahoe), from the West to the "externalized" frontier in Cuba—followed the direction of America's own history, from Jamestown to Vietnam. But the Corleones, like all Left heroes, arrived late, finding their frontiers closing as they reached them. Thus, the New Land's promise became the teeming, predatory world of Little Italy, and the West's landscapes had shrunk to dark rooms where men discussed "business" behind heavy curtains that shut out views of the mountains. Even Cuba failed the Corleones; Michael arrived to witness Batista's fall and Castro's beginnings.

Like the other Left films, *The Godfather II* depicted a postfrontier world of scarcity and violence. Unlike them, it sought to avoid idealizing its protagonists as last representatives of a glorious past. *The Godfather II*, in fact, suggested that America had been a postfrontier world from the beginning, and that perhaps the very idea of a condition that could accommodate extreme individualism without violence was the most fundamental illusion of all. Initially, the film's organization seemed to suggest a pastoral past in which Vito appeared in a favorable light. His pre-organization-man, Robin Hood banditry, interventions against corrupt landlords, and devotion to his family all implicitly criticized the coldly efficient Michael. Their contrast suggested the basic outlaw hero-official hero dichotomy, with Vito's energy invoking, in Philip Rahv's terms, the appeal of life conceived as an opportunity rather than as a discipline.[12] But ultimately, the Vito sequences revealed that behind the Corleones' rise lay Vito's own brutal murder of Fanucci. While the Left heroes had fought in the open, Vito hid in the darkness to ambush his enemy, shooting him with a revolver carefully wrapped in a towel to muffle the sound.

As Pauline Kael observed, the Vito sections of *The Godfather II* "satisfied an impossible yet basic human desire to see what our parents were like before we were born and to see what they did that affected what we became."[13] These sequences, then, worked like the imaginary movie in Delmore Schwartz's story "In Dreams Begin Responsibilities," providing a vision of the past whose consequences could be felt in the present. While partially nostalgic, the Vito scenes also suggested that the entire structure of the Corleone family, and by implication of America itself, rested on a crime at the inception: they thus confirmed *Liberty Valance*'s notion (itself derived from *Red River*, and subsequently picked up by *Easy Rider, Little Big Man*, and *McCabe and Mrs. Miller*) that the American Dream had gone wrong from the start. Watching Vito stalk Fanucci, an ironic filmgoer might have felt like Schwartz's narrator, pleading with his parents to reconsider marrying: "Don't do it. It's not too late to change your minds, both of you. Nothing good will come of it, only remorse, hatred, scandal, and two children whose characters are monstrous."

In fact, however, almost no filmgoers did feel this way. First, by structuring *The Godfather II* around one sustained parallel figure whose juncture lay in a previous movie, Coppola unwittingly subverted the connections between Vito's crime and Michael's behavior, creating instead a dreamlike state in which causality seemed suspended. More important, despite Coppola's intended Marxist critique of America's predatory origins, DeNiro remained too attractive as Vito and Fanucci too one-dimensionally villainous as a character for the audience not to wish his murder. Indeed, as Vito fired, a purely subjective shot of Fanucci placed the viewer in the position of the killer. Throughout *The Godfather II*, the audience's indentification with the Corleones remained almost complete. As a consequence, the movie revived (while reversing) the standard problem of so many postwar films: clearly Coppola's intent did not coincide with his movie's actual effect. In fact, *The Godfather* glamorized its protago-

nists and contributed at least one phrase to the national idiom: "I'll make him an offer he can't refuse."

The Godfather's failure to become the subversive movie of Coppola's designs reconfirmed the *Cahiers du cinéma*'s point that an effective ideological critique occurs primarily at the level of style.[14] By restricting his challenge to a thematic attack on the traditional American mythology, Coppola failed to dislodge the representational system (especially the identification mechanisms) that sustained it. At its worst, therefore, *The Godfather* inadvertently resembled the Mafia itself, adopting a superficial cloak of respectability (chic, Watergate-era anticapitalism) to conceal its tactics of manipulation (maintained by its style's invisibility).

At its best, on the other hand, *The Godfather* recognized what the *Cahiers* critics had not: that cinematic "style" lies not only in filmic syntax, but also in the expectations created by the popular cinema's fundamental intertextuality. In reversing so many of those expectations, *The Godfather* effected a more subtle critique whose immediate result was the end of the intrinsically nostalgic Left cycle.

The power of this critique derived precisely from its traditionality. In many ways, in fact, *The Godfather*'s revisionism resembled that of *The Great Gatsby*, the script for which Coppola had written between his original film and its sequel. Michael was a kind of Gatsby, losing and finding his first love, trying to remake the past, attempting to undo the logic of an original crime. Like Fitzgerald's novel, Coppola's movie suggested that American tragedies resulted from a misguided interpretation of a promise that still existed. Not surprisingly, the movie's final image, with Michael sitting on a lawn chair beside his great empty house, alone by the lake in gathering darkness, recalled Daisy's green light and Gatsby's vigils, and Fitzgerald's concluding passage that suggested how much had been wasted and how much remained:

Most of the big shore places were closed now and there were hardly any lights except the shadowy, moving glow of a ferryboat across the Sound. And as the moon rose higher the inessential houses began to melt away until gradually I became aware of the old island here that flowered once for Dutch sailors' eyes—a fresh, green breast of the new world. Its vanished trees, the trees that had made way for Gatsby's house, had once pandered in whispers to the last and greatest of all human dreams; for a transitory enchanted moment man must have held his breath in the presence of this continent, compelled into an aesthetic contemplation he neither understood nor desired, face to face for the last time in history with something commensurate to his capacity for wonder.

And as I sat there brooding on the old, unknown world, I thought of Gatsby's wonder when he first picked out the green light at the end of Daisy's dock. He had come a long way to this blue lawn, and his dream must have seemed so close he could hardly fail to grasp it. He did not know that it was already behind him, somewhere back in that vast obscurity beyond the city, where the dark fields of the republic rolled on under the night.

Gatsby believed in the green light, the orgiastic future that year by year recedes before us. It eluded us then, but that's no matter—tomor-

row we will run faster, stretch out our arms farther. .... And one fine
morning—
And so we beat on, boats against the current, borne ceaselessly into
the past.

TAXI DRIVER

Even in hindsight, the most surprising thing about *Taxi Driver*
remains its commercial success (twelfth at the box office in 1976).
With its X rating, heavy doses of violence and profanity, and
failure to use major stars, it seemed automatically destined for
a relatively small audience. More important, as a "corrected"
Right film, it faced a far more treacherous problem of balance
than had *The Godfather*. For the Left movies originally pitched
at the developing ironic audience, "corrections" had always been
not only part of the basic marketing strategy, but also the key
to acquiring "legitimacy." In the Right cycle, on the other hand,
aimed at the naïve audience, "corrections" always threatened to
appear "artsy," the most damning adjective possible in that context. As a result, the Right movies had generally limited their
revisionism to injecting naturalist detail into traditional stories
of police and revenge. Formally, these films almost entirely eschewed New Wave devices, preferring instead to refine conventions inherited from Classic Hollywood.

The Right cycle's standard procedures appeared to suggest the
impossibility of making a heavily "corrected," commercially successful Right movie. Worse, even if someone *could* do it, *Taxi
Driver*'s Martin Scorsese (director), Paul Schrader (scriptwriter),
and Robert DeNiro (principal actor) seemed an unpromising team.
All had strong previous associations not only with the Left cycle,
but also with a highly revisionist style of filmmaking that borrowed extensively from the New Wave.[15] None (except DeNiro,
who had appeared in *The Godfather II*) had found any major
commercial success. And yet together they produced the most
popular "corrected" movie in the American Cinema since *Citizen
Kane*.

Like *Kane*, *Taxi Driver* mounted its challenge to Hollywood's
paradigms on both formal and thematic fronts. Also like *Kane*,

however, *Taxi Driver* preserved its accessibility by locating its revisions within a popular genre and an accepted style. Thus, on its surface, *Taxi Driver* seemed to fit comfortably into the Right cycle's basic variant, what Pauline Kael called "the street westerns."[16] In fact, with its New York setting, violent loner hero, and standard revenge plot, it clearly traded on the surprising popularity of *Death Wish* (1974), a low-budget Charles Bronson movie originally intended for the drive-in trade.

More important, *Taxi Driver*'s New Wave borrowings never became either merely cosmetic or utterly freed from the demands of storytelling. In making these stylistic defamiliarizations narratively functional, Scorsese, of course, betrayed Godard's original desire to expose cinematic forms as themselves the perpetuators of ideological attitudes. To suggest style's role, Godard had often employed ways of filming that had no recognizable narrative purpose, but whose very arbitrariness called attention to form itself as a perceptual determinant. *Masculine-Feminine*, for example, followed one nearly six-minute take (of Paul in an amusement arcade) with a laundromat sequence that developed from a series of rapid jump cuts, without in either case making the viewer sense the formal procedure's inevitability or even appropriateness. *Taxi Driver*, on the other hand, softened Godardian ruptures by integrating them into the story, where they recovered most of their invisibility.

Two examples will suffice. In an all-night diner sequence, Scorsese conveyed his hero's intensifying introspection by adopting his perspective to zoom in on a glass of Alka Seltzer until the bubbling water filled the screen in an enormous close-up. This shot came directly from Godard's *2 or 3 Things I Know About Her*, where a steady zoom-in on a cup of coffee had accompanied Godard's own voice-over. Despite their superficial similarities, however, the two sequences remained profoundly different. In Godard's sustained series (nearly 3½ minutes), the shots of the coffee cup had issued not from the main character's point of view, but from that of a stranger without narrative consequence. As a result, the close-ups of the coffee's surface had provided no character insights, but only the occasion for a meditation on subjectivity, objectivity, language, and, not incidentally,

the role of objects as links between two shots taken from different angles. Scorsese's single, relatively brief shot, on the other
hand, prompted no abstract musings; instead, it graphically suggested the hero's self-absorption and growing isolation. In another borrowing, Scorsese panned away from his hero's telephone conversation to an empty hallway whose desolate disrepair
implied the protagonist's own mental condition. By contrast, Godard's similar shot in *A Woman Is a Woman* had worked against
the narrative by reducing it to the caricature of his inserted title:

BECAUSE THEY LOVE ONE ANOTHER, EVERYTHING WILL GO WRONG FOR
EMILE AND ANGELA. THEY HAVE MADE THE MISTAKE OF THINKING THEY
CAN GO TOO FAR. BECAUSE THEIR LOVE IS BOTH MUTUAL AND ETERNAL.

By making his stylistic departures functional, therefore, Scorsese kept the naïve audience from seeing them as purposelessly
"arty." In fact, narrative motivations rendered such departures
largely invisible. Thus, when the hero scanned a room filled with
blacks, the slight slow motion that made them appear threatening remained unnoticed. Similarly, because the movie offered
them as correspondents for its hero's state of mind, the unrealistic, hallucinatory colors, blurred focus, and antimelodic score
provoked no challenges to Right filmgoers. Even Scorsese's jump
cuts, so visible in Godard, seemed a natural way to express the
protagonist's incipient breakdown.

Taxi Driver, in other words, abided by the American Cinema's
fundamental assumption that style should serve narrative. It also
clearly advertised itself as a genre movie. Having thus avoided
scaring off the naïve audience, the film could then attack that
audience's sustaining myth, the belief in the continued applicability of western-style, individual solutions to contemporary
complex problems.

Taxi Driver's basic story followed the Right cycle's loyalty to
the classical western formula: a reluctant individual, confronted
by evil, acts on his own to rid society of spoilers. As played by
Robert DeNiro, *Taxi Driver*'s protagonist had obvious connections with western heroes. Even his name, Travis, linked him to
the defender of the Alamo. Rangy and bowlegged, he wore jeans
and cowboy boots. His origins remained unspecified: like Shane,

he merely appeared on the scene, where he lived alone and kept to himself. The story suggested a typical gunfighter's background, mysterious, yet with hints of violence and familiarity with weapons: he had been a marine (the script indicated Vietnam service), and other cabbies called him "Killer." The pimp, Sport, used a more mythologically explicit nickname: "You're a real cowboy," he kidded Travis. "That's nice, man."

Like all outlaw heroes, Travis immediately recognized his new community's problems. Driving a cab through New York, he described what he saw in a voice-over that modernized the stock western line, "What kind of town is this?"

All the animals come out at night—whores, skunk pussies, buggers, queens, fairies, dopers, junkies . . . sick, venal. Someday a real rain'll come and wash all this scum off the street.

Like the standard western hero, however, he remained reluctant to get involved. He was, he told his superintendent, willing to go with his taxi "anytime, anywhere," and in the middle of an obviously decaying city, he expressed only disinterest:

I go all over. I take people to the Bronx, Brooklyn, I take 'em to Harlem. . . . I don't care, don't make no difference to me. . . . It does to some— some won't even take spooks. Don't make no difference to me.

Travis's attempt to connect with a woman fell into the pattern of irreconcilability established by Godard's *Breathless*. A campaign worker for a presidential candidate, the woman was clearly a joiner who destroyed her own mystique with her opening words during their first date: "*Christ*, the organizational problems." Like *Breathless*'s Patricia, she was also a culture-monger, inevitably provoking another cross-purposes conversation resembling the Godardian original (Patricia: "Do you know William Faulkner?" Michel: "No, who's that? Someone you slept with?"):

Betsy: You know what you remind me of?
Travis: What?
Betsy: That song by Kris Kristofferson.
Travis: Who's that?
Betsy: A songwriter. "He's a prophet and a pusher, partly truth, partly fiction, a walking contradiction."

TRAVIS: You sayin' that about me?
BETSY: Who else would I be talking about?
TRAVIS: I'm no pusher. I never have pushed.

Clearly, they lived in different worlds. Worse, her campaign job identified her with a legal, institutional solution to society's problems that here, as in all westerns, was represented as inadequate, incapable of taking the decisive action necessary for dealing with what Travis saw on the streets. Betsy's obviously overmatched candidate, Senator Charles Palantine, was another in the long line of good-hearted community men shown by the western to be too weak to deal with the real problems. During a cab ride with Travis, Palantine's failings became clear:

PALANTINE: Can I ask you something, Travis?
TRAVIS: Sure.
PALANTINE: What is the one thing about this country that bugs you the most?
TRAVIS: Well, I don't know, you know, I don't follow political issues that closely, sir. I don't know.
PALANTINE: There must be something. . . .
TRAVIS: Well, whatever it is, he should clean up this city here because this city here is like an open sewer, you know? Whoever becomes the President should just . . . really clean it up, you know what I mean? Sometimes I go out and I smell it—I get headaches it's so bad, you know? So I think the President should just clean up the whole mess here, you know? Just flush it down the fuckin' toilet.
PALANTINE: Well, I think I know what you mean, Travis, but it's not going to be easy. . . . We're going to have to make some radical changes.
TRAVIS: Damn straight.

The movie made obvious the inadequacy of Palantine's hedging, suggesting, like all westerns, the need for decisive action.

Taxi Driver followed the Right pattern by implying that such action could only come from an individual hero. Arming himself with black-market guns (including Dirty Harry's favorite Magnum), Travis began training, practicing fast-draws like the wounded Brando in *One-Eyed Jacks*. Watching himself in the mirror, he rehearsed a street version of the western showdown:

Huh? Huh? Faster 'n you, son-of-a-bitch. . . . Saw *you* comin'. . . . shitheel.

I'm standin' here. You make the move. You make the move. It's your move. . . . Try it, you. . . .

You talkin' to *me*? You talkin' to me? You talkin' to me? Well, who the hell else are you talkin' to? . . . You talkin' to me? Well, I'm the only one here. Who the fuck do you think *you're* talkin to? Oh yeah? Yeah? O.K. . . .

In this scene, *Taxi Driver* brought into the open the western myth that had sustained *Dirty Harry, Death Wish, Walking Tall*, and the other cop/vigilante movies of the Right cycle. Like the heroes of those films, Travis would act for an emasculated society. "Listen, you fuckers, you screwheads," he swore to himself, "here is a man who would not take it any more. . . . here is a man who stood up against the scum, the cunts, the dopes, the filth, the shit. Here is someone who stood up."

Up to this point, *Taxi Driver* seemed a standard Right movie, a verification of reasons for law-and-order postures, and a satisfying reaffirmation of western-style responses. From Travis's perspective New York appeared as a jungle: a man ran crazily through the streets shouting almost incomprehensibly, "I'll kill her, I'll kill her, I'll kill her." Two old men fought obscenely on a street corner, one apparently trying to rob the other. Street gangs hurled eggs at Travis's windshield, and teenage girls taunted subteen prostitutes. But most of Travis's rage concentrated on Sport, a pimp who kept a twelve-year-old prostitute named Iris. Trying to persuade her to leave Sport, Travis invoked the outlaw hero's traditional distrust of the law:

IRIS: What should I do? Call the cops?
TRAVIS: The cops don't do nothin', you know that.
IRIS: Sport never treated me bad, honest. Never beat me up once.
TRAVIS: But you can't leave him to do the same to other girls. You can't allow him to do that. He is the lowest kind of person in the world. Somebody's got to do something to him. He's the scum of the earth. He's the worst sucking scum I have ever seen.

Travis's need to pin all of society's problems on one locatable source (that could be dealt with straightway) represented the typical Right movie's displacement strategy. Given the other views of New York afforded by the movie, Travis's concentration on Sport appeared extreme even for the Right cycle, but the movie to this point had carefully insured the audience's identification with Travis by holding closely to his point of view. The few scenes not including him, in Betsy's office, merely prepared for his entrance. (The one jarring departure from this circumscribed point of view, Sport's slow seduction-dance with Iris, was added to satisfy Harvey Keitel, who played Sport.)

Scorsese had also structured the film around skillful juxtapositions that encouraged the audience to regard Travis as the one honest, genuine character. One typical sequence set the stage for Travis by showing Betsy and her fellow office worker, Tom, trying to light a match while simulating missing two fingers on one hand: such silliness made Travis's brooding intensity seem a sign of grace. Scorsese then cut directly to a parallel scene, as a gabby driver, the Wizard, told tall tales about screwing a woman passenger in the back seat of his cab in the middle of the Triboro Bridge. Again, Travis's silence suggested depths of feeling unavailable to the others in the movie.

The most telling undermining of attitudes that might have opposed Travis's occurred in a later juxtaposition. Having gone to the Wizard for advice, Travis received the following counsel:

Look at it this way, you know—a man . . . a man takes a job, and that job, you know, that becomes what he is. You know, like . . . you do a thing and that's what you are.

I've been a cabbie for seventeen years, ten years at night, and I still don't own my own cab. You know why? 'Cause I don't want to. That must be what I want, you know?, on the night shift, drivin' somebody else's cab. Understand? You become . . . you get a job, you become the job.

I mean, one guy lives in Brooklyn, one guy lives in Sutton Place, you get a lawyer, another guy's a doctor, another guy dies, another guy gets well, and you know, people are born. . . . I envy you, you—go on get laid, get drunk. You know, do anything. 'Cause you got no choice anyway. I mean, we're all fucked. More or less, you know?

To this speech, a devastating parody of Hollywood's normally sanctified common sense, Travis could only respond, "I don't know; that's about the dumbest thing I ever heard." The very next scene offered nothing better, only a higher-class version of similar rhetoric. At home watching TV, Travis heard Palantine sum up his platform:

We came up with our slogan, "We are the people." When I said "Let the people rule," I thought I was being overly optimistic. I must tell you that I am more optimistic than ever before—the people are rising to the demands that I have made of them. The people are beginning to rule. I feel it as a groundswell. I know it will continue through the primary; I know it will continue in Miami; and I know it will rise to an unprecedented swell in November.

This obviously shallow populism only reaffirmed the audience's attachment to Travis as the one truly moral force of the film.

Throughout its early sections, however, *Taxi Driver* had offered suggestions (typically conveyed by formal disruptions of the invisible style) of Travis's instability. Street scenes filmed from Travis's point of view used swirling, overripe colors accompanied by disquieting music that at times approximated a slightly accelerated heartbeat. An odd doubling effect, borrowed from Godard and Robert Bresson, provided a certain distance, as the sound track contained Travis's voice pronouncing words that filled the screen as he wrote them. Where the Right heroes' stolidness suggested their imperturbability, Travis's off-key platitudinizing implied his coming disintegration. Of Betsy: "They . . . cannot . . . touch . . . her." Of his own condition: "You're . . . only . . . as . . . healthy . . . as . . . you . . . feel." The jump cuts that accompanied Travis's preparations for the shootout further hinted at his fragmenting personality. Thematically, his predilection for porno movies also remained vaguely unsettling, particularly given his pronouncements about New York's venality.

Most troubling, however, was his loneliness, a stranger, more disquieting solitude than that of the other Right protagonists. "Loneliness has followed me all my life," he spoke in a voice-over soliloquy, whose recurring form reaffirmed his condition. "There's no escape; I'm God's lonely man." As an extreme isolate, Travis satisfied perfectly Tocqueville's ultimate predictions for American democracy:

> Thus not only does democracy make every man forget his ancestors, but it hides his descendants and separates his contemporaries from him; it throws him back forever upon himself alone and threatens in the end to confine him entirely within the solitude of his own heart.[17]

As a European, Tocqueville had characteristically distrusted radical solitude. The American mythology, on the other hand, had habitually portrayed it as the means to grace, and located the origin of sound decisions in the individual, isolated heart (see *Walden*). Thus, neither the Left nor Right films had questioned Patton's self-confident intuition: "I feel I am destined to achieve some great thing." *Taxi Driver*, however, made Travis's version of the instinctive urge less reassuring: "I just wanna go out and really . . . really do something," he confessed to the Wizard. "I just wanna go out . . . I really got some bad ideas in my head."

Subtly warned by these foreshadowing "corrections," therefore, the audience should not have been entirely unprepared when *Taxi Driver* abruptly withdrew its sympathy for Travis with a single shot. After identification with Travis had peaked with his attempts to "rescue" Iris, the film shifted to Columbus Circle where Palantine had begun a speech. Suddenly, the movie confirmed any incipient fears that Travis might represent a distorted version of the Right hero. The camera panned slowly from the podium through the crowd, moving at knee level, finally stopping on a pair of legs, obviously Travis's, stepping out of a cab. Then very slowly (in a shot whose atomization imitated *Breathless*'s policeman killing), the camera moved up his body, to the waist, then to the jacket bulging with guns, and at last to Travis's head, horribly shaved in a Mohawk haircut. The shock was terrific. By following the standard Right pattern, *Taxi Driver* had led its audience into an almost complete identification with a hero now revealed as recognizably insane. Like so many of Hitchcock's films, *Taxi Driver* had implicated the audience in any resulting violence, for the audience had willed this hero and trusted his impulses.

In aborting Travis's assassination attempt, however, *Taxi Driver* punished its audience more subtly. Having failed to kill Palantine, Travis turned his rage against Sport. In a long, harrowingly violent climax, he killed the pimp and two of his henchmen, and the camera rose and panned dispassionately over the carnage to show the audience the results of its vigilante fantasies. The final sequence contained still further ambiguities: a slow pan of Travis's apartment revealed newspaper headlines announcing his canonization ("Taxi Driver Battles Gangsters," "Taxi Driver Hero to Recover") and a letter from Iris's parents thanking him "for returning our Iris to us."

Presumably, *Taxi Driver* had fully "corrected" the Right cycle, indicating to the viewer that Travis's "heroism" resulted from chance: he could just as easily have killed Palantine; indeed, he had tried and failed. The movie thus implied that behind the Right cycle's fantasies lay madness. *Taxi Driver*, however, had so carefully reproduced the appearance of a standard Right film that even sophisticated observers missed the "corrections." Many objected to the extreme violence, which, by punishing the audience for eagerly desiring it, had actually provided the crucial revision. Joan Mellen even referred to the movie as "another vigilante film."[18]

In fact, *Taxi Driver* repudiated what Richard Slotkin has described as the basic myth in American culture: the myth of "regeneration through violence."[19] Scorsese's film even represented a modern version of the most traditional incarnation of that myth, the captivity narrative, which Slotkin calls "the first coherent myth literature in America for American audiences" (p. 95). These stories appealed to the Pilgrims' own ambivalent responses to the New World, which they perceived as both an abundant garden and a terrifyingly hostile wilderness. Their need was to subdue the wilderness without becoming like it, to participate in its freedom without yielding to its temptations.

In Slotkin's terms, "the captivity narratives embodied the dark side of the Puritan attitude toward the natural world in general and toward the American wilderness in particular" (p. 146). These stories of women taken prisoner by the Indians (who inevitably represented the unrestrained libido) allegorized sinful falls and saving restitutions. Removed to the wilderness by her captors, the woman prisoner was portrayed as being in hell, and the forest itself, once a symbol of promise, as the equivalent of the Inferno. "All interest in the landscape of the wilderness disappears," Slotkin writes. It is "seen only as a wasteland of starvation and hardship. Natural terrain is suggested in horrific abstractions; the landscape of the Puritan mind replaces the real wilderness" (p. 99).

The rescue of the woman inevitably depended upon violence and swift action, for frequently the captive women, tempted by the freedom of impulse, action, and sexual choice allowed by Indian society, wished to remain. The rescue was dangerous, for the hero had to "fight the enemy on his own terms and in his own manner, becoming in the process a reflection or double of his own dark opponent" (p. 563). Thus, the rescue became a perverse marriage-hunt converted into a murderous exorcism.

The paradigm of the captivity narratives exactly fitted *Taxi Driver*. Iris appeared to be held prisoner by Sport, who significantly dressed and looked like an Indian, with high cheekbones, slanted eyes, and long straight black hair held in place by a headband. She was characteristically reluctant to leave her "captivity." Scorsese replaced the real New York with a series of "horrific abstractions" corresponding to the landscape of Travis's mind. The city became a wilderness hell, in which Iris's home with Sport was a particularly terrible corner. Like the Pilgrims, Travis was an emigrant whose experiences confirmed the Right audience's anxieties about American urbanization. Hunting Sport, Travis became like him, violent, unrestrained, even taking on an Indian appearance with his Mohawk haircut. "Go back to your fuckin' tribe," Sport told him, confirming the reference.

Taxi Driver suggested, however, that the myth of "regeneration through violence" that lay behind the Right cycle had become inapplicable in modern society. As a solution, it was madness. To the extent that this myth had also provided the basis of Classic Hollywood's thematic paradigm, and the traditional American ideology itself, *Taxi Driver* undertook to challenge the whole of American culture. In doing so, it followed the lead of D. H. Lawrence, whose description of the essential American soul perfectly fitted Travis: "hard, isolate, stoic, and a killer." Similarly, Travis's rantings ("Listen, you fuckers, you screwheads, here is a man who stood up against the scum, the cunts, the dopers, the filth, the shit") recalled Norman Mailer's description of Sam Croft the Hunter in *The Naked and The Dead*:

A lean man of medium height but he held himself so erectly he appeared tall. His narrow triangular face was utterly without expression. There seemed nothing wasted in his hard small jaw, gaunt firm cheeks and straight short nose. His gelid eyes were very blue. . . . He hated weakness and he loved practically nothing. There was a crude unformed vision in his soul but he was rarely conscious of it. . . .

His ancestors pushed and labored and strained, drove their oxen, sweated their women, and moved a thousand miles.

He pushed and labored inside himself and smoldered with an endless hatred.

(You're all a bunch of fuggin whores)

(You're all a bunch of dogs)

(You're all deer to track)

I HATE EVERYTHING, WHICH IS NOT IN MYSELF[20]

Here, *Taxi Driver* implied, was the reality behind the Right movies, and indeed, the reality behind the Right's continued reliance on unilateral, individualistic responses to complex, contemporary problems. In many ways, *Taxi Driver* allegorized the American experience in Vietnam: detached isolationism followed by violent, and ultimately ineffective, intervention. More immediately, its equation of the impulse to vigilantism with the impulse that led to assassinations put an end to the Right cycle. Had *Taxi Driver* been more popular, or its "corrections" less ambiguous, its critique of the reluctant hero story might have put an end to the American Cinema's "certain tendency" as well.

Conclusion

IN THIS BOOK's Introduction, I suggested that the most interesting question posed by the American Cinema concerned those marginal, dissident moments (formal or thematic) contained in films otherwise controlled by the traditional paradigms. In the chapters on *Casablanca, It's a Wonderful Life, The Man Who Shot Liberty Valance, The Godfather*, and *Taxi Driver*, I examined such moments and their capacity to call into question the ideological position sustained by Hollywood's normal procedures. Here in the Conclusion, I would reformulate my original suggestion by broadening it: as historically the most powerful, visible, and influential sector of popular culture, the American Cinema presents us with the ideal case for studying popular culture's relationship both to its own tradition and to the ideology that its tradition embodies. In an age that has seen popular culture become, for most people, the *only* culture, our need to understand that relationship has become urgent.

I am not sure that our understanding of that relationship will ever become complete. I do know that it is customary at this point in a book for the author to offer his own solutions to the issues he has raised. I am tempted myself by the prospects of such an ending, one in which all previous contradictions would vanish in a reconciliation confirmed by a certain emotional correctness—in precisely the kind of ending, in other words, repeatedly afforded by the American Cinema. In offering such a conclusion, I would, of course, be renewing rather than challenging the ideological effect produced by that cinema's principal tradition.[1] In the place of such an ending, I will provide a short review of the problems that remain unsolved but that seem to

indicate the right direction for future work. Here is a "conclusion," then, that I hope will serve as an introduction.

We might begin with the following question: if, as is generally
agreed, the American Cinema has been largely a conservative
cinema, functioning to subdue those conflicts capable of generating dissent, what would a genuinely radical cinema look like?
The answer taking shape over the last decade has derived from
a combination of sources, most prominently Brecht's drama theory, Lacan's psychoanalysis, and old-fashioned avant-gardism. In
particular, this polemic (for it has always been that more than a
simple answer) has organized itself around three oppositions:
Brecht's dramatic/epic theaters, Lacan's Imaginary/Symbolic
realms, and film's dominant/counter cinemas. Within this theoretical strand, the first term of each of these oppositions has become identified with a regressive passivity resulting from a massive, unquestioned identification of the self with a fictional
representation.[2] While the notions of dramatic theater and dominant cinema turn simply on delineating those types of transparent, continuity-based modes that discourage the spectator's
critical intervention, Lacan's terms, by being more comprehensive, have remained fluid and capable of sustaining increasingly
different types of arguments.

In brief, Lacan means by the "Imaginary" that first period when
an infant remains incapable of distinguishing himself from his
image in the mirror; the child's ultimate recognition of the difference, on the other hand, marks his permanent accession to
the Symbolic order. Clearly, the diachronic aspect of this thesis
accounts for part of its appeal, for it locates undesirable passivity
in a past that the organism has outgrown. Indeed, at first glance,
this distinction seems to explain the American Cinema's evolution from the Imaginary innocence of *Casablanca* to the Symbolic irony of *Taxi Driver*.

Such an account, however, would satisfy no one. *Taxi Driver*
fails to convince the proponents of "counter cinema" whose model
is the Godardian/Straubian film of unmitigated dislocation, disruption, and estrangement. For that group, *Taxi Driver* remains
too situated within Hollywood's traditional paradigms to produce
an effective critique of the ideology those paradigms sustain. What

counter cinema's advocates have consistently neglected, however, is Lacan's warning that the images produced during the Imaginary stage are not abandoned upon entry into the Symbolic. Indeed, those images form the absolute basis of an organism's specific personality, and the semiotic skills characteristic of the Symbolic order serve only as the means for controlling, ordering, and deriving meaning from those images.[3] By that account, a radical American Cinema would necessarily make use of American culture's Imaginary—that store of myths and means of representation that I have called Hollywood's "certain tendency." By not drawing on that Imaginary bank, an American radical cinema would risk being the ineffectual, unattended blind alley that too much of counter cinema has become.

In other words, precisely because *Taxi Driver* draws on both Hollywood's thematic and formal paradigms, only to criticize them, it seems to me a model for a "radical" American movie. Diachronic logic would then propose *Casablanca* as an example of the Imaginary. But if counter cinema's champions will not accept *Taxi Driver* as radical, I cannot accept *Casablanca* as "innocent." Despite our persistent determination to see the past (whether individual or cultural) as the naïve realm of the Imaginary, we have seen that in relation to its own moment, *Casablanca* called into question its own resolution of the anxiety produced by World War II. Is that self-criticism the cause of its abiding popularity? I don't know. It does appear that a significant number of American movies that have remained popular contain some sort of internal critique which, in contesting these films' displacements, have continually "modernized" them. Or perhaps as Barthes's *S/Z* demonstrates, contemporary criticism practices a deliberate alchemy, resuscitating works it likes by transforming them from Imaginary dross into Symbolic gold.

We should in any case be wary of labeling *Casablanca* as "innocent," a term that, even if correct, would not properly describe the film's text, but rather a specific audience's relationship to it. Forty years after the fact, how can we possibly say whether *Casablanca*'s first audiences saw it "innocently"? What would we mean by such a designation? That the audience was unaware of, or unaffected by, what I (perhaps alone) perceive as the movie's internal self-doubts? That the audience had not yet attained the Symbolic realm and thus could not recognize the play of differences that constitute cinema's formal and thematic codes?

In fact, we cannot even answer the most basic question about the American Cinema's audience: does industrialized, commercial popular culture reflect the tastes of its audience or impose them? We should remember that the Frankfurt School in general, and Theodor Adorno in particular, repeatedly criticized the notion that "popular culture" resulted from an ongoing negotiation between producers and audience, citing instead the captive audience's powerlessness in an age of capital-intensive, highly centralized media production. Adorno attacked even the term "popular culture" itself as being an ideological weapon serving to disguise the products of a dominant minority as "the people's art."[4] And yet, Hollywood's continuously demonstrated ability to respond quickly to immediate historical crises seems to confound Adorno's pessimism. In the wake of the 1973 oil embargo, for example, the cycles of disaster, horror, and science fiction movies all appeared to reflect the American audience's sudden awareness of its vulnerability to "the Other," typically personified as at once senseless and destructive. We should remember, however, that in Althusser's terms, the American Cinema has never reflected "real" events but at most its audience's relation to those events, and, as I have argued, that relation has at no point been free of cultural conditioning. That is, the very categories of perception that constitute the audience's relation to material events themselves derive overwhelmingly from the culture that purports merely to reflect them.

I would settle here for a middle position that defines the industry-audience relationship as a reciprocal one. I am more pessimistic, however, about the possibilities for mass intervention in the production process. Despite the optimism of such media theorists as Walter Benjamin and Hans Enzensberger,[5] the average person in the twentieth century has less access to the means of cultural production than he would have had a hundred years ago. We might describe this problem as "the ownership of the image."

Recently, Sony has announced the imminent arrival of an

enormously sophisticated television monitor and video camera whose image will equal or surpass the quality of even 35mm film. Most mentions of this prototype have discussed its advent in merely technical terms. In fact, however, such a development would perpetuate a political control of the image that has existed since the early 1920s.

Technological improvements in photography, film, and television have always carried concealed political implications. Each improvement, in effect, has redefined what counts as an acceptable (and therefore "realistic" and "unbiased") picture of the world, escalating the standard so as to keep it always just out of reach of all but the most powerful. Those images that fall short of the accepted norm appear not only as amateurish, but more importantly, as less "real." While the images produced by those in power seem to be merely an "objective" record of the way things are, less-than-standard images always appear as the products of special interests.

The history of Hollywood itself illustrates how the image's proprietors will quickly and consciously erect barriers to entry in order to establish a costly norm. On the eve of World War I, before such barriers had been erected, the American movie business was still largely a cottage industry, with hundreds of independent filmmaking groups. That competitive situation depended primarily on the absence of a general agreement about what a "movie" should be. Producers argued about such fundamentals as the proper length, stories versus documentaries, stars versus anonymous actors, and the budgets for individual films. By 1920, all those issues had been decided, and a "movie" became defined as an expensively produced, ninety-minute fictional narrative that used recognizable stars. Not coincidentally, that definition effectively excluded from commercial filmmaking everyone but the increasingly oligopolistic Hollywood movie industry, which had thereby gained complete control of the acceptable image.[6]

Recently, we have been repeatedly told that video will rapidly redistribute the image to a larger population. Video is cheap; portable color cameras designed to work with home VCR systems lie within reach of most of the middle class. The rapid refinement of the video image, however, once again effectively withdraws the image from its audience. Indeed, the quality of the picture produced by the networks' $35,000 cameras disenfranchises everyone without access to similar equipment, branding images produced by cheaper cameras as not merely inferior, but as less than a "true" record of reality.

Given the steadily narrowing ownership base of cinema's means of production, it may be that the best possibility for audience intervention lies in what Sylvia Harvey calls "radical readings,"[7] those interpretations (for which Barthes's *S/Z* and the *Cahiers du cinéma*'s analysis of *Young Mr. Lincoln* provide the models) that subvert a text's apparently intended effect by emphasizing precisely those internal marginal elements that contest it. The contemporary college audience's disrespectful, camp reading of the U.S. government's antimarijuana movie *Reefer Madness* seems to have implemented Umberto Eco's call to arms:

In my *La struttura assente*, I proposed, also, the possibility of a "semiotic guerrilla warfare"; the gap between the transmitted and the received message is not only an aberration, which needs to be reduced—it can also be developed so as to broaden the receiver's freedom. In political activity it is not indispensable to change a given message: it would be enough (or, perhaps better) to change the attitude of the audience, so as to induce a different decoding of the message—or in order to isolate the intentions of the transmitter and thus to criticize them.[8]

After quoting this passage, Sylvia Harvey asks simply, "how is this 'semiotic guerrilla warfare' to be disseminated?" I would answer with one word: television. I have argued in this book that the chief means by which the ironic audience has acquired its distance from Hollywood's conventions has been television, with its indiscriminate recycling and baroque deployment of the American Cinema's basic paradigms. At the same time, however, television has perpetuated the most conservative incarnations of those codes. As a result, we may be on the verge of witnessing the creation of a mass audience with a truly double system of consciousness, by turns (or simultaneously) straight and ironic.

The election of Ronald Reagan symbolizes that double consciousness. For whatever else Reagan may represent to his supporters (a return to traditional values, a refusal of modernity), he remains, even for them, vaguely a figure of camp, a poor man's cowboy most often associated with movies in which he shared billing with a chimpanzee. Reagan's ambivalent image only offers another sign of American culture's growing mythological self-consciousness. Indeed, perhaps only a former movie star could satisfy an age that is at once so nostalgic for, and so cynical about, clear-cut action and straightforward heroes.

Certainly, the contemporary American Cinema reflects, and furthers, that self-consciousness. Where television now perpetuates the "sincere" versions of the traditional mythology (as in "Bonanza," "Little House on the Prairie," "The Waltons," and any situation comedy), the movies have increasingly reproduced that mythology in forms either explicitly or implicitly ironic. Such films inevitably draw on Classic Hollywood's established paradigms, but the literalness of their transcription becomes itself a source of distance. No film illustrates this effect more than *Star Wars* (1977), one of the most successful movies of all time, and one whose plot reads like the ur-version of the reluctant hero story. Reviewing it, Stanley Kauffmann complained about the absence of irony: "I kept looking for an 'edge,'" he wrote, "to peer around the corny, solemn comic-book strophes; [but Lucas] was facing them frontally and full."[9] In fact, however, regardless of its creator's intentions, *Star Wars*, with its elephantine score (that seemed to parody Max Steiner's *Casablanca* music) and cartoon characters, was inescapably camp for anyone over twelve.

Lucas's use of the abiding "Star Trek" cult as a selling device for *Star Wars* confirmed Hollywood's steadily increasing reliance on television as a silent partner in the mythologizing process. Where initially television had single-mindedly wanted to be the movies, adopting all of Hollywood's traditional genres and formulas, the movies now often wanted to be television, trading on personalities or subjects spawned by the network's shows. No figure understood this new relationship more than Burt Reynolds, the leading box office draw of the 1970s, and the first major Hollywood star to use television talk shows to "correct" an existing screen persona. Like the "corrected" genre picture, Reynold's resulting image (simultaneously straight machismo and a parody of machismo) proved the perfect means for satisfying the popular audience's combination of nostalgia and cynicism.

With the rise of cable networks and home videotaping units,

television seems destined to become the eventual repository of the American Cinema's "certain tendency." Almost certainly, television's ceaseless availability and neutralizing familiarity will subject that tendency to more and more irony, as it is forced to make its own place in an environment already swarming with images. In *2 or 3 Things I Know about Her*, Godard observed that "living in today's world is rather like living in the middle of a giant comic strip." The nature of film, with its discrete still pictures tricked into motion by projection, had always implied animation, but in Classic Hollywood's versions, America's traditional mythology had seemed genuinely alive. Strangely, that mythology, which began in folk tales and literature before finding its home in the movies, now survives primarily in private houses, where amidst the furniture and the smells of cooking, flickering images replace each other over and over, and continue to shape our lives in ways we still do not fully understand.

Notes

INTRODUCTION

1. "An Interview with Raymond Williams," *Screen Education* 31 (1979), 13. (Emphasis added.)

2. Roland Barthes, "Upon Leaving the Movie Theater," trans. Bertrand Augst and Susan White, in *Apparatus*, ed. Theresa Hak Kyung Cha (New York: Tanam Press, 1981), p. 3. Barthes's remark involves French psychoanalyst Jacques Lacan's distinction between the Imaginary and Symbolic realms. See my discussion of how Lacan's theory might apply to the American cinema, pp. 362-63.

3. See, for example, Pauline Kael's description of *Casablanca* as "a movie that demonstrates how entertaining a bad movie can be," and Andrew Sarris's backhanded compliment: "*Casablanca*, the happiest of happy accidents, and the most decisive exception to the auteur theory." Pauline Kael, *Kiss Kiss Bang Bang* (Boston: Little, Brown, 1968), p. 345. Andrew Sarris, *The American Cinema: Directors and Directions 1929-1968* (New York: Dutton, 1968), p. 176.

4. Cobbert Steinberg, *Reel Facts: The Movie Book of Records* (New York: Vintage, 1982), pp. 42-43.

5. *Edinburg '77 Magazine*, no. 2 (1977), 10. Despite the pessimism it expresses about the possibility of cinematic history, Nowell-Smith's article has proved valuable to me in emphasizing the various autonomous processes in which the movies find themselves immersed.

6. This listing derives from, while modifying, Nowell-Smith's. Ibid., p. 11.

7. *A Future for Astyanax: Character and Desire in Literature* (Boston: Little, Brown, 1976), pp. 284-85.

8. The most common source for Brecht's theoretical writings is *Brecht on Theatre*, ed. and trans. John Willett (New York: Hill and Wang, 1964). Perhaps more significant for the current debates within film theory is the "ideal Brecht" (the populist, politically correct modernist) propagated by leftist critics. See for example the Brecht issue of *Screen* 16 (Winter 1975-1976) and Alan Lovell's superb summary of the elements in this ideal portrait: "Epic Theater & Counter-Cinema's Principles," *Jump Cut* 27 (1982), 64-68.

After beginning as a pure formalist (*Theory of Film Practice*, trans. Helen R. Lane [Princeton: Princeton University Press, 1981], a new edition whose foreward recants on the book's premise), Burch has developed a thoroughly historical, materialist account of Hollywood cinema's stylistics. The crucial arguments appear in "Propositions" (co-written with Jorge Dana), trans. Diana Matias and Christopher King, *Afterimage* (London) 5 (Spring 1974), 40-66; *To the Distant Observer: Form and Meaning in the Japanese Cinema* (Berkeley: University of California Press, 1979); and "How We Got into Pictures: Notes Accompanying *Correction Please*," *Afterimage* (London) 8/9 (Spring 1981), 22-38.

9. George Mitchell, "The Consolidation of the American Film Industry 1915-1920," *Ciné-Tracts* 6 (Spring 1979), 28-36 and *Ciné-Tracts* 7/8 (Summer/Fall 1979), 63-70.

10. See the Burch pieces mentioned above in n. 8.

11. On shot-reverse shot, see the discussion of "suture" in *Screen* 18 (Winter 1977-1978) and Daniel Dayan's leading article, "The Tutor Code of Classical Cinema," reprinted in *Movies and Methods*, ed. Bill Nichols (Berkeley: University of California Press, 1976), pp. 438-51. On deep focus, see Brian Henderson, "Toward a Non-Bourgeois Camera Style," in *Movies and Methods*, ed. Nichols, pp. 422-38.

12. A general (and often obscure) account appears in Stephen Neale, *Genre* (London: British Film Institute, 1980). The essays collected by Rick Altman in *Genre: The Musical* (London: Routledge & Kegan Paul, 1981) provide the best ideological critique of a single genre.

13. Jean-Louis Baudry, "Ideological Effects of the Basic Cinematographic Apparatus," trans. Alan Williams, *Film Quarterly* 28 (Winter 1974-1975), 39-47. Baudry's article also appears in *Apparatus*, ed. Cha, pp. 25-37.

14. The most frequently cited article stating this position has become Colin MacCabe's "Realism and the Cinema: Notes on Some Brechtian Theses," *Screen* 15 (Summer 1974), 7-27.

15. *Film Quarterly* 35 (Winter 1981-1982), 2-16.

16. For a superb discussion of ideology which has greatly influenced my own thinking on the subject, see Michael Rosenthal, "Ideology, Determinism and Relative Autonomy," *Jump Cut* 17 (1978), 19-22. Rosenthal draws heavily on Nicos Poulantzas's theory of the modern state to refute the widely held notion of ideology as a "thing."

17. Louis Althusser and Etienne Balibar, *Reading Capital*, trans. Ben Brewster (London: New Left Books, 1970), p. 97.

18. "Contradiction and Overdetermination," in *For Marx*, trans. Ben Brewster (London: New Left Books, 1979), p. 113. Althusser's startling move clearly derives from Freud's cancellation of his own *prima causa*, the primal scene, in "The Wolf Man Case," officially known as "From the History of an Infantile Neurosis," in Sigmund Freud, *Three Case Histories* (New York: Collier Books, 1963). For an excellent discussion of this decentering move, see David Carroll, "Freud and the Myth of Origin," *New Literary History* 6 (Spring 1975), 513-28.

19. For a Marxist critique of Althusser, see Simon Clarke et al., *One-Dimensional Marxism: Althusser and the Politics of Culture* (London: Allison & Busby, 1980).

20. See Derrida's comments in the "Discussion" that follows his "Structure, Sign and Play in the Discourse of the Humanities," in *The Structuralist Controversy*, ed. Richard Macksey and Eugenio Donato (Baltimore: The Johns Hopkins University Press, 1972), p. 271.

21. See Derrida's "Hors Livre: Outwork," in *Dissemination*, trans. Barbara Johnson (Chicago: University of Chicago Press, 1981), pp. 1-59.

22. See Charles Eckert's prophetic remarks in 1974: ". . . film study is becoming increasingly demanding, just in terms of the organization of one's work, since everything needs to be pursued at once, presented at once, theoretically validated as it is presented, and subjected to scrutiny in terms of one's motivations for establishing categories and arriving at solutions (which in turn, in the interest

of truth, must be converted into problems of a new order). . . . there is a stiff, cold wind blowing against partial, outmoded, or theoretically unsound forms of film criticism—and it just might blow many of them away." "Shall We Deport Lévi-Strauss?" *Film Quarterly* 27 (Spring 1974), 65.

23. See James Turner, *The Politics of Landscape: Rural Scenery in English Poetry 1630-1660* (Cambridge: Harvard University Press, 1979), p. 187, making this point about literature.

24. The biggest influence on my argument in this book, and the article that seeks to combine these three discourses into a unified approach to film study, is Charles Eckert's "The Anatomy of a Proletarian Film: Warner's *Marked Woman*," *Film Quarterly* 17 (Winter 1973-1974), 10-24.

25. See Althusser's "Contradiction and Overdetermination," in *For Marx*.

26. See Lévi-Strauss's *The Raw and the Cooked: Introduction to a Science of Mythology: I*, trans. John and Doreen Weightman (New York: Harper & Row, 1975).

27. The crucial discussion appears in the chapter "The Dream Work" in *The Interpretation of Dreams*, trans. Dr. A. A. Brill (New York: Modern Library, 1950).

28. Marx and Engels, *The German Ideology*, in *The Marx-Engels Reader*, ed. Robert C. Tucker (New York: Norton, 1978), p. 172.

29. Raymond Geuss's *The Idea of a Critical Theory: Habermas and the Frankfurt School* (Cambridge: Cambridge University Press, 1981) provides an extremely useful taxonomy of the various usages of the term "ideology." Geuss's general schema distinguishes three principal connotations: 1) "ideology in the descriptive sense," implying that every human group has an ideology; 2) "ideology in the pejorative sense," offering the idea of ideology as a systematic false consciousness or delusion imposed on one group by another; and 3) "ideology in the positive sense," suggesting an enabling program adopted for the purposes of action. As Geuss summarizes: "Whereas an ideology in any of the descriptive senses is something one *finds* . . . and an ideology in the pejorative sense is something one finds and isolates in order to criticize, an ideology in the positive sense isn't something 'out there' to be found by even the most careful empirical investigation. It might be a desideratum for a particular society that it have an ideology in this sense, but the ideology is something *to be* constructed, created, or invented; it is a *vérité à faire*" (p. 23).

30. "Marxism and Humanism," in *For Marx*, p. 231.

31. Ibid., pp. 232-33.

32. See, for example, Terry Lovell, *Pictures of Reality: Aesthetics, Politics and Pleasure* (London: British Film Institute, 1980).

33. *Mythologies*, trans. Annette Lavers (New York: Hill and Wang, 1972), p. 11.

34. Raymond Williams, "Marxism, Structuralism and Literary Analysis," *New Left Review* 129 (September-October 1981), 51-66.

35. V. N. Vološinov, *Marxism and the Philosophy of Language*, trans. Ladislav Matejka and I. R. Titunik (New York: Seminar Press, 1973); P. N. Medvedev (M. M. Bakhtin), *The Formal Method in Literary Scholarship: A Critical Introduction to Sociological Poetics*, trans. Albert J. Wehrle (Baltimore: The Johns Hopkins University Press, 1978); Jan Mukařovský, *Aesthetic Function, Norm and Value as Social Facts*, trans. Mark E. Suino (Ann Arbor: Michigan Slavic Contributions, 1979).

36. Truffaut's phrase occurs in the title of his polemic, "A Certain Tendency of the French Cinema," which in attacking the cinematically hidebound "tradition of quality" then dominant in French film, provided the auteurists, and ultimately the New Wave directors, with their manifesto. Truffaut's 1954 article, originally appearing in the *Cahiers du cinéma*, has been reprinted in *Movies and Methods*, ed. Nichols, 224-37.

37. The Frankfurt School's landmark attack on popular culture appears in T. W. Adorno and M. Horkheimer's "The Culture Industry: Enlightenment as Mass Deception," a chapter from their book *Dialectic of Enlightenment*, trans. John Cumming (New York: Seabury Press, 1972). This article represents a late summary of positions developed by Adorno in the 1930s and 1940s.

38. Eberhard Knödler-Bunte, "The Proletarian Public Sphere and Political Organization: An Analysis of Oskar Negt and Alexander Kluge's *The Public Sphere and Experience*," trans. Sara Lennox and Frank Lennox, *New German Critique* 4 (Winter 1975), 51-52.

39. Anthony Trollope, *The Way We Live Now* (Indianapolis: Bobbs-Merrill, 1974).

CHAPTER 1. A CERTAIN TENDENCY OF THE AMERICAN CINEMA: CLASSIC HOLLYWOOD'S FORMAL AND THEMATIC PARADIGMS

1. Statistics taken from Cobbett Steinberg's *Reel Facts: The Movie Book of Records* (New York: Vintage, 1982), pp. 47-49.

2. For the extent of this domination in 1937, see Jeremy Turnstall, *The Media Are American: Anglo-American Media in the World* (New York: Columbia University Press, 1977), p. 284.

3. Joseph V. Mascelli, *The Five C's of Cinematography: Motion Picture Filming Techniques Simplified* (Hollywood: Cine/Grafic Publications, 1965), p. 8. (Emphasis partially added.)

4. In *Language and Cinema*, trans. Donna Jean Umiker-Sebeok (The Hague: Mouton, 1974), pp. 55-61, Christian Metz restates this distinction between external and internal elements, proposing the terms "filmic" (external elements nonspecific to the movies) and "cinematic" (internal elements specific to the movies— i.e., the cinema's own signs and codes). I find this distinction confusing and hard to remember. I also regard Metz's insistence on the "cinematic" as the proper object of film study a sign of his (now-renounced) desire to replace the messy complexities of a comprehensive approach with a neater formalism.

5. "Shirley Temple and the House of Rockefeller," *Jump Cut* 2 (July-August 1974), 1.

6. The best evaluation of technological/stylistic changes appears in three articles by Barry Salt: "Statistical Style Analysis of Motion Pictures," *Film Quarterly* 38 (Fall 1974), 13-22; "Film Style and Technology in the Thirties," *Film Quarterly* 30 (Fall 1976), 19-32; and "Film Style and Technology in the Forties," *Film Quarterly* 31 (Fall 1977), 46-57.

7. For this description, I am drawing on John Ellis's fine article, "The Institution of the Cinema," *Edinburg '77 Magazine*, no. 2 (1977), 62.

8. "Shirley Temple and the House of Rockefeller," p. 1. Eckert's point draws on F. D. Klingender and Stuart Legg, *Money behind the Screen* (New York: Arno, 1978), pp. 69-79. The Arno edition is a reprint of the 1937 original.

9. The seminal discussion of the American Cinema's tactic of displacement is

Charles Eckert's "The Anatomy of a Proletarian Film: Warner's *Marked Woman*," *Film Quarterly* 17 (Winter 1973-1974), 10-24.

10. Robert Sklar, *Movie-Made America: A Social History of American Movies* (New York: Random House, 1975), pp. 195-96.

11. Roland Barthes, *Mythologies*, trans. Annette Lavers (New York: Hill and Wang, 1972), pp. 148, 147.

12. This term, and its implications for a study of the American Cinema, form a crucial part of the *Cahiers du cinéma*'s famous collective essay "John Ford's *Young Mr. Lincoln*." The essay appears in *Film Theory and Criticism*, ed. Gerald Mast and Marshall Cohen (New York: Oxford University Press, 1979), pp. 778-831. The essay was first published in 1970.

13. *Movie-Made America*, pp. 196-97.

14. David Thompson, *A Biographical Dictionary of Film* (New York: William Morrow, 1976), p. 541.

15. François Truffaut, *Hitchcock* (New York: Simon and Schuster, 1967), p. 208. The *Cahiers* article on *Young Mr. Lincoln* analyzes another instance of concealed withholding that I discuss in the chapter on *Liberty Valance*.

16. See, for example, the following representative pieces: 1) Noël Burch, "Film's Institutional Mode of Representation and the Soviet Response," *October* 11 (Winter 1979), 77-96. 2) Burch, "Porter, or Ambivalence," *Screen* 19 (Winter 1978-1979), 91-105. 3) Burch, "A Parenthesis on Film History," in Burch's *To the Distant Observer: Form and Meaning in the Japanese Cinema* (Berkeley: University of California Press, 1979), pp. 61-66. 4) Burch, "How We Got into Pictures: Notes Accompanying *Correction Please*," *Afterimage* (London) 8/9 (Spring 1981), 22-38. 5) Colin MacCabe, "Realism and the Cinema: Notes on Some Brechtian Theses," *Screen* 15 (Summer 1974), 7-27. 6) MacCabe, "The Politics of Separation," *Screen* 16 (Winter 1975-1976), 46-61. 7) Stephen Heath, *Questions of Cinema* (Bloomington: Indiana University Press, 1981), which collects the articles Heath regards as his most important. A useful summary of this now well-developed position appears in Tony Stevens, "Reading the Realist Film," *Screen Education* 26 (Spring 1978), 13-34 and in the dissenting reply, Dick Hebdige and Geoff Hurd, "Reading and Realism," *Screen Education* 28 (Autumn 1978), 68-78.

17. *Writing Degree Zero*, trans. Annette Lavers and Colin Smith (New York: Hill and Wang, 1968).

18. The leading article on this point is Roland Barthes's "The Realistic Effect," trans. Gerald Mead, *Film Reader 3* (1978), 131-35.

19. Borrowing the term from Noam Chomsky, Jonathan Culler uses "competence" to describe an individual's internalized mastery of a system of meaning-producing signs or conventions. See Culler, *Structuralist Poetics* (Ithaca, N.Y.: Cornell University Press, 1975), pp. 113-30.

20. See, for example, Russell Merritt, "Nickelodeon Theaters 1905-1914: Building an Audience for the Movies," in *The American Film Industry*, ed. Tino Balio (Madison: University of Wisconsin Press, 1976), pp. 59-82.

21. Burch, "Porter, or Ambivalence" and "How We Got into Pictures: Notes Accompanying *Correction Please*," both cited above in n. 16. See also Burch's entry "Fritz Lang: German Period," trans. Tom Milne, in *Cinema: A Critical Dictionary, The Major Film-Makers, Volume Two*, ed. Richard Roud (New York: Viking, 1980), pp. 583-99; and Burch's modification of that article in "Notes on Fritz Lang's First *Mabuse*," *Ciné-Tracts* 13 (Spring 1981), 1-13.

22. Octave Mannoni, *Clefs pour l'Imaginaire ou l'Autre Scène* (Paris: Le Seuil, 1969), pp. 9, 163-64.

23. Apparently toward the end of his life, Theodor Adorno also formulated a notion of a "double system of consciousness" that enables a spectator to be temporarily spellbound by an event he ultimately regards as having no importance. Adorno, however, reverses the terms of Mannoni's "je sais bien, mais quand même . . ." by suggesting that the "nevertheless" applies not to the reconfirmation of one's faith in the illusion, but to the retroactive disavowal of what had previously been embraced. Adorno based his revised theory on empirical evidence that despite enormous TV audiences for the wedding of Dutch Princess Beatrix to German diplomat Claus von Amsberg, television viewers attributed relatively little importance to the event. See Andreas Huyssen, "Introduction to Adorno," *New German Critique* 6 (1975), 9-10. I would regard this conflicting evidence as resulting from the kind of leading questions I criticized in the Introduction as being inadequate for determining audience response.

24. See James Linton, "But It's Only a Movie," *Jump Cut* 17 (1978), 16-19.

25. The crucial article is Jacques Lacan, "The Mirror Stage as Formative of the Function of the I as Revealed in Psychoanalytic Experience," in *Écrits*, trans. Alan Sheridan (New York: Norton, 1977), pp. 1-7.

26. Burch, *To the Distant Observer*, p. 22.

27. For the best summary of the 180° system, see David Bordwell and Kristin Thompson, *Film Art: An Introduction* (Reading, Mass.: Addison-Wesley, 1979), pp. 163-71.

28. *To the Distant Observer*, p. 158. See also "Propositions," p. 66, n. 27.

29. Daniel Dayan, "The Tutor-Code of Classical Cinema," in *Movies and Methods*, ed. Bill Nichols (Berkeley: University of California Press, 1976), pp. 438-51. See also "Dossier on Suture" (including articles by Jacques-Alain Miller, Jean-Pierre Oudart, and Stephen Heath), *Screen* 18 (Winter 1977-1978), 23-76. For a dissenting view about the significance of the shot-reverse shot figure, see William Rothman, "Against 'The System of the Suture,'" in *Movies and Methods*, ed. Nichols, pp. 451-59.

30. Barry Salt, "Film Style and Technology in the Forties," *Film Quarterly* 31 (Fall 1977), 50-53.

31. Stanislaw Lem, *Return from the Stars*, trans. Barbara Marszal and Frank Simpson (New York: Harcourt Brace Jovanovich, 1980), pp. 31, 109-110.

32. The definitive grounding of the silents in Victorian melodrama is John L. Fell's *Film and the Narrative Tradition* (Norman: University of Oklahoma Press, 1974). Richard Chase, *The American Novel and Its Tradition* (Garden City, N.Y.: Anchor/Doubleday, 1957).

33. See Hugh Honour, *The New Golden Land: European Images of America from the Discoveries to the Present Time* (New York: Pantheon, 1975).

34. Erik H. Erikson, *Childhood and Society* (New York: Norton, 1963). p. 286.

35. Leading discussions of the individual-community polarity in American culture can be found in *The Contrapuntal Civilization: Essays Toward a New Understanding of the American Experience*, ed. Michael Kammen (New York: Crowell, 1971). The most prominent analyses of American literature's use of this opposition remain Leslie A. Fiedler's *Love and Death in the American Novel* (New York: Stein and Day, 1966) and A. N. Kaul's *The American Vision* (New Haven: Yale University Press, 1963).

36. Robert Bresson, *Notes on Cinematography*, trans. Jonathan Griffin (New York: Urizen Books, 1977), p. 12.

37. Leslie A. Fiedler, *No! In Thunder* (New York: Stein and Day, 1972), pp. 253, 275.

38. D. H. Lawrence, *Studies in Classic American Literature* (New York: Viking/Compass, 1961), p. 3. See also Fiedler's *Love and Death in the American Novel* and Sam Bluefarb's *The Escape Motif in the American Novel: Mark Twain to Richard Wright* (Columbus: Ohio State University Press, 1972).

39. Jerzy Kosinski, *Steps* (New York: Random House, 1968), p. 133.

40. See John G. Cawelti, *Apostles of the Self-Made Man: Changing Concepts of Success in America* (Chicago: University of Chicago Press, 1965), pp. 101-123.

41. Alexis de Tocqueville, *Democracy in America*, ed. J. P. Mayer, trans. George Lawrence (Garden City, N.Y.: Anchor/Doubleday, 1969), pp. 430, 506. Irving Howe has confirmed Tocqueville's point, observing that Americans "make the suspicion of ideology into something approaching a national creed." *Politics and the Novel* (New York: Avon, 1970), p. 337.

42. Daniel J. Boorstin, *The Americans: The National Experience* (New York: Random House, 1965), p. 337.

43. *Politics and the Novel*, p. 164.

44. *Childhood and Society*, p. 286.

45. *Love and Death in the American Novel*, p. 355.

46. *The Americans: The National Experience*, p. 337.

47. *The American Novel and Its Tradition*, p. 1.

48. Ronald H. Carpenter's "Frederick Jackson Turner and the Rhetorical Impact of the Frontier Thesis," *Quarterly Journal of Speech* 63 (April 1977), pp. 117-29, identifies the crucial passage: "To the frontier the American intellect owes its striking characteristics. That coarseness and strength combined with acuteness and inquisitiveness; that practical, inventive turn of mind, quick to find expedients; that masterful grip of material things, lacking in the artistic but powerful to effect great ends; that restless, nervous energy, that dominant individualism, working for good and for evil, and withal that buoyancy and exuberance which comes with freedom—these are the traits of the frontier, or traits called out elsewhere because of the existence of the frontier."

49. See William Appleman Williams, "The Frontier Thesis and American Foreign Policy," in *History as a Way of Learning* (New York: New Viewpoints, 1974), pp. 135-57.

50. Louis Althusser and Etienne Balibar, *Reading Capital*, trans. Ben Brewster (London: New Left Books, 1970).

51. Ronald H. Carpenter and Robert V. Seltzer, "Nixon, *Patton*, and a Silent Majority Sentiment about the Viet Nam War: The Cinematographic Bases of a Rhetorical Stance," *Central States Speech Journal* 25 (Summer 1974), pp. 105-110.

52. "The Carole Lombard in Macy's Window," *Quarterly Review of Film Studies* 3 (Winter 1978), 1-21.

CHAPTER 2. REAL AND DISGUISED WESTERNS: CLASSIC HOLLYWOOD'S VARIATIONS OF ITS THEMATIC PARADIGM

1. For discussions of "screen memory," see Sigmund Freud, *The Psychopathology of Everyday Life*, trans. Alan Tyson (New York: Norton, 1965), pp. 43-52

("Childhood Memories and Screen Memories"). In "The Wolf Man Case," Freud provides analyses of several "screen memories": see Freud, *Three Case Histories* (New York: Collier Books, 1963), pp. 201-211, 281-90. See also the entry on "Screen Memory" in J. Laplanche and J. B. Pontalis, *The Language of Psychoanalysis*, trans. Donald Nicholson-Smith (New York: Norton, 1973), pp. 410-11.

2. Robert Warshow, *The Immediate Experience* (New York: Atheneum, 1972), p. 140.

3. Jim Kitses, *Horizons West: Anthony Mann, Budd Boetticher, Sam Peckinpah: Studies of Authorship within the Western* (Bloomington: Indiana University Press, 1970), p. 11.

4. *Love and Death in the American Novel* (New York: Stein and Day, 1966), p. 289.

5. *The Movies* (New York: Simon and Schuster, 1970), pp. 92-93.

6. Andrew Bergman, *We're in the Money: Depression America and Its Films* (New York: Harper Colophon, 1972), pp. 133-34.

CHAPTER 3. THE CULMINATION OF CLASSIC HOLLYWOOD:
CASABLANCA

1. *Love and Death in the American Novel* (New York: Stein and Day, 1966), p. 349.

2. Ibid., p. 263.

3. *Democracy in America*, ed. J. P. Mayer, trans. George Lawrence (Garden City, N.Y.: Anchor/Doubleday, 1969), p. 430.

4. *The Immediate Experience* (New York: Atheneum, 1972), p. 138.

5. Quoted in Fiedler, *Love and Death in the American Novel*, p. 277.

6. *Democracy in America*, p. 507.

7. Ibid., p. 511.

8. *Love and Death in the American Novel*, pp. 464-65.

9. Molly Haskell, *From Reverence to Rape: The Treatment of Women in the Movies* (New York: Penguin, 1974), p. 213.

CHAPTER 4. CLASSIC HOLLYWOOD'S HOLDING PATTERN: THE
COMBAT FILMS OF WORLD WAR II

1. Basil Wright, *The Long View* (New York: Knopf, 1974), p. 153.

2. Manny Farber, *Negative Space* (New York: Praeger, 1971), pp. 26-27.

3. Peter John Dyer, "Sling the Lamps Low," in *Focus on Howard Hawks*, ed. Joseph McBride (Englewood Cliffs, N.J.: Prentice-Hall, 1972), p. 85.

4. "*Rio Bravo*," in *Focus on Howard Hawks*, ed. McBride, p. 129.

5. Richard Schickel, *The Men Who Made the Movies* (New York: Atheneum, 1975), p. 105.

6. *Negative Space*, p. 27.

7. Lawrence H. Suid, *Guts and Glory: Great American War Movies* (Reading, Mass.: Addison-Wesley, 1978), p. 53.

CHAPTER 5. THE DISSOLUTION OF THE HOMOGENEOUS AUDIENCE
AND HOLLYWOOD'S RESPONSE: CULT FILMS, PROBLEM PICTURES,
AND INFLATION

1. William Manchester, *The Glory and the Dream: A Narrative History of America 1932-1972* (Boston: Little, Brown, 1974), p. 539.

2. *Movie-Made America: A Social History of American Movies* (New York: Random House, 1975), p. 269. Other statistics in this paragraph taken from Cobbett Steinberg, *Reel Facts: The Movie Book of Records* (New York: Vintage, 1982), p. 272 and Charles Champlin, *The Flicks: Or Whatever Became of Andy Hardy?* (Pasadena, Calif.: Ward Ritchie, 1977), p. 21.

3. *The Glory and the Dream*, p. 724.

4. See Gerald Mast, *A Short History of the Movies* (Indianapolis: Bobbs-Merrill, 1976), pp. 327-28.

5. *The Statistical History of the United States* (New York: Basic Books, 1976), p. 796.

6. Quoted in Champlin, *The Flicks*, p. 46.

7. Richard Schickel, *Movies: The History of an Art and an Institution* (New York: Basic Books, 1964), p. 315.

8. Daniel Bell, "The End of American Exceptionalism," *The Public Interest* 41 (Fall 1975), 202-203.

9. Godfrey Hodgson, *America in Our Time* (Garden City, N.Y.: Doubleday, 1976), p. 17.

10. Quoted in Manchester, *The Glory and the Dream*, p. 514.

11. Eric F. Goldman, *The Crucial Decade—And After: America, 1945-1960* (New York: Vintage, 1960), p. vi.

12. *The Glory and the Dream*, p. 672.

13. *The Crucial Decade—And After*, p. 211.

14. *America in Our Time*, p. 18.

15. Eric Rhode, *A History of the Cinema from Its Origins to 1970* (New York: Hill and Wang, 1976), p. 431.

16. Pauline Kael, "Fantasies of the Art-House Audience," in *I Lost It at the Movies* (Boston: Little, Brown, 1965), pp. 31-44.

17. *Movies*, p. 162.

18. Quoted in Penelope Houston, *The Contemporary Cinema 1945-1963* (Baltimore: Penguin, 1963), p. 169.

19. The term is used by Peter Schrag, *The End of the American Future* (New York: Simon and Schuster, 1973), p. 287.

20. *The Flicks*, p. 38.

21. Leo Braudy, *The World in a Frame: What We See in Films* (Garden City, N.Y.: Anchor/Doubleday, 1976), p. 179.

22. It is possible to argue that this gap between popularity and quality has always existed in the American Cinema. During Hollywood's Classic Period, for example, the following movies did not make the top twenty box-office lists: 1930: *All Quiet on the Western Front, The Blue Angel*; 1931: *The Champ, The Front Page, Dracula, Public Enemy*; 1932: *I Am a Fugitive from a Chain Gang*; 1933: *King Kong, Dinner at Eight*; 1934: *The Thin Man*; 1935: *The Informer*; 1936: *Fury*; 1937: *Dead End, The Awful Truth, Nothing Sacred*; 1938: *Bringing Up*

Baby; 1939: *The Wizard of Oz, Only Angels Have Wings*; 1940: *My Little Chickadee*; 1941: *Citizen Kane, Maltese Falcon*; 1942: *The Magnificent Ambersons, Sullivan's Travels*; 1943: *Shadow of a Doubt*; 1944: *Double Indemnity*. Each period, however, detects its own shape in previous eras. To a large extent, our sense of these films' importance results from the postwar auteurists' revision of film history generated by the apparentness of the enormous discrepancy between commercial success and artistic worth that arose in the fifties. And too, far more ultimately important movies made the top box-office lists in the Classic Period than in the years between 1946 and 1966.

Not surprisingly, nineteen of Andrew Sarris's "Twenty-five Most Memorable Cult Films" date from the 1946-1966 period (*The Village Voice*, 18 December 1978, p. 61): *The Big Heat* (1953), *Bigger Than Life* (1956), *Black Angel* (1946), *Detour* (1945), *Forbidden Planet* (1956), *Forty Guns* (1957), *Gun Crazy* (1949), *Invasion of the Body Snatchers* (1956), *Kiss Me Deadly* (1955), *The Pitfall* (1948), *Ride the High Country* (1962), *Rio Bravo* (1959), *Ruby Gentry* (1953), *The Searchers* (1956), *Seven Men from Now* (1956), *Silver Lode* (1954), *Touch of Evil* (1958), *Vertigo* (1958), and *Wicked Woman* (1954). Only *I Walked with a Zombie* (1943), *Night of the Living Dead* (1968), *Once Upon a Time in the West* (1969), *The Shanghai Gesture* (1941), *Summer Storm* (1944), and *The Uninvited* (1944) were not made during the postwar period.

23. "Director John Huston: A Remarkable Man and the Movies in '56," *Newsweek*, 9 January 1956, pp. 67-70.

24. "Les Dix Meilleurs Films de l'Année," *Cahiers du cinéma* 12 (January 1957), 2-3.

25. *The Contemporary Cinema*, p. 36.

26. *Love and Death in the American Novel* (New York: Stein and Day, 1966), p. 281.

27. Alain Robbe-Grillet, "Order and Disorder in Film and Fiction," trans. Bruce Morrissette, *Critical Inquiry* 4 (Autumn 1977), 20.

28. *Movie-Made America*, p. 280.

CHAPTER 6. THE DISCREPANCY BETWEEN INTENT AND EFFECT: *FILM NOIR*, YOUTH REBELLION PICTURES, MUSICALS, AND WESTERNS

1. Andrew Sarris, "Notes on the *Auteur* Theory in 1962," in *The Primal Screen: Essays on Film and Related Subjects* (New York: Simon and Schuster, 1973), p. 51.

2. Manny Farber, "White Elephant Art vs. Termite Art," in *Negative Space* (New York: Praeger, 1971), pp. 131-44.

3. Andrew Sarris, *The American Cinema: Directors and Directions 1929-1968* (New York: Dutton, 1968), p. 57.

4. Joan Mellen, *Big Bad Wolves: Masculinity in the American Film* (New York: Pantheon, 1977), p. 191.

5. For a discussion of the musical along these lines, see Leo Braudy's *The World in a Frame: What We See in Films* (Garden City, N.Y.: Anchor/Doubleday, 1976), pp. 139-63.

6. "I Can't Be Bothered Now," Ira Gershwin and George Gershwin, Gershwin Publishing Co. (ASCAP), 1937.

7. Michael Wood, *America in the Movies* (New York: Basic Books, 1975), pp. 155, 149-50.

8. *The World in a Frame*, p. 131.

9. Robin Wood, *Howard Hawks* (Garden City, N.Y.: Doubleday, 1968), p. 124.

10. Quoted in Joseph McBride and Michael Wilmington, *John Ford* (New York: Da Capo, 1975), p. 148.

11. *Horizons West* (Bloomington: Indiana University Press, 1970), p. 43.

12. Peter Bogdanovich, *John Ford* (Berkeley: University of California Press, 1968), p. 86.

CHAPTER 7. *IT'S A WONDERFUL LIFE* AND *THE MAN WHO SHOT LIBERTY VALANCE*

1. Of *Variety*'s 225 top moneymaking films between 1930-1941, only three were gangster movies: *Little Caesar* (1930), *Bullets or Ballots* (1936), and *Angels with Dirty Faces* (1938). Among the now-famous gangster movies that failed to make *Variety*'s annual lists were *Public Enemy* (1931), *Scarface* (1932), *Manhattan Melodrama* (1934), *The Petrified Forest* (1936), *Dead End* (1937), *You Only Live Once* (1937), *The Roaring Twenties* (1939), *High Sierra* (1941), and *All Through the Night* (1941).

2. Charles Champlin, *The Flicks: Or Whatever Became of Andy Hardy?* (Pasadena, Calif.: Ward Ritchie, 1977), pp. 3-4.

3. See, for example, A. N. Kaul, *The American Vision* (New Haven: Yale University Press, 1963), on the individual-community dichotomy; William C. Spenglemann, *The Adventurous Muse: The Poetics of American Fiction, 1789-1900* (New Haven: Yale University Press, 1977), treating the adventure-domesticity polarity; and Lawrence Chenoweth, *The American Dream of Success* (North Scituate, Mass.: Duxbury Press, 1974), on conflicting attitudes toward success. Donald M. Kartiganer and Malcolm A. Griffith, eds., *Theories of American Literature* (New York: Macmillan, 1972) collects leading essays and excerpts whose frequent point is the antithetical character of American culture. For a more political, less literary, vantage point on the same theme, see Michael Kammen, ed., *The Contrapuntal Civilization: Essays Toward a New Understanding of the American Experience* (New York: Crowell, 1971).

4. James Agee, "*It's a Wonderful Life*," in *Frank Capra: The Man and His Films*, ed. Richard Glatzer and John Taeburn (Ann Arbor: University of Michigan Press, 1975), p. 157.

5. Robert K. Merton, "Social Structure and Anomie," in *Social Theory and Social Structure* (Glencoe, Ill.: Free Press, 1963), p. 134.

6. Daniel J. Boorstin, *The Exploring Spirit: America and the World, Then and Now* (New York: Vintage, 1977).

7. Erik H. Erikson, *Childhood and Society* (New York: Norton, 1963), p. 293.

8. Alexis de Tocqueville, *Democracy in America*, ed. J. P. Mayer, trans. George Lawrence (Garden City, N.Y.: Anchor/Doubleday, 1969), p. 536.

9. Mark Twain, *The Adventures of Tom Sawyer* (New York: New American Library, 1959), p. 61 (Chapter 8).

10. *The Portable Mark Twain*, ed. Bernard DeVoto (New York: Viking, 1946), p. 49 (Chapter 1).

11. Leo Marx, *The Machine in the Garden: Technology and the Pastoral Ideal in America* (New York: Oxford University Press, 1964), pp. 136-37.

12. *The Immediate Experience* (New York: Atheneum, 1972), p. 133.

13. See Marvin Meyers, "Venturous Conservative: On Tocqueville's Image of the Democrat," in *The Contrapuntal Civilization*, ed. Kammen, pp. 159-78, especially p. 164.

14. Barbara Deming, *Running Away from Myself: A Dream Portrait of America Drawn from the Films of the Forties* (New York: Grossman, 1969), p. 115.

15. John Ford won directing Academy Awards for *The Informer* (1935), *The Grapes of Wrath* (1940), *How Green Was My Valley* (1941), *The Quiet Man* (1952), and two wartime documentaries, *The Battle of Midway* (1942) and *December 7th* (1943).

16. William S. Pechter, "A Persistence of Vision," in *Twenty-four Times a Second: Films and Film-Makers* (New York: Harper & Row, 1971), pp. 231, 226.

17. *The Machine in the Garden*, pp. 31-32.

18. For an elaborate treatment of this horizontal-vertical motif and of other visual motifs in *Valance*, see J. A. Place, *The Western Films of John Ford* (Secaucus, N.J.: Citadel, 1974), pp. 214-27.

19. Joseph McBride and Michael Wilmington, *John Ford* (New York: Da Capo, 1975), p. 91.

20. For a discussion of the migratory nature of certain "realistic" landscape descriptions, see Alistair M. Duckworth, "Scott's Fiction and the Migration of Settings," *Scottish Literary Journal* 7 (May 1980), 97-112, an article which draws on the work of Ernst Curtius (*European Literature and the Latin Middle Ages*), Roland Barthes ("L'Ancienne Rhétorique" and *S/Z*), and Roman Jakobson ("Two Aspects of Language: Metaphor and Metonymy") to discuss Sir Walter Scott.

21. *The Immediate Experience*, p. 146.

22. Robin Wood, "Shall We Gather at the River?: The Late Films of John Ford," *Film Comment* 7 (Fall 1971), 8.

23. McBride and Wilmington, *John Ford*, p. 86.

24. See William Luhr and Peter Lehman, *Authorship and Narrative in the Cinema* (New York: Putnam, 1977), pp. 80-82.

25. William Faulkner, *Go Down, Moses* (New York: Modern Library, 1942), p. 193.

26. *Valance* mentions no specific dates, but one can estimate the story's time period. Andrew Sarris reveals that Tom's reference to "the Picketwire" is not to a "picket wire" but to the cowboy bastardization of the Purgatoire River in southeast Colorado. (*The John Ford Movie Mystery* [Bloomington: Indiana University Press, 1975], p. 179 n.) Colorado became a state in 1876. Since the movie takes place on the eve of statehood, we can say that its rough date is 1873-1875. The unmentioned state must be Colorado. The other possibility "south of the Picketwire," New Mexico, was admitted to the Union too late (1912) to fit the film's setting.

27. A. N. Kaul, *The American Vision* (New Haven: Yale University Press, 1963), p. 123.

28. James Fenimore Cooper, *The Pioneers* (New York: Signet, 1964), p. 13.

29. James Fenimore Cooper, *The Prairie* (New York: Signet, 1964), p. 388.

CHAPTER 8. THE 1960s: FRONTIER METAPHORS, DEVELOPING SELF-CONSCIOUSNESS, AND NEW WAVES

1. The questions and the critics' responses are found in "The Future of Film: A Symposium," in *Film 67/68*, ed. Richard Schickel and John Simon (New York: Simon and Schuster, 1968), pp. 282-305. Kauffmann's response, p. 292; Simon's, p. 304. Other critics quoted were Hollis Alpert, Brendan Gill, Philip T. Hartung, Arthur Knight, Joseph Morgenstern, Andrew Sarris, Richard Schickel, and Wilfrid Sheed.

2. Robert Sklar, *Movie-Made America: A Social History of American Movies* (New York: Random House, 1975), p. 301.

3. Daniel Bell uses this word in "The End of American Exceptionalism," *The Public Interest* 41 (Fall 1975), 202.

4. Knowledge as a function of "shared examples" is discussed by Thomas S. Kuhn, *The Structure of Scientific Revolutions* (Chicago: University of Chicago Press, 1970), p. 175.

5. Louis Althusser, *For Marx*, trans. Ben Brewster (London: New Left Books, 1977), pp. 233-35.

6. *The Structure of Scientific Revolutions*, p. 183.

7. See Herbert Marcuse, "Repressive Tolerance," in R. P. Wolff, Barrington Moore, Jr., and Herbert Marcuse, *A Critique of Pure Tolerance* (Boston: Beacon Press, 1965).

8. Quoted in Godfrey Hodgson, *America in Our Time* (Garden City, N.Y.: Doubleday, 1976), p. 68. Cantril's surveys are found in his book, *The Pattern of Human Concerns* (New Brunswick, N.J.: Rutgers University Press, 1966).

9. *America in Our Time*, pp. 14-15. (Emphasis added.)

10. Quoted in *Time Magazine*, 20 March 1978, p. 67.

11. See Kuhn, *The Structure of Scientific Revolutions*, and Michel Foucault, *The Order of Things* (New York: Vintage, 1973).

12. Nietzsche fathered this position, which has been taken up in the twentieth century by Martin Heidegger and Jacques Derrida.

13. Turner's famous sentence: "The existence of an area of free land, its continuous recession, and the advance of American settlement westward, explain American development."

14. Quoted in Hodgson, *America in Our Time*, p. 469.

15. Quoted in ibid., p. 484.

16. Walter Prescott Webb, *The Great Frontier* (Austin: University of Texas Press, 1952). A useful summary of Webb's ideas can be found in his two articles "Ended: 400 Year Boom: Reflections on the Age of the Frontier" and "Windfalls of the Frontier," in *Harper's Magazine*, October and November 1951.

17. Barry Commoner, *The Closing Circle: Nature, Man and Technology* (New York: Bantam, 1974); Donella H. Meadows et al., *The Limits to Growth: A Report for the Club of Rome's Project on the Predicament of Mankind* (New York: Signet, 1974); Paul R. Ehrlich and Anne H. Ehrlich, *The End of Affluence* (New York: Ballantine, 1974); Robert L. Heilbroner, *Business Civilization in Decline* (New York: Norton, 1976); E. F. Schumacher, *Small Is Beautiful: Economics as if People Mattered* (New York: Perennial Library, 1973); Fred Hirsch, *Social Limits to Growth* (Cambridge: Harvard University Press, 1976); Peter Schrag, *The End of*

the American Future (New York: Simon and Schuster, 1973); Rufus E. Miles, Jr., *Awakening from the American Dream: The Social and Political Limits to Growth* (New York: Universe, 1976); and Guido Calabresi and Philip Bobbitt, *Tragic Choices: The Conflicts Society Confronts in the Allocation of Tragically Scarce Resources* (New York: Norton, 1978).

18. "The End of American Exceptionalism," pp. 211-12.

19. *The End of the American Future*, pp. 34, 33.

20. Richard Schickel, "Mastery of the Dirty Western," in *Film 69/70*, ed. Joseph Morgenstern and Stefan Kanfer (New York: Simon and Schuster, 1970), p. 151.

21. Again, see Kuhn and Foucault on "breaks" in established world views. In addition, the personal experiences of Marx and Freud have often provided models for discussing "self-healing" and the difficulties involved in escaping from an inherited way of experiencing the world.

22. See Erik Barnouw, *Tube of Plenty: The Evolution of American Television* (New York: Oxford University Press, 1975), pp. 197-98.

23. For listings of annual prime time schedules, see Tim Brooks and Earle Marsh, *The Complete Directory to Prime Time Network TV Shows 1946-Present* (New York: Ballantine, 1979), pp. 705-771.

24. *The Time of Illusion* (New York: Knopf, 1976), p. 363.

25. For a discussion of the Left's relationship to the mass media, see Todd Gitlin, *The Whole World Is Watching: Mass Media in the Making and Unmaking of the New Left* (Berkeley: University of California Press, 1980).

26. Dennis Hopper, "Into the Issue of the Good Old Time Movie Versus the Good Old Time," in *Easy Rider*, ed. Nancy Hardin and Marilyn Schlossberg (New York: Signet, 1969), pp. 8-9.

27. *America in Our Time*, p. 337.

28. Andrew Sarris, "Introduction," in *A Hard Day's Night: A Complete Pictorial Record of the Movie*, ed. J. Philip Di Franco (New York: Penguin, 1977), p. xiii.

29. *Godard on Godard*, ed. Jean Narboni and Tom Milne, trans. Tom Milne (New York: Viking, 1972), p. 173.

30. François Truffaut, "We Must Continue Making Progress," trans. Paul Ronder, in *Film: A Montage of Theories*, ed. Richard Dyer MacCann (New York: Dutton, 1966), p. 371.

31. *Godard on Godard*, p. 216.

32. "The New Sentimentality," *Esquire* (July 1964), p. 25.

33. The following scenes show the influence of *Breathless*'s conversation-at-cross-purposes between Michel (Jean-Paul Belmondo) and Patricia (Jean Seberg):

Breathless (1959)
PATRICIA: [Pointing to a Renoir print] Do you like this poster?
MICHEL: Not bad.
PATRICIA: Renoir is a very great painter.
MICHEL: I said not bad. . . .
PATRICIA: Say what you want, I don't care. I'm going to put all that in my book.
MICHEL: What book?
PATRICIA: I'm writing a novel.
MICHEL: You?
PATRICIA: Why not me? What are you doing?

MICHEL: I'm taking off your shirt.

PATRICIA: Not now, Michel.

MICHEL: You're such a drag. What good is that?

PATRICIA: Do you know William Faulkner?

MICHEL: No, who's that? Some guy you slept with?

PATRICIA: No, my dear.

MICHEL: Then to hell with him, take off your shirt.

PATRICIA: He's a novelist that I really like. Have you read *The Wild Palms*?

MICHEL: I said no. Take off your shirt.

PATRICIA: Listen to the last sentence, it's very beautiful. "Between grief and nothing, I will take grief." And you, what would you take?

MICHEL: Show me your toes. The toes are a very important thing in a woman. Don't laugh.

PATRICIA: What would you take?

MICHEL: Grief's a waste of time; I'd take nothing. It's not much better, but grief, that's a compromise. You've got to have all or nothing.

Bonnie and Clyde (1967)

[Near the end, both recovering from wounds incurred during the last shootout]

BONNIE (Faye Dunaway): What would you do, what would you do if some miracle happened . . . and we could walk out of here tomorrow morning and start all over again. Clean. With no record and nobody after us? H'm?

CLYDE (Warren Beatty): Well, eh, I—I guess I'd do it all different. First off, I wouldn't live in the same state where we pull our jobs. We'd live in a, in another state, and stay clean there. And then when we wanted to take a bank, we'd go into the other state.

Taxi Driver (1976)

[In a coffee shop]

BETSY (Cybill Shepherd): You know what you remind me of?

TRAVIS (Robert DeNiro): What?

BETSY: That song, by Kris Kristofferson.

TRAVIS: Who's that?

BETSY: Songwriter. "He's a prophet and a pusher, partly truth, partly fiction, a walking contradiction."

TRAVIS: You sayin' that about me?

BETSY: Who else would I be talkin' about?

TRAVIS: I'm no pusher; I never have pushed.

Smokey and the Bandit (1977)

FROG (Sally Field): Do you know who I think has *really* revolutionized the American musical theater? That's Stephen Sondheim.

BANDIT (Burt Reynolds): Yeah?

FROG: Yeah.

BANDIT: Who's he, who's that?

FROG: Stephen Sondheim?

BANDIT: Yeah. Does, does he do a lot of musicals and stuff?

FROG: Yeah.

BANDIT: Ever do anything with Brenda Lee?

FROG: Does she dance?

BANDIT: She spins, she's a little spinner. . . .

FROG: Can I ask you something?
BANDIT: Sure.
FROG: Do you think we have anything in common? . . .
BANDIT: Yeah. Like what?
FROG: Did you ever see the Broadway show *Chorus Line*?
BANDIT: No.
FROG: Do you like Elton John?
BANDIT: No.

Saturday Night Fever (1977)
STEPHANIE (Karen Lynn Gorney): We saw Zeffirelli's *Romeo and Juliet*.
TONY (John Travolta): Shakespeare wrote that. I read it in high school.
STEPHANIE: Zeffirelli was the director. It was the movie . . . I mean film.
TONY: One thing always bothered me about that. Romeo, he could have waited a
    minute. I mean, he didn't have to take the poison so fast. I . . . that always
    bothered me . . .
STEPHANIE: This week I had business lunches with Eric Clapton at Le Madrigal
    and at Côte Basque with Cat Stevens.
TONY: Far out!
STEPHANIE: You, you heard of them, those restaurants?
TONY: No.
STEPHANIE: But you know who those artists are?
TONY: No. Well, maybe, sort of.
STEPHANIE: Then why'd you say "far out"?
TONY: It sounded far out. Wasn't it? . . .
STEPHANIE: You know who came in the office today? Laurence Olivier.
TONY: Who's that?
STEPHANIE: You don't know who Laurence Olivier is?
TONY: No.
STEPHANIE: He's only the most famous actor in the world, you know, the English
    actor who did the Polaroid commercials.
TONY: Oh, *him*. He's good.
STEPHANIE: Well, he was in the office, and I did a couple of errands for him, and
    he told everybody that I was really the brightest, most viv . . . viv . . . vivacious
    thing he's seen in years.
TONY: Could he get you one of those cameras, like at a discount, you know what
    I mean?

34. *Godard on Godard*, pp. 214-15.

35. Andrew Sarris, "After *The Graduate*," *American Film* 3 (July-August 1978),
32.

36. See David Newman and Robert Benton, "Lightning in a Bottle," in *The
Bonnie and Clyde Book*, ed. Sandra Wake and Nicola Hayden (New York: Simon
and Schuster, 1972), pp. 13-30. ". . . we were riding the crest of the new wave
that had swept in on our minds, and the talk was Truffaut, Godard, De Broca,
Bergman, Kurosawa, Antonioni, Fellini and all the other names that fell like a
litany in 1964. . . . Our minds most recently blown by *Breathless*, we addressed
ourselves more and more, during working and drinking hours, to the idea of
actually doing something about it. . . . Perhaps the heaviest influence on our
heads as we wrote was Truffaut, especially two films: *Shoot the Piano Player*,

with its wonderful combination of comedy and bleakness, gangsterism and humanity, and *Jules and Jim*, which managed to define the present as it evoked the past; their spirit informed us as we wrote" (pp. 13, 15).

37. André Labarthe and Jean-Louis Comolli, "The Arthur Penn Interview," in *The Bonnie and Clyde Book*, p. 171.

38. See Terry Eagleton's gloss on Brecht in "Aesthetics and Politics," *New Left Review* 107 (January-February 1978), 28: "You thus cannot determine the realism of a text merely by inspecting its intrinsic properties. On the contrary, you can never know whether a text is realist or not until you have established its effects—and since those effects belong to a particular juncture, a text may be realist in June and anti-realist in December." Quoted in Sylvia Harvey, *May '68 and Film Culture* (London: British Film Institute, 1978), p. 73.

See also Brecht's own remark: "Time flows on. . . . Methods wear out, stimuli fail. New problems loom up and demand new techniques. Reality alters; to represent it the means of representation must alter too. . . . The oppressors do not always appear in the same mask. The masks cannot always be stripped off in the same way." *Brecht on Theatre*, ed. and trans. John Willett (New York: Hill and Wang, 1964), p. 110. Quoted in Harvey, *May '68 and Film Culture*, p. 74.

CHAPTER 9. THE LEFT AND RIGHT CYCLES

1. Pauline Kael, *Reeling* (Boston: Little, Brown, 1976), p. 284.

2. Pauline Kael, *Deeper into Movies* (Boston: Little, Brown, 1973), p. 152.

3. Godfrey Hodgson, *America in Our Time* (Garden City, N.Y.: Doubleday, 1976), p. 363.

4. Quoted in Peter Schrag, *The End of the American Future* (New York: Simon and Schuster, 1973), p. 39.

5. Quoted in ibid., p. 171.

6. Ibid., p. 171.

7. *Deeper into Movies*, p. 314.

8. Quoted in Ralph Brauer, "Who Are Those Guys? The Movie Western during the TV Era," in *Focus on the Western*, ed. Jack Nachbar (Englewood Cliffs, N.J.: Prentice-Hall, 1974), p. 118.

9. Robin Wood, *Arthur Penn* (New York: Praeger, 1970), p. 75.

10. David Newman and Robert Benton, "Lightning in a Bottle," in *The Bonnie and Clyde Book*, ed. Sandra Wake and Nicola Hayden (New York: Simon and Schuster, 1972), p. 19.

11. Quoted by Pauline Kael in *Deeper into Movies*, p. 100.

12. See Leslie A. Fiedler, *The Return of the Vanishing American* (New York: Stein and Day, 1968), pp. 177-87.

13. André Labarthe and Jean-Louis Comolli, "The Arthur Penn Interview," in *The Bonnie and Clyde Book*, p. 168.

14. Quoted by Wilfrid Sheed, "The Movie South," in *Film 67/68*, ed. Richard Schickel and John Simon (New York: Simon and Schuster, 1968), p. 221.

15. *Film 71/72*, ed. David Denby (New York: Simon and Schuster, 1972), p. 127.

16. Ken Kesey, *One Flew Over the Cuckoo's Nest* (New York: Viking Critical Library, 1973), pp. 304-305.

17. Diane Jacobs, *Hollywood Renaissance* (New York: A. S. Barnes & Co., 1977), p. 77.

18. Robin Wood suggests this comparison in *Arthur Penn*, p. 98.

19. "Penn Interview," in *The Bonnie and Clyde Book*, pp. 168, 172.

20. Richard Schickel, *Second Sight: Notes on Some Movies 1965-1970* (New York: Simon and Schuster, 1972), p. 143.

21. *Arthur Penn*, p. 75.

22. Jacques Lacan, "The Mirror Stage as Formative of the Function of the I as Revealed in Psychoanalytic Experience," in *Écrits*, trans. Alan Sheridan (New York: Norton, 1977), pp. 1-7. For a useful background to Lacan's thinking, see Sherry Turkle, *Psychoanalytic Politics: Freud's French Revolution* (Cambridge: The MIT Press, 1978). For applications of Lacan to ideological studies of film and advertising, see Bill Nichols, *Ideology and the Image: Social Representation in the Cinema and Other Media* (Bloomington: Indiana University Press, 1981), pp. 29-34; Judith Williamson, *Decoding Advertisements: Ideology and Meaning in Advertising* (London: Marion Boyars, 1978), pp. 60-67.

23. Louis Althusser, "Freud and Lacan," in *Lenin and Philosophy*, trans. Ben Brewster (New York: Monthly Review Press, 1971), pp. 218-19. (My emphasis.)

24. In an explicitly Lacanian article, Christian Metz argues that such films-within-films typically encourage an uncritical response to the movie as a whole: "the distance it [a film-within-a-film] establishes between the action and ourselves comforts our feeling that we are not duped by that action: thus reassured, we can allow ourselves to be duped by [the film-as-a-whole] a little bit longer. . . . The included film was an illusion, so the including film was not. . . ." *The Imaginary Signifier: Psychoanalysis and the Cinema*, trans. Celia Britton et al. (Bloomington: Indiana University Press, 1982), pp. 73-74.

CHAPTER 10. *THE GODFATHER* AND *TAXI DRIVER*

1. The "new" American movies typically reserved freeze frames for endings, slow motion for scenes of violence or sentimentalized romance, and nondiegetic pop songs (e.g., *Easy Rider*'s rock score) for obvious underscoring of the image.

2. *Deeper into Movies* (Boston: Little, Brown, 1973), pp. 318-19.

3. By summer 1984 *The Godfather I* was the eighth highest earning film.

4. Quoted by Joan Mellen, *Big Bad Wolves: Masculinity in the American Film* (New York: Pantheon, 1977), p. 280.

5. Arthur Schlesinger, Jr., "*The Godfather* Plays on Our Secret Admiration for Men Who Get What They Want," in *Film 72/73*, ed. David Denby (Indianapolis: Bobbs-Merrill, 1973), p. 10.

6. "Windfalls of the Frontier," *Harper's Magazine* (October 1951), 71.

7. Quoted in Carlos Clarens, *Crime Movies: An Illustrated History* (New York: Norton, 1980), p. 289.

8. Quoted in Joseph Gelmis, "How Brando Brought Don Corleone to Life," in *Film 72/73*, ed. Denby, p. 12; William Murray, "*Playboy* Interview: Francis Ford Coppola," *Playboy* (July 1975), pp. 53ff.

9. "Made to Order" [a review of *Bonnie and Clyde*], in *Film 67/68*, ed. Richard Schickel and John Simon (New York: Simon and Schuster, 1968), p. 36.

10. "I felt I was making a harsh statement about the Mafia and power at the

end of *Godfather I* when Michael murders all those people, then lies to his wife and closes the door. But obviously, many people didn't get the point I was making. And so if the statement I was trying to make was outbalanced by the charismatic aspects of the characters, I felt *Godfather II* was an opportunity to rectify that." "*Playboy* Interview," p. 60.

11. Quoted in William S. Pechter, "*Godfather II*," *Commentary* (March 1975), p. 79.

12. Philip Rahv, "Paleface and Redskin," in *Literature and the Sixth Sense* (Boston: Houghton Mifflin, 1970), p. 1.

13. *Reeling* (Boston: Little, Brown, 1976), p. 398.

14. Jean-Louis Comolli and Jean Narboni, "Cinema/Ideology/Criticism," *Cahiers du cinéma*, no. 216 (October 1969), trans. Susan Bennett and reprinted in *Movies and Methods*, ed. Bill Nichols (Berkeley: University of California Press, 1976), pp. 22-30.

15. Paul Schrader had written a leading article on *film noir* and a study of Bresson, Ozu, and Dreyer: *Transcendental Style in Film* (Berkeley: University of California Press, 1972). DeNiro had recently appeared in Scorsese's "corrected" gangster movie, *Mean Streets* (1973) and Bertolucci's Marxist *1900* (1975).

16. *Reeling*, p. 286.

17. *Democracy in America*, ed. J. P. Mayer, trans. George Lawrence (Garden City, N.Y.: Anchor/Doubleday, 1969), p. 508.

18. *Big Bad Wolves: Masculinity in the American Film*, p. 309.

19. Richard Slotkin, *Regeneration through Violence: The Mythology of the American Frontier, 1600-1860* (Middletown, Conn.: Wesleyan University Press, 1973).

20. Quoted in ibid., p. 517.

CONCLUSION

1. See James Turner's "Conclusion" to his *The Politics of Landscape: Rural Scenery and Society in English Poetry 1630-1660* (Cambridge: Harvard University Press, 1979), p. 186, for a similar argument. I encountered Turner's book too late to affect the body of my own argument, but I have found that his approach (close ideological readings of individual texts founded on similar critical premises) resembles my own.

2. See as an example of this type of approach Peter Wollen, "Counter Cinema: Vent d'Est," *Afterimage* (London) 4 (Autumn 1972), 6-16.

3. The most graceful implementations of Lacan's insistence on retaining the Imaginary within Symbolic practice are Roland Barthes's late autobiographical works: *Roland Barthes by Roland Barthes*, trans. Richard Howard (New York: Hill and Wang, 1977) and *A Lover's Discourse: Fragments*, trans. Richard Howard (New York: Hill and Wang, 1978).

4. Theodor Adorno, "Culture Industry Reconsidered," trans. Anson G. Rabinbach, *New German Critique* 6 (Fall 1975), 12.

5. See Walter Benjamin, "The Work of Art in the Age of Mechanical Reproduction," in *Illuminations*, ed. Hannah Arendt, trans. Harry Zohn (New York: Schocken Books, 1969) and Hans Magnus Enzensberger, "Constituents of a The-

ory of the Media," in *The Consciousness Industry* (New York: Seabury Press, 1974).

6. In this paragraph, I am summarizing George Mitchell's superb article, "The Consolidation of the American Film Industry 1915-1920," *Ciné-Tracts* 6 (Spring 1979), 28-36, and *Ciné-Tracts* 7/8 (Summer/Fall 1979), 63-70.

7. Sylvia Harvey, *May '68 and Film Culture* (London: British Film Institute, 1978), p. 110.

8. "Towards a Semiotic Enquiry into the Television Message," trans. Paola Splendore, *Working Papers in Cultural Studies*, no. 3 (Autumn 1972), 121. Quoted by Harvey, *May '68 and Film Culture*, p. 115.

9. Stanley Kauffmann, *Before My Eyes: Film Criticism and Comment* (New York: Harper & Row, 1980), p. 290.

Bibliography

Adorno, Theodor. "Culture Industry Reconsidered." Translated by Anson G. Rabinbach. *New German Critique* 6 (Fall 1975), 12-19.

Adorno, T. W. and Horkheimer, M. *Dialectic of Enlightenment*. Translated by John Cumming. New York: Seabury Press, 1972.

Althusser, Louis. *For Marx*. Translated by Ben Brewster. London: New Left Books, 1977.

———. *Lenin and Philosophy*. Translated by Ben Brewster. New York: Monthly Review Press, 1971.

Althusser, Louis and Balibar, Etienne. *Reading Capital*. Translated by Ben Brewster. London: New Left Books, 1970.

Altman, Rick, ed. *Genre: The Musical*. London: Routledge & Kegan Paul, 1981.

Barnouw, Erik. *Tube of Plenty: The Evolution of American Television*. New York: Oxford University Press, 1975.

Barthes, Roland. *A Lover's Discourse: Fragments*. Translated by Richard Howard. New York: Hill and Wang, 1978.

———. *Mythologies*. Translated by Annette Lavers. New York: Hill and Wang, 1972.

———. "The Realistic Effect." Translated by Gerald Mead. *Film Reader 3* (1978), 131-35.

———. *Roland Barthes by Roland Barthes*. Translated by Richard Howard. New York: Hill and Wang, 1977.

———. "Upon Leaving the Movie Theater." Translated by Bertrand Augst and Susan White. In *Apparatus*, edited by Theresa Hak Kyung Cha, pp. 1-4. New York: Tanam Press, 1981.

———. *Writing Degree Zero*. Translated by Annette Lavers and Colin Smith. New York: Hill and Wang, 1968.

Baudry, Jean-Louis. "Ideological Effects of the Basic Cinematographic Apparatus." Translated by Alan Williams. *Film Quarterly* 28 (Winter 1974-1975), 39-47.

Bell, Daniel. "The End of American Exceptionalism." *The Public Interest* 41 (Fall 1975), 193-224.

Benjamin, Walter. *Illuminations*. Edited by Hannah Arendt. Translated by Harry Zohn. New York: Schocken Books, 1969.

Bergman, Andrew. *We're in the Money: Depression America and Its Films*. New York: Harper Colophon, 1972.

Bersani, Leo. *A Future for Astyanax: Character and Desire in Literature*. Boston: Little, Brown, 1976.

Bluefarb, Sam. *The Escape Motif in the American Novel: Mark Twain to Richard Wright.* Columbus: Ohio State University Press, 1972.

Bogdanovich, Peter. *John Ford.* Berkeley: University of California Press, 1968.

Boorstin, Daniel J. *The Americans: The National Experience.* New York: Random House, 1965.

———. *The Exploring Spirit: America and the World, Then and Now.* New York: Vintage, 1977.

Bordwell, David and Thompson, Kristin. *Film Art: An Introduction.* Reading, Mass.: Addison-Wesley, 1979.

Braudy, Leo. *The World in a Frame: What We See in Films.* Garden City, N.Y.: Anchor/Doubleday, 1976.

Brecht, Bertolt. *Brecht on Theatre.* Edited and translated by John Willett. New York: Hill and Wang, 1964.

Bresson, Robert. *Notes on Cinematography.* Translated by Jonathan Griffin. New York: Urizen Books, 1977.

Brooks, Tim and Marsh, Earle. *The Complete Directory to Prime Time Network TV Shows 1946-Present.* New York: Ballantine, 1979.

Burch, Noël. "Film's Institutional Mode of Representation and the Soviet Response." *October* 11 (Winter 1979), 77-96.

———. "Fritz Lang: German Period." Translated by Tom Milne. In *Cinema: A Critical Dictionary, The Major Film-Makers, Volume Two,* edited by Richard Roud, pp. 583-99. New York: Viking, 1980.

———. "How We Got into Pictures: Notes Accompanying *Correction Please.*" *Afterimage* (London) 8/9 (Spring 1981), 22-38.

———. "Notes on Fritz Lang's First *Mabuse.*" *Ciné-Tracts* 13 (Spring 1981), 1-13.

———. "Porter, or Ambivalence." *Screen* 19 (Winter 1978-1979), 91-105.

———. *Theory of Film Practice.* Translated by Helen R. Lane. Princeton: Princeton University Press, 1981.

———. *To the Distant Observer: Form and Meaning in the Japanese Cinema.* Berkeley: University of California Press, 1979.

Burch, Noël and Dana, Jorge. "Propositions." Translated by Diana Matias and Christopher King. *Afterimage* (London) 5 (Spring 1974), 40-66.

Calabresi, Guido and Bobbitt, Philip. *Tragic Choices: The Conflicts Society Confronts in the Allocation of Tragically Scarce Resources.* New York: Norton, 1978.

Cantril, Hadley. *The Pattern of Human Concerns.* New Brunswick, N.J.: Rutgers University Press, 1966.

Carpenter, Ronald H. "Frederick Jackson Turner and the Rhetorical Impact of the Frontier Thesis." *Quarterly Journal of Speech* 63 (April 1977), 117-29.

Carpenter, Ronald H. and Seltzer, Robert V. "Nixon, *Patton,* and a Silent Majority Sentiment about the Viet Nam War: The Cinematographic Bases of a Rhetorical Stance." *Central States Speech Journal* 25 (Summer 1974), 105-110.

Carroll, David. "Freud and the Myth of Origin." *New Literary History* 6 (Spring 1975), 513-28.

Cawelti, John G. *Apostles of the Self-Made Man: Changing Concepts of Success in America.* Chicago: University of Chicago Press, 1965.

Champlin, Charles. *The Flicks: Or Whatever Became of Andy Hardy?* Pasadena, Calif.: Ward Ritchie, 1977.

Chase, Richard. *The American Novel and Its Tradition*. Garden City, N.Y.: Anchor/Doubleday, 1957.

Chenoweth, Lawrence. *The American Dream of Success*. North Scituate, Mass.: Duxbury Press, 1974.

Clarens, Carlos. *Crime Movies: An Illustrated History*. New York: Norton, 1980.

Clarke, Simon, Terry Lovell, Kevin McDonnell, Kevin Robins, and Victor Jeleniewski Seidler. *One-Dimensional Marxism: Althusser and the Politics of Culture*. London: Allison & Busby, 1980.

Commoner, Barry. *The Closing Circle: Nature, Man and Technology*. New York: Bantam, 1974.

Comolli, Jean-Louis and Narboni, Jean. "Cinema/Ideology/Criticism." Translated by Susan Bennett. In *Movies and Methods*, edited by Bill Nichols, pp. 22-30. Berkeley: University of California Press, 1976.

Cooper, James Fenimore. *The Pioneers*. New York: Signet, 1964.

———. *The Prairie*. New York: Signet, 1964.

Coppola, Francis Ford. "*Playboy* Interview." Conducted by William Murray. *Playboy* (July 1975), pp. 53ff.

Culler, Jonathan. *Structuralist Poetics*. Ithaca, N.Y.: Cornell University Press, 1975.

Dayan, Daniel. "The Tutor Code of Classical Cinema." In *Movies and Methods*, edited by Bill Nichols, pp. 438-51. Berkeley: University of California Press, 1976.

Deming, Barbara. *Running Away from Myself: A Dream Portrait of America Drawn from the Films of the Forties*. New York: Grossman, 1969.

Denby, David, ed. *Film 71/72*. New York: Simon and Schuster, 1972.

Derrida, Jacques. *Dissemination*. Translated by Barbara Johnson. Chicago: University of Chicago Press, 1981.

———. "Structure, Sign and Play in the Discourse of the Humanities." In *The Structuralist Controversy*, edited by Richard Macksey and Eugenio Donato, pp. 247-72. Baltimore: The Johns Hopkins University Press, 1972.

"Director John Huston: A Remarkable Man and the Movies in '56." *Newsweek*, 9 January 1956, pp. 67-70.

"Les Dix Meilleurs Films de l'Année." *Cahiers du cinéma* 12 (January 1957), 2-3.

Duckworth, Alistair M. "Scott's Fiction and the Migration of Settings." *Scottish Literary Journal* 7 (May 1980), 97-112.

Eagleton, Terry. "Aesthetics and Politics." *New Left Review* 107 (January-February 1978), 21-34.

Eckert, Charles. "The Anatomy of a Proletarian Film: Warner's *Marked Woman*." *Film Quarterly* 17 (Winter 1973-1974), 10-24.

———. "The Carole Lombard in Macy's Window." *Quarterly Review of Film Studies* 3 (Winter 1978), 1-21.

———. "Shall We Deport Lévi-Strauss?" *Film Quarterly* 27 (Spring 1974), 63-65.

———. "Shirley Temple and the House of Rockefeller." *Jump Cut* 2 (July-August 1974), 1, 17.

Eco, Umberto. "Towards a Semiotic Enquiry into the Television Message." Translated by Paola Splendore. *Working Papers in Cultural Studies* 3 (Autumn 1972), 103-121.

The Editors of *Cahiers du cinéma*. "John Ford's *Young Mr. Lincoln*." Translated by *Screen*. In *Film Theory and Criticism*, edited by Gerald Mast and Marshall Cohen, pp. 778-831. New York: Oxford University Press, 1979.

Ehrlich, Paul R. and Ehrlich, Anne H. *The End of Affluence*. New York: Ballantine, 1974.

Ellis, John. "The Institution of the Cinema." *Edinburgh '77 Magazine*, no. 2 (1977), 56-66.

Enzensberger, Hans Magnus. *The Consciousness Industry*. New York: Seabury Press, 1974.

Erikson, Erik H. *Childhood and Society*. New York: Norton, 1963.

Farber, Manny. *Negative Space*. New York: Praeger, 1971.

Faulkner, William. *Go Down, Moses*. New York: Modern Library, 1942.

Fell, John L. *Film and the Narrative Tradition*. Norman: University of Oklahoma Press, 1974.

Fiedler, Leslie A. *Love and Death in the American Novel*. New York: Stein and Day, 1966.

———. *No! In Thunder*. New York: Stein and Day, 1972.

———. *The Return of the Vanishing American*. New York: Stein and Day, 1968.

Foucault, Michel. *The Order of Things*. New York: Vintage, 1973.

Freud, Sigmund. *The Interpretation of Dreams*. Translated by Dr. A. A. Brill. New York: Modern Library, 1950.

———. *The Psychopathology of Everyday Life*. Translated by Alan Tyson. New York: Norton, 1965.

———. *Three Case Histories*. New York: Collier Books, 1963.

Geuss, Raymond. *The Idea of a Critical Theory: Habermas and the Frankfurt School*. Cambridge: Cambridge University Press, 1981.

Gitlin, Todd. *The Whole World Is Watching: Mass Media in the Making and Unmaking of the New Left*. Berkeley: University of California Press, 1980.

Glatzer, Richard and Taeburn, John, eds. *Frank Capra: The Man and His Films*. Ann Arbor: University of Michigan Press, 1975.

Godard, Jean-Luc. *Godard on Godard*. Edited by Jean Narboni and Tom Milne. Translated by Tom Milne. New York: Viking, 1972.

Goldman, Eric F. *The Crucial Decade—And After: America, 1945-1960*. New York: Vintage, 1960.

Griffith, Richard and Mayer, Arthur. *The Movies*. New York: Simon and Schuster, 1970.

Hardin, Nancy and Schlossberg, Marilyn, eds. *Easy Rider*. New York: Signet, 1969.

Harvey, Sylvia. *May '68 and Film Culture*. London: British Film Institute, 1978.

Heath, Stephen. *Questions of Cinema*. Bloomington: Indiana University Press, 1981.

Hebdige, Dick and Hurd, Geoff. "Reading and Realism." *Screen Education* 28 (Autumn 1978), 68-78.

Heilbroner, Robert L. *Business Civilization in Decline*. New York: Norton, 1976.

Henderson, Brian. "A Musical Comedy of Empire." *Film Quarterly* 35 (Winter 1981-1982), 2-16.

———. "Toward a Non-Bourgeois Camera Style." In *Movies and Methods*, edited by Bill Nichols, pp. 422-38. Berkeley: University of California Press, 1976.

Hirsch, Fred. *Social Limits to Growth*. Cambridge: Harvard University Press, 1976.

Hodgson, Godfrey. *America in Our Time*. Garden City, N.Y.: Doubleday, 1976.

Honour, Hugh. *The New Golden Land: European Images of America from the Discoveries to the Present Time*. New York: Pantheon, 1975.

Houston, Penelope. *The Contemporary Cinema 1945-1963*. Baltimore: Penguin, 1963.

Howe, Irving. *Politics and the Novel*. New York: Avon, 1970.

Huyssen, Andreas. "Introduction to Adorno." *New German Critique* 6 (1975), 9-10.

Jacobs, Diane. *Hollywood Renaissance*. New York: A. S. Barnes & Co., 1977.

Kael, Pauline. *Deeper into Movies*. Boston: Little, Brown, 1973.

————. *I Lost It at the Movies*. Boston: Little, Brown, 1965.

————. *Kiss Kiss Bang Bang*. Boston: Little, Brown, 1968.

————. *Reeling*. Boston: Little, Brown, 1976.

Kammen, Michael, ed. *The Contrapuntal Civilization: Essays Toward a New Understanding of the American Experience*. New York: Crowell, 1971.

Kartiganer, Donald M. and Griffith, Malcolm A., eds. *Theories of American Literature*. New York: Macmillan, 1972.

Kauffmann, Stanley. *Before My Eyes: Film Criticism and Comment*. New York: Harper & Row, 1980.

Kaul, A. N. *The American Vision*. New Haven: Yale University Press, 1963.

Kesey, Ken. *One Flew Over the Cuckoo's Nest*. New York: Viking Critical Library, 1973.

Kitses, Jim. *Horizons West: Anthony Mann, Budd Boetticher, Sam Peckinpah: Studies of Authorship within the Western*. Bloomington: Indiana University Press, 1970.

Klingender, F. D. and Legg, Stuart. *Money behind the Screen*, New York: Arno, 1978.

Knödler-Bunte, Eberhard. "The Proletarian Public Sphere and Political Organization: An Analysis of Oskar Negt and Alexander Kluge's *The Public Sphere and Experience*." Translated by Sara Lennox and Frank Lennox. *New German Critique* 4 (Winter 1975), 51-75.

Kosinski, Jerzy. *Steps*. New York: Random House, 1968.

Kuhn, Thomas S. *The Structure of Scientific Revolutions*. Chicago: University of Chicago Press, 1970.

Lacan, Jacques. *Écrits*. Translated by Alan Sheridan. New York: Norton, 1977.

Laplanche, J. and Pontalis, J. B. *The Language of Psychoanalysis*. Translated by Donald Nicholson-Smith. New York: Norton, 1973.

Lawrence, D. H. *Studies in Classic American Literature*. New York: Viking/Compass, 1961.

Lem, Stanislaw. *Return from the Stars*. Translated by Barbara Marszal and Frank Simpson. New York: Harcourt Brace Jovanovich, 1980.

Lévi-Strauss, Claude. *The Raw and the Cooked: Introduction to a Science of Mythology: I*. Translated by John and Doreen Weightman. New York: Harper & Row, 1975.

Linton, James. "But It's Only a Movie." *Jump Cut* 17 (1978), 16-19.

Lovell, Alan. "Epic Theater & Counter-Cinema's Principles." *Jump Cut* 27 (1982), 64-68.

Lovell, Terry. *Pictures of Reality: Aesthetics, Politics and Pleasure*. London: British Film Institute, 1980.

Luhr, William and Lehman, Peter. *Authorship and Narrative in the Cinema.* New York: Putnam, 1977.

MacCabe, Colin. "The Politics of Separation." *Screen* 16 (Winter 1975-1976), 46-61.

———. "Realism and the Cinema: Notes on Some Brechtian Theses." *Screen* 15 (Summer 1974), 7-27.

McBride, Joseph, ed. *Focus on Howard Hawks.* Englewood Cliffs, N.J.: Prentice-Hall, 1972.

McBride, Joseph and Wilmington, Michael. *John Ford.* New York: Da Capo, 1975.

Manchester, William. *The Glory and the Dream: A Narrative History of America 1932-1972.* Boston: Little, Brown, 1974.

Mannoni, Octave. *Clefs pour l'Imaginaire ou l'Autre Scène.* Paris: Le Seuil, 1969.

Marx, Karl and Engels, Friedrich. *The Marx-Engels Reader.* Edited by Robert C. Tucker. New York: Norton, 1978.

Marx, Leo. *The Machine in the Garden: Technology and the Pastoral Ideal in America.* New York: Oxford University Press, 1964.

Mascelli, Joseph V. *The Five C's of Cinematography: Motion Picture Filming Techniques Simplified.* Hollywood: Cine/Grafic Publications, 1965.

Mast, Gerald. *A Short History of the Movies.* Indianapolis: Bobbs-Merrill, 1976.

Meadows, Donella H., Dennis L. Meadows, Jorgen Randers, and William W. Behrens III. *The Limits to Growth: A Report for the Club of Rome's Project on the Predicament of Mankind.* New York: Signet, 1974.

Medvedev, P. N. (M. M. Bakhtin). *The Formal Method in Literary Scholarship: A Critical Introduction to Sociological Poetics.* Translated by Albert J. Wehrle. Baltimore: The Johns Hopkins University Press, 1978.

Mellen, Joan. *Big Bad Wolves: Masculinity in the American Film.* New York: Pantheon, 1977.

Merritt, Russell. "Nickelodeon Theaters 1905-1914: Building an Audience for the Movies." In *The American Film Industry,* edited by Tino Balio, pp. 59-82. Madison: University of Wisconsin Press, 1976.

Merton, Robert K. *Social Theory and Social Structure.* Glencoe, Ill.: Free Press, 1963.

Metz, Christian. *The Imaginary Signifier: Psychoanalysis and the Cinema.* Translated by Celia Britton, Annwyl Williams, Ben Brewster, and Alfred Guzzetti. Bloomington: Indiana University Press, 1982.

———. *Language and Cinema.* Translated by Donna Jean Umiker-Sebeok. The Hague: Mouton, 1974.

Miles, Rufus E., Jr. *Awakening from the American Dream: The Social and Political Limits to Growth.* New York: Universe, 1976.

Mitchell, George. "The Consolidation of the American Film Industry 1915-1920." *Ciné-Tracts* 6 (Spring 1979), 28-36; and *Ciné-Tracts* 7/8 (Summer/Fall 1979), 63-70.

Morgenstern, Joseph and Kanfer, Stefan, eds. *Film 69/70.* New York: Simon and Schuster, 1970.

Mukařovský, Jan. *Aesthetic Function, Norm and Value as Social Facts.* Translated by Mark E. Suino. Ann Arbor: Michigan Slavic Contributions, 1979.

Nachbar, Jack, ed. *Focus on the Western.* Englewood Cliffs, N.J.: Prentice-Hall, 1974.

Neale, Stephen. *Genre.* London: British Film Institute, 1980.

Newman, David and Benton, Robert. "The New Sentimentality." *Esquire* (July 1964), pp. 25-31.

Nichols, Bill. *Ideology and the Image: Social Representation in the Cinema and Other Media.* Bloomington: Indiana University Press, 1981.

Nowell-Smith, Geoffrey. "On the Writing of the History of the Cinema: Some Problems." *Edinburg '77 Magazine*, no. 2 (1977), 8-12.

Pechter, William S. "*Godfather II.*" *Commentary* (March 1975), pp. 79-80.

————. *Twenty-four Times a Second: Films and Film-Makers.* New York: Harper & Row, 1971.

Place, J. A. *The Western Films of John Ford.* Secaucus, N.J.: Citadel, 1974.

Rahv, Philip. *Literature and the Sixth Sense.* Boston: Houghton Mifflin, 1970.

Rhode, Eric. *A History of the Cinema from Its Origins to 1970.* New York: Hill and Wang, 1976.

Robbe-Grillet, Alain. "Order and Disorder in Film and Fiction." Translated by Bruce Morrissette. *Critical Inquiry* 4 (Autumn 1977), 1-20.

Rosenthal, Michael. "Ideology, Determinism and Relative Autonomy." *Jump Cut* 17 (1978), 19-22.

Rothman, William. "Against 'The System of the Suture.' " In *Movies and Methods*, edited by Bill Nichols, pp. 451-59. Berkeley: University of California Press, 1976.

Salt, Barry. "Film Style and Technology in the Forties." *Film Quarterly* 31 (Fall 1977), 46-57.

————. "Film Style and Technology in the Thirties." *Film Quarterly* 30 (Fall 1976), 19-32.

————. "Statistical Style Analysis of Motion Pictures." *Film Quarterly* 38 (Fall 1974), 13-22.

Sarris, Andrew. "After *The Graduate.*" *American Film* 3 (July-August 1978), 32-37.

————. *The American Cinema: Directors and Directions 1929-1968.* New York: Dutton, 1968.

————. "Introduction." In *A Hard Day's Night: A Complete Pictorial Record of the Movie*, edited by J. Philip Di Franco, pp. xiii-xiv. New York: Penguin, 1977.

————. *The John Ford Movie Mystery.* Bloomington: Indiana University Press, 1975.

————. *The Primal Screen: Essays on Film and Related Subjects.* New York: Simon and Schuster, 1973.

————. "Those Wild and Crazy Cult Movies." *The Village Voice*, 18 December 1978, pp. 60-61.

Schell, Jonathan. *The Time of Illusion.* New York: Knopf, 1976.

Schickel, Richard. *The Men Who Made the Movies.* New York: Atheneum, 1975.

————. *Movies: The History of an Art and an Institution.* New York: Basic Books, 1964.

————. *Second Sight: Notes on Some Movies 1965-1970.* New York: Simon and Schuster, 1972.

Schickel, Richard and Simon, John, eds. *Film 67/68.* New York: Simon and Schuster, 1968.

Schrader, Paul. *Transcendental Style in Film: Ozu, Bresson, Dreyer.* Berkeley: University of California Press, 1972.

Schrag, Peter. *The End of the American Future*. New York: Simon and Schuster, 1973.

Schumacher, E. F. *Small Is Beautiful: Economics as if People Mattered*. New York: Perennial Library, 1973.

Screen 16 (Winter 1975-1976). (Brecht issue.)

Screen 18 (Winter 1977-1978). (Suture issue.)

Sklar, Robert. *Movie-Made America: A Social History of American Movies*. New York: Random House, 1975.

Slotkin, Richard. *Regeneration through Violence: The Mythology of the American Frontier, 1600-1860*. Middletown, Conn.: Wesleyan University Press, 1973.

Spenglemann, William C. *The Adventurous Muse: The Poetics of American Fiction, 1789-1900*. New Haven: Yale University Press, 1977.

The Statistical History of the United States. New York: Basic Books, 1976.

Stead, C. K. *The New Poetic*. London: Hutchinson, 1964.

Steinberg, Cobbett. *Reel Facts: The Movie Book of Records*. New York: Vintage, 1982.

Stevens, Tony. "Reading the Realist Film." *Screen Education* 26 (Spring 1978), 13-34.

Suid, Lawrence H. *Guts and Glory: Great American War Movies*. Reading, Mass.: Addison-Wesley, 1978.

Thompson, David. *A Biographical Dictionary of Film*. New York: William Morrow, 1976.

Tocqueville, Alexis de. *Democracy in America*. Edited by J. P. Mayer. Translated by George Lawrence. Garden City, N.Y.: Anchor/Doubleday, 1969.

Trollope, Anthony. *The Way We Live Now*. Indianapolis: Bobbs-Merrill, 1974.

Truffaut, François. "A Certain Tendency of the French Cinema." In *Movies and Methods*, edited by Bill Nichols, pp. 224-37. Berkeley: University of California Press, 1976.

————. *Hitchcock*. New York: Simon and Schuster, 1967.

————. "We Must Continue Making Progress." Translated by Paul Ronder. In *Film: A Montage of Theories*, edited by Richard Dyer MacCann, pp. 368-76. New York: Dutton, 1966.

Turkle, Sherry. *Psychoanalytic Politics: Freud's French Revolution*. Cambridge: The MIT Press, 1978.

Turner, James. *The Politics of Landscape: Rural Scenery and Society in English Poetry 1630-1660*. Cambridge: Harvard University Press, 1979.

Turnstall, Jeremy. *The Media Are American: Anglo-American Media in the World*. New York: Columbia University Press, 1977.

Twain, Mark. *The Adventures of Tom Sawyer*. New York: New American Library, 1959.

————. *The Portable Mark Twain*. Edited by Bernard DeVoto. New York: Viking, 1946.

Vološinov, V. N. *Marxism and the Philosophy of Language*. Translated by Ladislav Matejka and I. R. Titunik. New York: Seminar Press, 1973.

Wake, Sandra and Hayden, Nicola, eds. *The Bonnie and Clyde Book*. New York: Simon and Schuster, 1972.

Warshow, Robert. *The Immediate Experience*. New York: Atheneum, 1972.

Webb, Walter Prescott. *The Great Frontier*. Austin: University of Texas Press, 1952.

Williams, Raymond. "An Interview with Raymond Williams." *Screen Education* 31 (1979), 5-14.

———. "Marxism, Structuralism and Literary Analysis." *New Left Review* 129 (September-October 1981), 51-66.

Williams, William Appleman. "The Frontier Thesis and American Foreign Policy." In *History as a Way of Learning*, pp. 135-57. New York: New Viewpoints, 1974.

Williamson, Judith. *Decoding Advertisements: Ideology and Meaning in Advertising*. London: Marion Boyars, 1978.

Wolff, R. P., Barrington Moore, Jr., and Herbert Marcuse. *A Critique of Pure Tolerance*. Boston: Beacon Press, 1965.

Wollen, Peter. "Counter Cinema: *Vent d'Est*." *Afterimage* (London) 4 (Autumn 1972), 6-16.

Wood, Michael. *America in the Movies*. New York: Basic Books, 1975.

Wood, Robin. *Arthur Penn*. New York: Praeger, 1970.

———. *Howard Hawks*. Garden City, N.Y.: Doubleday, 1968.

———. "Shall We Gather at the River?: The Late Films of John Ford." *Film Comment* 7 (Fall 1971), 8-17.

Wright, Basil. *The Long View*. New York: Knopf, 1974.

Index

Library of Congress Cataloging in Publication Data

Ray, Robert B., 1943-
A certain tendency of the Hollywood cinema, 1930-1980.

Bibliography: p.
Includes index.
1. Moving-pictures—United States—History. I. Title.
PN1993.5.U6R38 1985   791.43'0973   84-42901
ISBN 0-691-04727-8 (alk. paper)   ISBN 0-691-10174-4 (pbk.)

Robert B. Ray is Assistant Professor of English at the
University of Florida, Gainesville.